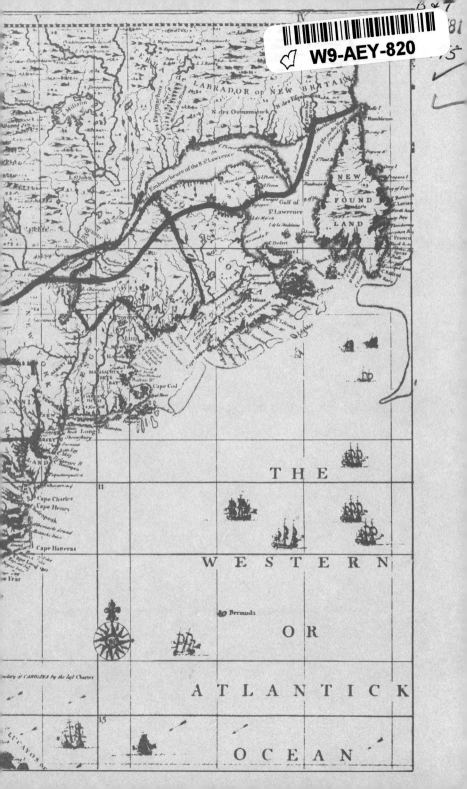

PORTRAIT OF CANADA

Portrait of
CANADA

June Callwood

DOUBLEDAY & COMPANY, INC.
GARDEN CITY, NEW YORK
1981

ISBN: 0-385-05746-6
Library of Congress Catalog Card Number 77–25579

To Bill

Contents

Introduction

When the province of Québec elected a government, on November 15, 1976, that promised to take Québec out of Canada, Canadians were too stunned to believe it, though the country has never been without a strong secessionist movement since its beginning. Nova Scotia's first reaction to the birth of Canada in 1867 was to vote to leave it. In the wake of the re-election in February 1980 of Pierre Elliott Trudeau, the country's stylish, haughty prime minister, a prominent western Progressive Conservative, Richard Collver, leader of the party in Saskatchewan, resigned and said he would work to take western Canada out of federation and join the United States.

It isn't true that Canadians don't care about Canada. Canadians dislike (a) other Canadians, and (b) their governments, but will fight to the death if either is threatened. They reserve their most intense loyalty for the landscape of their own neighborhoods, for the certain lovely light of a winter dawn, for a skyline that lifts the eye, for waves ruffled white in a bay. Canadians, excepting only those descended from the French and living in Québec, have never created a myth that would unify them into nationhood.

The country was not designed that way. The base for its existence was a strong aversion to being absorbed into the United States following the Civil War, together with the anxiety of the founding fathers, many of whom were railway speculators, to make money from building a transcontinental railway. To that end they patched together four wary, doubtful, newly self-governing British colonies and called them Canada.

To add to the difficulty of poor carpentry, the country is illogical. It runs east and west on a continent where rivers and moun-tains, commerce and people flow north and south. Canada is uneconomic and absurd in its demographic outline: its 23 million people live along the United States border in a band about 100 miles wide and 3,987 miles long. The peculiar population distri-bution makes Canadians world-class masters of communication. Since there are too few customers to attract private industry, the government has been obliged to subsidize or own outright an air-line, a railway, television networks (French and English), radio networks (French and English), oil and gas pipelines; enthusiasm for public enterprise overflowed into a government-owned oil company, government ownership of all beer and liquor sales, government-owned hydroelectric power, nuclear power, and a third of all Canadian-controlled corporations.

Canada has centralist churches, banks, insurance companies, and businesses, a theme dating to the country's beginnings when it was a fur farm owned by European monopolies. French and English investors controlled all commerce and had feudal author-ity over every living creature. Settlers had no civil rights but re-ceived protection from invading Americans, start-up supplies and copious amounts of law and order provided first by agents of the monopolies, then by armies, and then, today, by paramilitary police.

At a hint of trouble, the Canadian custom is to call out the Army, jail all suspects, all relatives of suspects, all associates of suspects, all whose names or addresses resemble those of suspects, and, human nature being what it is, all to whom none of the above applies but who have offended the authorities.

No nonsense about *habeas corpus;* suspects go to jail and stay there. In Canada, 85 percent of those charged with indictable offenses are convicted. Small wonder: in Canada courts allow il-legally obtained evidence. Canadian police have been opening pri-vate mail illegally for years. When Canadians heard of it in 1979, they were indignant: they demanded that the law be changed so that police could open mail freely, without breaking the law. When Canadians also learned that police bugged the conversations of cabinet ministers, they approved.

The Supreme Court of Canada recently rejected the tradition in English law that an accused person has the right to remain silent.

In Canada, if you don't reply to the police, you go to jail. Juries in the 1970s twice found a man innocent of the crime with which he was charged. Each time higher courts ruled he should go to jail anyway—and he did.

Those arrested for offending the government customarily are held without bail, without being allowed to notify relatives or lawyers, without visits from anyone but teams of interrogators, without appearing before judges, and without being informed what the charge might eventually be. Canadians who *looked* as though they might disagree with the government have been deported to the country of their birth, or their parents' birth; also without trial.

In 1970 in Canada, those who protested such draconian methods were described by Prime Minister Pierre Elliott Trudeau as "bleeding hearts." The occasion was his invocation of the War Measures Act after terrorists in Montréal had kidnapped two people. As a result of the act, 465 people were put in jail, almost none even remotely connected with the kidnapping.

Canada teemed with Vietnam War draft resisters then, most of whom had imagined themselves in a liberal Utopia. When Trudeau invoked the War Measures Act, they were among the few residents of Canada dismayed by it. A Gallup opinion poll showed 87 percent of Canadians in favor of the War Measures Act, making it the single most popular piece of legislation in the country's history. Canadian university students, fresh from picket lines protesting the Vietnam War, or for boycotting California grapes, or demonstrating solidarity with the Selma, Alabama, march for black rights—all causes romantically distant—turned out by the thousands after the War Measures Act *to support it.*

Employees in the Canadian Embassy in Washington tried to explain to astonished Americans how a modern democracy could impose behavior appropriate to Vlad the Impaler without provoking riots. The United States, which had just survived a presidential assassination without violating the rights of its citizens, began to feel it hadn't understood Canada at all.

Unlike Americans, whose natural response to an invasion of rights by the state is to fill Washington with demonstrators, Canadians tolerate even brutal use of authority with approval. Unless it is directed at them personally, they don't mind. They trust the government and police to act in the best interests of society even when they do not seem to be doing so. They trust that authority knows best.

When a train spill in Mississauga released chlorine gas over that Toronto suburb in 1979, 250,000 people left their homes without fuss at the request of the police. The largest peacetime evacuation in world history, the refugees slept for a week on the floors of shopping plazas, uncomplaining. Meanwhile, though their homes and businesses were deserted, the crime rate went *down*.

The Royal Canadian Mounted Police celebrated its hundredth birthday in 1973 and was honored across the country. An Ottawa columnist, Charles Lynch, was impressed. He could not imagine, he wrote, a similar outpouring of good wishes on the anniversary of Scotland Yard or the FBI. Later it was revealed that the RCMP at that time was stealing dynamite to create an illusion of an active underground, forging seditious documents, burning down a barn, copying membership lists of legitimate political parties, and burglarizing a newspaper. Canadians defended the police. If Mounties were breaking the law, Canadians reasoned, the law was wrong.

Alan Borovoy, general counsel for the Canadian Civil Liberties Association, an organization with an almost unblemished record of failure in such a climate, describes the Canadian style as "autocracy with decency," a tribute to the government's restraint. The government limits retaliation to a target group, wipes it out, and withdraws well short of tyranny.

Canadians are not Americans who live in a colder climate: they are different people. While they resemble Americans—wear the same jeans, use the same expletives, drink the same booze, bet the same point spread, pop the same pills for the same reasons, watch Johnny Carson, and goggle at the same center folds—they are not the same. In a clutch, an American goes for a gun; a Canadian calls the police, who arrive promptly and in great numbers.

A Canadian who doesn't care for that kind of passive reliance on authority, one who has uppity feelings about private enterprise and individual freedom, can always move south of the border to an environment as familiar-looking as his own where his quirks will be appreciated. A radio pioneer in Canada, Graham Spry, once observed, "The state or the United States."

The U. S. economist-statesman John Kenneth Galbraith, Canadian-born, expressed a similar sentiment. "In southwestern Ontario," he wrote, "we were taught that patriotism should not withstand anything more than a $5-a-month wage difference. Anything more than that and you went to Detroit."

Canadians drift back and forth over the border. Always have. Only in recent years have they been obliged to confide their intentions to customs or immigration officers. In 1885 a harried official in Washington declared, "No further reference will be made to the subject (of Canadian immigration) till a more effective system can be devised for enumeration."

Officially, "Canadian foreign stock" in the United States is calculated at 3 million, an unlikely figure. Estimates are that there are close to 2 million of French-Canadian heritage in New England alone. There are more Québécois in the Los Angeles area (200,000) than there are in Québec City (186,000).

The United States often forgets to identify Canadians as a racial entity. When the American Museum of Immigration in New York City was opened in 1972, Canada was not represented. The explanation was that Canadians aren't really foreigners. The U. S. Bureau of Statistics does recognize them as such: it reports Canadians are the third-largest ethnic group in America.

In the late 1890s, the governor-general's lady, wandering among her countrymen on the Québec City docks to welcome newcomers to Canada, was disconcerted that the question she was asked most frequently was the direction to the United States border. In the 1950s, when Canada was developing a middle class, the expression "the brain drain," referred to the scholars, scientists, actors, inventors, manufacturers, doctors, writers, and engineers flowing south.

Canada has received two mass migrations moving the other way, one after the War of Independence in 1776, and one during the Vietnam War of the late 1960s. Both times, Canada got American conservatives in search of stability and structure.

Culture, however, travels in but one direction: north. Canada is afloat in American films, American television, American music, American books, American magazines, American sport, American fads—all of which stimulate defensive government support of artists, publishers, dance companies, theaters, magazines, galleries, orchestras, and radio and television networks in order to nourish the frail flower of indigenous culture. To offset the fact of the deluge of Americana, Canadian schools in the 1970s began to stress Canadian history and offer Canadian literature in English courses. The country now is festooned with ceremonies in which Canadians receive awards for singing Canadian songs, or writing Canadian books, or for some aspect of the Canadian identity, the pursuit of which is a national obsession.

All this applies to English-speaking Canada. Québec, a French island in English North America, is steeped in its own culture. Writers, singers, and artists have been dowsing for the wellspring of the Québécois sense of *patrie* for more than a century. Before that, the Roman Catholic Church held people together in defiance of a Protestant anti-Catholic British Empire. For a very long time, French-speaking Canadians have known, and admired, themselves; English-speaking Canadians have no similar imploded racial commonality and pride.

Communication problems are a result of treaty makers in the eighteenth century who constructed the border to give maximum advantage to the United States. In all such negotiations, Canada was never represented. Instead, the British team speaking for Canada usually was made up of men with close financial ties to the United States, men who had no interest in Canada but were determined to help America prosper.

Accordingly, Canadians got two million square miles of lunar rock, some treeless tundra, and a thin strip of arable land so eccentrically arranged that transportation between the parts was almost impossible. The British had given the United States the Mississippi-Ohio valley, Maine, upper New York State, and the Oregon country, all once legitimately part of Canada.

For most of history, the fastest and most comfortable way to travel from central Canada to another part of Canada or to Britain was through the United States. This meant that Canadian politicians from Toronto went down the Hudson in order to get to London, and British governors-general bound for Ottawa got off the boat at Portland, Maine. Such accommodations had to be suspended during those periods when the United States was actively invading Canada, or planning to, at which time British redcoats had to march the longer all-Canada route over terrain that killed many of them.

Pressed by the weight of ice and rocks at their backs, most Canadians live as close to the American border as they can without changing citizenship. Their communities form a chain of beads; if one, say Québec, drops off, the necklace comes apart.

Some Canadians are resigned to the inevitability of dissolution, even after a referendum in Québec in May 1980 rejected separation by a margin of 60–40. The Atlantic provinces resent that Ontario has prospered in Canada at their expense. Alberta, rich in oil and gas pegged by the Ottawa government well below world prices, seethes with resentment. British Columbia, remote beyond the mountains, has never felt itself very Canadian. And Newfoundland in 1980 observed the thirty-first anniversary of its joining Canada with a suggestion in its largest newspaper that the island separate.

Only Ontario, which profited most in 1867 from confederation which provided markets for its factories and a high tariff wall to enrich manufacturers, shows any real passion for keeping the country together. Everywhere else, Canadians talk mutinously of leaving. Vancouver Island has a group ready to leave British Columbia. The *Parti Acadien* has its own flag and talks of leaving New Brunswick. Newfoundlanders have a new flag (June 1980) and an anthem they sing with tears in their eyes; when they became Canada's tenth province, they donned black armbands in grief. Labrador has a secessionist movement; northern Ontario has an element hopeful of separating from southern Ontario.

"I can report to you that national unity is far from being a dead issue," wrote Dalton Camp, former head of the Progressive Conservative party of Canada, after a coast-to-coast tour in November 1979. "Instead, there may be as many as 23 million people out there ready and eager to march against it."

Efforts to control the runaway pieces of the country are hampered by damage to the constitution committed by members of the Judicial Committee of the British Privy Council. For most of Canada's history they functioned as a supreme court on constitutional matters. Almost without exception, they dismantled the authority of the central government.

The founding fathers, almost all of them immigrants except for the French-Canadians, drew up a constitution that is a business agreement, a dispersal of powers. They were lawyers and railway speculators, not philosophers. When the Canadian constitution was drafted in 1864, the American Civil War was raging. Fearful that they would be invaded by the victorious Union Army, Canadians wrote clauses to invest most authority in the central government. To sell federation to the locals, particularly French-Canadians nervous of assimilation, provinces got authority over minor matters like culture. Thanks to the Privy Council, culture turned out to be the whole ball game.

The constitution could not be enacted in Canada because the provinces then were colonies of the British Empire. So it was addressed to the House of Commons in London, England, which passed what it called the British North America Act only moments before considering the big business of the day—a tax on dogs. Disputes over interpretation had to be referred back to the British Government, which effectively eroded federal authority.

Thus, modern Canada is almost ungovernable. Every matter touching the personal lives of Canadians is in limbo between federal and provincial jurisdiction. Thousands of federal and provincial civil servants ponder the pieces. Hundreds of federal-provincial conferences are held annually—a good many ending without agreement.

Deplorable evidence of this awkwardness came to world attention in the fall of 1948, when Canada abstained from signing the first draft of the United Nations Declaration on Human Rights. Six other dissenting countries were from beyond the Iron Curtain: Byelorussia, Czechoslovakia, Poland, the Ukraine, the Soviet Union, and Yugoslavia. Canada eventually endorsed it but the signature is technically unconstitutional. In Canada civil rights fall within provincial jurisdiction, not federal. A federally enacted Canadian Bill of Rights makes a handsome wall hanging but rarely intrudes upon the solemn deliberations of Canadian judges.

Still, the peculiarities of sailing a ship of state with eleven captains pacing the bridge have developed in Canadians a genius for compromise. During the Suez Crisis of 1956, when it seemed that a third world war was inevitable, Canadian diplomat and later Prime Minister Lester B. ("Mike") Pearson produced in the United Nations a resolution that received unanimous support, ended the crisis, and won him the only Nobel Peace Prize ever awarded a Canadian. Another Canadian who became prime minister, William Lyon Mackenzie King, earned a generous cash payment for teaching John D. Rockefeller a better way to get along with labor unions than by shooting strikers.

That was the same prime minister who, when confronted during World War II with a country violently divided on the issue of sending draftees overseas, pronounced that his government's quintessentially Canadian policy was "conscription if necessary, but not necessarily conscription."

As a legacy to hand down the generations, in the way that Americans believe in their gift for enterprise and the English in their grit, the Canadian ability to straddle issues lacks snap. So does the suggestion that English-speaking Canada derives from discards of the American Revolution. The Revolutionary War of 1776 created not one but two nations. The United States of America grew from the Revolution, Anglo-Canada from the counterrevolution.

The central fact of North American history is that there were fifteen British colonies before 1776. Thirteen rebelled and two did not. "The great refusal," Canadian historian Frank Underhill called it. In truth, neither northern colony had much choice. The Royal Navy was based in one, Nova Scotia, and the British Army in the other, Québec.

The characters of both new nations were molded in the crucible of that revolution and in the migrations that followed. The thirteen colonies that became a republic rid themselves of conservatives, change resisters, traditionalists: American Tories moved north and reestablished under a monarchy in a military state, blissful to have order and security. The two British colonies gradually emptied of dissenters, authority shakers, individualists, free enterprisers, liberty mongers. Nova Scotian Congregationalists with a taste for egalitarianism went back to New England, passing New Englanders who couldn't abide disorder and were moving to Halifax.

Canada developed from people who consciously, and with some considerable sacrifice, chose structure rather than individualism and wanted a powerful state rather than citizen rights. While the American constitution speaks of liberty, the Canadian one says "peace, order and good government."

xviii   INTRODUCTION

Northrop Frye, an esteemed academic at the University of Toronto, has written extensively on what he describes as "the garrison mentality" of Canadians. Frye's theory is that because Canadians have lived for more than two centuries in fear of an American invasion, they are scarred. Generations of Canadians depended on first the British Army and now on a faintly militaristic government. The concept of citizen justice, of vigilantes and posses, is as foreign to Canada as to Switzerland.

Even the word *liberty* was alien to early Canadians. It was as reviled as *communist* is in North America today, since it represented a sloganeering and dangerous enemy. In the Canadian context, democracy was an outside agitator.

The United States put its faith in the individual American and got dazzling achievement at the cost of independent Americans choosing to become muggers. Canada put its faith in a paternalistic state and police power, at the cost of flair and private enterprise.

"Anemia was their heritage," grumbled Canadian novelist Mordecai Richler, who frequently despairs upon contemplating his countrymen's amiable lassitude. Kaspar Naegele, a Canadian sociologist, put it more gently: "There is less emphasis in Canada on equality than there is in the United States. In Canada there seems to be a greater acceptance of limitation, of hierarchial patterns. There seems to be less optimism, less faith in the future, less willingness to risk capital or reputation. In contrast to America, Canada is a country of greater caution, reserve, restraint."

One side of the border has a policeman for a hero, the red-coated Mountie. The other celebrates mavericks. One country believes father is always right; the other may put a bullet in father's head. In the United States the entrepreneur, the person who stands out from the crowd, becomes immortal; the Canadian ideal is the one who emerges from a snowdrift with the toes intact—a survivor.

Differences in style were sharper in the last century. American miners who stampeded north from California in 1860 were met by soldiers and a British judge who hospitably cautioned them to "remember on which side of the line the camp is—for boys, if there is shooting in Kootenay, there will be hanging in Kootenay." When the great cattle drives of the American Midwest flowed north to railheads in Canada, cowboys adjusted to the shock of being asked to surrender their guns to the single policeman who met them at the border. One Mountie rode into Sitting Bull's camp a few days after the Battle at Little Big Horn, noted fresh American scalps and horses with U. S. cavalry brands, and advised Sitting Bull to obey Canadian laws or he, the Mountie, would deport the whole tribe. And Sitting Bull nodded.

During the Klondike gold rush of the nineties, the American town of Skagway in the Alaskan panhandle was run by a ruthless American gangster and gunfights in the streets were common. Across the border in Canada, Yukon mining towns were so law-abiding that a miner safely could leave his poke of gold in an unlocked cabin.

Canadians don't even litter. Office workers eating picnic lunches in city squares pick up every scrap. The Canadian crime rate is startlingly lower than that in the United States. Detroit policemen visiting their Toronto counterparts noted a chart listing eighteen murders in July. "Pretty heavy weekend," one observed. Toronto police were shocked. Eighteen was the score for the *year*.

Good behavior, while laudatory, makes people yawn. The world appears to be little impressed with Canada as an important power. The impression is widespread that Canadians, despite some differences with the United States over matters such as scallop fishing in the Atlantic, are in America's hip pocket. There was little surprise during the Vietnam War that Canadians on the United Nations International Control Commission used the opportunity to spy for the American Army. Third World nations, which twenty-five years ago looked to Canada for moral leadership against the Big Powers, no longer count Canada as a neutral.

Also, there is a tendency abroad to dismiss Canada as a small country which isn't too bright. Canadians protest that what seems a pathological willingness to be conned is instead only anxiety to be liked. And, assuredly, the world is wrong about the size. Canada is big, the largest country in the world except for the Soviet Union. It is larger by 300,000 square miles than all of the United States, including Alaska. It stretches from sea to sea to sea— Atlantic, Arctic, and Pacific—giving it the longest coastline of any nation on earth.

"The immense searching distance," Northrop Frye once called

it. Few Canadians live more than an afternoon's drive from wilderness. Beyond the towns are woods and lakes, and then rock, tundra, and ice that stretches to the top of the world. The country's small population of 23 million is lost in the big land. There are fewer Canadians than there are people in the Philippine Islands or South Korea; Canada's population is approximately the same as that of Yugoslavia or New York State. But South Korea could be floated on one of Canada's anonymous lakes without disturbing the fish, Yugoslavia is about half the size of Baffin Island, and if New York State were transported north a little, it would find itself lost in the Otish Mountains without a road map, since the Otish Mountains have almost no roads.

The crushing problem the economy has faced since the first commerce, fur trading, is that distances are too enormous for cheap distribution, making private enterprise an endeavor highly likely to lead to bankruptcy. Canadians therefore are employees. What the government doesn't own, multinationals do; no one else can afford costs of transportation. Canadians welcome multinationals: the government gives bonuses and tax breaks; the combines legislation is as weak as that of an African dictatorship; natural resources can be taken from the ground with negligible interference from royalty collectors. For instance, 90 percent of gold taken from the Canadian Klondike at the turn of the century wound up in Fort Knox, the Canadian Government pocketing pennies in return.

The Canadian civil service has been described as the country's only growth industry. It administers extensive welfare services paid, in good part, by foreign investment in Canada. Canada has been providing monthly allowances for mothers for more than thirty years, hospital insurance since 1947, medical insurance since 1962. It supplies unemployment insurance, disability benefits, rape-crisis centers, day-care centers, pensions for the elderly, and, in one province, compensation for victims of crime, and, in two provinces, state-run car insurance.

Canadians expect no less. A semi-feudal system with paternalistic *seigneurs* existed in Canada for a century after it had been abolished in France. Also, Canada through most of its development had no middle class. There was the top of the ladder and there was the bottom of the ladder; in between, there was no ladder. States with a rigid ruling class not uncommonly bestow broad social services to the masses.

By contrast, America's backwardness in such fundamental considerations as Medicare owes much to the Horatio Alger myth of individual invincibility and the American dream of upward mobility for all.

The high cost of Canada's welfare services resulted in the 1980s in a government picturesquely sinking into unmanageable debt, borrowing extravagantly on natural resources fast being leeched from the ground, mostly by the United States. America controls 99.4 percent of Canada's oil and gas deposits, and almost all the coal, iron, asbestos, nickel, pulp and paper mills. Most of Canada's manufacturing sector is U.S.-owned. The country's largest industry, automobiles and automotive parts, is wholly owned by Americans; Americans own 89 percent of all chemical producers, 88 percent of all electrical products, 87 percent of all machinery, 87 percent of all rubber products; only 5 percent of all patents registered in Canada are held by Canadians. Canada is the only country where the dominant labor unions have headquarters in the United States.

Since most Canadian industry is a branch plant of an American conglomerate, Canadians find it almost impossible to compete. There is no Canadian-designed car, few Canadian-designed appliances, and a Canadian clothing industry that would collapse like a three-dollar suit without a tariff wall to protect it. In recent years, as multinational corporations have relocated in Third World countries with right-wing, union-bashing governments, Canada has seen a sharp decline in industry. Whole communities in Canada are thrown out of work when the U.S. parent makes a better business deal in Guatemala or the Philippines.

Canada and the United States are each other's major trading partners, but the exchange is ominous for Canadians. While 70 percent of Canadian exports go to the United States, most are non-renewable natural resources, shipped raw and providing few jobs. But 70 percent of American exports to Canada are manufactured labor-intensive goods.

Canadians appear to have little confidence in their country. Small businesses and factories find it easier to borrow money in New York than in Toronto, while Canadian investors have plunged $20 billion into *American* enterprise, a sum exceeded in the United States only by the Netherlands and Britain.

Canadians see themselves as hewers of wood and drawers of water, first for France, then for Great Britain, and now for the United States. When the country's natural resources give out, as they will begin to do in the 1980s, the country will be destitute.

Frank Underhill, Canadian historian, once wrote that Canadians are the world's oldest continuing anti-Americans. There are still Canadian nationalists who talk of buying back the country's industries and resources from Yankee carpetbaggers, but most people accept that Canada hasn't enough money for such a grand design. Irritation with the United States in the 1980s was focused instead on border problems. Canadians drink water full of asbestos dumped by Silver Bay, Minnesota, the American switch to coal meant acid rain in Ontario, the U.S.-Canada fish treaty was being held up in the U. S. Senate for years while New England fishing fleets depleted the scallops in contested waters, and the Garrison Dam in North Dakota threatened to back pollution into Manitoba. An American judge, pondering a project in Washington State that would flood British Columbia, raised hackles when he mused aloud, "We have a third dimension here and it's called Canada, and every time I look at it I wonder what I'm going to do about it."

Canadians like to say that when the United States catches a cold, Canada sneezes; also, that being on the same continent as the United States is like being a guppy in a tank of piranhas—it's okay so long as the piranhas aren't hungry. Prime Minister Pierre Elliott Trudeau once observed that Canada is a mouse in bed with an elephant.

Canadians, in truth, admire and envy Americans and imitate them wistfully. Success within Canada is often suspect: most Canadians reason, if the person is *really* good, why isn't he or she in the United States?

Still, the *Parti Québécois* victory in 1976 created an invisible shift along the old fault lines. English-speaking Canadians were amazed by their depth of feelings as the country neared the precipice in the weeks leading to the 1980 May referendum. A *Péquiste* cabinet minister, Lise Payette, emerged shaken from a federal-provincial conference. A man wept on her shoulder and said, "Lise, don't go." She reflected, "We had expected English

Canadians to react to separatism with cool arguments. We were not prepared for the sheer emotion."

English-Canadians were equally surprised. Their patriotism has been a slow process. Canada was ninety-eight years old before it had its own flag. It was sixty years old before it started to handle its own negotiations with the United States. It was eighty-two years old before it stopped allowing Britain to rearrange its constitution. It was eighty years old before there were Canadian passports and Canadian citizenship. It was eighty-five years old before the governor-general was a Canadian. As recently as 1959, Queen Elizabeth II signed a United Nations document on behalf of Canada; she is the Canadian head of state. Only in 1977 did Canada take power from the Queen of England to accredit and recall diplomats, declare war, and sign peace treaties for Canada. In June 1980 the Canadian Parliament decided to make *O Canada* the national anthem.

"What do you think of a country that has no flag?" an irate nationalist asked American comedian Mort Sahl during a show on Canadian television in the 1950s.

Sahl considered carefully. "Well," he offered, "it's a start."

A national disinterest in Canadian history has created a vacuum in which a variety of desultory emblems and anthems have found accommodation. The beaver, which has come to represent Canada as the eagle does the United States and the lion Britain, is a flat-tailed, slow-witted, toothy rodent known to bite off its own testicles or to stand under its own falling trees.

The maple leaf, another Canadian symbol and the natural choice for the design-a-flag contest in 1965, does not take well to city life in Canada. When Canadians wish to foliate downtown parks with the national tree, they import hardier species from Norway.

As a tourist attraction, Ottawa stages in summer a changing-of-the-guard ceremony in front of the Parliament buildings. The uniforms worn in this operetta are patterned on those last seen on a British expedition on the Nile in 1884. The country's internationally recognized red-coated Mountie is encased in a montage of European cavalry castoffs topped with a hat adapted from the Texas Rangers of the last century.

There are nearly twenty English versions of the national anthem, *O Canada*. In 1972 the government considered 615 suggestions for lyrics, and finally, in 1980, chose one. No Canadian adult is yet certain which one is official; on formal occasions the last three lines are an incomprehensible babble as loyal Canadians sing whichever version they know best. The French lyrics of *O Canada* bear no similarity to the English. In any event, separatists won't sing it; they prefer *Gens du Pays*.

In the spring of 1973 the *Canadian Magazine* sponsored a contest asking Canadians to submit a better set of lyrics for the national anthem. The editors abandoned the project when two thirds of the suggestions were derisive or obscene, and the word *bland* was overused. The music for *O Canada* was written by a French-Canadian who subsequently moved to the United States and spent his money on pamphlets urging his countrymen to do likewise.

His defection is not unique. Louis Riel, a rebel hanged in Regina, Saskatchewan, in 1885 and commemorated as a hero in 1973 on a Canadian stamp, died an American citizen. Alexander Graham Bell, of Brantford, Ontario, inventor of the telephone, couldn't interest Canadians in backing his device. He's buried under a tombstone inscribed, as he wished, "Died a Citizen of the U.S.A." The first man to sail alone around the world, Joshua Slocum, was born in Nova Scotia in 1844 and was raised there; his thirty-seven-foot yawl flew the Stars and Stripes.

Yet Canada is populated by people who will live nowhere else. They are held in good part by the land. All Canadians share a rapture about the beauty of their country. Canadian calendars usually feature scenery. Until the 1930s, Canadian artists painted little else. During the American bicentennial of 1976, Canada's official gift to the United States was a book of superb photographs of—what else?—scenery.

Canadians are attached to their country by private ecstasies: small, religious experiences that dissolve the senses, as when a loon cries across a still northern lake, or the ocean thunders against the rocks of Cape Breton, or the Rockies leap up out of the prairies at Calgary, or wheat fields under the aching blue arch of the great sky, or the eerie flickering of the aurora borealis above the ice, or even the monotonous tundra that author Farley Mowat described as "a terrestrial ocean whose waves are the rolling ridges."

Canadians tend to be fanatical about the particular part of the country they inhabit: it's the best. In 1973 residents of a desolate Labrador village named Black Tickle refused to relocate on a better site only twelve miles away.

Some of the bliss that Canadians feel contemplating a view is charged with pure pride. The geography everywhere is unforgiving; to survive is an achievement. Half of Canada is covered by the Canadian Shield, the oldest exposed rock on earth. It sprawls in boomerang shape from Labrador to the Great Lakes, covering four fifths of Québec and nine tenths of Ontario. It is rock, the age of which in places is measured at 2.5 billion years, ideal for U.S. astronauts to practice sample-gathering before setting off for the moon.

Only 4 percent of Canada is under cultivation. Another 3 percent is marginally arable but isn't farmed because the yield would be uneconomic. A semi-desert covers the north, a treeless waste carpeted in summer by moss and exquisite miniature flowers. Prairie wheat must grow in a latitude frost-free a mere ninety days a year. The heart of the western plains is a potential dust bowl. A glacier covers 75,000 square miles of Canada, and in Saskatchewan there is a patch of shifting sand stretching for 115 square miles.

People who choose to remain in such a land are magnificently perverse. What the cruel land doesn't clobber the climate will. Though parts of Canada lie as far south as Madrid and Istanbul, and parts are farther south than northern California, it is not apparent in winter. Between the Rockies and the Maritimes, Canada is a scoop that catches the polar cold and hurls it at school-children.

Only Siberia and northern Scandinavia are as cold as most of Canada in winter. Montréal spends more money on snow removal than the entire budgets of some emerging nations. Canadians are not surprised that a man ice-fishing in Canada, Clarence Birdseye of Massachusetts, was inspired there to discover the principle of fast-freezing food. Inuit on Baffin Island find it *really* cold only when the temperature drops to −80° F. When it's a mere −40° F and breath frosts eyebrows, Canadians at bus stops exchange looks of pure pleasure: they are feisty; they are invincible; they can take it.

No one on earth appreciates the first warm day of spring as intensely as a Canadian does. The west coast, where golf courses never close, takes spring for granted, but elsewhere it is an armistice. The war is over for a while.

Summers can be torrid with heat waves in the nineties. Even the Yukon has days when the temperature reaches the seventies (or 21° Celsius: to their disgust, Canadians were compelled to begin converting to metric measure in the mid-1970s). Resolute, a weather station five hundred miles north of the Arctic Circle, has two weeks under the midnight sun in July when there is no frost.

Climate shapes character. Climate extremes shape character profoundly. Remorseless winters have forged in Canadians fortitude, endurance, and an ingenuity for survival. The special qualities of Canadians are nowhere more dramatically evinced than in wartime. The only soldiers who didn't run from humankind's first poison gas attack in World War I were Canadians; later, the person who designed a gas mask to withstand the deadly fumes was a Canadian. The army selected by the British to be slaughtered on the Dieppe beaches in World War II was Canadian. The air crews who took the heaviest casualties in that war were Canadians. The men in the dirtiest convoy duty, sailing the North Atlantic in little minesweepers and corvettes, were Canadians.

A character in a Bernard Malamud novel asks, in essence, "Why are you doing this insane thing?"

The answer is, "Because I can."

Military historians agree that Canadians are among the best fighters in the world, not as predictable as the British, not as erratic as the Americans. Instead, they think hard and they don't bolt. That's what Canadians at a bus stop are doing when glittering ice sheathes the city and a wind shrieks mercilessly all the way from the arctic, thinking hard about Florida, but *staying*.

Canadian novelist and poet Margaret Atwood explored Canadian literature in search of the theme. In a book *Survival* she demonstrated that the essence of Canadianism is endurance. Canadians, she maintained, are an endangered species, which is why they empathize readily with the plight of baby seals, whooping cranes, and miners trapped in cave-ins. Survival is a Canadian's ideal of epic achievement. She concluded that, if a Canadian had written *Moby Dick,* the book would have been done from the perspective of the whale.

Canadian bush pilots flew in the arctic in open-cockpit planes
in winter. Canadians fish on the Atlantic from open dories so exposed their hands freeze to the nets. It was a Canadian who put
on a wet suit and went first under the ice at the North Pole. Canadians walked all over North America a century before Americans
dared to leave the safety of the Atlantic coast.

That's heroism on a grand scale. But somehow it hasn't per-
meated the country's psyche in a way that emerges as national
self-esteem and identity. Canadian unity founders on particu-
larism. People who come to Canada do not surrender the past and
don a new nationality as immigrants to the United States do.
They come to Canada because it's available, because it's all right,
because it's preferable to whatever they left. In Canada they keep
their roots; there is little repotting even to the third generation.
They remain Scots, Ukrainians, Haitians; no altered loyalty seizes
their imaginations.

The Melting Pot is American. Immigrants there dissolve in
bubbling assimilation; they become Americans. Canada has the
Mosaic. The country doesn't assimilate and never aspired to. The
pieces of the Canadian Mosaic are beautiful, as in Cape Breton
towns where people converse in Gaelic still, or the spanking clean
Hutterite villages of Alberta, or the Portuguese neighborhoods
of Toronto where black-eyed babies wear tiny gold rings in their
ears. But the parts don't merge as a coherent whole.

Canadians suspect that an invasion by the United States would
unite them overnight. The country's fingers closed into a fist in the
1970s when an American ship, *Manhattan,* took liberties in Canadian territorial water in the arctic. Such an event, however gratify-
ing to nationalists, is hardly likely. American presidents since
Franklin Delano Roosevelt have been unable to restrain their
speech writers from admiring the world's longest undefended border. In truth, the United States doesn't arm the border because it
doesn't need to, and Canada doesn't arm the border because people would fall down laughing at the presumption.

The border indeed is undefended. It is porous. The Haskell
Free Library in Vermont, for instance, has black tape across the
floor to designate the border. The librarian is Canadian, but her
office is on the American side of the tape. A fire in the bathroom

in 1976 brought a surveyor to determine whether a Canadian or an American firm would pay.

Pinecreek, Minnesota, has a binational airport. Planes landing on the Canadian end of the runway finish their taxiing in the United States. In Washington State, Metcalfe's Cafe in Point Roberts straddles the border. When patrons imbibe too much in the Canadian end of the room, the proprietor calls the Canadian police. Patrons then pick up their glasses and move to the other end of the bar. There's a woman in Edmundston, New Brunswick, whose parlor is in Canada and kitchen in the United States.

A Canadian general in the 1920s drafted a contingency plan for the invasion of the United States by Canada. He based it on military intelligence obtained by asking for the free road maps available at American gasoline stations. Eventually he was led away with a butterfly net over his head. The Pentagon, on the other hand, has detailed campaigns designed for the invasion of Canada which were adjusted in 1976 when the separatists won the election.

If Québec ever leaves Canada the new nation will call its people *Québécois;* Canadians will be foreigners. That's ironic. Canada is the name French settlers insisted upon in the seventeenth century. They rejected the king's efforts to call their country La Nouvelle France. They were not French, they said. They were a new breed of people, *Canadiens.*

The word *Canada* comes from a journal of the sixteenth-century explorer Jacques Cartier, who spelled it *Kanata.* The most accepted translation of the lost Iroquois word is that it meant "a collection of huts." When Cartier indicated by sign language that he wanted to know what natives called their land, the Iroquois told him "Kanata." Etymologists now believe the Iroquois thought Cartier referred to the nearby village, a collection of huts.

The other plausible explanation is that the Iroquois used a phrase picked up from Portuguese fishermen who made annual voyages to catch cod and whales long before Cartier's time. According to this theory, the visitors impressed the natives with the fervent comment, *"Aca nada, aca nada!"* which means, "There is nothing here, *nothing!"*

"No one knows my country," historian Bruce Hutchison wrote sadly. "My country has not found itself."

Québec has. Alberta has. Newfoundland has. The Yukon is in the process. Vancouver Island has. Cape Breton has. Northern Ontario is in the process. . . .

A collection of huts.

1

Fish, Furs, and Foreigners

A full six hundred years before Columbus, Vikings blown each spring by eastern winds off Europe put colonies on Iceland and Greenland, and probed farther south on the North American continent. Tough, sea-smart sailors out of Bristol, England's most western harbor town, followed the trail in about 1480. While kings and traders ached to find a short route to the silks and spices Marco Polo unveiled, the men of Bristol and partners in Lisbon were indifferent to the glories of opening a sea route to the Orient. They were after cod, seals, polar bears, narwhal horn, whale oil, and walrus tusk.

Though the voyage that threaded through floating cliffs of ice was perilous and expensive, profits were worth the risk. Europe's rivers were polluted with excrement and carrion, the fish gone or a source of plagues, and starvation was bringing some nations to the verge of extinction. Oily herring caught in the Baltic took so long to absorb the salt meant to preserve it that Europe's Roman Catholics, bound by law to eat no meat 153 days of the year, rarely tasted fish that wasn't in an advanced stage of putrefaction.

In Bristol, the land near the fishing banks—where cod swam so thick that a man almost could walk on them—was known as "Brasil." Though men of learning declared the world was flat, sailors knew otherwise. Over the western horizon, the ocean lapped on some out-islands of Asia where cod teemed. Plump and tasty, they absorbed salt thirstily and remained edible for months after.

By the closing years of the fifteenth century, marine technology made mariners bolder. A magnetic compass was developed and astrolabes were installed in ships to fix their position by sighting the stars. Improved sails held the wind better, and navigators began to court backers who would finance expeditions of discovery. After 1453, when Moslem Turks closed Constantinople to Christians and barred caravan commerce with the Orient, a seaman's tale of far-off islands could catch a royal ear.

In 1493 Europe was astonished at the news that Cristoforo Colombo had sailed into the setting sun and found India. "The people all go naked, even men and women . . . They are artless and generous with what they have to such a degree as no one would believe it but he who has seen it."

Artless and generous with what they have! A compatriot of Colombo, Giovanni Caboto, knew of the shuttle out of Bristol and hurried to England. His study of Marco Polo's journals convinced him that Colombo had hit nothing more than some outer islands barring the way to the Asiatic mainland. The English route, he thought, might hit Cipangu, Marco Polo's name for Japan.

England, however, appeared to be excluded from the search. The Borgia politico who was Pope, Alexander VI, received the news of Colombo's journey by deeding all the new world to Spain. The following year Portugal, Spain's most powerful rival, wrested from Spain a piece of the prize, a concession that turned out, when the cartographers were finished, to be Brazil. It would be a brazen act to challenge that authority.

Henry VII, a practical man interested in commerce, was happy to try. He granted to Bristol merchants who would back Caboto, whom he called John Cabot, a trade monopoly and freedom from import taxes. In May 1497, Cabot left Bristol in the *Matthew,* crewed by eighteen convict slaves. On June 24, St. John the Baptist's Day, he stepped ashore on land he named St. John's Isle after the saint. Then he fumbled along the coast of a heavily wooded land, saw no humans or sign of habitation, and returned to Bristol as the lion of the hour.

Cabot declared that he had been to "the country of the Grand Kahn." Henry VII gratefully settled a pension on him for reaching the "new founde land." Cabot believed that Cipangu lay south of St. John's Isle and sailed the following spring to reach it. There is no record of his fate, but Spanish explorers brought back stories of an English expedition in their waters, which sent a flurry of Spaniards north to find the challenger.

Cabot's son Sebastian followed his father west in 1508 but tried to sail north around what mariners were beginning to recognize as a solid land mass blocking a direct approach to Asia. The young Venetian, then about twenty-four, led an optimistic expedition of two ships crewed by three hundred men and loaded with trade goods. He followed open water through cliffs of ice and probably entered Hudson's Bay, which he took to be the Pacific Ocean.

Meanwhile, a peasant from Portugal, João Fernandes, given the title of Llavrador, in 1499 followed the American coastline north and gave Labrador its name. The next year another Portuguese, Gaspar Corte-Real, followed and sighted Greenland. On his second voyage his ship was lost. A brother, Miguel, went in search of him and also disappeared. A third Corte-Real brother was refused permission to continue the hunt.

By 1507 the confounding sprawl of land that blocked Asia had a name, America, in honor of the Florentine, Amerigo Vespucci, who charted it from Chesapeake Bay to the region of the Amazon and calculated, with an error of only fifty miles, the circumference of the globe.

Through it all, Portuguese and English ships swarmed west for something better than adventure: fish. The cod banks of New Founde Land, or Terra Nova, drew fishing fleets that found a marvelous natural harbor, a long key protected on three sides by steeply rising rock, that was called St. John's. Spanish and French ships next joined the summer shuttle; by mid-century the Basques alone sent two hundred ships every season to the Grand Banks.

The shore base introduced sailors to the native people of New Founde Land, light-skinned, small Beothuks, a people so long without a predator that they had lost any skill for self-defense. Their communal ethic of sharing prompted them to pick up whatever European goods they saw. To protect property, sailors began to kill Beothuks on sight.

The abundance of whale and cod kept seamen from killing one another unduly: There was plenty for all. In 1509 England's new king, Henry VIII, sought to appropriate St. John's excellent harbor for Bristol's fleets by establishing a small wintering colony. In the

spring there was no trace left. Sailors stranded on New Founde
Land as punishment for insubordination never survived the harsh
winter and scurvy-producing diet. In 1528 Henry VIII tried a second colony, but it also perished.

England, fighting France for supremacy on the fishing grounds,
had recovered from a severe disadvantage in the matter of the
fish-preservative, salt. France, with sun-drenched briny marshes in
Brittany, could recover sea salt cheaply while foggy England was
obliged to pay dearly for imported salt. In the sixteenth century,
sailors developed a new technique of drying fish in the sun and
wind before putting it into salt barrels, a method that greatly reduced the amount of salt needed to avoid putrefaction.

England and France, emerging from plagues and pestilence, fed
their populations on cod, and so flourished that a robust people
challenged Spain and Portugal. In 1523 France's king, François I,
commissioned Giovanni da Verrazzano, a gifted navigator from a
prominent Florentine family, to find for France the route west to
Cathay. The *Dauphine* carried him to Florida and he sailed north,
past New York harbor and Narraganset to Cape Breton. A region near Virginia was so beautiful he called it Arcadia, a name
that migrated north until it settled inside Nova Scotia's claw.

"The New World which above I have described is connected
together, not adjoining Asia or Africa," he reported.

In 1528 Verrazzano returned to the new world, landed in the
Lesser Antilles, and there was killed and eaten by a Carib tribe.

François I agreed to try again in 1534 at the urging of the
bishop of Saint Malo. He hired a Breton, Jacques Cartier, an experienced seaman familiar with the route of the fishing fleets. Cartier's task was to look for gold—France was unwilling to believe
that the gold of America was confined to territories controlled by
Spain and Portugal—and to test Verrazzano's conclusion that
there was no passage to China.

Cartier sailed from Saint Malo, crossed the ocean in twenty
days, rounded the northern tip of New Founde Land, and sailed
into a vast salt gulf where whales played. He charted its outline—
missing the opening of the enormous river that empties into the
gulf—and assigned names to the bays and promontories he found.
In the Baie des Chaleurs his ship was surrounded by a swarm of
small craft made from tree bark filled with excited, naked, dark-

skinned people, the Micmacs. A tribe accustomed to trading with European fishermen, they displayed for Cartier their most cherished goods, beaver pelts. He turned away in disinterest but farther along the coast, at Gaspé, met Iroquois who were there for the fishing. Cartier persuaded the chief, Donnacona, to allow him to take two of the chief's sons for training as interpreters.

When Cartier returned to France, François I excitedly provided him with a second expedition almost twice the size of the first. He returned to the gulf and bestowed the name Baie Saint-Laurent on a cove, from which the entire gulf received its name. Donnacona's sons led Cartier to the Saint Laurent River, past a tributary they said led to the Saguenay where copper could be found, and to the Iroquois village of Stadacona where they were reunited with their father.

Cartier had encountered one of North America's great trading tribes, an agricultural nation that had developed beyond nomadic hunting because of food crops grown by women. Stadacona was a populous village of long houses set among fields of corn, tobacco, marijuana, squash, and beans, currency with which the Iroquois traded along a chain from Florida to the Arctic Circle. Donnacona was anxious to establish trading relations with Cartier for the astonishing metal tools of the Europeans, and Cartier's anxiety to explore the river beyond Stadacona worried him: Another Iroquois village, Hochelaga, lay upstream and would offer competition.

Despite Donnacona's protests, Cartier found Hochelaga, climbed a nearby hill he called Mont Royal, and was ecstatic to learn there was a sluice of rapids beyond Hochelaga which he took to be the opening to the Pacific. He thought a Kingdom of Saguenay lay farther on, rich in gold, silver, and copper.

He wintered at Stadacona in a fort his men built to guard against Donnacona's increasing hostility. The Frenchmen had never known such cold. The inside walls of their shelter were coated with six inches of solid ice. Of Cartier's 110 men, 100 had scurvy by February; 25 died of it. A native medicine made from white cedar bark saved the others.

In the spring Cartier took Donnacona and nine other Iroquois prisoners and returned to France. His record shows that when he asked the name of the region, a native waved an arm and said *kanata,* which possibly referred to the Iroquois village nearby. In any case, Cartier had his own name for the river, Rivière de Canada, and the country, La Nouvelle France.

Though Cartier's voyage created a stir in France, the king was preoccupied with a war against Spain. But in the fall of 1540 François I was ready to establish a French colony to claim the Saguenay wealth and the gateway to Asia. All that winter a rich Protestant nobleman, Jean-François de La Rocque, sieur de Roberval, intrigued against Cartier to get the charter.

Preparations were made with great secrecy as the legend of the Saguenay kingdom grew. A fleet was prepared in the sumptuous style of Roberval's entourage, with wines, brocades, fine-carved furniture, and costumes for masked balls. Musicians and hairdressers were hired; in the hold were slaves in chains, and on the decks cattle and other livestock to feed the passengers.

However, Roberval wasn't ready to sail in the spring, so Cartier left ahead of him. No Iroquois had survived the six years in France. Cartier went directly to Stadacona and demanded to be taken to the Saguenay. He was rebuffed but found along the river rock veined with gold and chips of what seemed to be diamonds. He wintered again at Stadacona and sailed for France when ice released him in spring.

The only other Europeans in North America were also leaving that spring. Hernando de Soto of Spain, leading six hundred soldiers overland as far as Oklahoma, was withdrawing in disgust at finding no gold.

Cartier put in at St. John's in New Founde Land and met the Roberval expedition there. Cartier slipped away by night and took samples of the treasure to France where the gold was found to be iron pyrites, known as fool's gold, and the diamonds worthless quartz.

Roberval's mandate to establish French civilization in America began with a scandal. His niece, Marguerite de Roberval, outraged her uncle, a hard-nosed Calvinist, by having an affair on shipboard. He put her ashore on Îles des Démons in the Gulf of St. Lawrence with her lover and a maid. Though the lover, the maid, and the infant Marguerite bore died, the woman survived for two years until rescued by a passing ship.

Roberval's colony selected Charlesbourg-Royal as its base, not far from Stadacona, and wintered there—in shock. Roberval had not been able to locate the fabled Saguenay kingdom. In his rage, he flogged and hanged his subjects without mercy. By spring the subdued survivors returned wearily to France to face derision and debt. For the next fifty years, La Nouvelle France and Canada were regarded as synonymous with foolishness.

England had no such disillusionment. Henry VIII's daughter Elizabeth was anxious to start a year-round colony in America. Sir Humphrey Gilbert, half-brother of Sir Walter Raleigh, pored over skewed maps and selected as his base an island in the Gulf of St. Lawrence called Anticosti. Elizabeth, smitten by Raleigh, nonetheless had reservations about his half-brother, who was too profligate. She granted him a patent with reluctance and he set off from Plymouth in June 1583. Raleigh, who was supposed to accompany him, stayed at home for lack of interest.

Gilbert's fleet of five ships, one of which was the *Golden Hind,* arrived in St. John's to find the harbor jammed with ships, mostly French and Portuguese. Undaunted, Gilbert issued each of the thirty-six ships in harbor an English license to fish, assigned each captain a section of the rocky hillside for drying fish, and took possession of New Founde Land. The seamen, almost all of them Roman Catholic, accepted philosophically Gilbert's decree that only the Church of England would prevail.

That done, Gilbert sailed out of St. John's. He was last seen on the deck of his smallest ship, the ten-ton *Squirrel,* having refused all suggestions that the larger *Golden Hind* was safer. When the *Squirrel* went down in a storm, so did Gilbert.

When Raleigh learned of his half-brother's demise, he applied to Elizabeth for transfer of the patent. Since New Founde Land officially was England's, he selected a site as far south as he dared —a verdant stretch of the Spanish coast of America that he called Virginia—for his queen. For the remainder of his life, until James I had him beheaded, he claimed the title of Lord of New Founde Land as well.

The English claim to St. John's proved difficult to maintain without an armed colony. Bristol merchants hired pirates to attack Spanish fishing fleets and succeeded in driving them to find ports elsewhere on the island. France festooned the Gulf of St. Lawrence with drying racks in such numbers that Bristol's fleets felt threatened. In 1610 merchants hired an English colony to winter on a harbor now known as Cupids. English investment in Grand Banks fishing was considerable, as many as 250 ships every summer. The summer population of St. John's was in the thousands, sufficient to hunt the bewildered Beothuks to near extinction.

French sailors who encountered Micmacs traded trinkets for beaver pelts. The market in Saint Malo and Nazaire was small but steady. Dressmakers and tailors bought furs for trimmings. In time, Paris milliners learned of the cheap supply of prime beaver and were elated. The pelts, made up of fine barbed hairs, were superior sources of felt for hats.

Milliners gave sailors commissions to carry trade goods to the Indians and return with furs. Micmacs and their allies, the Malecites, were overjoyed at the upward turn in their fortunes. They had no way of knowing the goods were worth a fraction of the value of the furs in European terms, but they bargained shrewdly within the limits of their experience. They wanted utensils, particularly needles, axes, and iron pots, to replace the traditional cooking method of heating food in wooden containers by adding heated stones. Especially, they wanted metal arrow heads to keep competitors away from the meeting places with European ships. Thus, a curious industry was created in seventeenth-century France: the manufacture of ancient weapons to Micmac specifications.

As demand for beaver felt increased and ownership of a wide-brimmed, high-crowned, and plumed felt hat became such a status symbol that men wore them to have portraits painted, Huguenot merchants in the seaports found it profitable to equip ships solely for the fur trade. By 1569 French ships passed up the lucrative cod fishing and went straight to prearranged trading sites around the mainland.

The effect on Micmacs and Malecites was dramatic. The tribes abandoned prudent conservation habits of centuries and in a few years wiped out all the beaver in their hunting grounds. Fur traders then passed them by and contacted inland tribes of Montagnais, Naskapis, and Algonkians. Historians deduce that in the commercial upheaval that followed, the Iroquois Cartier met on the St. Lawrence were displaced. In the sixteenth century some were farming south of the Great Lakes—the Mohawks, Oneidas, Onondagas, Cayugas, and Senecas. Another agricultural confederacy, the Hurons, had villages near Georgian Bay, and a third, appropriately called the Neutrals, were concentrated along Lake Erie between the two. The Hurons in particular were in a dominant position because they could contact canoe tribes of the northwest to offer in trade essential portable food: corn mashed and preserved in animal fat.

Every spring the northwest tribes headed for Tadoussac, the contact point with French and Portuguese fur traders at the junction of the Saguenay River and the St. Lawrence. Every summer Tadoussac became a brawling town of tents and campfires as Algonkian, Montagnais, some Huron, French-speaking Micmacs, and Malecites converged for barter and celebration, well lubricated with the French brandy they found irresistible.

Natives rapidly learned that Europeans would bid against one another and began to hold out for ever-higher prices. Merchants in the French ports, French Protestant Huguenots skilled in business practices, begged the king for a monopoly charter to eliminate bidding. In 1599 Calvinist Pierre Chauvin obtained a ten-year monopoly from Henry IV of France in return for a promise to place a colony of French in the new world to establish France's claim.

Chauvin, known as the founder of Tadoussac, chose that hotbed of the fur trade for his all-male colony. By spring most were dead from scurvy. In 1602 Henry IV widened the monopoly to some traders in Rouen and Saint Malo, but competitors were protesting hotly. Nevertheless, Henry IV, in 1603, granted a vast charter to another French Protestant, Pierre du Gua, sieur de Monts, because monopolies represented a painlessly cheap method of planting French colonies.

Although De Monts regarded Tadoussac as too full of poachers to be a profitable colony, he had a wide choice of location. The king had granted him "the coasts, lands and confines of Acadia, Canada and other places in New France," a territory extending roughly from the Hudson River to Newfoundland. His geographer, Samuel de Champlain, was experienced. Champlain was familiar with the St. Lawrence River as far upriver as Trois-Rivières. He had guessed the outline of the Great Lakes from descriptions given him by natives, knew there was salt water west of the St. Lawrence (Hudson Bay), and had admired the scenery and milder climate of the Gaspé and Nova Scotia.

De Monts sent two ships to carry his colony to L'Acadie, far from poachers. His preparations were impressive. The colonists, 60 healthy beggars recruited from the streets of Paris together with 125 craftsmen to do construction, were divided almost equally between Protestants and Catholics and, therefore, were served by two clergymen. They detested one another. Another passenger was Matthew de Costa, a black who had learned the Micmac language while enslaved on a Portuguese fishing vessel. De Costa was the colony's interpreter.

De Monts selected an island in a river he called Sainte Croix south of Passamaquoddy Bay, a location he judged safer from Indian attack than a site on the mainland. It proved a disastrous choice in a bitter winter that imprisoned the colony in snow from early October to April. Forty men were dead by spring.

De Monts and Champlain cruised the New England coast that summer looking for a better location. They admired Plymouth and Boston harbors but decided on the lovely Annapolis valley on the shores of the Bay of Fundy. The prefabricated buildings of Sainte Croix were dismantled and moved to the new site, which De Monts called Port Royal.

The first permanent European settlement in North America, Port Royal was two years older than the first English settlement in Virginia, nineteen years before the Walloon settlement on Manhattan Island, twenty-one years ahead of a fur-trading post that would be called Salem. As the walls of Port Royal went up, Lord Baltimore, the Roman Catholic colonizer of Maryland, was being born.

Twelve Frenchmen died of scurvy that winter and seven the next, despite the repasts prepared by the continent's first social club, the Order of Good Cheer, which offered diversions during the evening meal. Champlain spent the summer of 1606 charting the coast to the south and produced flawless maps of such landmarks as Nantucket Sound. De Monts, beset by enemies and unexpected poachers, was in dire financial trouble. He lost his charter. Port Royal learned in 1607 that the colony was being withdrawn on almost the very day that 105 Londoners set foot on the shore where they built Jamestown.

De Monts wangled a one-year extension on the charter. He hired Champlain as his lieutenant and skipped the requirement for a colony. Champlain headed for Tadoussac, paused to note with horror the debauchery around the campfires, and hurried up-river. To defend the monopoly he built a medieval butternut castle at a place where the river narrowed sharply. He called it Québec, after an Indian word meaning narrow waters, and his fortress was complete with a moat fifteen feet wide and the severed head of a traitor displayed on a pike staff mounted on the walls. (Champlain had caught the man aiding a Basque plot to take over the fort.)

Algonkians and Hurons bound for Tadoussac, a long weary paddle down the river, stopped in amazement at the sight. Champlain profitably did business with them on the spot. The ship for France carried away a groaning cargo of furs just ahead of the winter freeze. Scurvy then struck the butternut castle's occupants and by spring only Champlain and seven others were alive. Still Champlain unhesitantly committed himself to stay. A stubborn, driven man, he wanted wealth, he wanted a place in history as an explorer, and he dreamed of converting *les sauvages* to Catholicism in order to save his soul.

France's toehold on the continent at Québec and tumbled-down Port Royal existed only as business offices run from France, while England's colonies on the Atlantic seaboard already had a different character. Settlers in Jamestown asserted their independence of colonial authorities by electing their own leader, Captain John Smith, and planting crops to sustain themselves through the vagaries of English supply ships.

Agriculture had tragic consequences for non-whites. Short of manpower, the English colonists needed slaves to work the land and the fields they cultivated had to be taken from tribes by violence. In one part of the continent Europeans from England hunted natives to the death; in another, La Nouvelle France, Europeans from France feasted by tribal campfires: cooperation between white traders and natives was essential for business.

In the summer of 1609 Champlain took a step that delivered one native nation to the side of the English. The fateful event began innocently. As part of a trade-off to improve access to furs, Champlain agreed to join some Montagnais and Algonkians in a

war party to teach the Iroquois to stay out of the way. Sixty natives, painted for battle, and three Frenchmen armed with a few
obsolete guns called *arquebuses* stopped at Mont Royal to admire
the view of the rapids, which Champlain named La Chine in anticipation of finding the route to China beyond them, and then
slipped along a river he called Richelieu, as a gesture to the most
powerful priest in France, and into a lake Champlain named for
himself.

They were in the heart of the Iroquois nation of 60,000 people,
a well-governed society with 50,000 acres under cultivation and
communication lines stretching a thousand miles over which they
traded corn meal, tobacco, and hemp in exchange for canoes,
furs, and seashells. Two days after Champlain entered their land,
two hundred Iroquois showed themselves at Ticonderoga. Champlain stepped forward dressed for war in bloomers and long hose,
an iron plate protecting his breast and gut, a gleaming plume-
topped metal bonnet on his head. He raised his gun and aimed at
the most prominent men standing the length of a football field
away. He fired the load, four pellets, and two Iroquois chiefs
dropped dead. Demoralized by the shock of an unthinkable
weapon, the Iroquois ran.

Henry Hudson of the Dutch East Indies Company was at that
moment on the river he named for himself. When Dutch traders
later contacted Iroquois, they were astounded by the sophistication of the demands. Instead of metal arrow heads that had
satisfied Micmacs, the Iroquois wanted only guns to kill the
French.

Though Iroquois ambitions to take over the Hurons' role in the
fur trade were thwarted by Champlain's display of technology,
Hurons were still unwilling to cooperate with the geographer's
scheme for pushing on to the Pacific. The only concession he
could gain was to plant one of his men, eighteen-year-old Étienne
Brûlé, in the Huron villages with instructions to gather information and promote the fur trade.

Brûlé went off gladly, grateful to escape a scurvy-ridden winter
in the butternut fortress, and probably was the first European to
see the Great Lakes. When Champlain encountered him next, the
young Frenchman was tanned, naked, fluent in Huron, and could
handle a canoe with dexterity. Brûlé lived with the Hurons for

twenty years—until they tired of his promiscuity, chopped him up, and ate him.

In 1610 the cause of religious tolerance was lost in France when Henry IV was assassinated. Champlain hurried home to make certain his business contacts would withstand the rising anti-Huguenot feeling. There, he married twelve-year-old Hélène Boullé, promising her parents he would not consummate the marriage until she reached fourteen. He spent her dowry securing his place in the fur trade.

The forty-year-old Champlain returned to the St. Lawrence and picked as a location for a future trading post the old site of Hochelaga where Montréal would begin thirty-one years later.

Years of financial uncertainty followed until 1614 when Champlain received from Louis XIII an eleven-year contract to exclusive rights to all the fur trade in La Nouvelle France. As a Christmas present to himself he had deflowered his thirteen-year-old wife, who ever after detested him. She ran away from him so often that eventually her mortified parents disowned her.

Champlain's contract was obtained by granting a Bourbon prince, Henri, Prince de Condé, a sizable kickback. The man called "the father of New France" was a supple and devious master of financing. Harold Innis, historian of the fur trade, calls Champlain North America's first successful promoter. An annoying condition of his charter was that he was to bring six families of colonists annually to La Nouvelle France on the understanding they would keep their hands off the fur trade. The requirement was one which Champlain tended to brush aside.

The French colony in the St. Lawrence basin consisted of little more than Étienne Brûlé and a handful of other French fur traders living among the Hurons. The monopoly's fur warehouse was at Québec, guarded by a few employees while the peripatetic Champlain commuted to Paris to keep his fragile mandate from collapsing. Port Royal, De Monts' deserted settlement in L'Acadie, was reoccupied in 1610 by an indigent nobleman, Biencourt de Poutrincourt, an ardent farmer, who had obtained the entire peninsula as a gift because he admired the scenery.

Named the colony's lieutenant-governor after putting together some shaky financing, De Poutrincourt brought good French peasants to till the fields around Port Royal. The French administrator was impressed by natives and managed to cultivate the land without losing the respect and affection of Micmacs and Malecites. De Poutrincourt was pleased when the amity resulted in a substantial number of baptisms.

Priests who presided at the conversions in L'Acadie were Jesuits, to De Poutrincourt's chagrin. He would have preferred clerics of an order less inclined to commercial aggrandizement and political interference. But when he returned to Paris after the assassination of Henry IV, he found the Jesuits more entrenched in court circles than before. Many of France's aristocrats were in the grip of a growing fervor for evangelical Catholicism, which directed itself to such good works as sending missionaries to America.

The Marquise de Guercheville, wife of the governor of Paris and an admirer of the Jesuits, raised money for priests and a missionary colony near Port Royal called Saint Sauveur. Before construction of either community, however, L'Acadie met with disaster. First, De Poutrincourt was driven from the colony by disputes with his creditors, who put him in prison. Then the Jesuits prevented him from punishing a Frenchman who had raped a native woman, souring relationships with the locals. Soon after De Poutrincourt's departure, a Virginian buccaneer turned up in L'Acadie and destroyed the colony.

The Virginian was Samuel Argall, hired in Jamestown in 1613 to rid the coast of French settlements. He caught the colonists of Port Royal building a fortress and easily captured them, moving on to take an unprepared Saint Sauveur and then to rob Sainte Croix's ruins of salt stored for the French fishing fleet. Argall carried off the Jesuits to Virginia as trophies and packed the other settlers back to France.

Champlain's colony, meanwhile, was something less than the six families per year he had promised. In 1617 there was but one family in residence in all La Nouvelle France, Louis and Marie Hébert and their three children. Hébert was an apothecary from Paris, an open, friendly man with a peasant's passion for farming. In 1609 Hébert was a member of De Monts' expedition and was so anxious to prove the soil of America fertile that he cultivated land where Gloucester, Massachusetts, now stands.

Champlain visited Hébert in Paris in 1616 and offered him a

handsome salary as an officer in the fur trade if he would move his family to Québec. Hébert discovered as he was about to sail that he had been duped. The promised salary was cut by half. It was late for him to turn back so he sailed, having experienced the unifying tribulation of most of France's colonists who followed, that of being cheated.

The loneliness of Québec did not disturb the Héberts as much as the diet of eels three times a day. The fur trade syndicate in France discouraged farming, seeing such domesticity as erosion of the wilderness designed for furs. Hébert asked every year for agricultural implements and was refused. Years passed before he got a farm cart he wanted. He was dead before the first plow was delivered in La Nouvelle France.

Samuel Argall's raids on L'Acadie gave James I of England the impression that the peninsula was his. In 1621 he gave it to a court favorite, Sir William Alexander, a Scot poet of small talent. Alexander bestowed the name Nova Scotia (New Scotland) on his realm and obtained a handsome inducement for settlers: all heads of households who would undertake to colonize Nova Scotia would be given the title of knight-baronet.

Even so, few were interested in trusting their lives to a wilderness. Six years later Charles I took the throne of England and noted that Alexander was conducting a thriving business in the sale of baronies but transported no people. Champlain, meanwhile, had done little better in persuading Frenchmen to emigrate. In 1620 his colony at Québec was augmented only by the addition of his reluctant wife. She endured the isolation and the eels for four years and then insisted on returning to France. When Champlain turned up in Paris on business trips, she permitted him to stay in her house on the understanding that he keep out of her bed.

In 1627 the first English colony, "70 men and twa women," landed at Port Royal, astonished to find Acadiens still there. After Argall's raids, they had returned to their farms and patiently rebuilt. The newcomers and the Acadiens made the best of it, neither having anywhere else to go, until a war between England and France made their situation untenable.

Charles I hired the Kirke brothers to fight the war on his behalf in America. David, Lewis, Thomas, John, and James—the

Kirkes—were Scot Presbyterians raised in Dieppe and renowned for their ferocity as pirates. With instructions to capture "Canida" from France, the dashing Kirkes had little difficulty taking the fur trade port of Tadoussac. By luck they surprised a fat fleet of supplies and French settlers in the gulf, bound for Québec, and took it as a bonus. Champlain, cut off by the Kirke blockade, surrendered his starved garrison on July 19, 1629, unaware that the war had ended and the Kirkes had no business taking a French fort.

The kings of England and France were three years sorting out the legal mess, the negotiation made more complex by a family squabble between them. Charles I, married to Louis XIII's sister, complained that his brother-in-law still owed half the dowry. Louis said he would pay only if he got back La Nouvelle France and L'Acadie.

In 1632 Québec and Port Royal took down the flags of England, and Alexander's Scots, their numbers reduced by half by scurvy, went home on the same ship that brought French colonists to Port Royal. France had reconsidered the long neglect of its holdings on the American continent. It was recruiting settlers in earnest. Cardinal Richelieu, Louis XIII's astute chief minister, had come to appreciate the economic usefulness of a colonial empire.

Rather than have the state pay the horrendous cost of transporting and sustaining colonies, Richelieu organized the Compagnie des Cent-Associés. In return for exclusive right to furs in North America in the region stretching from Florida to the North Pole, the Compagnie agreed to put living Frenchmen, not promises, in the French colonies. The Compagnie des Cent-Associés campaigned vigorously for settlers, offering to those audacious or desperate enough free land, access to the fur trade, rapid promotion and, as William Alexander had done, a title, seigneur, and most of the feudal trappings. The result was a boom of emigrants, richly seeded with priests and nuns. Richelieu had no intention of allowing the morals of the colony to collapse under the temptations of a pagan frontier.

— 2 —

The First
French Connection

Champlain enthusiastically supported the missionary movement that swept France after Henry IV's death. In 1615 he imported Recollet priests to live among the Hurons to convert the natives. Young French fur traders in Huronia who had married Huron women according to tribal rites were uncomfortable in the presence of the scandalized clergy, but otherwise the mix went well. The Huron language was unable to accommodate the subtle mysteries of Catholicism that the priests were struggling to unfold, but Hurons accepted the priests as a guarantee that business relations with the French would prosper.

Jesuits arrived, young idealists tormented by Huron nudity, a diet of half-raw meat, and spring portages waist-deep in ice-choked marshes. There was also the danger of Iroquois harassment, especially as beaver grew scarce and Iroquois felt pinched by a French-Huron wall that blocked them from the rich pelts available over the northwest portages.

In the 1630s a foe more formidable than marauding Iroquois shook the Huron nation. Jesuits pouring into their villages brought smallpox, which wiped out half the population. Despite a suspicion that holy water used in last rites contributed to the deaths, Hurons continued to tolerate the priests. Conversions increased so rapidly that the nation soon was divided between traditionalists and new Catholics. Jesuits sent Huron boys to the college they had founded in 1635 in Québec, the first educational institution in the French colonies, an integrated seat of learning to instill habits of piety in all.

On Christmas Day 1635 Samuel de Champlain died in Québec,

first thoughtfully disinheriting his wife. When she learned that she was free of her vows, she left Paris and founded a convent.

Four years later a remarkable Frenchwoman, Marie Guyart, known in the Ursuline order she founded as Marie de l'Incarnation, established a school to provide religious instruction for daughters of colonists and natives. A determined woman who shared the mystical evangelism of her time, she was accompanied to Québec by a close friend, Madame de Chauvigny de la Peltrie. Both were widows who had disliked marriage intensely.

Marie de l'Incarnation remained in La Nouvelle France until her death thirty-three years later and loved it dearly, writing as many as six hundred letters a year to France begging for help at a time when the colony was almost extinct. She learned Algonkian and Iroquois and wrote dictionaries and catechisms. She suffered without complaint the desertion of her friend, Mme. de la Peltrie, who left her for Jeanne Mance, founder of the hospital on the island of Montréal.

Jeanne Mance, an experienced nurse, was part of a religious colony that grew out of a series of visions that came to an Anjou tax collector. A pious philanthropist donated funds, and a group of missionaries bought Montréal for the Société de Notre Dame de Montréal, building there in 1642 a village they called Ville-Marie. Their leader was Paul de Chomedey de Maisonneuve, and the community consisted of fanatical laymen determined to "labor there solely to bring about the glory of God and the salvation of the Indians."

The undertaking was daft in the extreme. The location at the crossroads of freight canoes carrying furs to the Québec warehouse was more suited to commerce than to a village given over to prayers. Worse, Ville-Marie was on the border of the Iroquois nation, which each summer sent war parties into Huronia and the St. Lawrence to dislodge competition.

Hurons desperately sent a peace delegation to the Iroquois. Jesuits helped fur traders to block it, agreeing that a Huron-Iroquois alliance would mean a diversion of furs to the Dutch and English. For their part Hurons stopped Neutrals from making a treaty with the French because they feared it would mean their displacement as France's middlemen.

By 1648 the frightening Iroquois military machine was rolling over Huron villages. In two years, Huronia had vanished. Thousands died and the rest were scattered.

French fur trade came to a stop for five years of horror as Iroquois, chiefly Mohawks, sent warriors to drive their remaining competitor, the French, off the St. Lawrence. In Ville-Marie, Jeanne Mance tended hideously hacked Hurons, Algonkians, and French, while Maisonneuve went to France to plead for help from a noblewoman, a friend of Mlle. Mance. He returned with a hundred soldiers and Marguerite Bourgeoys, a nun who founded the Congrégation de Notre-Dame de Montréal and became deeply attached to Jeanne Mance.

The devout residents of Ville-Marie dared go no farther than four steps from their doors: The village was surrounded by Iroquois. Trois-Rivières, halfway to Québec, often was abandoned. Farms along the river stood deserted and gutted. Marie de l'Incarnation, besieged in Québec where refugees crowded, wrote, "Either we must die or we must return to France."

In 1654 France sent four companies of soldiers from West Indies posts and followed them with four more, enough to save the colony but not to break the Iroquois blockade of the fur trade. Destitute, La Nouvelle France turned to the colony's young men. The governor asked Frenchmen to slip around the Iroquois and make contact with hunting tribes. *Coureurs de bois,* they were called. Adventurous youths left in such numbers that the colony was stripped of defenders.

The alarmed governor belatedly issued savage laws against men leaving the St. Lawrence without his permission. They had little effect against the pull of wilderness excitement, mystery, native women, and promise of profitable poaching. Iroquois raids, suspended while the confederacy dealt with competing tribes on its flanks, resumed in 1660 to dampen temporarily the foraging *coureurs de bois.*

On May 1, 1660, a twenty-five-year-old French soldier new to the colony, Dollard des Ormeaux, gathered seventeen volunteers of his age, all unmarried, and with forty Algonkians and four Hurons dug in on the Long Sault rapids where the Ottawa River joins the St. Lawrence. Evidence indicates they expected to ambush an Iroquois hunting party returning exhausted from portages and low on ammunition in order to relieve the hunters of their winter catch. In all likelihood Dollard expected as well to protect the colony's missing *coureurs de bois,* also due on the river that spring. Médard Chouart des Groseilliers and his brother-in-law, Pierre-Esprit Radisson, were among those who hadn't returned from a search for furs.

Instead, Dollard and his small band encountered the main body of eight hundred Iroquois braves headed from the Richelieu River to attack Ville-Marie. Dollard has become a legend in Québec as the savior of Canada, his reputation resting on the doubtful theory that he knew of the advancing Iroquois and recruited his forces to make a suicide stand. Whatever the truth of his motives, he held out gallantly for a week before the position was overrun. Dollard and twelve other Frenchmen were killed in the fighting; the remaining five Frenchmen were tortured to death.

The incident diverted the Iroquois army, giving La Nouvelle France time to harvest a crop against winter famine and allowing Radisson and Groseilliers to slip home with a fortune in furs that revived France's interest in its orphan child.

France was locked in religious clashes as the age of tolerance under Henry IV came violently apart. Persecution of French Protestants extended to a ban against Huguenots in La Nouvelle France. While religious differences in England were a rich source of colonial emigration to America, the powerful Jesuits of France made certain that no dissenters would be allowed in pious L'Acadie or on the St. Lawrence. Eventually Huguenots were forbidden even to sail to Québec: Priests complained that devotions were disturbed because sailors sang Protestant hymns on the decks of ships.

Meanwhile, Virginia attained a population of thousands of feisty colonists who demanded their own legislature. Pilgrims and Puritans poured into New England, outraged at Charles I's high church leanings and about to turn Massachusetts Bay's colony into a self-governing commonwealth. Dutch settlers to the south built energetic colonies at the mouths of the Hudson, Connecticut, and Delaware rivers. The French counterparts to these mercantile-minded uppity emigrants, the vigorous Huguenots, prohibited from entering France's American colony, went instead to England and Prussia where most of them prospered.

France grew indifferent to L'Acadie, resulting in a near abandonment of the settlements. Except for a few French on Cape Breton, the peninsula had been left to English colonists, who called it Annapolis after 1654.

Louis XIV of France in 1663 received a desperate delegation from La Nouvelle France: either withdraw from the colony entirely or support it. At the urging of his colonial administrator, Jean Baptiste Colbert, Louis decided on the latter course. Among the reforms that ensued were the integration of monastic Ville-Marie into the rest of the colony and appointment of a sovereign council and two heads of government, an intendant to control finance and administration and a governor to lead the army.

A militia was raised to defend the colony, and in 1665 the king sent a regiment, the crack Carignan-Salières, fresh from a campaign against the Dutch in the West Indies, and planted French settlers and governors from New Orléans to Guadeloupe. As the army marched to church for the Thanksgiving service, bells pealed in the village of Québec. That winter the regiment went looking for Iroquois and got lost, stumbling upon a settlement at Corlaer, present-day Schenectady, where Dutch and English took them in and fed them. The following summer their directions were better. They swept through abandoned Iroquois farms and destroyed the crops, a calamity which crippled the Iroquois economy for years.

The colony's first business manager was the intendant Jean Talon, thirty-nine, who found the colony at its lowest ebb, its enthusiasm even for the fur trade broken by the long ordeal of defending itself against the Iroquois. He counted only 3,000 French and Canadiens in the entire colony and began to pump in fresh blood: 1,500 indentured servants who would get land after three years' employment, and French immigrants who would be launched with two acres of seeded land.

The land, Talon noted, was "fruitful in natural-born Frenchmen, the women bearing nearly every year." Colbert, his chief and a cattle-breeder, applied the techniques of animal husbandry to the underpopulation of La Nouvelle France. He shipped fertile women, *filles du roi,* to Québec. Louis XIV provided the dowry, a bull and a cow, a dog, a sow, a cock and a hen, two barrels of salt meat, and eleven crowns in cash.

Jesuits and nuns preferred to select only women recommended

for piety and virtue, but when quotas were unfilled women were culled from sick wards, Paris beggar gangs, and whorehouses. Supervised on the voyage by what one observer described as "some stale old nuns" and purified on the way by a baptismal service, the women were sorted into three grades: well-born women were offered to officers of the Carignan-Salières, presentable women to soldiers, and the least attractive women to wastrels. Women were not permitted to reject a suitor. In a room adjoining the showroom, a priest performed marriage ceremonies. Dowries were paid upon consummation. Men who refused to marry were forbidden to hunt, fish, or trade in furs. Men whose wives bore a child every year were rewarded. There was a bonus for ten children, a larger bonus for twelve. The birth rate in La Nouvelle France boomed.

Colbert, who hated to see France depleted of its human stock to expand the colony, saw America as a breeding farm. Once he wrote Talon that he was shipping "four hundred stout fellows, fifty females, twelve mares, and two stallions." Jean le Moyne commented that Nouvelle France "manufactured enough people to disconcert history."

Talon attempted to diversify the one-industry economy by building a tannery, a brewery, a shipyard, and workshops that employed as many as 350. He imported hemp and coaxed farmers to grow the unfamiliar plant by providing looms and teaching women to weave. Hundreds of Pawnees and black slaves came with the developing seigneurial class as Talon distributed fiefs generously, as many as ten in a day. The island of Montréal was deeded over to the Séminaire de Saint-Sulpice. The Compagnie des Cent-Associés, which had title to most of North America, disappeared in 1663 and the colonies came under the direct control of Louis XIV.

Talon's fledgling commerce collapsed from lack of interest in the French court when he returned to France after five and a half years. A shipyard, factories, brewery, business contacts with Boston, beef trade with L'Acadie, and a commercial fishing co-op languished and disappeared. Québec's emerging middle class of merchants and seigneurs, who had formed a council to direct local matters, were ordered by Louis XIV to dissolve. He viewed the council as incipiently revolutionary. Many Carignan-Salières remained in the colony, wooed by free land, when the regiment was withdrawn; their property was seeded along the Richelieu River where they could make themselves useful if the Iroquois attacked.

Pierre Boucher, a visitor in 1664, warned Frenchmen who considered migration, "Good people may live here contentedly, but not bad people, because they are too closely looked after here."

The scourge of "bad people" was François-Xavier de Montmorency-Laval, Jesuit and first bishop of Québec. Laval's appointment bypassed, for the first time in La Nouvelle France, the authority of the church in France and placed colonial clergy under direct papal control, an arrangement historians view as responsible for the preservation of the Roman Catholic faith in Québec a century later.

Laval was an outstanding administrator but a fanatical puritan. He fought the temptations of the flesh by refusing communion to women who wore their hair provocatively in topknots, and he wanted to flog women who attended masked balls. He fought with the Sulpicans of Montréal, whom he suspected of undermining his authority, and with the governor over brandy trade to natives. To the horror of fur traders, Laval sought a royal edict against trafficking in brandy and planned to excommunicate *coureurs de bois* who violated it. The governor who fought him, and succeeded in having the ban rescinded, was a lusty old soldier, Louis de Buade, Comte de Frontenac.

Frontenac, a profligate deep in debt, obtained the posting to pay creditors and lay up a nest egg for his old age. He left in France a wife who had disgraced him, Anne de la Grange-Trianon, a rich beauty who left him for a princess, the granddaughter of Henry of Navarre. Whatever Frontenac's shortcomings in managing his household, he was the perfect foil for the Iroquois. On his arrival in 1672 he displayed the full panoply of his army to the Iroquois and obtained from the impressed confederacy an agreement that they would remain south of the Great Lakes and allow him to expand the French fur trade north.

Frontenac built a warehouse west of Ville-Marie at present-day Kingston, which the natives called Cataracoui and later became Fort Frontenac. Impatient for the profits he would skim off the fur trade, he encouraged *coureurs de bois* licensed by him to fan into the interior. Though Colbert complained about the cost, within twenty years there were French forts and Canadien fur traders from Tadoussac on the Gulf of St. Lawrence to Orléans on the Gulf of Mexico.

Under the circumstances it was almost impossible to prevent illegal *coureurs de bois* from stealing into the wilderness to bootleg furs to English traders. Though penalties were as harsh as to be chained for life to the oars of a French galleon, temptations were irresistible to the bold. Outlaw *coureurs,* hidden by their delighted families, were the colony's heroes, Canadiens who dared defy the omnipresent authority of the king.

Frontenac's business enterprise was entrusted mainly to a single astonishing man, René-Robert Cavelier, sieur de La Salle, a restless, well-born, former Jesuit priest who at twenty-four left the order. The following year, 1667, he was in Montréal, where the Sulpicans gave him a seigneury. He announced he was ready to find the Ohio River and the route to China, sold his seigneury, and departed. There is some doubt that the greenhorn achieved his goal, but in 1673 La Salle met Frontenac, and the adventure, wealth, and acclaim he had been seeking began.

Cataracoui was given him as a seigneury, where he could intercept furs intended for the Iroquois. He put another post above the falls at Niagara and one at Michilimackinac on the strait between lakes Michigan and Huron. Louis Jolliet, another ex-Jesuit favored by Frontenac, probed the necklace of lakes and rivers in 1673 with a Jesuit, Père Jacques Marquette, and discovered near Michigan's toe the headwaters of the Mississippi, which they followed as far as the Arkansas River.

La Salle and a Recollet priest, Louis Hennepin, traced the Illinois River in 1680. Hennepin independently traveled the tributaries, making note of the falls near the site of Minneapolis. Two years later La Salle followed a trail of an Iroquois war party's path through Illinois tribes, reached the Mississippi, and stopped to build a fort where Memphis now stands. He took possession of the Arkansas for France, passed through the territory of the Koroas and Natchez, and in April reached the Mississippi delta, which he called Louisiana, for the king of France.

La Salle was murdered in 1687 after a failed attempt to locate Louisiana by sea. He missed it by fifteen leagues and went ashore at Texas to look for a Mississippi tributary. He bungled the expedition badly and was killed by some of his own men.

Frontenac's vigor in pushing his fur trade across Iroquois routes was certain to lead to violence. The colony's growing problems with resentful Iroquois were minor, however, compared with that from a new competitor: Two renegade *coureurs de bois* had put England at the back door of La Nouvelle France.

— 3 —

Stand-Off

Pierre-Esprit Radisson and his brother-in-law, Médard Chouart des Groseilliers, known happily to Canadian schoolchildren as "Radishes and Gooseberries," could share credit with the slain hero Dollard des Ormeaux for saving La Nouvelle France in 1660. Dollard's stand on the Long Sault opened a hole in the Iroquois line that allowed Radisson and Des Groseilliers to slip into Ville-Marie with the most luxuriously thick beaver pelts the colony had ever seen: a haul that filled sixty canoes.

The governor pounced on the catch and confiscated it, ruling that the traders had left without his permission. His decision changed the history of North America. The infuriated Radisson, twenty, and Des Groseilliers, forty-two, were formidable men. At thirteen, Radisson was captured by the Iroquois, who adopted him. His band later rescued him as a rival band was torturing him to death. Des Groseilliers also had lived with natives, the Hurons, from whom he heard stories of the "great sea" to the west.

So both men were adept at living in the wilderness and fluent in native languages, an advantage that they determined to use. In August 1659 they slipped secretly from Trois-Rivières, eluded the Iroquois blockade, and probed the Great Lakes where Europeans had never been. That winter on the north shore of Lake Superior they camped with a Sioux tribe and learned geography. Natives told them rivers ran north into a large sea; Radisson guessed it was Hudson Bay.

Scores of Englishmen had been lost looking for a northern route to Japan. After the Cabots, there was Martin Frobisher, in 1576, who entered a cul-de-sac called Frobisher's Bay. In 1587 John Davis sailed the coast of Baffin and Greenland and met the

Inuit tribe. In 1611 Henry Hudson died in an open boat, set adrift by his own crew in James Bay. Then Thomas Button, in 1612, tried to penetrate the arctic ice, and three years later William Baffin, the finest navigator of them all, circled the island that bears his name.

While England was disappointed that a Northwest Passage still eluded traders, the voyages established a general outline of the inland sea, Hudson Bay. Radisson and Des Groseilliers had stumbled across a clue that tied beaver trade in the continent's center to ports accessible to ocean-going ships.

Bitter at their reception by the unsympathetic governor of La Nouvelle France, the renegade fur traders shopped for backing elsewhere. They were rejected in Gaspé and Boston, though their description of the wealth of furs available in the interior contributed to New England's resolve to eliminate Dutch competition for the prize by attacking New Holland. Radisson and Des Groseilliers next failed to interest backers in France. In England, Radisson improved their chances by marrying a well-connected woman whose father, while detesting his new son-in-law, put the Frenchman in touch with Prince Rupert.

Rupert, an aging but dashing cavalier, was a favorite cousin of Charles II because of his courage against the armies of Oliver Cromwell in battles that restored the English monarchy. Rupert, deep in debt for his extravagant style of living, was willing to gamble on the chance that the *coureurs de bois* could make him rich in the fur trade.

Radisson and Des Groseilliers left England in two tiny ships, Radisson in the *Eaglet* and Des Groseilliers in the *Nonsuch,* captained by a New Englander, Zachariah Gillam. Radisson's ship was damaged and forced to turn back, but the *Nonsuch* was guided masterfully into James Bay, where the men wintered among Cree hunters who had never before seen Europeans. In the spring Des Groseilliers and Gillam returned to England laden with thick furs: In exchange for £650 of trade goods, he brought back £19,000 of prime pelts.

Rupert gathered eighteen investors in a group of "adventurers" called the Hudson's Bay Company. For less than £300 apiece, the partners launched the richest and longest-running monopoly in world history. Founded twenty-four years before there was a

Bank of England, it is still the world's largest fur-trading company, and in 1977 did a $317 million business in furs alone.

Charles II was generous with his cousin. On May 2, 1670, he gave the Hudson's Bay Company perpetual title over the entire Hudson Bay watershed, to be known as Rupert's Land, a territory that technically belonged to France.

None of the signatories to the grant realized the magnitude of the gift. Rupert's Land proved to be thirty times larger than the kingdom and equal in size to European Russia. Extending 1.5 million square miles, it covers 38 percent of modern Canada.

The existence of native nations in the ice, tundra, plains, and forests of the huge tract was ignored. In the north were Esquimaux tribes; on the tundra, Chipewyans hunted caribou; Algonkians and Crees lived nomadically in the woods; on the prairies there was the great Dakota nation: all now deeded to Rupert and his partners.

Charles II gave his relative more power than he had himself. The Hudson's Bay Company could write its own laws without interference by any parliament. The king asked in return only that when a monarch visited Rupert's Land, a gift would be made of skins from "two elkes and two black beavers," a promise kept for the first time three centuries later when a ruling British monarch finally did come to Canada.

A fleet of English ships left for James Bay only weeks after the document was signed. Des Groseilliers built Fort Rupert and Radisson established Port Nelson. The transatlantic shuttle which followed horrified La Nouvelle France, which immediately felt the diversion of prime furs to the more conveniently located northern ports. Jean Talon was back in the colony as intendant in 1670, bringing Recollet priests to challenge the officious Jesuits.

He came into conflict with Bishop Laval when he succeeded in restoring brandy to the fur trade. England was flooding the hunting tribes with rum, obliging the French to provide brandy in order to compete. The French groaned under a burden of disadvantages. For one, English rum was a cheap product produced by slave colonies in the West Indies, while French brandy tediously was aged in the cask. Louis XIV's Sun King extravagances were supported by a ruinous 25 percent tax on furs, which the English escaped. Also, there were disparities in transportation cost:

French furs came over a long, exhausting, and expensive network of portages in small canoes to reach an ocean-going ship, while English furs made a short, Iroquois-free jaunt to inland seaports.

England was prospering on a golden triangle: slave colonies were sustained on a diet of substandard cod obtained off Newfoundland, which kept them healthy enough to produce rum for the North American fur trade, and all profits of rum, beaver, and fish went to London. St. John's, Newfoundland's best harbor, had grown to a permanent community in order to shelter England's cod fleet every season.

French trading posts, however, had a compelling attraction that the English lacked: they were hospitable to natives. English traders openly detested hunters. They did business through an open window, with the doors barred. Canadien outposts, in contrast, were joyful camps marked by feasts shared by *coureurs de bois* and the tribes, where the Canadiens would purchase native women as mates. Living with natives as they did, Canadiens understood the hardships of the hunt and how narrowly survival was maintained. While English traders contemptuously rejected low-quality pelts, Canadiens bought everything.

Prodded by New Englanders, the Iroquois renewed efforts to knock out the French competition that blocked them from the thick northern pelts. Frontenac was gone from the colony in 1682, recalled because of his scandalous efforts to milk the fur trade and his quarrels with the clergy and intendants. As well, the old soldier had failed to keep the Iroquois in check. Nervous of provoking a war with England, he did not interfere as Iroquois attacked the colony's tribal allies and French outposts. The governor who replaced him, Le Febvre de la Barre, observed that the Iroquois were "the bravest, strongest and shrewdest in all North America" as Iroquois ravaged the Ottawas and Saulteaux, canoe tribes essential to the fur trade's transportation system.

The colony's economy, wholly dependent once again on the fur trade, was in such straits that an intendant was forced to issue the first paper money, currency the shape and firmness of a playing card which the official promised doubtful Canadiens would be redeemed in full in better times.

To add to the stress, Radisson was switching sides. He and Des Groseilliers built Fort Bourbon on the western shore of Hudson

Bay at the mouth of the Nelson River and brought a sumptuous load of furs to Québec. The governor imposed an equally sumptuous tax, which the two refused to pay. Radisson then went back to the HBC in a righteous huff; Des Groseilliers chose to remain and end his days on the St. Lawrence.

The next governor of La Nouvelle France was Marquis de Brisay de Denonville, for twenty years a soldier. Soon after his arrival in 1685 he toured his domain and found much to dislike. Mixed marriages and rough frontier manners affronted him deeply. He thought the youth of the colony would be straightened out in the army, and he therefore obtained permission to grant commissions.

The stagnant colony, forbidden to establish any industry that might compete with the mother country, was pleased when its young men took military careers. Horrified to learn that six hundred Canadien *coureurs de bois* were working in the fur trade and certain that some were bootlegging furs to the English, Denonville put a limit of twenty-five licenses on the colony and restricted the number of *voyageurs*—canoemen, who could leave on fur-trade ventures.

He dealt the English competition on James Bay a stunning military blow. Claiming he was embarking on a police action to arrest Radisson, he sent a French officer, Pierre Chevalier de Troyes, to lead a small force six hundred miles overland from Ville-Marie and knock out the English. Of De Troyes' force, thirty were French marines and the rest Canadiens and natives. Prominent among the Canadiens were three of the twelve sons of Charles le Moyne, the wealthiest seigneur in the colony. The most famous of Le Moyne's extraordinary brood was the third son, Pierre le Moyne d'Iberville, then twenty-five. With him on Denonville's expedition were his brothers: Jacques, twenty-three, and Paul, twenty-one. D'Iberville's military zeal for the battles of James Bay was whetted by his anxiety to escape an imminent paternity suit.

The force left Montréal by canoe in the spring of 1686 armed with muskets, swords, and pikes. They paddled up the tumbling Ottawa, crossed portages where black flies stung their faces beyond recognition, sank cursing in spongy moss up to their hips. Eighty-five days later, they burst upon the thunderstruck defenders of Moose Fort, on an island at the mouth of the Moose River and protected by walls and palisades eighteen feet high.

De Troyes sent D'Iberville and a battering ram against the main door. With a sword in one hand and a musket in the other, the Canadien crashed through the barrier. The door slammed behind him and he was alone inside the garrison, fighting off English on every side in swashbuckling fashion until reinforcements broke down the door again.

Two weeks later D'Iberville was at Fort Rupert. With musket and sword, he leaped aboard a supply ship and captured it, while De Troyes took the fort. Three weeks later they located Fort Albany by the sound of the sunset gun. The astonished HBC governor surrendered in panic. De Troyes then withdrew most of his force, leaving D'Iberville to hold the northern posts for the French.

In the summer of 1689 Iroquois learned France and England were at war. Fur traders in the English colonies sent them against La Nouvelle France, which was unaware that King William's War was raging in Europe. Iroquois therefore surprised the village of Lachine, a stroll away from Montréal, and killed two hundred Canadiens, taking another ninety as prisoners to be tortured. Three Iroquois captured by Canadiens were tortured to death slowly in Place Royale as pitiless inhabitants watched.

Denonville, an able officer, was needed at home, and Frontenac, again mired in debt, returned to Québec. The strategy he recommended to Louis XIV was a naval and ground assault on New York, but the French king refused to send ships or men. The French colony's position appeared hopeless. Isolated half of the year by ice in the St. Lawrence, exposed to Iroquois, dependent on fur trade, the entire population numbered less than 12,000, roughly equivalent to that of Rhode Island. Against them were more than 200,000 English colonists whose coast was accessible year-round to English supply ships.

Frontenac decided to borrow the Iroquois tactic of hit-and-run terrorist attacks along the English border. Early in 1690 he sent small war parties of Canadiens and natives on snowshoes against Schenectady, where Jacques le Moyne de Sainte-Hélène was a leader, Salmon Falls, and Fort Loyal (now Portland, Maine).

The raids were conducted in the style of the frontier, which was cruel. Survivors described with horror how white Canadiens joined natives in depredations. Butchery by natives could be understood as vengeance for tribes destroyed by English settlers, such as the Narraganset nation's destruction by a New England confederacy fifteen years earlier, or the Tuscaroras who were driven out of the Carolinas, or others who simply disappeared. Participation in the savagery by Canadiens, many of whom wore crucifixes, was not forgiven in New England for centuries.

King William's War bonded the English colonies in America into a coalition aimed at driving the French off the continent. Sir William Phips, a born-again Christian of his day whose wealth came from finding sunken treasure ships in the West Indies, sailed from Massachusetts in May 1690 and paused at L'Acadie, long neglected by Louis XIV, to plant England's flag over Port Royal, vandalize the Catholic church there, and rename the place Annapolis Royal.

The military strategy for taking La Nouvelle France was to catch Québec in a pincer, one force led by Phips coming by sea and the other marching overland from New England. Colonial militia, however, inspired in part by William Penn's proclamations about liberty of conscience and unwilling to leave their farms at harvest time to serve in a foreign war, grumbled and shirked and would not go. Phips, therefore, was left alone to take Québec. Delayed when supplies from England were slow, he anchored off Québec in October and demanded that Frontenac surrender. The old soldier, then sixty-eight, replied to Phips's emissary, "I will answer your general only with the mouths of my cannon and the shots of my musketry."

Québec was bristling with the colony's new Canadien militia, 3,000 strong. Jacques le Moyne de Sainte-Hélène led resisters who repulsed Phips's attempt to put men ashore. De Sainte-Hélène later died of wounds. Phips had to content himself with lobbing 1,500 cannon balls into the town and then withdraw.

D'Iberville, described by historian Mason Wade as "a brilliant one-man war," was leading commando attacks against England all over the map. In 1694 he knocked the HBC out of James Bay trading posts the company had reoccupied and was given monopoly rights to the fur trade as a reward. A Le Moyne brother,

Louis, died there. D'Iberville, in 1696, knocked out English ships blockading L'Acadie, took Fort William Henry, an English fort on the border of L'Acadie, and in winter lashed on snowshoes to take St. John's, Newfoundland, from the rear and burn it to the ground. He demolished thirty-six English fishing villages in Newfoundland's coves and was about to win all of Newfoundland for France when he was dispatched to retake HBC trading posts, once more in English hands. En route, D'Iberville's single ship fought off three English vessels, sunk two of them and drove the other away, an action which enabled France to hang on to Hudson Bay forts for another sixteen years.

D'Iberville next was chosen to secure France's claim to Louisiana. He built a fort at Biloxi and laid down the foundations for Canadien-style relations with tribes from the Gulf of Mexico to Lake Michigan. He was unable to persuade France to become more aggressive in the south to stop English expansion, but he built a base at Mobile. Between military and colonizing engagements, he had no scruples about selling furs or illicit cod in New York. He was occupied with a dubious deal in Havana involving iron in 1706 when he died of malaria.

King William's War was good for the French fur trade, and Frontenac lived lavishly in Québec, quarreling with bishops over such puritanism as the banning of Molière's comedy *Tartuffe* and the excommunication of its star. The only literature allowed in the colony was devotional. When a priest found a nobleman reading *The Adventures of Petronius,* he ripped the book to shreds. Harvard, meanwhile, founded in 1636, was moving from Calvinism to an examination of "all good literature, arts and sciences."

Groaning French merchant ships glutted the Paris market with furs. When King William's War ended, French warehouses were clogged with furs. To cut costs, some posts were ordered closed. The fury this provoked among hunters abruptly deprived of markets resulted in France hastily re-opening the posts. Under Frontenac's direction, the network of trading posts in the Mississippi valley actually grew, and Canadien traders broke trail as far west as Lake Winnipeg.

Moreover, Canadien *voyageurs* eliminated the need for canoemen from the Ottawa tribe, who then appealed to the Iroquois, their former enemy, to clip French expansion. Frontenac, seventy-three and confined to a sedan chair, led an army against the Iroquois in the summer of 1696. He shattered the Iroquois nation by burning farms and harvests.

Two years later the old warrior died in bed in the governor's Château St. Louis in Québec. To his satisfaction, France, alarmed because English colonies showed lively interest in moving west, supported his decision to expand in the Mississippi valley. Canadien and native war parties continued to harass English colonies along the border, keeping colonial militia too busy to help the Iroquois. La Nouvelle France's cradles easily replaced the casualties of battle: The population reached almost 13,000 by 1696.

The war between France and England ended and the Peace of Ryswick was signed, an ignominious defeat for France which lost most of D'Iberville's gains, some forts on Hudson Bay and Newfoundland, but retained L'Acadie for France. War broke out again in 1702, Queen Anne's War or the War of the Spanish Succession. Canadien raids on New England resumed. Deerfield, Massachusetts, was the scene of a brutal encounter. Newfoundland again was taken from England. New Englanders in return recaptured vulnerable L'Acadie but failed in three attempts to take Québec.

The treaty of Utrecht of 1713 ended the war that marked the beginning of France's decline as a world power. With England ruling the ocean, France was forced to give up L'Acadie and withdraw from all HBC forts. Newfoundland was returned to England, even the French colony at Placentia, which was scattered to islands in the Gulf of St. Lawrence that France was allowed for its fishing fleets. Furious New Englanders accurately predicted that France would use the bases on St. Pierre, Miquelon, and Cape Breton for pirate ships to prey on Boston merchant fleets.

With France reduced to a long ribbon within the continent from Labrador to the Gulf of Mexico, Louis XIV was obliged to protect the vulnerable gateway to Québec with a naval fortress. He commissioned France's leading engineer, Vauban, to design a fortress that would be impregnable. Vauban drew plans for a massive star-shaped wall thirty feet high and in some places seventy feet thick to protect a town of 6,000 inhabitants, 4,000 of them

permanent army. The location was a bleak and foggy shore of
Cape Breton, and the fort was called Louisbourg. Construction
dragged on for twenty-five years, in good part because even the
stones were imported from France. "I expect to awaken one
morning in Versailles and see Louisbourg surging over the horizon," the king is said to have complained.

In a venture of such magnitude so far removed from scrutiny,
graft was on breathtaking scale to match the specifications of the
fort. Food, ammunition, and even army pay were mysteriously
missing, and worthless materials regularly were substituted for
those of quality. The rot of corruption spread along the far-flung
line of French trading forts. Governors grew rich, along with
contractors and suppliers while forts crumbled from the shoddiness
of construction materials, and men complained that food supplies
were short-weighted and unfit to eat.

Even more serious was France's neglect of trade goods. Natives
in America traded the fur robes off their backs and were desperate
for something only the HBC supplied: woolen blankets. England
shrewdly subsidized mills to make the blankets to native specifications, dyed in bands of scarlet, blue, white, and black. To meet the
demand, Scottish chieftains began to turn the highlands into sheep-
grazing grounds.

Harold Innis, Canadian economic historian, noted that "the
English woolen industry was of fundamental importance to the fur
trade, and eventually to the control of Canada by England."

But eighteenth-century France responded with a massive level
of neglect. Though fur traders begged for blankets, and tried to
import English ones, France was deaf to the need. Instead fur
trade goods were hopelessly out of date. Instead of lightweight
cooking pots, Canadiens facing a thousand miles of portages were
given massive iron pots suited to the coastal Micmac trade a century earlier.

English colonies on the Atlantic meanwhile flourished in the
thirty years of peace between France and England that followed
Utrecht. Newcomers picked up the colonial mood of spunky as-
sertiveness. In Philadelphia, Benjamin Franklin talked of colonial
union. Newspapers proliferated and Williamsburg had a theater
and art gallery.

La Nouvelle France also multiplied, thanks to the fertility of its women. Immigration almost stood still. Vigilant priests and nuns maintained decorum, though Canadiens dared to be open in their resentment of the French civil service that ruled them, especially after France redeemed the paper currency forced on the colony at half its face value and ruined Canadien merchants. The populace also was outraged by the venality of administrators and the behavior of wastrel sons of French nobility, exiled to La Nouvelle France, who pretended to be tutors in order to seduce the daughters of well-to-do Canadiens. Such misdeeds created a conviction in the minds of the bourgeoisie that literacy and sophistication equated with depravity.

Over a forty-year period, fewer than 5,000 left France for Québec. The colony had no jobs to draw Frenchmen except to unload furs and the climate was ill-suited to agriculture. Newcomers usually were castoffs. "Do not send such people," begged the bishop of Québec in 1725. "To continue to send such may cause the colonies to lose their faith and make them like the English and even the infidels."

The birth rate was phenomenal, amply replacing the five hundred *voyageurs* who were gone in canoes, risking early death by ambush or rupture. By the 1750s, the last decade of French rule, La Nouvelle France had a population of a mere 55,000, all but a fraction from fecundity alone.

Although L'Acadie was known as Acadia after the treaty of Utrecht, the 2,000 French colonists farming in the Annapolis valley chose to remain under English rule rather than give up their farms. England uneasily allowed them to stay, but banished priests and demanded an oath of allegiance. Included in the oath was a vow to defend the colony against all aggressors, including France.

The Acadiens insisted on a status of "French neutrals." Some swore allegiance to the English king, but they wouldn't promise to fight Frenchmen. Outlawed priests, living with the Abenakis nation and prodding Micmacs, Malecites, and Penobscots to harass English settlers, brought messages from Louisbourg counseling Acadiens to remain firm.

English administrators executed some Acadiens and flogged others, but the effort was futile: Acadiens neither moved to Louisbourg nor promised to be loyal subjects. In the end, the matter was dropped. New Englanders flocked to Acadia in such numbers that it seemed likely Acadiens would in time be assimilated.

Congregationalists laid out townsites in the Massachusetts way, built schools and town meeting halls, broke soil for gardens, and erected graceful frame homes in Georgian style. The communities did not mingle, separated by language, religion, and bitter memories of Acadiens and Abenakis who fell on New England villagers.

Louis XIV's death in 1715 was celebrated in Paris, relieved to be rid of a greedy, oppressive regime, but his successors were worse. Taxes were raised and currency devalued. The affairs of the colony were marked by opportunism and fraud. Poor management increased in the fur trade, producing chaotic pricing, overstocking, deterioration of stored furs, and a swarm of smugglers. European fashion dictated smaller hats, but beaver still made up 40 percent of exports from America, with mink, lynx, otter, deerskin, seal, and fox in great demand. In 1722, France solved some of the mess by establishing a monopoly, the Compagnie d'Occident, that created another period 'of rapid expansion.

New York traders put a rival fort on Lake Ontario at Oswego, across from Fort Frontenac, which was so attractive to Canadien smugglers that the Compagnie was obliged to plug the leaks all over the Great Lakes. In 1745 it built Fort Rouillé on a main commercial route where Toronto now stands. Two years later there was a fort at Sault Ste. Marie. Fort Niagara's wooden palisade on the east banks of the river were reinforced with stone to discourage competitors from Albany. The most audacious French forts were in Iroquois country, Chambly on the Richelieu River guarding Montréal and St. Frédéric and Carillon on Lake Champlain.

Despite the militant precautions, Canadiens continued to smuggle furs to Albany, where they brought a higher price. A notorious swindler, Antoine Laumet de Lamothe Cadillac, in 1701 the founder of Detroit, used the location to divert a heavy traffic of French furs to New York. Subsequently he was confined briefly in the Bastille.

To get ahead of the opposition, the French monopoly embarked on a new policy: selling fur-trading licenses to Canadiens who would open up new territory. The first Montrealer to send a scouting party west of the Great Lakes was a woman, Madame

Marie Verchères, widowed mother of a Canadien heroine, fourteen-year-old Marie-Madeleine, who, in 1692, when left in charge of the family home, held off an Iroquois siege for a week.

Next came the remarkable Vérendrye men, Pierre Gaultier de La Vérendrye and his eldest son, Jean-Baptiste, who went west in 1731 and built a fort on Rainy River that autumn. Jean-Baptiste wintered the next year at Lake of the Woods and went with his father in 1734 to mix in tribal wars between Crees and Prairie Sioux on the side of the Cree. That summer Jean-Baptiste built a fort on the Red River and the following year had another on Lake Winnipeg. In June 1736 Sioux caught him at Lake of the Woods and killed him; he was twenty-three.

His brother Pierre founded Fort Dauphin in 1741. Another brother, François, was twenty-four when he stood on the lazy-S bank of the Saskatchewan River in 1739, the first European to see it. In 1742 François and a younger brother, Louis Joseph, pushed west to the foothills of the Rockies, and on the return trip camped in South Dakota where they lost a lead plate that was unearthed two centuries later. Two years and three months after they started the historic journey, they were back on the Red River, disappointed men. They had hoped to reach the Pacific or at least locate a river artery running west. Instead, all North America's rivers appeared to run maddeningly north and south.

In 1744 the Vérendryes were summoned to La Nouvelle France: France and England were at war again. This one, King George's War, gave New England its opportunity to rid itself of Louisbourg, which had become a haven for pirate ships preying on Boston's merchant fleet. Sir William Pepperrell, son of one of New England's wealthiest traders, raised a force of 4,000, which the Royal Navy carried up the coast to Louisbourg.

Formidable as the reputation of the fortress was, gossip held that graft had weakened the garrison. Head of the commissary for five years was François Bigot, who plundered munitions and food and stole even the army payroll, flinging into prison those who complained.

Pepperrell's armada arrived off Louisbourg just as Bigot was suppressing a mutiny. Bigot opened the dungeons and promised amnesty to those who would help defend the fortress. Pepperrell blockaded the harbor for forty-six days while Louisbourg starved.

Then New Englanders landed three miles from the fort and brought cannon ashore. Straining, sweating men, one hundred to a cannon, dragged the guns through a swamp and bombarded Louisbourg from its vulnerable backside. All its main guns were fixed in stone, pointing at the sea. Cheering, the English stormed over the walls and took the fortress. Pepperrell left the *fleur de lis* flying from the battlements and twenty plump supply ships sailed innocently into harbor before the world learned that impregnable Louisbourg had fallen.

William Shirley, governor of Massachusetts, moved into Louisbourg's exquisitely appointed château and sent letters to England's colonial administrator, the Duke of Newcastle, begging for an army and navy to take Québec and complete the conquest of New France. But England, preoccupied with the frightful defeat of Prince Charlie and Catholic highlanders at Culloden and threatened by an invasion of Dutch, could not help.

King George's War ended inconclusively in 1748. England wanted the return of Madras, India's great center for spices and silk. France would yield the prize only if some face-saving was provided, so England gave back Louisbourg.

New England's wrath at the betrayal obliged England to atone. A naval base south of Louisbourg was promised to provide protection against pirates. A natural harbor was located and named Halifax for the family whose founding of the Bank of England had contributed to England's emergence as a world power.

The London *Gazette* carried the government's advertisement for English settlers and offered free passage, free land, and some supplies, with preference for military and building trades. Londoners leaped at the choice opportunity to rid themselves of the poor. They directed beggars to the colonial office.

"The number of settlers, men, women and children, is 1,400," wrote Edward Cornwallis, commander of Halifax in 1749 when the first batch arrived, "but I beg leave to observe to your Lordships that among these the number of industrious, active men proper to undertake and carry out a new settlement is very small. Of soldiers there is only 100, of tradesmen, sailors or others willing to work not above 200 more. The rest are poor, idle, worthless vagabonds."

His warning went unheeded. English taxpayers, crushed by

costly wars and the expense of supporting poorhouses, unloaded
indigents into ships bound for Halifax. In 1753 one settler was an
eighty-year-old. The commander wrote testily about the em-
barkation: "There were about thirty of them that could not stir
off the beach, eight of them orphans. Two died."

A better source of immigrants was New England. Cape Cod's
merchants, agents, tavernkeepers, whores, ship owners, and hab-
erdashers moved to Halifax in search of navy contracts and contacts. Congregationalists, though miffed when they were refused
permission to establish a town council in what England considered a military base, turned themselves anyway to good works.
With their own funds, they built an orphanage and hospital for
England's derelicts. The garrison's first church, St. Paul's, served
Church of England adherents, Halifax's English establishment, on
Sunday mornings and American "dissenters" in the afternoons.

Acadiens who ventured into Halifax looking for work risked severe abuse. Fertility had increased the population to 6,000, most
of whom stuck to farming and fishing. On the Île Royale, Louisbourg's governor considered them his subjects and sent instruction
by way of the busy priest-couriers. When King George's War
broke out, Acadiens defied the governor's orders to fight and
remained neutral. A few underground militants helped by building
scaling ladders and guiding French warships in the direction of
Annapolis.

France continued to make threatening gestures toward Halifax
and Acadia. A fort, Beauséjour, was built within marching distance of the English naval base, a challenge that Cornwallis met
by sending a force to destroy it. Acadiens in the path of the army
could remain indifferent no longer. Abbé la Loutre, priest-
provocateur, set fire to the Acadien village of Beau Bassin to
force homeless Acadiens to move to Beauséjour. The English assault failed, however, so the new governor at Halifax, Charles
Lawrence, ordered a confronting fort built in his name. Prudent
Acadiens, accurately reading the portents, began to slip away.
Two thousand were on Île St. Jean (Prince Edward Island) by
1752 and seven hundred around Louisbourg.

Meanwhile Anglo-Americans were clashing with Canadiens and
French in the Ohio Valley. Pennsylvanians tested the waters in
1748 and found tribes eager to trade for "certain red and blue

cloths, an ell and a quarter wide" and better prices. Word spread that the French network was porous. Londoners put up money so Virginians could claim a half-million acres stretching to the banks of the Ohio. A scruffy lot of American freebooters—"abandoned wretches," Governor Hamilton of Pennsylvania called them— filtered into the Ohio basin with rum and blankets.

Tribes generally preferred Canadiens, who learned their languages and didn't want their land, but English goods were irresistible. In 1752, however, American prestige suffered a severe setback. A Miami chief so closely allied with the Americans that he was called "Old Briton" was captured by some Chippewa led by a Frenchman, who then cooked Old Briton and ate him.

American stock on the frontier plunged sharply. Two prominent Pennsylvanian traders went bankrupt in a year. The Marquis de Duquesne, France's governor at Québec in 1753, sent soldiers into the Ohio to build forts and stop the Americans. The Battle of the Wilderness had begun.

— 4 —

The Conquest

Robert Dinwiddie, a Scot who was acting governor of Virginia, had plunged on land speculation on the Ohio. In January 1754 he sent a young surveyor, George Washington, twenty-one, to establish an English fort near the site of present-day Erie, Pennsylvania, to keep France off his claim. Washington walked three hundred miles in winter and reported that French soldiers were already there and had constructed nearby Fort le Boeuf, with a wagon road running to Fort Presqu' Île, and showed no inclination to leave.

Dinwiddie ordered construction crews to build an English fort, to be called Virginia, at the junction of the Monongahela and the Allegheny rivers where Pittsburgh now stands. Washington and a few Virginia militia followed, unaware that it already had been captured by the French who renamed it Fort Duquesne.

Canadiens and French, advised of Washington's approach, sent a small party to advise him he was on foreign territory. Nervous Virginians opened fire at the sight of them, killing or taking prisoner all but one, who escaped to warn the fort. Apprehensive, Washington ordered his men to build a palisade they grimly called Fort Necessity. They were scattered by a furious Canadien and tribal attack before they could complete the task.

The colonies dispatched delegates to Albany to discuss the crisis. Among them was Benjamin Franklin, long an advocate of colonial union, and a genial and wealthy Irish squire, William Johnson, owner of an estate in the Mohawk valley, who brought with him a handsome and significant ally, some Iroquois in war paint.

Colonial delegates could not agree. Pacifist Quakers from Pennsylvania refused to fight the French. Maryland, amused that Virginians were about to lose their shirts, showed no inclination to help. Despite huge investments in the Ohio, Virginians weren't willing to take on the French Empire alone. Eventually, England was obliged to send a rusty old general, Edward Braddock, sixty, and 1,400 redcoats.

With seven hundred Virginia militia, among them George Washington, Braddock moved ponderously across the Alleghenies toward Fort Duquesne, building roads where feasible to take the weight of his munitions and a line of men that stretched for miles. At the Monongahela crossing, an ambush of nine hundred shrieking Canadiens and Indians fired from ambush. In the carnage called the Battle of the Wilderness, Braddock was killed and other Anglo-Virginian casualties amounted to a thousand killed, scalped, or wounded. Washington was one of the few officers to survive.

English military strategy for the summer campaign developed on three other fronts: one an assault against Fort Niagara, crossroads of the fur trade; another aimed at French forts in the Mohawk valley on Lake Champlain; and the third against Beauséjour in Nova Scotia. William Johnson, chosen by Braddock to be Indian superintendent for New York, bumbled through a chance victory over the French at Lake George. Taking Fort St. Frédéric near Crown Point, he bagged a French general. New Englanders captured Beauséjour, but William Shirley of Massachusetts failed at Niagara.

In Nova Scotia, Acadiens were enjoying the greatest prosperity of their history. They had succeeded in finessing both the English, over the matter of the oath, and the French, who wanted them to move to Louisbourg. Their flocks had multiplied; they had developed a culture based on close-knit families, songs, and stories. Though still known as "the French Neutrals," their presence alarmed the English military establishment at Halifax. Charles Lawrence, the governor, was beset with pleas to take control.

He called for surrender of Acadien boats and guns, and demanded that all take an oath to fight against France or be deported. Acadiens were skeptical: How could 10,000 people be deported by a handful of English? As months passed in the summer of 1755, they grew less confident; Lawrence clearly was assembling ships to carry out his promise.

The exile of the Acadiens began on October 8, 1755, accelerated in 1758, when Louisbourg fell, and ended only in 1762. In 1767, when England called for all Acadiens left in Nova Scotia to swear allegiance, the count was 165 families. In the intervening years, Acadiens rounded up at gunpoint were flung around the world. The original intent to scatter them throughout the English seaport colonies was opposed violently. Boston turned back two shiploads; Virginia rejected a thousand stateless Acadiens. Some were sent instead to England; two ships loaded with refugees sank and all perished.

Finally, it was agreed to dump most of them in the distant French colony of Louisiana. Acadiens there received a chilly welcome from French plantation owners, who found their customs alien. The shattered Acadiens withdrew to mosquito-infested bayous to make a new start as a race Americans would call Cajuns.

Families were separated in the uprooting, few to be reunited again. Some hid in the woods around the Miramichi or on the gulf islands of Île Royale or Île St. Jean. Some fled as far as the western prairies to live among the *voyageurs* on Lake Winnipeg.

An American poet, Henry Longfellow, later heard of the expulsion while attending a dinner and used it for a poem he called *Evangeline,* which brought attention and sympathy for the exiles. Despite the tragedy, Acadiens proved capable of endurance. Cajun women passed along the oral heritage of legend and song and kept it alive through two centuries of efforts to make them American, while Acadiens in Prince Edward Island and New Brunswick emerged after two hundred years and showed themselves to be a whole people, with a heritage, flags, and anthems of their own.

The expulsion of the Acadiens achieved a degree of legitimacy as a military necessity when France and England in 1756 launched what was to be called the Seven Years' War. England was unprepared and parliament in chaos when shifts in European alliances brought on the conflict. William Pitt, disliked by George II but adored by the English public for remaining honest while holding the position of army paymaster, had been deposed. The Whig prime minister, Robert Walpole, had turned England's army into a sorry mess by encumbering it with officers whose promotions were secured by bribes.

France took swift action to defend its colonies, dispatching to Québec to replace the general captured at Crown Point Marquis de Montcalm, Louis Joseph de Montcalm-Gozon, forty-four. A soldier from the age of nine, Montcalm bore on his body a half dozen saber scars from wounds received in hand-to-hand conflict.

Montcalm viewed his new command with a sinking heart. The infamous François Bigot had escaped scandal for his depredations in Louisbourg and was intendant of La Nouvelle France, a position that enabled him to skim off fur-trade profits and plunder harvests, military supplies, and trade goods. His confederate, Joseph-Michel Cadet, a Canadien cattle dealer, held the post of purveyor-general for the army. The colony's governor, for the first time someone native-born, was fifty-eight-year-old Pierre de Rigaud, Marquis de Vaudreuil-Cavagnal, and a staunch supporter of Bigot. As a result of Bigot's corruption, the colony's defenses were appalling. Vaudreuil and Montcalm quarreled. The Canadien governor was furious that French soldiers sat by the fireside in winter, while Canadiens went with native allies to the dirty raids along the border.

Despite the havoc Bigot created, Montcalm's army had early successes. A few months after reaching Québec, he captured the American trading post at Oswego. Montcalm was unprepared for the aftermath of frontier victory, the torture of prisoners to their death. When he heard screams of agony, he hurled himself on those who were dismembering living prisoners, but was helpless to stop it.

New Englanders sent a fast ship to London to demand help. Montcalm captured Fort William Henry the following summer. Fighting in his shirtsleeves in the heat, he was ready this time when victory came. He ransomed prisoners from his native allies and saved some four hundred American lives.

William Pitt was returned to power as England's prime minister when the country suffered defeats in what Winston Churchill once described as "the First World War." Pitt fired incompetent generals and replaced them with young blood. James Abercromby, forty-nine, was sent to push Montcalm out of the Lake Champlain country; Fort Duquesne was the target of another force; and a third, under a promising thirty-nine-year-old Guards officer, Jeffery Amherst, was appointed at Louisbourg.

To balance, because Amherst was cautious, Pitt picked as his aide a flashy, mercurial officer, James Wolfe, thirty-one. Wolfe, white-skinned, redhaired, and frail, was a demon in battle but too outspoken about the stupidity or cowardice of his superiors to be popular with generals. Amherst and Wolfe captured Louisbourg in July 1758, after Wolfe found an unguarded spit of beach on which to land the English army and repeat Pepperrell's feat of hauling cannons to bombard the fortress from the rear. When Louisbourg surrendered, Wolfe took tea with the ladies of the town, noting that the code of war forbid him to rape when a garrison surrendered. He wrote his mother, "A day or two more and they would have been entirely at our disposal."

Abercromby meanwhile marched redcoats and militia from Massachusetts and New Hampshire to take the French fort Carillon (Ticonderoga). Montcalm, finding the fort too dilapidated to defend, arranged breastworks in the path of the English advance. With Canadiens and native allies setting up a din of war cries, Abercromby's forces were demoralized. Thousands died. Montcalm, whose forces were greatly outnumbered, marveled, "What a day for France! I never saw the like."

Fort Duquesne was captured by Anglo-Americans and renamed Pittsburgh for England's war leader. Montcalm, recognizing the impossibility of defending the long line of forts in the Ohio and Great Lakes, gave orders that they were to be abandoned at the first sign of redcoats. An early loss was Fort Frontenac, taken with its bulging fur warehouse by John Bradstreet and renamed Kingston.

Though New England was ecstatic at news that Louisbourg had fallen, celebrants were not so blinded by patriotism as to overlook business opportunities. Ships from Boston brought food and fresh water to French warships at midocean trysts, and Montcalm purchased beef and grain from farmers in New York.

That winter, the French general made preparations for the spring attack on Montréal and Québec. Wolfe went back to England a hero, and Pitt gave him another promotion: He would lead

the combined army and navy of England against Québec. Wolfe
promptly introduced reforms he'd planned for years. He eliminated the anachronistic lace cuffs on infantry uniforms and rescinded orders that soldiers powder their hair, which he knew attracted rats when the men slept. He replaced tight britches with
trousers of a more humane cut and introduced a cross-webbed
harness to give better weight distribution to fifty-pound back-
packs.

England's finest navigators huddled that winter in Halifax over
maps of the St. Lawrence Gulf and River. One was James Cook,
thirty-one. In ten years he would set off on his famous voyages of
the Pacific.

Montcalm argued with Vaudreuil all winter. Vaudreuil opposed
the decision to abandon the outer forts and objected to Montcalm's insistence that Canadiens fight under French officers.
Montcalm thought the Canadiens too unruly to be trusted otherwise. A military traditionalist, he scorned the Canadien-style
ambushes and raids.

Montcalm's second-in-command was an indigent nobleman,
François de Lévis, a Gascon of courage and good sense. His aide
was an indifferent soldier but brilliant mathematician, Louis Antoine, Comte de Bougainville, who at twenty-seven had been
elected to the Royal Society in London. Bougainville was dispatched to France to beg for reinforcements but found the court
absorbed in an ambitious scheme to send an invasion fleet to England instead.

Louis XV is said to have commented coldly, "When the house
is on fire, one doesn't bother about the stables." Bougainville
brought a convoy of food ships and supplies, news of a promotion
for Montcalm, and word there would be no French naval support
to defend the colony. In July, Fort Niagara fell to the English and
Montcalm split his forces, sending Lévis to guard Montréal.

Montcalm prepared to defend the shore of the river around
Québec against landing parties. Though the citadel looked impregnable on the top of 200-foot cliffs, its walls were in poor condition. Canadiens labored to dig trenches in the heat of early summer; if the English gained the high ground, Montcalm felt he was
lost.

The full might of the Royal Navy appeared on the St. Lawrence below Québec, forty-nine warships bristling with cannon, and 119 transports. Wolfe placed cannons on the undefended sloping ground opposite the citadel and began a daily barrage, turning the town to rubble.

Montcalm concentrated on repulsing English landing parties. His most spectacular trick, setting fire to ships loaded with pitch and gunpowder and allowing them to drift into the enemy's mooring, was thwarted when a sluggish current gave the English time to avoid the floating holocaust.

The bombardment and stalemate went on all summer. Priests sang *misere mei Deud* and stood watch with fire buckets. During one of Wolfe's attempts to land, he witnessed a French officer rescuing a wounded English soldier who was about to be scalped. He sent a courier to Montcalm with a reward, which Montcalm returned with a courteous note: the officer, he explained, was only doing his duty.

Wolfe's Scots acquitted themselves valiantly in that engagement, refusing to withdraw until their wounded were safe. The Fraser clan were there because Wolfe had admired the courage of highlanders at the slaughter of Culloden and persuaded Pitt that they would be useful in foreign wars—particularly this one, since some spoke French.

Wolfe was often ill, his pallor ghastly. He stopped communicating with his sneering generals. To satisfy the need for action, he released American Rangers to pillage the Canadien countryside; "the worst soldiers in the universe," he had called them. He was repelled by the American fondness for scalping and gave orders that no one was to be scalped except Indians or Canadiens dressed as Indians. Columns of smoke rose in the summer heat to show where the Rangers were.

Montcalm tried the fireboat trick again. This time English sailors put grapples on the conflagration and towed it harmlessly away. Though Amherst had control of most of the fur-trade network, and such posts as Rouillé (Toronto) had followed orders to give up at first sight of the English, Canadiens began to believe that they would survive: the English navy would have to withdraw soon to avoid being frozen all winter.

Wolfe wrote disconsolately to Pitt, "I have never serv'd in so disagreeable a campaign." He feared for his brief, meteoric career: After the debacle of Carillon, Abercromby had been sacked.

Bougainville and a crack French regiment, the Guyennes, were stationed a few miles upriver from the English fleet to protect Montcalm's line of communication with Lévis. Montcalm, inclined to pessimism, wrote his wife, "I think I should have given up all my honors to be back with you, but the king must be obeyed. The moment when I shall see you again will be the finest of my life. Goodbye, my heart."

In September rain fell, day after day. Wolfe borrowed the coat of a grenadier and joined a party of workmen erecting tents across the river from the cliffs so he could examine them for an opening. A Canadien sentry put a spy-glass on him and recognized his red hair.

On the night of September 12 Wolfe tried a final, desperate plan. He had learned of a broad diagonal path leading up the 180-foot cliffs at a cove called Anse au Foulon, west of Québec, the top of which was guarded by thirty men. The young navigator assigned the task of finding the cove in the dark was so uncertain of his chances that he asked Wolfe to write a letter absolving him of responsibility if he failed.

That night the navy made a show of preparing to land at Beauport, east of Québec, to fool Montcalm. Montcalm watched the bustling activity while Wolfe was rowed silently up the dark river miles away. Bougainville, in bed with his cousin's wife at Cap Rouge, neglected to warn Montcalm of a change in plan: Supply ships from Montréal, due to slip through the English blockade that night, had been unable to leave Cap Rouge because they needed repairs. Sentinels along the river, expecting the food barges, softly hailed the dark shapes on the water and were answered in French by the Fraser highlanders.

A half hour before daylight, Wolfe's army had climbed the path up the steep cliffs at Anse au Foulon. Colonel William Howe, thirty, rushed the picket while a highlander distracted the guard. Wolfe was on the height a few minutes later, incredulous at his luck. Montcalm, who had just retired after a sleepless night, was awakened by distant shots as the picket was overcome. Then silence fell; the English were hauling cannon up the path.

Wolfe arranged his army in two long parallel lines, advised

them to rest, and issued a tot of rum for their breakfast. In front of them was a pasture that had been granted in 1635 to Abraham Martin, a rascal later sent to prison for seducing a child. The field was known locally as the Plains of Abraham.

Some hours passed before Montcalm had a report on the disaster. He sent word to Bougainville to come at once with the Guyennes to attack the English rear, but Bougainville could not be found. Montcalm decided he could not delay, though he had only a third of his forces at hand. He led his army to the Plains of Abraham and arranged them within sight of the English for battle.

His movements were heavy and listless. An aide said, "It seemed as though he felt his fate upon him." Drooping in the saddle of his big black horse, he placed his regulars in the middle of his line and the Canadiens on the flanks. Natives flitted into the brush to fight from concealment, baffled by the European military style of full visibility.

Montcalm gave the order to advance. Wolfe's men a quarter of a mile away rose and aimed five-foot Brown Bess muskets. Canadiens yelling Iroquois war cries started unevenly across the field. "Much too fast," an observer commented. As shot dropped among them, Wolfe's army remained still. The French and Canadiens were forty yards away when Wolfe ordered his soldiers to fire. Four thousand muskets exploded and the French-Canadien line went down as though a scythe had sliced it. "Upon which," a British officer reported, "a total rout of the enemy ensued."

Wolfe, conspicuous in the full rig of an English general, had placed himself near the front of his army, a handsome target. A grape shot passed through his right wrist while the French were running toward him. He wrapped a handkerchief around the wound and kept his place. After the command to fire, two more shots hit him. One caused a minor wound in his thigh and the other tore a hole in his chest. Still he held his post and remained composed. An aide supported him and said, "They run, see how they run!" Wolfe asked who was running. Informed it was the French, he gave orders to cut off the retreat. Then he died.

Fraser highlanders, howling the clan battle cry, slashed the fleeing French with claymores as Canadiens covered the escape.

Montcalm was hit three times. He left the field in his saddle, his gut hideously open, supported on either side by officers.

The battle on the Plains of Abraham lasted but fifteen minutes. Four years later it resulted in a single statement written in a treaty by Louis XV: "His most Christian Majesty cedes and guarantees to his Britannick Majesty, in full right, Canada."

5

A Matter
of Adjustment

It wasn't immediately clear on the morning of September 13, 1759, that a single volley on the Plains of Abraham had lost France half of North America. Demoralized by the death of their general, Wolfe's officers failed to cut off the French army's retreat. Bougainville and the Guyennes were hurrying to Québec and might clear the English off the cliff before more cannon could be brought up. As Montcalm lay dying in the citadel, it fell to Vaudreuil to decide what to do.

There was a meeting at six that night. Vaudreuil brought Montcalm's opinion: there were three choices; surrender, fight, or withdraw the army from the citadel to join Bougainville at Jacques-Cartier and fight elsewhere. French army officers preferred the last option. That night the army left Québec with only the arms each man could carry. Jean-Baptiste Nicolas Roch de Ramezay, a Canadien from a distinguished Montréal family, was left in command with permission to surrender if necessary to prevent rape and looting.

Montcalm died at four in the morning, surrounded by weeping Ursuline nuns, and was buried in a crater in the floor of their roofless convent. Ramezay ordered that half rations be cut in half again. Three days passed with no sign of relief. On September 17, Ramezay raised a white flag over the citadel. Vaudreuil cursed. Another day and the army would have been ready; Lévis was at Jacques-Cartier.

The next morning the Royal Artillery came through the gates of Québec with a Union Jack mounted on a field piece. The English gave generous terms in the surrender since the fleet was preparing to sail, agreeing to Ramezay's request that the victors preserve the "exercise of Catholic, Apostolic, and Roman religion." In England priests often were hunted and hanged, but in Québec English soldiers stood guard duty at Catholic shrines.

The navy made ready. One of Wolfe's officers, Scottish-born James Murray, thirty-seven, of the Royal Americans, would remain at Québec with 6,000 men. The English were appalled by the misery and desolation of the inhabitants. "To describe it is really beyond my powers," one wrote, "and to think of it is shocking to humanity."

Cold rain fell on gaunt people dying in the open, too weak from wounds and hunger to move to shelter. Murray put his men on reduced rations to release food for civilian use. With Lévis' army still in the field, he was anxious to be harsh on possible rebels and conciliatory to the larger population he hoped to win over. They "hardly will hereafter be easily persuaded to take up arms against a nation they admire," he observed.

Wolfe's body went home pickled in a barrel of rum to preserve it and was given a hero's funeral as England celebrated "the wonderful year." The campaigns in America all had been victorious and the French invasion fleet was turned back at home. Antimonarchists in France also were jubilant to see Louis XV discomfited. Voltaire gave a dinner party to celebrate the fall of Québec. He complained, "These two nations at war over a few snowbound acres in the region of Canada are spending more than all of Canada is worth." The king's mistress, Madame de Pompadour, agreed. "Canada is useful only to provide me with furs," she said.

Lévis hoped France would blockade the Gulf of St. Lawrence to keep England from sending help to Murray and Amherst. His agents told him conditions in the citadel were dreadful. Two thousand were dead from scurvy and the rest severely weakened. Late in April Lévis attacked. Murray, like Montcalm unwilling to trust the citadel's fortifications, went out to meet him at Sainte Foy and was resoundingly defeated.

Lévis waited to follow up his victory, watching the river for French warships. In May the first ship from Europe appeared: it was English. Lévis, bottled up within North America and surrounded by English, withdrew to Montréal to make a last stand there. Amherst and Murray rolled their armies through Canadien villages, burning everything, and met at Montréal in September 1760. Lévis ordered the regimental colors burned to save them from disgrace as Vaudreuil accepted ignominious terms of surrender. On September 8, Montréal fell.

The provisional government established under James Murray to rule Canada was shaped by military expediency. Though George II still equated religious dissent with sedition, it was clearly impossible to convert 60,000 French-speaking Catholics overnight to the Church of England. Instead, the church and French civil law were permitted, but other measures, such as abolition of church tithes and seigneurial powers, were introduced as a taste of Anglicization.

French administrators, Vaudreuil and François Bigot included, were among three hundred leaders of La Nouvelle France allowed to return to France. Bilingual Swiss and Huguenots busily filled administrative posts. Canadien seigneurs and officers discovered that England was prepared to invest money in the colony's development. Canadiens who were willing to put aside antipathy for the enemy could get government appointments and contracts.

William Pitt's magnificent war machine had "subdued the world," as Prime Minister Walpole put it, but put England in staggering debt. As George II died in October 1760, heavily taxed landowners and industrialists in England were plotting his eclipse. In 1761 France and Spain made an alliance, Pitt resigned, and England captured Havana and the Philippines. England went to the treaty table in 1763 nervously holding an overextended empire.

The last battle of the Seven Years' War had been fought in America. In 1762 France sent a fleet from Brest to capture St. John's in Newfoundland in order to keep a fishing industry that employed 14,000 men. The harbor's permanent population, mostly Irish Catholic refugees, cheered the French victory, but it was short-lived. William Amherst, brother of England's commander-in-chief in America, slipped by chilled French sentries and attacked the fort on Signal Hill, overcoming the defenders.

England's Duke of Bedford, inexperienced and inept head of the British empire's delegation to the treaty talks, blundered and gave back pieces of the globe to France on whim. Though France had been driven from all of America except Louisiana, Louis

XV's delegates succeeded in retaining France's fishing rights. Bedford also gave France half of Newfoundland and two islands in the Gulf of St. Lawrence—St. Pierre and Miquelon.

When Royal Navy officers complained that France now had a major naval force and bases in North America, England marked off a large piece of Canada called Labrador and donated it to Newfoundland as reparation. The French brazenly wanted Canada back as well. Or perhaps Guadeloupe, richest sugar-producing island in the West Indies, or Goree, a rock off Dakar strategic to the slave trade.

Pitt groaned. "Some are for keeping Canada, some Guadeloupe. Who will tell me which I shall be hanged for not keeping?"

The deciding factor was unrest in England's American colonies. Certainly New Englanders would riot if France was left to threaten them again. There was already dramatic evidence that the colonies didn't trust the mother country. Soon after the victory at Louisbourg, Massachusetts sent a work force under Admiral Jack "Foul Weather" Byron, grandfather of the poet, to plant enough gunpowder in the French fortress to blow it to rubble rather than risk that England would give it back to France once more.

England therefore kept Canada, but Havana, where most of Wolfe's army died of malaria, was returned to Spain, as were the Philippines. England kept Spanish Florida, so France gave Spain a consolation present—Louisiana.

England rearranged the interior of the continent on the basis of guesswork, since there were no reliable maps. An army survey team headed by Major Robert Rogers went no farther west than Detroit. Colonel Thomas Gage, commanding officer at Montréal, reported that Canada extended to Vincennes (Indiana), but his description arrived too late. England asked for only the territory east of the Mississippi, leaving everything west of the river to Spain. To keep Canadiens from making a dangerous alliance with the tribes and to restrict the Atlantic colonies, the inner core from the Great Lakes to Louisiana was declared an English protectorate reserved for natives.

Speculators from Virginia and Pennsylvania, among them Benjamin Franklin, had planned to make deals with the tribes and sell land to settlers. Virginians had taken over Canadien trading posts,

killing or driving out the inhabitants. The vast real estate operation halted, aghast, at word that Anglo-Americans were to get out.

Canada lost not only the Mississippi valley and Labrador, but
the area later known as New Brunswick and the Île St. Jean
(Prince Edward Island), both of which were made parts of Nova
Scotia. Nova Scotians had no cause to rejoice. New Brunswick
was so thickly treed that it was uninviting for farmers, while
Prince Edward Island was given away, a Tory pork barrel. On the
day after the Treaty of Paris was signed, political cronies gathered
in London to draw lots for sixty-six of the sixty-seven tracts that
comprised the island.

Young men in search of adventure and fortune flocked to
Montréal from New York, Scotland, and England, some with
money to invest in the fur trade. The old French monopoly lay
open to the brave and fast-footed. Joseph and Benjamin
Frobisher, brothers born in Yorkshire, both in their early twenties, set up business in 1765. James McGill, twenty-two, a Scot,
was on the western plains the following year. They found Canada
a shrunken military garrison. General James Murray, the officer
in charge, was immune to suggestions that British citizens were
accustomed to electing a self-governing body: Britain saw Canada
as enemy territory requiring discipline and control.

Army occupation proceeded with remarkable smoothness. Canadiens, it appeared, were not particularly attached to France. Like
Americans, they felt the mother country was remote, insensitive,
ignorant, exploitive, and tyrannical. England in many respects
was a better friend. Canada hummed. Construction gangs built
houses, forts, and roads; prices stabilized. Benjamin Franklin
came to Québec to establish the colony's first postal system. The
Gazette appeared, the colony's first newspaper, bilingual and run
by the government. The colony's first book was published, a
catechism.

Still it couldn't compare with the other English colonies. The
Boston *Gazette* was full of articles by John Adams railing at
English taxation. Jonathan Mayhew, author of the line, "Britons
will not be slaves," was preaching a doctrine of reason that
would lead to Unitarianism. Philadelphia had a medical school,
America's first, and a company of actors performing Shakespeare.
John Winthrop of Harvard was teaching calculus based on New-
ton. Patrick Henry, a Virginian from the backwoods who was an

early example of the New World's phenomenal opportunity for upward mobility, stood in the House of Burgesses and shook his fist at George III.

James Murray advertised in colonial newspapers for settlers to move to Canada. The results were disappointing. Though the seaboard colonies were becoming congested, few found the invitation attractive. Canada, with its French-speaking Roman Catholic population and intolerable winters, was repugnant to most English colonists; as well, there was the matter of a military government that would allow no elections.

Murray found the brawling community of fur traders in Montréal an obnoxious group. He spent his time in Québec, where priests and seigneurs proved to be agreeable social company. His prejudices eased. When disputes between Canadiens and British soldiers clogged the courts, he appointed Canadiens to the bench. Priests gently implored him to allow them a bishop; the post was vacant. Though England detested "all popish hierarchy," he was sympathetic. The decision rested between a Sulpican priest, who would be responsible to his order in France and might therefore be expected to be a spy, or a priest linked to Rome. Murray picked a mild man, Jean-Oliver Briand, ultramontane vicar of Québec, who reported to the Pope.

As the announcement of the Treaty of Paris in 1763 was being made, an alarming development distracted the American colonies: a coalition of native tribes was preparing to go to war to stop the line of European settlement. An Ottawa chief, Pontiac, had united tribes along the Mississippi-Missouri-Ohio spine of the continent. In the summer of 1763 they struck at several Canadien trading posts occupied by Americans and killed the occupants. Detroit, a crossroads and supply depot of portable food—corn mixed with animal fat—for canoemen, was under terrifying siege for six months. Defenders had a ghastly view of the opposite shore of the Detroit River where the Ottawas spent the summer torturing prisoners until they died. In the fall, tribes resumed the hunt on which their lives depended and Detroit celebrated deliverance.

Murray learned of the uprising at the same time as he received instruction on how a truncated Canada was to be governed. English settlers would be allowed to elect a government of what was to be called the Province of Québec, since the word Canada had odious connotations. Canadiens would not vote or hold office unless they renounced Catholicism.

Murray was shocked by the prospect of unruly traders at Montréal governing some 70,000 Canadiens. He called the fifty eligible voters there "rapacious fanaticks" and regarded Canadiens as "perhaps the bravest and best race upon the globe."

The governor's fears were confirmed when Montrealers gained control of the courts and inflicted savage punishment on soldiers in revenge for the contempt officers displayed toward traders. One evening British officers burst into the home of one tormentor, Thomas Walker, interrupting him at dinner, and cut off his ear.

Murray found excuses to postpone an election that would exacerbate the situation. When Montrealers put pressure on London, Murray was recalled in 1766 to face charges. He survived the investigation but never returned to Québec.

Montréal quarrels with the army did not interfere with the enterprise they were showing in taking over the fur trade from Canadiens. The Hudson's Bay Company, rooted for a century in its ports, was stirring to meet the competition. In 1750 the Company hired its first scout, Anthony Henday, an outlaw from the Isle of Wight, who left York Factory in 1754 and traveled as far as the foothills of the Rockies, wintering with the most feared nation on the plains, the Blackfoot tribes. On his return he dropped in at one of the Vérendrye forts on the Saskatchewan, giving the occupants a nasty surprise.

Benjamin and Joseph Frobisher tracked from one old Vérendrye fort to another in 1769 and found the network anxious to resume operation. James McGill financed a second run, since the Frobishers were robbed in their first trial, and was rewarded when the Frobishers paddled into Montréal's landing places that autumn near-millionaires.

Montrealers were practical enough to hire Canadien *voyageurs,* "those natural water dogs," but the Hudson's Bay Company preferred to use small men from the Orkneys. The Orkneys, like Canadiens, married native women, who traveled in the canoes, carried as much weight as the men, and cooked and made clothing as well. The Company, though shocked, had to accept the frontier's miscegenation, and even Canadiens. Besides, as one

HBC official noted, "The Canadians have greatly the advantage . . . in getting goods inland, as five of their men with one canoe will carry as much goods as ten of the Honorable Company's can with five canoes."

The penalties were high. *Voyageurs* rarely lived beyond thirty, victims of syphilis, rupture, starvation, ambush, drowning, exposure, and scurvy. By Company regulations, they were no taller than five-foot-two, making more room in the canoes for goods, and they were expected to carry two, and sometimes three, ninety-pound bales across portages as long as ten miles. There were thirty-five portages between Montréal and Michilimackinac, fifty beyond that to Grand Portage, the turn-around warehouse on Lake Superior where the *canots du maître* (the freight canoes) transferred loads to the light *canots du nord* that commuted to the western plains.

"These poor people are so much attached to the country that they seldom or ever complain," a fur trader observed approvingly.

Voyageurs established families in mating with comely women of the tribes. A copper pot would buy a woman slave, who could be sold when the *voyageur* was bored. More often, the unions were for life. Their children, called métis, or mixed-blood, grew up among tribal cousins in camps on the Red River, where buffalo was the diet staple.

Alexander Ellice, English-born partner in the Schenectady, New York, firm Phyn, Ellice and Co., investors in the fur trade, became a major bankroller of the thriving and competitive industry based in Montréal. In 1779, a rich man, he moved to London to represent the network and left his younger brother, Robert Ellice, in charge of the Canadien end of the operation. With solid Ellice backing, such traders as Cuthbert Grant and Peter Pond pushed far across the plains; in one season they returned with 12,000 beaver skins.

The Hudson's Bay Company, outflanked, hired another scout, Samuel Hearne, twenty, a sailor. In 1770 Hearne left the James Bay post of Churchill with a Chipewyan, Matonabbee, and several of Matonabbee's wives, since women were "made for labor." Matonabbee, raised around HBC posts and invaluable for his skills in diplomacy with the Crees, guided Hearne over 5,000 miles of the most inhospitable land on earth. They reached the Coppermine River and stood on the shore of the Arctic Ocean. Hearne was dejected; he had hoped to find a route to the Pacific.

Four years later Hearne built the first HBC post inland on an island in Cumberland Lake that dominated the Saskatchewan River routes to Churchill. The Company had its first presence among Montrealers swarming on the prairies.

Montréal traders rid themselves of James Murray but were no happier with his successor, Guy Carleton, forty-two. Carleton, a veteran of the Seven Years' War, was Wolfe's friend and had fought on the Plains of Abraham. His first inclination as governor of Québec was to be severe with Canadiens, but he rapidly changed. He detested the tiny crude English community in Mont-réal, describing residents as "Quakers, Puritans, Anabaptists, Pres-byterians, atheists, infidels, and even Jews" and saw no reason why they should have elections.

Nova Scotia's colonial administrators were looking to joining state and the Church of England, since the naval establishment on which Halifax depended was solidly Anglican. A law required the reading of the Book of Common Prayer, and Yankee Congre-gationalists supplying the fleet were given strong hints to convert. The effort foundered. Dissenters were so numerous and deter-mined that English governors were obliged to tolerate "liberty of conscience."

Carleton concluded in Québec, as English governors had in L'Acadie, that edicts against Catholics were unrealistic. He de-scribed Canadiens as "that brave, hardy people" and recom-mended that English-speaking immigrants be discouraged. "Bar-ring a catastrophe too shocking to think of," he wrote, "this country must to the end of time be peopled by the Canadian race."

When the Board of Trade protested, he went to London. His argument proceeded from military realities: He was trying to keep order with only 1,500 soldiers in a colony of 70,000 French-speaking Catholics. Further, the adjacent English colonies were full of treason, and England might require a loyal Québec. Canadiens, he said, would be content if they were given positions of "trust and profit."

Carleton at forty-eight married a beautiful noblewoman, French-speaking Lady Maria Howard, who subsequently bore him eleven children, and they returned to Québec to await the Québec Act. It was an astonishing piece of eighteenth-century legislation, giving Roman Catholics in Canada rights they were denied in England. The conquered colony was restored to a seventeenth-century level of development, with tithes and seigneurial powers revived, French civil law in place, and elected government forbidden. The only concessions to English colonials in Montréal was retention of English criminal law and a provision that the governor would appoint a council, which turned out to be composed of Canadien seigneurs loyal to England and English Army chums.

When the Québec Act was proclaimed in 1774, there were riots in Montréal and New England over the ban of elected government. Groups calling themselves Sons of Liberty held rallies urging a revolution. In Boston the measures in the Québec Act were seen as a message intended for New England's rebels, the mother country's hard reply to agitators in the colonies who were protesting British taxes levied to pay for the Seven Years' War and the garrison in Canada. *Behave,* the Québec Act was saying, *or we'll take away the franchise.*

Another outrageous aspect of the Québec Act was the new border established for Québec. The Mississippi valley was returned to Canadiens, the entire Missouri-Mississippi-Ohio watershed from the Great Lakes to upper Louisiana and west to Vincennes (Indiana) and the Rockies, together with Labrador, rich as a base for seal and whale hunters. The restoration of Canada to its former shape was England's recognition that the colony had no economic hope without fisheries and the fur trade.

American land developers exploded. Negotiations to take over the land from tribes already were proceeding. William Johnson, who lived among the Mohawks, in 1768 signed a treaty with the Iroquois at Fort Stanwix and obtained the Mohawk valley. A Virginian, John Stuart, paid an insignificant sum for Cherokee land. George Washington acquired 33,000 acres in the Ohio-Illinois territory expecting that land given to the tribes "as a temporary expedient to quiet the minds of the Indians" would soon be released. Thomas Jefferson, another Virginia planter, and Philadelphia's Benjamin Franklin also had invested in the upper Mississippi.

The outrage of the Québec Act was followed rapidly by "Coercian Acts" passed by England's parliament to punish Anglo-American dissenters. Massachusetts called a colonial conference, the First Continental Congress, to respond. It met in Philadelphia in September 1774. Three colonies did not attend: Québec, which was not invited, and Nova Scotia and Georgia, the poorest colonies, for whom England spared the tax burden. The first item on the agenda was the odious Québec Act. Congress declared it was "the worst of laws . . . dangerous to an extreme degree." Catholicism, it continued, was a papal conspiracy that "dispersed impiety, bigotry, persecution, murder and rebellion throughout every part of the world."

Delegates were dispatched to urge Nova Scotia and Georgia to strengthen the Congress. As an afterthought, a note was sent to Montrealers resentful that the Québec Act denied them a vote. "Your province is the only link that is wanting to complete the bright strong chain of union," Congress wrote enticingly. Montrealers, however, noting the prevalence in Congress of land speculators who wanted to take the Ohio valley from Canada, were unimpressed.

Samuel Adams, a leading colonial protestor, John Hancock, whose sloop *Liberty* had been stopped and searched by Royal Customs officers six years earlier, and John Brown, a Yale lawyer and hero of the protest that set fire to an English customs ship, were assigned the task of recruiting Québec for Congress. In Montréal they found sympathetic English-speaking dissidents and, to their surprise, a Canadien underground supported by French agents.

Adams, Hancock, and Brown met with them. "You have been conquered into liberty if you act as you ought," they promised. When Canadiens asked if the Catholic church would be protected, the New Englanders replied evasively, "The rest of North America [will be] your unalterable friends."

Alarmed, Carleton took what measures he could to persuade Canadiens to support England. Rumors said he was prepared to deport every Canadien. Priests helped by telling their parishes the anti-Catholic statements issued by the first Congress.

In April 1775 the British governor of Massachusetts attempted to arrest Samuel Adams and John Hancock. Redcoats collided with seventy youths at Lexington. An officer cried, "Disperse, you rebels, immediately." In a tense moment of indecision, someone fired "the shot heard around the world" and the American Revolution began.

Ethan Allen led men from the Green Mountains of Vermont to seize the star-shaped former French fort at Ticonderoga for its guns, while Benedict Arnold, a merchant from Connecticut, moved in with militia to help take nearby Crown Point. Sheer momentum suggested that they continue and capture Canada.

Carleton was in Québec when he heard that Allen and Arnold were moving up the Richelieu, recruiting Canadien insurgents as they approached Montréal. Fort Saint Jean, an old French trading post, was garrisoned with English regulars and Canadien militia. Ethan Allen slipped around the fort with thirty Green Mountain men and eighty *Congressistes* and marched up the post road to Montréal, confident of a welcome. Carleton, however, raised a force of clerks and fur traders to fight Allen's small army and defeat it. The hero of Ticonderoga was marched in chains through the streets of Montréal, where he was pelted with garbage.

Canadiens were so impressed that a thousand men left surrounding villages to help Carleton defend Montréal. Carousing happily in taverns, they awaited the outcome of the siege of Fort Saint Jean.

A second Continental Congress met in Philadelphia, shaken by the events at Lexington. Colonial merchants who hoped only to rid themselves of taxes and other English interference with profits were aghast that young radicals had pushed them into a war with their principle trading partner. Virginian Landon Carter hated Patrick Henry more than he did George III.

Thomas Jefferson and Benjamin Franklin soothed such concerns. The colonies weren't disloyal, they said, but were never so English as when demanding English justice. George Washington, appointed head of the Congressional Army, and his officers toasted the king every night at dinner. Sir Guy Carleton, they maintained, was the culprit. The English general was preparing to use Frontenac's old tactic of sending Canadiens and natives on border raids. To prevent such depredations, it was necessary to invade Canada at once.

In Montréal, Carleton was fuming. Canadiens had wearied of

waiting for action and were slipping back to their farms, leaving
the city undefended. He raged that they fought like Indians, inclined "to strike a sudden blow and then go home." When Saint
Jean fell on November 3, 1775, after fifty-five days of siege,
Montréal was exposed. American rebels moved north jubilantly
under the command of an experienced British officer, Richard
Montgomery, a former friend and comrade of Carleton's. Montgomery was persuaded to switch sides by his American father-in-
law, Judge Robert Livingston, a prominent New Yorker and a
leading opponent of the Stamp Act.

As Montgomery advanced, Carleton learned that Benedict Arnold was attacking Québec. Leaving Montréal to its fate, he
disguised himself as a Canadien farmer and departed downriver
that night in a boat with muffled oars. Montgomery led his army
into Montréal the next day, a triumphant parade of ragged men,
some barefoot, some dressed in bloodied English uniforms taken
from the defenders of Fort Saint Jean. The victors carried two
flags, being undecided about the Revolution's banner. One was
solid red, denoting liberty, and the other red bordered in black,
signifying liberty in mourning.

"Our chains are broken," a Canadien spokesman thanked
Montgomery, who left a few men to garrison Montréal and hurried
to Québec to join Arnold.

The decision to attack Québec was Arnold's, forced on a reluctant George Washington who much preferred an easy march into
Nova Scotia, whose English troops were drawn off for the defense
of Boston. New Englanders in Nova Scotia clamored for the Congressional Army and raised militia to help, but Arnold argued
with Washington that England would send an army to Québec in
the spring and pour troops down the funnel of Lake Champlain to
attack the American rear.

Accordingly, Washington agreed to send a thousand Cambridge
men overland to Québec to meet with Montgomery's forces outside the citadel. Arnold left Newburyport on September 25, 1775,
and staggered through the woods beyond the Kennebec River.
Food ran out. "This day killed my dog and another dog and eat
them," Henry Dearborn wrote stoically. Hundreds turned back.

The remnants broke out of the woods on November 9 near the
Chaudière River and fell ravenously on a herd of cows, which

they slaughtered and ate. Canadiens fed the gaunt men along the route to Québec. Montgomery's Virginians and Canadiens linked with Arnold's Yankees on December 2. Militiamen were setting deadlines; enlistment ended at year's end. Montgomery promised Christmas dinner within Québec and they could then go home.

"I think our fate extremely doubtful," Carleton wrote. He expelled Canadiens whose loyalty he doubted and drilled the remaining valets and cobblers. Much of his army had been lost at Fort Saint Jean. An American deserter adjusted the odds against him by telling the time and place, Lower Town, where Montgomery and Arnold would attack.

Just before dawn on the last day of 1775, Americans opened the assault in a dense snowstorm. Carleton placed snipers in second-story windows to pick off Virginians, dark shapes in the street below. Montgomery was killed, Arnold wounded, and four hundred rebels were trapped and captured. "As compleat a little victory as ever was gained," a participant gloated.

Aaron Burr collected the shattered survivors and ordered a retreat. In the morning Carleton hunted among a hundred corpses frozen in snow drifts. He buried Montgomery, his friend and former neighbor, with full military honors. His soldiers gathered souvenirs: the Americans, lacking uniforms, wore badges of paper in their hats which read LIBERTY OR DEATH.

Benedict Arnold, recovering from a torn leg, sent to Washington for help. He had few supplies and no cannon to bombard Québec. His camp was riddled with smallpox and scurvy; sentries froze toes and fingers. But Washington, laying siege to Boston with cannon dragged from Ticonderoga, could not be diverted from victory over William Howe.

That winter David Wooster of Connecticut commanded the Congressional Army in Montréal, pleased at the opportunity to show his opinion of Catholicism. Yankees were free to urinate on shrines and savage priests, and Wooster filled Chambly prison with Canadiens who protested. Hungry and cold, the Congressional Army begged and stole food and firewood. Wooster paid his soldiers with the paper currency of the Revolution, which Canadiens profoundly mistrusted.

Benjamin Franklin was sent from Philadelphia to investigate tales of Wooster's excesses. To placate Canadiens he brought with

him two Catholics, John Carroll, later first Catholic archbishop of
Baltimore, and Charles Carroll of Carrollton, a cousin and one of
the wealthiest supporters of the Revolution. With Samuel Chase,
the delegates made a rough crossing of Lake Champlain, an agony
for Franklin's inflamed gout. They then were refused a carriage by
a Canadien liveryman, who spurned their paper money, and arrived in Montréal after ignominiously hitchhiking.

Wooster was removed, Chambly prison was emptied, and anti-
Catholic edicts rescinded, but reparation came too late. Cana-
diens no longer had faith in the decency or fiscal soundness of the
American Revolution.

Boston's defense collapsed in March 1776, and William Howe
fled with a thousand New England refugees, most of them prosperous merchants with business links to England, and his army.
Hundreds of ships brought him to the only safe English harbor
on the coast, Halifax, a village unprepared to feed or house
them. Washington, free to help Arnold, sent his army with its
temporary flag of thirteen red and white stripes. When it reached
the St. Lawrence, it was too late by days. The Royal Navy's
frigate, appropriately named *Surprise,* broke through the ice on
May 6, 1776, and anchored at Québec, sending Arnold's army
fleeing with Carleton in ambling pursuit.

"Poor creatures," Carleton called the Americans. Anxious to
defuse the Revolution, he treated captured stragglers kindly. On a
June day the Congressional Army decided to abandon Montréal
to the British. It marched away with 150 *Congressistes,* Canadiens
still loyal to the Americans. Carleton behaved mildly toward
those who had wavered, removing from office militia captains
created by Canada's first experience with democracy and putting
only a few to the lash.

That done, he followed the Congressional Army across the border. He decided to protect the traditional invasion route to Canada by building a navy on Lake Champlain, dragooning Canadien farmers to cut trees and saw timber. George Washington
spent a frustrating summer, wary of Carleton on Lake Champlain
and unable to move against Howe in Halifax, where Yankee
sympathizers were filling the prisons.

The Continental Congress, all inclination to reconcile with England gone on July 4, 1776, issued a Declaration of Independence,

authored in the main by Thomas Jefferson, a liberal touched by eighteenth-century humanism and optimism, who believed, as would Jeremy Bentham and John Stuart Mill, that a government based on justice and equality for all would provide happiness.

Thirteen English colonies thereby cut the cord. When Betsy Ross sewed the new nation's flag that winter, it had thirteen stripes and thirteen stars. The remaining two English colonies in America would not be part of the Revolution.

— 6 —

The Map Makers

American Revolutionaries did not give up hope of liberating Nova Scotia and Québec until Benedict Arnold was defeated by Carleton at Lake Champlain and a Nova Scotian Yankee, Jonathan Eddy, failed in an attack on the fort the French called Beauséjour. William Howe, reinforced at Halifax by his younger brother, Admiral Richard Howe, pitted 25,000 trained men against the rebels, took Staten Island, and pushed George Washington out of the town of New York, sending Benjamin Franklin scurrying to France for help.

Halifax boomed, jammed with wealthy refugees awaiting ships to take them to England, merchant ships bringing supplies through the cordon of New England privateers, tall ships of the line bringing Hessians and cannon, and a raw harborfront of grog shops and brothels.

St. John's in Newfoundland felt the surge every summer when fishing boats brought their catch into port to dry cod on wooden racks in "rooms" reserved on the hillside. "As everything here smells of fish, you cannot get anything that does not taste of it," grumbled the British governor Sir Joseph Banks. Like Newfoundland's best-known governor of the period, Sir Hugh Palliser, Banks was supposed to keep French and English fishermen from killing one another over rights to the coves along a stretch of Newfoundland coast England unaccountably had given to France. The appointment was seasonal, ending in the fall, when governors were to ensure that seamen returned to England for service in the navy and merchant marine.

Though summer governors imposed ruthless regulations to discourage permanent settlement, on one occasion banning chimneys so shelters couldn't be heated, on another burning all shacks in St.

John's to the ground, stranded fishermen and their families clung to the rocks. In the season, 12,000 English fishermen came to fish. Hunting for Beothuks was no longer a shore-leave recreation: The tribe was destroyed. Palliser in 1768 found only a child, "so young as to be of little use."

St. John's attracted Irish-Catholic refugees fleeing British purges and poverty. At the beginning of the American Revolution, there were hundreds who found work with the summer influx and stayed behind when the fishing fleets left.

Most emigrants from Britain preferred the established and thriving colonies on the seaboard. They moved north to Nova Scotia only when they found conditions too crowded or expensive. In that way, Ulster Irish established themselves around Truro. Yorkshire families also moved in, and in 1773 a foul little barge, the *Hector,* moored off Pictou to deposit 186 Scots to the lonely wail of bagpipes. The Highlanders were forerunners of thousands of clansmen pushed off tribal heaths by their own chiefs, avid to turn over the countryside to grazing sheep and make a fortune selling wool to English mills. In this case, a sharp Philadelphia land developer lured them to Nova Scotia, "New Scotland." The name had a homey ring but when they staggered ashore they were forbidden ocean-front land and were denied provisions. Still, at the outbreak of the American Revolution, the men went to war on the side of England.

The two occupied colonies, Québec and Nova Scotia, had courageous resistance movements working for the Revolution. Nova Scotia was full of Yankees whose philosophic and familial ties bound them to the Continental Congress. Under cover of fog or darkness, spies shuttled to New England with news of British ship movements. Yankee privateers fell upon plump Halifax merchant ships bound for the West Indies. Since many owners secretly favored the Revolution, capture of the ships was an affront which turned many Congregationalists into ardent Tories.

Yankee raiding parties against isolated fishing villages, particularly John Paul Jones's destruction of cod oil stores in Canso, also lost the Congressional Army its friends behind the lines. Gangs calling themselves "Army of Liberation" created havoc along the Maine border, prompting Nova Scotia's Yankees to apply to the Royal Navy for permission to become pirates themselves. Fast colonial clipper ships ranged as far south as Florida hunting Americans and putting raiding parties ashore to rob and destroy, backed by such Royal Navy ships as the H.M.S. *Albemarle,* whose crew in those years included Horatio Nelson, twenty-four, a love-sick hero-to-be who was recovering from an unsuitable passion for a sixteen-year-old in Québec.

In 1777 a rival general, "Gentleman Johnny" Burgoyne, succeeded in ousting Guy Carleton as commander of a campaign that would bring the British through the Lake Champlain gateway to the Hudson valley. Carleton soon resigned as governor of Québec. Burgoyne ruthlessly conscripted Canadiens between the ages of sixteen and sixty, sending press gangs to hunt through haystacks for shirkers.

Burgoyne's strategy to take Albany bore no relationship to William Howe's plan that summer to capture Philadelphia, a fact not immediately clear to Burgoyne. He led an impressive, ungainly army of more than 10,000 redcoats and conscripted Canadiens, together with the normal army baggage of wives, children, whores, cows, and chickens, down the Richelieu. The flying wedge of Burgoyne's army was something new in British military annals: Seneca braves under their great chief Old Smoke.

The Senecas held Fort Stanwix for the British advance, which was made more secure when Mary Brant, head of the Iroquois matriarchy, former mistress to William Johnson and mother of eight of his children, sent a warning that American rebels were on the way. Among those present at the victory that resulted was John Butler, a farmer in the Mohawk valley, frequently an interpreter in colonial dealings with the Six Nations.

Burgoyne advanced beyond abandoned Ticonderoga and was caught at Saratoga on October 17, stunned that Howe's army was elsewhere. Hessian mercenaries quit, and Burgoyne was obliged to surrender the rest of his army, a loss that marked the turning point in the Revolution. Americans treated Canadien conscripts with generosity and sent them home.

Louis XVI, hearing of the defeat of the British at Saratoga, in 1778 signed an alliance that Benjamin Franklin had been seeking. A twenty-year-old dandy, the Marquis de Lafayette, already was fighting for the Revolution for the thrill of it. Useful work was found for him after France officially entered the war. The Frenchman sent agents to Québec to encourage a Canadien underground to overthrow the English.

Québec's new governor, Carleton's replacement, was Swiss-born Frederick Haldimand, an experienced officer in the British Army who could rise no higher because of his foreign birth. Haldimand worried that Canadiens would join the Revolution. He attempted to atone for the harsh methods of his predecessors, granting pensions for those pressed into the army and payment for damages to property. But he was tough on suspected rebels, throwing them into prison without trial. Among those jailed were Charles Hay, a Montrealer with business connections in the other colonies, and Fleury Mesplet, a friend of Benjamin Franklin's and founder of the first French-language newspaper in Canada, the *Gazette de Montréal*.

Haldimand instructed John Butler to recruit other dispossessed New Yorkers into a striking force. With the help of Mary Brant, who pleaded successfully with the Iroquois, he was joined by Senecas and other tribesmen. Known as Butler's Rangers, the combined force spread desolation along the frontier during the summer of 1778, culminating in Pennsylvania in the Wyomissing valley, where the cruelty was frightful.

The frontier was open to Butler's Rangers because the Congressional Army was busy on the seaboard. In 1779 General John Sullivan was dispatched from Philadelphia to stop Butler. In August his forces met the Rangers at Newton (Elmira, New York) and defeated them. Iroquois refugees retreated to the shelter of Fort Niagara to await the outcome of the war.

Mary Brant's handsome brother Thayendanegea, known as Joseph Brant, was war chief of the Mohawks. He was welcomed as an exotic diversion by London society when he went to England to ask George III to return to the Iroquois the land overrun by American rebels. Brant, dressed in feathers and deerskins, with bracelets on his biceps and with flashing eyes, sat for a portrait by George Romney, a court favorite. George III gave the Mohawk a gold watch and a promise that the Six Nations would have their farms back.

Meanwhile, Iroquois and American refugees huddled around Fort Niagara, putting strain on Haldimand's food supply. The governor asked John Butler to select some of his former neighbors to begin farming, and Butler, his property lost behind enemy lines and anxious to find government employment, carried out his instructions with zeal. A community developed centered on a village on the Niagara which was first called Butlersbury and then Newark.

General George Cornwallis surrendered the British Army in October 1781, and a wave of revulsion against the war swept Britain. The Tory government, blamed for the Revolution, was thrown out of office and replaced with Whigs whose political and philosophic sympathies were pro-American. Charles Rockingham, a long-time friend of American dissenters, took charge of the government and opened negotiations for the peace settlement.

Guy Carleton was sent to Long Island to take charge of the American refugees gathering there. Some were patricians who for business reasons or respect for traditional values had chosen the side of the monarchy. These whiled away the hours of tedious confinement by laying plans for an ideal society they would construct to replace the debacle of republicanism. They hoped England would secure Maine for their purpose; Carleton suggested they would be better advised to consider Nova Scotia's undeveloped "back part."

They couldn't wait to begin. "Halifax or Hell" was their slogan. English ships were depositing refugees from every seaboard colony, people set upon by mobs of looters on suspicion that they held loyalist views or because a relative fought with an English regiment. Others trapped inland sent desperate cries for help. Twenty-four families of Glengarry highlanders, Jacobites who had settled near Lake Champlain, were abused because their men enlisted in the Royal Highland Emigrant Regiment.

Carleton counted more than 35,000 refugees, some in deplorable shape, in the Long Island camp. England offered a choice of destinations: England, the West Indies, or Halifax. Wealthy Americans tended to favor the first two, certain their connections would enable them to resume their lives in comfort. Others, tied to America, chose Halifax. Ships came to carry them to Nova Scotia; 5,000 at a sailing.

In preparation for their arrival, a surveyor laid out a dozen streets in the military-grid style, and emergency housing popped up overnight to shelter the fortunate. "Nova Scarcity," they called the colony, rampant with inflation and shortages. Rum was a common comfort, so cheap that shopkeepers kept open barrels of it and gave customers a free ladleful. Typhus, tuberculosis, and smallpox raged and streets ran with excrement. Every message to England was filled with pleas for help.

Treaty talks in Versailles began in April 1782. Rockingham, on the verge of death, entrusted the assignment to a man who would succeed him as prime minister that year, William Petty Fitzmaurice, Earl of Shelburne. Shelburne, an Irish intellectual and liberal, deeply admired the American Revolution and said openly that the Declaration of Independence was the finest document ever produced by any government. In his view, and that of British businessmen who supported the Whigs, the theories of the economist Adam Smith were persuasive. In Smith's doctrine, a prosperous America would make England richer. Shelburne intended to be as generous as he dared to the new nation and knew he had the support of such powerful financiers as John Dunning, the first Baron Ashburton.

The British team at the negotiating table therefore consisted entirely of Adam Smith devotees eager to please the brilliant American team headed by John Jay and Benjamin Franklin. Franklin declared he was delighted by England's selection; all had business connections in the United States. The most urgent matter was the sole unpleasantness Shelburne imposed on the sessions—the refugee problem. Though both parties knew the United States was penniless, a promise to make good property lost by American loyalties was accepted in good faith. That settled, the delegates unrolled a thirty-year-old map of North America drawn by John Mitchell when half of the continent belonged to France. Though it was grossly inaccurate it was deemed adequate for the purpose, which was to give the United States as much land as possible.

Benjamin Franklin suggested the simplest course was to cede the entire continent to the United States. Shelburne's delegates regretted that it was impossible to oblige since Nova Scotia was full of American Tories for whom land must be found, and Québec under Haldimand was receiving refugees as well. They agreed, however, that the residual English colonies need not be large.

Vermont was given the mountains on the northern border, and Maine was expanded to the Sainte Croix River where Champlain

had wintered almost two centuries earlier. New York received the
Mohawk Valley that George III had promised Joseph Brant and
all the land west of it to the Ohio. Québec lost the upper Mississippi watershed that had been Canada for a century, the fertile
land covering a quarter of a million square miles that would become the states of Ohio, Illinois, Indiana, Michigan, Wisconsin,
and Minnesota. It was the slaughter of one nation, Canada, to
feed another.

Where natural borders of rivers or lakes were impractical, as in
the unsettled and almost unknown reaches west of Lake Superior,
peace teams decided to use the 49th parallel. The 49th figured in
earlier boundary discussions between England and France when
England insisted that Canada should not extend farther *north*
than the 49th parallel to protect the Hudson's Bay Company. In
Versailles, England arranged that Canada would have the 49th
as a southern border.

Benjamin Franklin observed that the operative word at the
treaty table was *reconciliation*. "It is a sweet word," he said, as
England stripped the two colonies which had remained loyal in
order to enrich the thirteen which had fought England to the death.

England threw in the fur-trade network: Fort Niagara, Detroit,
Michilimackinac, and priceless Grand Portage, the hinge on Lake
Superior on which the prairie posts and Montréal depended. John
Adams, alert to the needs of New England fishing fleets, secured
unlimited access to Nova Scotia's waters and the right to use any
unsettled part of the coast.

A century later when Theodore Roosevelt examined the deals
made by eighteenth-century liberals, he marveled. He found it
odd that the Thirteen Colonies had secured the Ohio-Mississippi
basin which had never been part of the Revolution. "When independence was declared," he commented, "it was as much a foreign
territory as Florida or Canada."

As the tide of liberalism turned in England, Shelburne finally
grew concerned. So much land had been gouged out of Canada
that the interior was beyond communication in winter except via
Maine, and Montrealers were cut off from trading posts in the
west. He dispatched a new delegate to Paris, Henry Strachey, with
last-minute orders to regain concessions from the Americans.

Strachey was able to restore to Canada that part of the continent which became Ontario, but nothing more.

Shelburne's radical Whigs were out of power after a reign of only eight months, ousted by a horrified coalition of Tories and moderates, but the period was exactly sufficient to conclude the boundary agreements with John Jay and Benjamin Franklin.

Loyalist Americans wretchedly sorted themselves out. Some found they hadn't fled far enough north: Richard Cartwright of Albany selected an island in Lake Ontario that was British when he started to farm it and American when the treaty was signed. Loyalists on the Penobscot in Maine dragged their houses north to the Sainte Croix and found it had three tributaries emptying into Passamaquoddy Bay. The distance between one Sainte Croix and another represented about one third the whole "back part" of Nova Scotia. The treaty had failed to define which Sainte Croix was the real one.

In Nova Scotia, Shelburne's choice for governor was obese John Parr, a Whig who applauded the American Revolution and thought the loyalists who rejected it were fools. His attitude did not endear him to the 35,000 American refugees waiting in Halifax and environs for him to assign them their land in the "back part." The vanguard of loyalists and the most vociferous were the wealthy New Englanders, among them Edward Winslow, whose family had been governors of the Plymouth Bay colony, and John Coffin, who could trace his lineage back to the *Mayflower*.

The next wave consisted of tradesmen and soldiers, also with slaves. Entire loyalist regiments crowded the streets of Halifax: the King's American Dragoons, the Queen's Rangers of Virginia, the King's American Regiment of North Carolina, the New York Volunteers, the Loyal American Regiment, New Jersey Volunteers—known as "Skinner's Cowboys" for their commander, Cortlandt Skinner—the Pennsylvania Loyalists, the Prince of Wales American Regiment, the King's Orange Rangers of New York, the Scots from Pictou who fought in the Royal Highland Emigrant Regiment, and former slaves freed to fight in black regiments.

Most came in the winter of 1782–83 while peace talks continued in Paris. "About or near 20,000 have already arrived from New York and they are to be followed by many more," Parr wrote Shelburne. "Those who came early in the year have got under tolerable shelter and are doing very well, but those who have lately come and are to come must be miserable indeed."

Conditions grew worse. Newcomers in 1784 were "in a sick and weakened condition and without clothing." A few hundred came from St. Augustine, "the poorest and most distress'd of all beings, without a shilling, almost naked, and destitute of every necessity of life."

Parr gave a chilly reception to the petition of Fifty-five Associated Loyalists headed by Abijah Willard of Boston, who requested land grants of 5,000 acres each on the grounds that they had suffered most in the Revolution; "a pack of rascals replete with gross partialities," he called them.

Loyalists were assigned crudely surveyed land in the Annapolis valley and the "back part," which they called New Ireland. The King's American Dragoons hammered stakes in the ground along the shore of the major river, the St. John, at its farthest navigable point, the site of the future capital, Fredericton. By the end of 1783 there were 14,000 loyalists in the "back part," and a strong separatist movement to break away from Governor Parr was growing.

The dispute over the Sainte Croix was no longer a minor backwoods quarrel. New Brunswick turned out to be a forest of white pine, some of it 115 feet high and straight as a plumb line, ideal for masts for the Royal Navy in case a blockade cut off supplies of timber from the Baltic.

"Tough, clean, durable, clear of sap," one observer reported. "The Baltic produces nothing like it."

The contentious region embraced the headwaters of the St. John River system, the corridor on which trees were floated to the thriving town of Saint John on the Bay of Fundy. A surveyor sent to examine the "northwest angle" found Acadien refugees in an abandoned Micmac village called Madawaska and gave a garbled report that only inflamed the argument. England and America concluded that an international committee would have to arbitrate.

Governor Haldimand in Québec was sorting out his refugee problem, his soldier's mind on defense. Some 7,000 Americans

were trekking north to the upper St. Lawrence and Great Lakes.
He thought it best to settle them away from Canadiens, so his
only alternative was to put them west of Montréal, with demobilized soldiers seeded along the border where American attack
could be expected.

The Glengarrys, who walked from Lake Champlain with children on their backs, were given lots on the north shore of the St.
Lawrence. Butler's Rangers received the fruitlands along the Niagara River. Haldimand's biggest headache, the dispossessed Indians whom George III had forgotten, were assigned a reserve six
miles wide on either side of a wide river flowing south into Lake
Erie. John Johnson, white son of William Johnson, had been
stripped of 170,000 acres in the Mohawk valley, most of which
had been given him by Mohawks or bought for token cash from
the Oneidas. He was comforted with the post of superintendent of
the colony's Indian department.

Mary Brant, still dominating Six Nations' war councils, moved
into a house Haldimand gave her near Kingston and was given a
pension of a hundred pounds a year, the highest yet paid to any
Indian. Joseph Brant led the homeless Six Nations over a blazed
trail to the place of their exile. They built long-house villages on
a river called La Tranche, which became a refugee camp for tribes
fleeing the westward movement of American settlers. Not until the
natives needed cash for food some sixteen years later did they discover they didn't really own the land.

The shock felt in Montréal by the terms of the 1783 Treaty of
Paris, which cost every major trading post linking it to the west,
was softened by the news that England would keep the forts
and posts until America settled its debt to the loyalists. Simon
McTavish, a Scot in his twenties who supplied rum to the fur
trade, had moved from Albany at the outbreak of the Revolution.
Together with his brother-in-law, Duncan McGillivray, he raised
a storm in England against the imminent loss of Grand Portage
and about Haldimand's autocratic Privy Council government
made up of Canadien seigneurs and army favorites. With thousands of English-speaking Americans breaking land along the
Great Lakes, Montrealers clamored to become a colony separate
from Québec with an elected government run by businessmen.

Elsewhere in the remaining British colonies, the mood was for amalgamation. William Smith, former chief justice of New York and a Tory, became a crony of Guy Carleton's during the wait on Long Island for transport. The two sailed for England in 1783 with a plan to unify the remaining English colonies. Carleton would be the first governor and Smith the first chief justice. Smith imagined that such a colony, serene, solid, and impregnated with Britishness, would be so attractive that Americans would repent of their folly.

Charles Inglis, former rector of Trinity Church in New York (which the rebels burned), had a similar vision in which he would be the first Anglican bishop. The flow of British policy, however, was in the opposite direction. England already had lost thirteen colonies, in part because they united, and more revolution was on the way. France was full of radicals on the verge of over-throwing Louis XVI.

The portents from British colonies in America were bad: Complaints poured in from fur traders, from American Tories shocked at primitive conditions and disgruntled that free land in Prince Edward Island wasn't available, from others furious that Cape Breton's coal deposits had been appropriated by the Royal Navy, and from Anglicans fighting for power and parishioners. There was evidence that the French revolt and anti-clericism could spread to Québec, while in Nova Scotia "New Light" evangelical missionaries were offering ecstatic conversion in the backwoods that smacked of another American plot against the flag.

In 1783 George III picked as prime minister a brilliant twenty-four-year-old, William Pitt the Younger, addicted to two bottles of port a day and probably homosexual, who was to steer the empire through the rocky period of liberalism unrest. Pitt decided that the remaining colonies in America should be small and manageable, with soldiers for governors.

He started with Nova Scotia, which was broken in half. The "back part," named New Brunswick rather than New Ireland because Ireland was an annoyance, in 1784 received its first governor, Guy Carleton's youngest brother Thomas. Cape Breton was separated as well, though without any decision about its government, and Prince Edward, another fragment, also was parted from Nova Scotia. In London, a Scot millionaire philanthropist, the young Earl of Selkirk, bought a tract on Prince Edward Island to settle a thousand evicted countrymen there.

Guy Carleton, elevated to the peerage as first Baron Dorchester after intense lobbying, was named governor-in-chief of British North America in 1786 over the colonies of Québec, Nova Scotia, and New Brunswick; his brother accordingly was demoted to lieutenant-governor. Smith went with Dorchester as chief justice and at once fell into quarrels with affronted judges. More upsetting still was the appointment of Charles Inglis as Anglican bishop of all the colonies the following year, a move which some feared presaged the imposition of an Anglican state.

Inglis, like Smith, was soon embroiled in disputes with furious clerics, particularly independent-minded American Methodists. Inglis established King's College in Nova Scotia to train Anglican priests and closed its doors to "dissenters," a move which gave Roman Catholics bargaining power to establish schools of their own and build the first Roman Catholic church in Halifax.

Dorchester visited the aged and ailing Catholic bishop in Québec, his old friend Jean-Olivier Briand. Both were aware that at one time or another in the Revolution most Canadiens had hoped the Americans would win. He cultivated the seigneurs who had remained loyal to Britain and ignored businessmen with progressive views, a group he abhorred. When American loyalists continued to pour into the colony, reaching an estimated 15,000, he opened the townships along the New York border south of Montréal to them. Depressed, angry, bitter, and prone to quarrel with Canadiens they regarded as backward, the newcomers created ill will that tended to unite Canadiens against them. William Smith exacerbated the conflicts by establishing English law for the Americans instead of the law of the land, which was French.

New Brunswick also brimmed with competition. Possibilities for wealth for the well-connected were breathtaking. Britain closed the West Indies trade to Americans, a policy which brought merchant fleets to Saint John, the village that grew so quickly at the mouth of the St. John River that within the year it was incorporated as a city. At the same time the Royal Navy, vulnerable to a wartime blockade of Baltic timber, was placing orders for masts. Yankee speculators snapped up mill sites along the rushing rivers that carried logs to port, fuming that Britain put a hold on huge tracts for the exclusive use of the navy. "Britain's private woodpile," historian Arthur Lower described Canada.

In 1789 William Pitt made William Wyndham Grenville his Home Secretary with orders to straighten out colonial discord in America. Grenville's answer two years later was the Constitutional Act of 1791. Dorchester and Smith were disappointed. Their dream of one British colony stretching from the Arctic Ocean to the Gulf of Mexico fell apart. England had cut the colonies into even smaller bits.

— 7 —

Moving West

Adam Smith proved to be right: A stronger America meant a richer Britain. Fifteen years after the Revolutionary War, England and the United States were one another's best customers. Ninety percent of America's imports were British, the tariff an important source of revenue for a young government of a citizenry touchy about taxes, and England bought almost half of America's exports.

London's bankers, Whig sympathizers whose grasp of business enterprise put them more in tune with American hustlers than with British Tory landowners, were pleased to have commerce with America restored. Such giants as the Barings, a banking family, offered cash to hard-pressed American enterprise in return for partnerships and facilitated government policy in America's direction whenever they could.

American Tories in exile in the fracturing British colonies felt neglected. England actively was discouraging their economic revival. A group of whaling families from Nantucket was refused permission to settle in Nova Scotia and went to Dunkirk instead. The Royal Navy had a fist-hold on New Brunswick's timber and Cape Breton's coal; Prince Edward Island was owned by Londoners. American loyalists, homesick and miserable, felt envy and regret. Since they had sacrificed all to remain in the British Empire, their pride would not allow that their mother country was abusive. While grumbling about the absence of elected government and the grip of monopolies, they created out of their wretchedness an attachment to a mythic Britain, all wonderful and worth the pain.

The real Britain was forced to give direct help in the form of land, seed, livestock, utensils, and transportation in ways that were unusual in an era not renowned for welfare services. These measures, necessary to keep the population from perishing, inspired a level of dependency and expectation in government services and government wisdom that came to be a Canadian characteristic. Only two pockets of fiery private enterprise existed, the West Indies trade out of ports in Nova Scotia and New Brunswick, with its attendant shipyards, and the fight Montrealers were waging to wrest the fur trade from the Hudson's Bay Company.

The competition took resources beyond those of any single trader, so Montrealers formed partnerships and combinations to stretch available funds. In 1784 the Frobisher brothers alone had 50,000 pounds of trade goods at Grand Portage, making their banker, James McGill, exceedingly nervous. Simon McTavish tried a sixteen-share alliance in 1779 that was called the North West Company. It worked so well that it was established on a permanent basis in 1783, and a few years later McTavish went into partnership with the Frobisher brothers to supply trade goods.

Fur trading was hard on the nerves of investors but a thrill that became addictive for the scouts on the plains. A North West Company partner, twenty-three-year-old Alexander Mackenzie, a New York Scot whose family fought on the British side of the Revolution, was given command of the remote post on Lake Athabaska in 1787. There he met an American, Peter Pond. Pond, a seasoned fur trader, described a great river that flowed west. Mackenzie was obsessed from that moment with the dream of finding the water route to the Pacific that Hearne had sought in vain.

He hired *voyageurs* and natives, including four women, and set out in 1789 with a rough map Pond drew for him. They paddled a great river that wound west from Great Slave Lake and then turned north. Mackenzie, disappointed, followed it in the hope it would curve west again. It flowed north, always north; he named it the River of Disappointment.

The expedition saw caribou in the hundreds of thousands. On the shore where they camped Mackenzie found traces of oil and coal and the naked, emaciated people of the Dog-rib and Slave tribes with pierced noses and tattooed cheeks, the most poverty-stricken natives he had ever seen. Fifteen hundred miles from the journey's beginning, he reached the frozen, salty delta where the river emptied into the Arctic; the wrong ocean. Map makers later traced the river he decided to name for himself and measured it at 2,653 miles. Draining 700,000 square miles of prairie and frozen tundra, it is a river rivaled in America only by the Mississippi.

On his return trip up the river, Mackenzie passed a tributary that ran west. It haunted him. Perhaps it connected to the Pacific. That winter he went to England with the North West Company's shipment of furs and bought a sextant and compass. In the spring of 1793 he tried again from Great Slave Lake, took the fork that bore west and rode the Peace River through the mountains, full of terror that hostile natives would kill him.

He finally found his way to the Dean Channel and stood on the shore of the Pacific Ocean, a satisfied man, eleven years ahead of the second overland trek to the Pacific that Lewis and Clark would make for America. He carved on a rock, "Alexander Mackenzie, from Canada, by land, the twenty-second of July, one thousand seven hundred and ninety-three."

He was not the first European to see that coast. England, consumed with scientific curiosity and an eagerness to increase its commercial realm, in the 1770s commissioned its best navigator, James Cook, to explore the little-known Pacific Ocean. Using Marco Polo's ancient maps, Cook came back in 1771 with Europe's first charts of the South Seas. In 1776 he was sent around the Horn to examine the west coast of America and find a river that would give passage from the interior to China.

Cook sailed with two ships, the *Resolution* and the *Discovery,* south around Africa, east to Australia, and across the Pacific to the area of present-day San Francisco, too close for comfort to the Spanish in Mexico. His masts and spars rotting, he sailed north in search of timber and put in at Nootka Sound on Vancouver Island.

His landing party that day in March 1778 included William Bligh of the Royal Navy (who one day would command the legendary *Bounty* whose crew mutinied) and twenty-one-year-old George Vancouver, who later gave his name to the island. The whaling tribe of Nootkas greeted them, prosperous people who wore nose rings and kept their family history on carved totem poles. Cook observed evidence that the Nootkas had been trading with Europeans, probably Spanish.

His crew gave them trinkets and syphilis and left the cove a few weeks later to sail north as far as Bering Strait. It was named for the Russian Vitus Bering, who reached it in 1721, unaware he was in the water gap between Asia and America. Ice in the polar sea turned Cook back. He wintered in the paradisiacal Hawaiian islands he had seen on his crossing. He was tired and, at fifty-one, crotchety. There was an argument concerning a small boat, perhaps taken by a native. Cook interfered and the dispute became violent. On a February day in 1779 he was killed on the beach of Kealakekua Bay.

Though Spain claimed the western coast of America as early as 1493, England's East Indies Company used Cook's voyage as justification to extend its monopoly there. Sea-otter pelts traded by the Nootkas were a sensation in China. Word of them spread by clipper ships to Spain, New York, Boston, Russia, and London. As investors prepared merchant ships for the long voyage, the East Indies Company announced it would levy fines on poachers. It built a fort among the Nootkas in 1786, using fifty Chinese slaves for labor.

Spain protested and three years later the Union Jack was hauled down by Don Esteban Martinez, who had been told that the offending fur traders were Russian. He found instead Americans and British ships posing as Portuguese. A garbled report of the confrontation reached London and eroded relations with Spain. In view of the expense to maintain an army so far distant, it was agreed that Russia could have the Aleutians, and Spain the coast as far as San Francisco. The rest, temporarily, was left to free traders.

England, hoping to put a colony among the Nootkas to nail down the claim, dispatched George Vancouver to chart the coast in 1791. Vancouver missed the mouth of the Columbia River, which he judged to be an unimportant delta, and sailed by it just two weeks before Robert Graves, an American trading sea otter between the Nootkas and Canton, came across the river and sailed it, naming it for his ship, the *Columbia*.

Vancouver meticulously surveyed Oregon and Washington and

over the next three seasons charted as far north as Alaska, which he established was not an island but part of the continent. He was deep in Russian territory, where the Russian American Company, a coalition of Russians and Yankee traders, was laying claim not only to Alaska but the entire coast south to San Francisco.

Poachers made life miserable for the Russian American Company and the British claim. In 1811 John Jacob Astor's Pacific Fur Company aggressively built a fort at the mouth of the Columbia, calling it Astoria. The North West Company of Montréal arrived four months later. David Thompson, a former Hudson's Bay Company clerk who used his savings to buy into the North West Company, floated down the Columbia on a cedar-plank boat and found a bright new Stars and Stripes flying over Fort Astoria.

Thompson was a foundling raised in an orphanage, a bright lad picked at fourteen as an apprentice in the HBC's London office. When his employers offered him a suit of clothes as a bonus, the boy asked for a sextant instead; he dreamed of being an explorer.

Thompson has been described as "the greatest practical land geographer who ever lived." A tiny black-haired man in deerskins, he married a métis woman, Charlotte Small, who bore sixteen children and often paddled while pregnant. David Thompson covered a territory of America estimated at two million square miles, the first European to see much of what is now the Canadian plains, Idaho, Montana, Wyoming, Washington, and Oregon. He charted the headwaters of the Mississippi and proved that the map used by England and America to establish boundaries after the Revolution was inaccurate. He was also the first to map the length of the Columbia. Because he always knew exactly where he was, he led a charmed life among warring tribes: They thought him a shaman.

When he skidded down the Columbia in 1811, Charlotte Small was with him, an infant at her breast and two toddlers packed among the supplies. Simon Fraser, son of an American Tory who had died in an Albany prison, a North West Company partner in charge of the territory west of the Rockies, also had been searching for the Columbia. Three years earlier, in 1808, he traced the roaring river which almost parallels the Columbia and named it for himself.

Exploration was heady excitement for Mackenzie, Thompson,

and Fraser but shockingly expensive for the backers in Montréal, especially with so many competing partnerships in the field. Rum that left McTavish's warehouse in Montréal to return two years later as a sea-otter pelt passed through "three sets of men" coming and going. England made matters worse in 1794 when Jay's Treaty was signed, by which England and the United States resolved their final difference, reparation for loyalist losses, and the trading posts vital to the network had to be given to John Jacob Astor's powerful American Fur Company, which then ran the North West Company off the Mississippi.

At a cost of more than £10,000, the North West Company built a replacement for Grand Portage. The new location was farther north on Lake Superior at the head of a difficult chain of portages that took six days longer than the old one. Known to natives as Kaministikwia and to traders as "Kam," it saved on overhead by sharing space with the North West Company's chief rival, the XY Company of Montréal, a forced arrangement notable for the irritation it produced on both sides.

Inevitably the expense of operating trading posts from Montréal to the Pacific Ocean proved too much, and the North West Company merged with XY in 1804. The most powerful figure in the merger was Alexander Ellice, former Schenectady, New York, trader, whose fortune was enormous. He died the following year and left his son, Edward Ellice, twenty-two, known in London as "Bear" Ellice because he was slippery, rich enough to try to buy the Hudson's Bay Company.

He was rejected, but the HBC was taking a bruising from the Nor'westers of Montréal. An HBC factor, Colin Robertson, commented, "It is not many years since the Canadian establishments of the fur traders in America extended no farther than the banks of Lake Superior, but now their boundaries are the Atlantic, the Pacific and the frozen oceans."

The HBC was indignant that the food supply that maintained the prairie operation of the Nor'westers came from the Lake Winnipeg region, which the HBC regarded as its own preserve. There, Cree and métis women prepared pemmican out of strips of buffalo dried in the wind, pounded into buffalo fat, and sometimes flavored with blueberries. Hunters and traders consumed eight pounds a day, their diet staple and often their only food.

Guy Carleton, Lord Dorchester, found the Nor'westers unattractive, even when they attempted to raise the tone of their Montréal social group, the Beaver Club, by ejecting those too far gone in alcoholism. Grenville's Constitution Act of 1791, by which England moved from Dorchester's goal of a united British colony and created instead even more pieces, was a disappointment he was obliged to suffer. He was given the title of governor-general, but his authority over the lieutenant-governors was dubious since he was aging and travel was difficult.

"I miss the expected Establishment," he sighed. Where there had been two British colonies after the Revolution, there were now six. The newest was called Upper Canada and included the territory west of the Ottawa River where American loyalists and Scots, evicted from their clan land, were clearing primeval forest to make farms. What was left of Québec was called Lower Canada, and included Montréal.

England's decision to leave the North West Company's base inside a colony dominated by Canadiens had produced furious lobbying. The Company preferred to be included in the all-English colony west of them, where the new lieutenant-governor, John Graves Simcoe, was trying to decide where to put his capital.

Simcoe, who commanded the Queen's Rangers of New York, a loyalist regiment in the American Revolution, and was wounded at Brandywine, made a fortuitous marriage during his convalescence to a fifteen-year-old, Elizabeth Posthuma Gwillim—Posthuma because she was delivered after her mother died in childbirth. Elizabeth Simcoe's family connections ten years later gained the posting in Upper Canada for her husband.

Since there were no roads in Upper Canada when the Simcoes and their six children arrived in 1792, all 10,000 American, German, Quaker, and Scot settlers lived along the lakes and rivers. Simcoe joined his old regiment at Fort Niagara, which still flew the Union Jack even though the Treaty of Paris decreed the area to be the United States. Simcoe unpacked the family's effects on the British side at a village he called Newark; he detested the tendency of his colony to retain native and French names. Among his belongings was a spacious, prefabricated, half-canvas house that had been the property of James Cook; the Simcoes bought it at an auction in London because they thought it might be useful in Upper Canada. They were to live in it during most of their stay.

Simcoe concluded that Newark was too close to the United States border to be a safe capital. Kingston, with fifty houses, some of them stone, was the colony's largest center. It was also too accessible to American raiders. His choice was far up the La Tranche River, which he renamed the Thames, where he hoped to established a town he would call New London. Dorchester had other ideas. He wanted the gateway of a heavily used portage, the only defensible harbor west of Kingston, to be fortified. Simcoe was commanded to establish the government at Fort Rouillé, which the natives called Toronto. Simcoe named it York and consoled himself with the excellent salmon fishing there.

Elizabeth Simcoe, a cultivated, enterprising, and fearless twenty-five-year-old, had opinions on everything and recorded them in a diary. She was amazed that the women of Newark wore gauze ballgowns on the edge of a wilderness teeming with poisonous snakes, bears, wolves, and passenger pigeons in such numbers that people killed enough for dinner by throwing rocks through the flock. Her small son, rude and difficult most of the time, adored the native chiefs who came to pay their respects; so did his mother. "I never saw so handsome a figure," she wrote of Jacob the Mohawk, who danced Scottish reels "with more ease and grace than any person I ever saw," wearing a black blanket, scarlet leggings, and silver bands on his head and arms.

Her husband was a decisive and practical administrator. Though he loathed Americans, whom his wife described as "perfectly democratic and dirty," he could see no other source of settlers. While building forts and reinforcing existing ones to keep out an American army, he invited American farmers to migrate north. He got so into the spirit of competition that he complained when land speculators in the Genesee valley in New York intercepted settlers bound for Canada.

The first law he passed in York was the abolition of slavery, fourteen years ahead of Britain itself. Americans who brought slaves to help clear the land were aghast. As concession to them, Simcoe ruled that the legislation would prohibit importing slaves and would free children of existing slaves, but adult slaves already in Upper Canada would not be freed.

The Constitutional Act of 1791 presented each of the British colonies in America with a semblance of elected government, well tempered by Britain's concern that soldier-governors keep control of the colonies to prevent American agitators from stirring trouble. Dorchester and his lieutenant-governors were empowered to establish executive committees, below which was an executive council picked by the governor, and below that a landowner-elected House of Assembly, which the governor could overrule. It bore striking similarities to the government of the United States which also followed a colonial model, except that the legislative council, or Senate, was appointed rather than elected.

The governors used their powers to elevate friends and American Tories who impressed them as loyal and useful to the crown. Simcoe, for instance, favored Thomas Talbot, an eccentric alcoholic with a mysterious connection in George III's court. Talbot later was given a large tract of land on Lake Erie. John Scadding, a family retainer from Devonshire, was given a sinecure. William Osgoode, an Oxford lawyer and friend of Simcoe's, became chief justice.

The interior colonies, devoid of commerce except the fur trade which monopolies almost completely controlled, offered no other prospects for aspiring American Tories than government appointments or land speculation. American developers hustled in ahead of them, buying millions of acres in Lower Canada. They promised William Smith to put settlers on it, but instead they resold undeveloped land to high bidders, who also had no intention of putting themselves to the expense and trouble of finding farmers.

Colonial governors anxious to populate the impenetrable forests were obliged to find another source of immigrants: Scotland. Mixed with "late loyalists" drawn by free land were penniless Scots driven off the highland to make room for sheep. Nova Scotia's governor John Parr found the newcomers in deplorable state. He wrote in September 1791 about 650 Scots who had landed at Pictou "in wretched condition." He used his own funds to feed them "to prevent their emigration to South Carolina."

Competition for the Scots was intense, with land speculators holding huge tracts in the new territory. England, nervous that the French Revolution would spread to discontented Scotland, created more refugees. Henry Dundas was ordered to stamp out all traces of *egalité* and *liberté,* a task he performed with such ruthlessness that Scot liberals jammed the jetties trying to get a ship to America. The cheapest passage, they discovered, was to allow themselves to be packed heel to head in the fetid infested holds of timber ships returning empty to New Brunswick and Lower Canada. If they still had the strength after a crossing where the ship's wake was strewn with corpses, the Scots could continue on to the United States.

Frustrated Canadiens, excluded from commerce by Americans, Scots, and Englishmen in Montréal, ignored by the British government establishment at Québec, drew encouragement from news of the French Revolution. Dorchester, concerned at the unrest developing, decided not to issue guns to the Canadien militia. A *Club de Patriotes* made up of two hundred young Canadiens dazzled by Rousseau and the French Revolution's Declaration of the Rights of Man met in Montréal in defiance of Dorchester's edict that France was not even to be discussed in Lower Canada.

When France declared war on England in February 1793, some Canadiens began to hope. A mutinous French fleet in Chesapeake Bay was expected to burn Halifax and restore French rule in America. Few British soldiers were left in the colonies; most were gone to defend the West Indies. Even the king's son, Prince Edward, Duke of Kent, had been transferred. Edward had enriched the social life of Québec during his posting, despite Catholic disapproval of his open relationship with a mistress who took the alias Julie de St. Laurent. Though Julie and the prince lived in domestic bliss for twenty-seven years, some of it in Québec and Halifax, they parted in tears when duty required Edward to marry a German princess and produce an heir to the throne, who turned out to be Queen Victoria.

Saber-rattling by the United States increased. The French Revolution's notoriously overzealous "Citizen Genêt" spread stories of Canadien unrest under British rule. Efficient spies kept Dorchester informed through the winter of 1793–94 as Canadiens absorbed the news that the Bastille had fallen and Louis XVI had gone to the guillotine. Québec's clergy sided with Dorchester; French republicans were anti-church as well as anti-king. But when Dorchester appealed for volunteers to defend the colony against the scare of a French-American invasion from Vermont, Canadiens stayed home.

Dorchester used repressive measures against Canadien republicans and banned the Montréal *Gazette,* which had been stirring up liberalism. The expected American invasion didn't materialize. Americans decided to delay in order not to upset Jay's Treaty negotiations by which forts and trading posts along the new border would be given to the States.

With 156,000 Canadiens in Lower Canada and only 10,000 English-speaking residents, and an Assembly which consisted of thirty-four French and sixteen English, William Grenville decided to adjust some of the provisions of the Constitutional Act of 1791. "It will be experience that will teach them that English laws are best," he commented, lifting the restriction against speaking French in the Assembly. James McGill, William Grant, and other Montrealers protested, though they numbered only sixteen in a House of fifty. Pierre Bédard, a leading Canadien assemblyman, told them, "If the conquered should speak the language of the conqueror, why don't the English still speak Norman?"

When British soldiers pulled out of forts from Niagara and Detroit to Sandusky and Grand Portage, the tribes in the Ohio-Mississippi were exposed to an influx of American land agents and settlers. They saw the end of their nations. Shawnees and Miamis, Algonkian people scattered by the upheavals of the fur trade and Anglo-France wars, met on the Sandusky River to consider their alternatives: fight or flight.

Joseph Brant (Thayendanegea) attended, fresh from a meeting with George Washington in Philadelphia. Washington had promised that if the tribes would yield the Ohio valley peacefully, the United States would make no further demands. The region between the Ohio and the Muskingum rivers was the farthest western expansion that Americans contemplated, he said.

Shawnees, displaced from their land by the agreement signed at Fort Stanwix in 1768 and driven from their claims by Virginians in 1774, were unimpressed. John Graves Simcoe sent soldiers to the Maumee River to build a British fort in Ohio to protect Upper Canada from American cavalry sent to deal with the Indians.

General "Mad Anthony" Wayne, so-named at a battle at Stony

Point in 1779 where his men killed 699 of the seven hundred defenders, led the American attack against the tribes, burning Shawnee villages. Shawnees and Miamis made a stand at Fallen Timbers and suffered a massive defeat. With Wayne in pursuit, survivors fled toward Detroit, still a British fort.

To their astonishment, they found a spanking new fort on the way, with a Union Jack on the flagpole. The commanding officer at Maumee refused them refuge, nervous of provoking an American attack. Wayne and the cavalry galloped into view, equally amazed to encounter an English fort. He sent a message asking the English to surrender. The commanding officer said no.

A soldier held a burning taper a few inches from the fuse of a cannon trained on Wayne's chest. Stillness fell, as Wayne debated whether to start a war between the United States and England. He decided to withdraw.

Elizabeth Simcoe, evacuated to Québec in the emergency, wrote tartly, "If the Gov. [Simcoe] had waited until the opening of navigation of the lakes to have gone to the Miami *as Lord Dorchester proposed,* the fort would not have been rendered defensible by this time to have intimidated Mr. Wayne and war would have commenced with the U. States."

Wayne's victory at Fallen Timbers shattered the tribes. Shawnee, Delaware, Miami, Chippewa, Ottawa, Wyandot, Sac, and Fox chiefs signed an agreement in 1795 by which they yielded the Ohio valley to America. Young men felt betrayed and fell out with their elders. Joseph Brant's son attacked him with a knife, and in the struggle the Mohawk killed his boy.

— 8 —

Smugglers and Sabers

Jay's Treaty of 1794 averted what appeared to be the real likelihood that Britain and the United States would go to war again. American traders, frustrated by being banned from Indies trade, were breaking the embargo. When the Royal Navy retaliated, it appeared Mad Anthony Wayne's discretion on the Maumee was in vain. George Washington sent Chief Justice John Jay to meet with England's William Grenville to find a peaceful solution.

The answer was to give more of Canada to the United States. Canadiens living near trading posts that became American soil had until June 1, 1796, to move or become American citizens. American traders were permitted into the West Indies, a blow to New Brunswick and Nova Scotia since neither were allowed to trade outside the British network and both depended on preferential arrangements.

Jay's Treaty also established that an international commission would examine the border dispute on the Sainte Croix River. The outcome was in little doubt: two of the three commissioners were Americans and the third was from Halifax, a maritime rival of New Brunswick.

Maine produced aged Indians who swore the Sainte Croix of their boyhood was the northern tributary. New Brunswick countered with the ghost of Samuel Champlain, his drawings of the 1604 French settlement which placed the Sainte Croix on the southern alternative. The commission could not escape the old geographer's evidence and awarded the rich timber tract to New Brunswick. Americans homesteading there complained bitterly; so did land speculators in New York and London. In the end, Maine was allowed to keep the Sainte Croix of its choice while giving up claim to the Madawaska hinge, vital for rafting timber to Saint John and keeping communication with interior Canada.

Timber smuggling and poaching involved highly placed men on both sides. Though American customs men tried to stop them, Vermonters hired Canadien rivermen to take logs to Lord Dorchester for the Royal Navy. The traffic caused confusion about allegiance. Americans in Lower Canada's eastern townships found it difficult to think of themselves as British; Vermont, its commerce linked to Canada, considered a choice of flags: American, British, or Vermont.

Some Americans changed citizenship in the interest of business. Philemon Wright of Woburn, Massachusetts, went to the upper Ottawa River in 1797, climbed to the tops of a hundred trees without seeing anything but trees in every direction, and bought land. He built a mill at Hull, learned from Canadiens how to raft logs, and competed with Vermont for navy contracts.

British colonial policy in America at the turn of the century consisted of enabling a ruling class to evolve as a bulwark against republicanism. The colonial patronage system was used to elevate loyal Tories and, at the governor's discretion, the governor and his friends. In a dozen years at the beginning of the nineteenth century, a few people were given 1,500,000 acres of Upper and Lower Canada. Most were members of the governor's executive council or had connections to it. Envious outsiders called the group in Upper Canada the "Family Compact" and in Lower Canada the "Château Clique."

James McGill got 38,000 acres; the Frobisher brothers 57,000. In Upper Canada Thomas Talbot ruled like a monarch over 65,000 acres on Lake Erie, lecturing his settlers on the evils of temperance and Methodists. The Jarvis cousins, American loyalists who lost a vast estate in Connecticut, received land and government positions.

A Lower Canada governor of the period, Robert Shore Milnes, explained frankly that the grants and appointments were made to ensure "a due proportion . . . between the aristocracy and the lower orders of people, without which it [the House of Assembly] will become a dangerous weapon in the hands of the latter."

The activities of the governors and their friends tended to drive up the cost of land artificially. Much of it was vacant, held by

English and American investors waiting for a population boom. To add to the difficulties faced by newcomers in colonies still without roads, land was reserved for the crown, one lot in every seven, and for the clergy, another lot in every seven, leaving stretches of impenetrable forest between farms. Under such conditions, communication was almost impossible and settlers did without villages, churches, and even schools.

In Lower Canada where the Jesuit order had been dissolved in 1773 without disposition of land owned by priests, the Jesuit estates emerged as a political issue that divided Canadiens and English-speaking citizens of Lower Canada for almost a century. Canadiens wanted money from the sale of some ten seigneuries to be used to educate Catholic children, pointing out that such use was consistent with the work of the Jesuits. Montrealers and the Château Clique demanded that it be applied to Protestant schools only, arguing that the prevalence of illiteracy among Canadiens demonstrated that education was wasted on them.

In 1806 anguished Canadiens founded a nationalist newspaper, *Le Canadien,* with the motto *Fiat justitua ruat caelum,* "Our language, our institutions, our laws." Pierre Bédard, leader of the Canadiens in the Assembly, was an editor. Two others, Jean-Thomas Taschereau and Joseph Borgia, were lawyers, and the fourth, François Blanchet, was a doctor. In Lower Canada where commerce was in the hands of English-speaking citizens, Canadien men of ability and education either went into British colonial administration, if their families supported the governor, or entered medicine or law, the careers open to Canadien dissidents.

In 1810 the British governor, Sir James Craig, closed *Le Canadien* and put the four founders in prison without trial. The following year Canadiens defied the governor and elected Bédard and Blanchet to the Assembly though the two were still in jail.

British governors also had trouble in the maritime colonies. After Jay's Treaty, New Brunswick suffered so drastically because of the losses in the Indies trade that growth virtually stopped. In 1803 the population was 25,000 and dropping fast. Except for the profits from smuggling British goods to New Englanders, a major source of income for prominent colonials, New Brunswick would have asked to be annexed to the United States.

In 1806 and 1807, when Napoleon's European campaigns cut

off England's supply of timber from the Baltic, New Brunswick suddenly prospered. In one year, exports for the wooden ships of the Royal Navy doubled; the next year, 1808, they tripled. Shipyards in Saint John reopened and boomed, attracting swarms of Yankee shipwrights.

Alexander Baring, later the first Baron Ashburton and head of London's powerful Baring brothers financial house, took a personal interest in New Brunswick's prosperity. He was married to the daughter of a U. S. Senator, William Bingham, whose dowry included a million acres of Maine timber. By deft lobbying, Baring got legislation that fixed a low tariff on timber from the United States and the British colonies. Baltic timber's tariff was fixed so high that whatever eluded Napoleon's blockade was more expensive than the North American product.

Edward Ellice shrewdly invested North West Company profits in mills on the Miramichi River in New Brunswick. So did Montrealers, McTavish and Inglis.

Newfoundland, ignored and abused by England for two centuries, received sudden attention. The efforts of summer governors had failed to uproot the stubborn colony of emigrant Irish Catholics and disgruntled seamen who clung to St. John's, though the town was a reeking slum. Even the governor's residence was a disgrace, its sagging slate roof porous to the rain. In 1811 shopowners were given deeds to their land. In 1817 the first year-round governor arrived. He was an admiral, Francis Pickmore, who had pulled every string to avoid the posting. Despondently, he moved into his official residence where snow drifted into the bedrooms.

Timber ships continued to bring refugee Scots to New Brunswick and Lower Canada by the thousands as the ignoble Scottish clearances continued. Except for a steady influx of Americans moving to Upper Canada, Scots were the only colonists to be had.

A philanthropist, the fifth Earl of Selkirk, Thomas Douglas, gave impetus to the migration. A millionaire at twenty-eight, he devoted himself to helping his starved and homeless countrymen. The first Selkirk colony was on land he purchased in Prince Edward Island, the next on some dreadful site in Upper Canada. Then Selkirk read Alexander Mackenzie's journals about exploration and fur trading and bought controlling interest in the Hudson's Bay Company at a time when the stock was off. He wrested from the other directors title to 45 million acres in the Red River valley where he intended to establish dispossessed highlanders.

Selkirk was aware that his proposed community would cut across North West Company trade routes and would be planted in the heart of the North West Company food supply. Collision was inevitable: Either the North West Company would be ruined, or the fur traders would wipe out the Scot settlers.

He called the territory Assiniboia. It stretched over 166,000 square miles from Lake Winnipeg to the headwaters of the Mississippi, taking in much of what is now Manitoba, Minnesota, and North Dakota. The first shipment of Scots arrived late in 1811 at the Hudson's Bay Company post of York Factory. Ragged and ill, they came ashore on the forbidding coast behind a piper who had been at Culloden. The following spring they straggled south to the fork of the Red and Assiniboine rivers where, among the Crees and métis, they built homes.

Nor'westers grew increasingly alarmed as Selkirk's agent, Miles Macdonell, built a fort he named Douglas, for his chief. More Scots came. Macdonell hastened the looming crisis by decreeing in January 1814 that pemmican could not be sold to fur traders. In 1815 the Nor'westers scattered the Scots with inducements to move to Upper Canada and threats of extermination if they didn't. That winter Colin Robertson, a North West Company deserter to the HBC, found remnants of the colony hiding on the Jack River and persuaded them to return.

Selkirk sent the fifth shipment of Scots in 1816 under a new governor, William Semple. A nineteen-year-old métis, Cuthbert Grant, son of a Nor'wester of the same name, approached Fort Douglas with an armed band of Cree and métis. Semple left his meal to meet them, accompanied by men from the fort. They argued in the shade of oak trees. Someone made a threatening move and the Nor'westers opened fire, leaving Semple and twenty others dead. The Massacre of Seven Oaks, as it is called in history, was followed by attacks by Nor'westers against the remnants of Selkirk's colony.

The laird himself was on the way with help, a force of one hundred mercenaries of the Swiss-German-Italian De Meurons regiment, described by one observer as "a rough and lawless set of blackguards." Selkirk and the De Meurons were at Sault Ste. Marie when they learned of the killings at Seven Oaks. They changed course for the Nor'wester warehouse at the western tip of Lake Superior, the former Kaministikwia, renamed Fort William for the Nor'wester chief William McGillivray. Selkirk and the De Meurons caught two wintering partners in residence, William McGillivray himself and Simon Fraser. Selkirk arrested them, on doubtful authority, and sent them to Montréal for trial for the murder of William Semple and other HBC employees.

Cuthbert Grant attempted an ambush of Selkirk and the De Meurons when they continued their journey west in the spring, but the Saulteaux came to the rescue. The tribe was waiting eagerly for Selkirk's arrival. He was the rich man the settlers promised who would give money for the land they were farming.

The Red River valley in question was the ancestral home of Crees and Assiniboins, but Saulteaux canoemen carried on commerce in the area and took a proprietary view. They escorted Selkirk to Fort Douglas where he collected his demoralized settlers, bestowed free land on the De Meurons, and sat down with Saulteaux and Crees to discuss settlement of the twenty-four miles of riverfront farms his colony would occupy. The tribes were assured that Selkirk would return with silver to pay for the land, so they put their mark on a deed surrendering claim to Assiniboia in return for a token payment of ammunition and tobacco. In fact, it was all they were to get.

Selkirk left the Red River by way of the United States to face the legal mess of charges and countercharges the Hudson's Bay Company and the North West Company were laying. Since judges and juries in the colonies tended to be Nor'westers or their relatives, Selkirk formed a low opinion of local justice. The trials dragged through courts in York, Montréal, Sandwich, Detroit, and London for four years, a feast for lawyers that eventually reduced the North West Company to bankruptcy and made the Earl of Selkirk penniless and deathly ill.

The events in Assiniboia seemed remote from the larger drama that unfolded at the same time in the other British colonies of

America. The Napoleonic wars in Europe created a trade blockade against England that forced the British to depend on North America. The United States and the colonies were selling timber to the Royal Navy and food to Wellington's army in the Spanish peninsula.

The U. S. President, Thomas Jefferson, concerned that the United States might become involved in another war, steered a bill through Congress in 1807 prohibiting Americans from trading with the belligerents. The result was the end of cotton shipments from Virginia, which caused cotton mills in Manchester to close and unemployed workers to riot. Britain desperately issued special licenses to smugglers to break the blockade, a decision applauded in New Brunswick, Nova Scotia, and New England.

In 1808 the British Board of Trade had granted 5,000 such licenses; in 1810, 20,000 were granted. Wellington's army in Europe relied on American supplies, a situation which greatly stimulated shipbuilding and drained the pool of experienced seamen. With the U.S. merchant fleet offering top wages, the Royal Navy was hit by desertions. British warships began stopping U. S. ships at sea to search for missing crew and to take as prizes all American ships suspected of trading with Napoleon. Furious owners demanded that President James Madison put a stop to the outrage.

Other forces also were urging that the United States declare war. Young Republicans, called "War Hawks," led by John C. Calhoun of South Carolina, saw the British presence in North America as an impediment to western expansion. So long as hostile tribes could get guns from fur traders, it would be unsafe for Americans to settle in the west. Calhoun pointed out that Upper Canada was populated almost entirely by Americans. If the United States went to war with Britain, he estimated it would take no more than four weeks until the colonies would be "in our possession."

Tribes caught between the United States and its new acquisition, Louisiana, were under no illusions that they would be left in peace. An Ohio-born Shawnee, Tecumseh, was forming a tribal coalition to defend the land. Tecumseh, an imposing man in his forties who once had an American mistress who read him Shakespeare, sent messages along the tribal network that natives must rally for a final stand against white aggression. With his brother, known as The Prophet, he organized a tribal conference in the Shawnee village where the White and Tippecanoe rivers meet in Indiana, about eighty miles south of Lake Michigan.

William Henry Harrison, governor of Indiana and a former Indian fighter, a rakish, aggressive man who wore an ostrich plume in his beaver hat, was impatient with orders to avoid confronting the Shawnees. When Tecumseh visited him in Vincennes, the capital, to ask for recognition of tribal claims, he treated him rudely. Tecumseh announced he would take his grievances to Washington.

Harrison, judging The Prophet to be a weaker opponent, took advantage of the Shawnee chief's absence. With a thousand men, some of them U. S. infantry, he went up the Wabash and camped near Tippecanoe. The Shawnees attacked at night, inflicting heavy casualties on the Americans. Afterward Harrison rode into the almost abandoned village, killed those who hadn't joined the evacuation, and put homes and food stores to the torch. Tippecanoe was reported as a resounding victory, and the legend of the encounter carried Harrison to the White House. Running against John Tyler in 1840 with the slogan "Tippecanoe and Tyler too," he won.

Andrew Jackson, lawyer-soldier, sided with the War Hawks. War with Britain, he declared, would reestablish "our national character." The United States lacked only an army, since the founding fathers viewed the military as "inconsistent with the principles of republican government." In January 1812 Congress authorized money to raise a militia. Isaac Brock, British soldier-administrator in Upper Canada, in 1811 was made a major-general. He tried to push a Militia Bill through a reluctant House of Assembly but the crisis didn't appear real enough to warrant pressing farmers into the military at seeding time. In truth, it seemed highly unlikely that Americans could be stopped if they wanted Canada. The U. S. population stood at 7.5 million, while the British colonies had fewer than a half million, most of whom were Canadiens who might side with Americans, and many of the rest were Americans who certainly would.

On June 4, 1812, the U. S. Congress declared war on Britain by a vote of 79 to 49. The Senate debated setting a time limit on the war, but this was rejected as being impractical. The war bill was passed by a narrow margin 19 to 13. On June 19, President Madison signed it, unaware that Britain had just decided to lift the trade embargo that had created most of the anti-British sentiment along the seaboard.

9

The War of 1812

The U. S. Secretary of State, James Monroe, sent a message to London at once that America was willing to negotiate peace. It was too late to stop the military. Along the border between the United States and the British colonies, smugglers feared for their livelihoods. Residents of Eastport, Maine, sent a note to Saint John, New Brunswick, promising to "preserve the good understanding," a decision that most other colonials and Americans reached without committing themselves in writing.

Napoleon retreated from Moscow, and Wellington was stalled in Spain. The British prime minister, Spencer Perceval, was assassinated by a man driven mad by debts. The British public was aghast to learn that it would have to pay for another army to fight in America. Isaac Brock, who had hoped the confrontation would be avoided when traders stopped selling guns to Tecumseh, regarded his prospects as poor. British military strategy assumed that Upper Canada could not be held. The shores of the Great Lakes were too open and accessible everywhere to enemy landings and the colony was filled with Americans, even in the House of Assembly.

News of the war came to the garrison at Fort George on the Niagara River at an embarrassing moment. The British were hosting American officers from Fort Niagara to a banquet. After a few minutes of consternation, the sensible decision was made to finish the meal and start the war the next day. British officers saw the Americans into their boats and waved them a cordial farewell.

The war in North America could not be allowed to interfere with supplies for Wellington in Spain. U.S. merchant ships were issued permits to allow them through the British blockade of the peninsula, while New Englanders met with the Royal Navy at sea to sell provisions.

John Jacob Astor, the American fur trade mogul, was caught by the war in Montréal doing civil business with the rival North West Company. Despite the inconvenience of the hostilities, negotiations continued for the sale of Fort Astoria to the Nor'westers. Vermont, doubtful of its allegiance, declared itself a neutral and continued to sell timber at Québec for Britain's navy. Massachusetts honored British bills of exchange and, like Connecticut, refused to raise its militia quota. New York farmers drove cattle across the border for delivery to Brock's army in the field against Americans. The Barings in London, who had arranged the financing of the Louisiana Purchase a few years earlier, kept in anxious contact with their many partners and investments in the States throughout the war.

In any case, it was accepted that the war wouldn't last long. The U. S. Secretary of War, William Eustis, boasted, "We can take the Canadas without soldiers; we have only to send our officers into the provinces and the people, dissatisfied with their own government, will rally round our standards." Thomas Jefferson, recalled to Washington to help in the crisis, agreed. "The annexation of Canada this year as far as the neighborhood of Québec will be a mere matter of marching, and will give us experience for the attack on Halifax next."

The British governor-general of the colonies, Sir George Prevost, allowed Brock to declare martial law in Upper Canada. Brock distributed the thin resources at his command, 1,200 British soldiers and some highly reluctant militia, many of them American-born. Brock realized that command of the Great Lakes was the key to defending Upper Canada, which was still largely without roads. Americans had a fleet of fast, sleek clipper ships on Lake Erie and Lake Ontario. These were converted to warships by mounting cannons on the decks. Britain had nothing like them, only ungainly boxcar-shaped boats intended for fur traffic.

George Prevost doubted that even Lower Canada could withstand an American invasion. Like Brock, he had few soldiers; England was concentrating on Napoleon. Canadiens seethed with revolutionary plots, appalled that the government once more was issuing paper money. When Prevost's press gangs tried to force

Canadiens into a militia, there were riots. Prevost threatened to deport everyone who failed to show loyalty; one of his officers complained that most English-speaking settlers were Americans who "retain those ideas of equality and insubordination so prevalent in that country."

The British could depend on Catholic Scots. The Glengarry clan of Macdonells turned out to a man, accepting in their ranks other Scots from the Atlantic colonies but refusing those considered doubtful, Canadiens and ex-Americans. Though Prevost raised 11,000 Canadiens for the militia, he decided to trust only 4,000 with guns.

Brock, a handsome bachelor, blond, courtly, six-foot-two, received a visit from a Nor'wester. Robert Dickson, a Scot married to the sister of a native chief, offered to lead fur traders and natives to Michilimackinac, Dickson's former post until Jay's Treaty gave it to the United States. Since it was likely Americans there didn't know war had started, they could be overcome easily. Brock agreed.

That victory at Michilimackinac sent British prestige soaring among colonists who expected America to win easily in Upper Canada. Iroquois on the Grand River reconsidered a decision to remain neutral and instead volunteered to help the British. Tecumseh, with four hundred Shawnee fresh from raids against Americans in revenge for Tippecanoe, offered his army to Brock.

The two met at Fort Amhertsburg south of Detroit, where Brock expected an American attack. They admired each other on sight. Brock said of the Shawnee, "A more sagacious or a more gallant warrior does not, I believe, exist." William Hull, almost sixty, like most American generals a retread from the Revolutionary War, led the American army across the Detroit River and announced to farmers in Upper Canada that "the arrival of friends must be hailed by you with cordial welcome." He wandered across the countryside until an ambush by Tecumseh's warriors sent him flying for safety to Fort Detroit. When the U. S. Secretary of War asked why he wasn't invading Canada, Hull replied that England controlled "the water and the savages."

Henry Adams, nineteenth-century historian, observed of the campaigns in 1812, "The country refused to take the war seriously."

Brock and Tecumseh moved to Detroit. Aware that Hull was in terror of Shawnee, Brock warned the American that the Indians "will be out of control the moment the contest commences." He recommended that Hull surrender. The next morning, seeing natives and redcoats all around, Hull did. Tecumseh kept the Shawnee in check, and the Ohio militia went home unharmed. Some five hundred American soldiers, however, were put in chains and paraded through every community of any size between Detroit and Québec, making a deep impression on those who had discounted Britain's chances.

"The people of Canada could scarcely believe events, even after they were known to be true," Reverend Michael Smith marveled. "The army now became respectable."

Brock, knighted for the victory at Detroit, moved to the Niagara frontier where the next attack was expected. Prevost sent a message to the American general, goutish Henry Dearborn, asking if he wanted an armistice. Dearborn consulted President Madison. While he awaited the President's testy reply that he get on with the invasion of Canada, Dearborn's short-term militia reached the end of its enlistment period and went home.

Brock prepared to defend Fort George. Farther down the river, a picket guarding a clifftop at Queenston grumbled that he would miss the action. On the night of October 10, 1812, British soldiers on guard duty heard Americans cursing the rain and the turbulent river. The next morning they could see an invasion fleet massing on the opposite shore. Brock was notified. He was unimpressed, believing the blatant maneuver could only be a decoy.

But three nights later he heard gunfire at Queenston and knew he had erred. Dawn showed Americans on the top of the cliff and more crossing the river in tossing boats. Brock didn't wait for his army from Fort George to catch up. He ordered an attack by the handful of Iroquois, militia, and regulars at his disposal. Waving his sword, he ran up the sloping ground toward the enemy and was killed by a Virginia marksman.

Winfield Scott, twenty-six, commander of the landing party, future hero of the war with Mexico, was cool and steady under the first fire of his career. As he calculated the favorable odds, he was shocked to note that his militia was climbing down the cliff and piling into boats to return to the American shore. They were exercising their democratic right: They hadn't volunteered to fight on foreign soil.

Robert Runchey of York, leading a platoon of freed slaves, the Company of Coloured Volunteers, raced up the slope with bayonets gleaming. On the flanks were Mohawks, screaming war cries, and in the distance the sound of Brown Bess muskets indicated that Brock's army was near. Scott pulled a handkerchief from his sleeve and surrendered.

Roger Sheaffe, the Boston-born Tory who succeeded Brock as commander-in-chief of the British Army in Canada, uncomfortably accepted Scott's sword; Americans outnumbered his force two to one. He followed Brock's example and sent the American militia home, while displaying chained American regulars as a propaganda weapon through the colonies.

Sheaffe, sixty and newly married to a daughter of blue-blood Bostonian John Coffin, spent the winter hunting American sympathizers in Upper Canada to prepare the colony for a spring invasion. Expecting little help from England, he offered inducements of free land and high wages to volunteers. Military courts conducted fast trials of suspected traitors. Following the "Bloody Assizes" at Ancaster, a hamlet near present-day Hamilton, eight men went to the gallows.

Canadiens were awed at the sight of American soldiers miserably in chains. Priests exhorted them to support England, while radicals cried for help for the invaders. Pierre Bédard, though recently released from a British prison, agreed with the priests. "If the Canadas come under the domination of the United States," he wrote the British government, "their population will be submerged . . . and they will become nothing, without any influence in their government, unable to protect their religion."

Young Louis-Joseph Papineau, twenty-six and an orator who could sway the House of Assembly, represented the *patriotes,* young educated Canadiens who urged neutrality. But even Papineau was tempted to fight Americans when Prevost named a Canadien officer to head an all-Canadien regiment. The man was Charles-Michel de Salaberry of an aristocratic Québec family with ties to the British establishment. Four De Salaberry sons joined the British Army and three died serving England in foreign wars.

De Salaberry, thirty-four, was trusted to form a regiment called the *Voltigeurs Canadien. Patriotes,* even Papineau, could not resist the chance to serve in the first all-French unit since the conquest. The Assembly's Canadien majority endorsed Prevost's army bills, though the American-dominated Assembly in Upper Canada was still resisting Sheaffe. That winter Lower Canada funded the defense of Upper Canada.

Dearborn, ill and cranky, crossed the Canadian border in November in an attempt to reach Montréal, but got lost. De Salaberry's *Voltigeurs* saw action for the first time. When they set up a whoop of Iroquois war cries, Dearborn's unhappy army fled in disarray.

With New England actively helping Britain, Nova Scotia or New Brunswick seemed in no danger of attack. Prevost sent to New Brunswick for volunteers to defend Upper Canada. The colony's militia, the Fencibles, set off on snowshoes in the coldest winter in a decade and spent fifty-two days struggling across Maine to get to the St. Lawrence. Some froze to death in their sleep: "All the hardest drinkers," someone observed.

The port town of Ogdensburg, New York, continued to be a shopping mecca for the British Army and Canadian housewives. Matrons crossed the ice carrying white flags and bought groceries, while Prevost's commissary sent agents to buy U. S. beef. When Captain Isaac Chauncey of the U. S. Navy announced his intention to make Ogdensburg a base for his newly armed clipper ships, "Chauncey's spiders," Ogdensburg was no less distressed than the British. The location was ideal for naval raids, close to the river mouth where the North West Company's furs came every spring. Chauncey caught exhausted *voyageurs* at Gananoque and captured enough furs to fill a warehouse.

Oliver Hazard Perry's fleet on Lake Erie also was enjoying success against the clumsy ships of the provincial marine, cutting Sheaffe's communication with Detroit. Prevost hurriedly installed shipyards at York and Kingston to lay down the keels of warships.

William Henry Harrison clamored for a chance to assault Detroit, which was isolated by American naval supremacy. An army sent to retake Detroit was intercepted at Frenchtown and surrendered when cautioned that otherwise "the Indians might get out of hand." Tecumseh was absent, however, and prisoners were killed.

Chauncey's fleet was driven from Ogdensburg that spring and moved to a new base at Sackett's Harbor. On April 26, 1813, it anchored off Upper Canada's capital, York. The town of nine hundred people was mired in deep mud, its trademark every spring. The American fleet of fourteen ships carrying 2,000 men had come to capture the thirty-cannon battleship *Sir Isaac Brock* which was almost ready for launching. Chauncey brought with him American carpenters to finish the job.

Sheaffe concluded it was hopeless to fight. He ordered a retreat on foot toward Montréal. That night he set gunpowder charges to destroy the *Isaac Brock* and readied other charges in the stone-walled magazine so the powder wouldn't fall to the Americans. Just as longboats brought the American army to shore in the morning, five hundred barrels of gunpowder exploded, "the nearest thing to an atomic blast seen in that age," as historian C. P. Stacey described it some 160 years later. Trees and tons of stone fell on Americans, killing or maiming more than three hundred. Among the dead was the explorer Zebulon Pike, thirty-four, after whom Pike's Peak is named, a man whose career was expected to culminate in the White House.

Raging, grieving, and drunk, Americans looted abandoned homes, opened the jail, and set fire to churches and public buildings, including Government House. They roistered in the taverns, singing *Yankee Doodle*. John Strachan, thirty-four, a Scot and one of five Church of England clergymen in Upper Canada, became spokesman for the terrified inhabitants of York. He shook his cane at Dearborn and Chauncey, raining Gaelic curses on them for the vandalism in his church.

Because the winds remained unfavorable, the American fleet was obliged to wait a week before recrossing the lake. It left so heavily laden with booty that some had to be thrown overboard to prevent the ships from capsizing. York's Royal Standard, part of the spoils, is still displayed in the U. S. Naval Academy at Annapolis.

That summer of 1813 Prevost, a poor general at offense, bungled an attack on Sackett's Harbor and lost most of his army. Winfield Scott crossed the Niagara River and took Fort George, pushing up the peninsula with 4,000 men. They were camped at

Stoney Creek near the eastern tip of Lake Ontario on the night of June 5, 1813. A peddler among them, a tall man with a brogue, was British soldier James FitzGibbon, Brock's "favorite sergeant-major," a man who had gone into debt to purchase a commission. FitzGibbon took note of the sentry posts, rejoined his regiment, and at 2 A.M. guided the British into the American camp. In the melee, Americans shot one another. When the confused battle ended, two U.S. generals were prisoners.

FitzGibbon's reward was to pick fifty skilled men to wage guerrilla war on American positions. An American colonel, C. G. Boerstler, led a detachment to FitzGibbon's command post. Mohawks brought word of the enemy's approach, news confirmed by Laura Secord, American-born wife of a wounded settler, who walked a circuitous route, found FitzGibbon, and gave him the warning.

Some four hundred Mohawks prepared an ambush at Beaver Dam and were fighting Boerstler when FitzGibbon and his forty-six men arrived. Approaching with a white flag, FitzGibbon told the Americans he would have difficulty keeping the Iroquois in check unless they surrendered. They did, all 462 of them.

The American navy, however, was in clear command of the Great Lakes. Despite a tragedy when two of Chauncey's top-heavy spiders rolled over in a squall and sank in Lake Ontario with all hands aboard, Lake Ontario belonged to him, and Lake Erie to Perry. The summer was hot and wet, a breeding ground for fevers. The British Army in the Niagara peninsula could not be supplied. "Most are near naked," an officer complained.

Henry Proctor, twenty-six, a Welshman in the British Army, commanded Detroit with increasing nervousness. As harvest approached, his militia began to desert. Proctor decided to abandon the fort, with Harrison in pursuit.

Shawnee retreated with the British. Tecumseh begged the young officer to make a stand, since his force outnumbered Harrison's. "We are determined to defend our lands and, if it is His will, to leave our bones upon them," Tecumseh said, referring to the Great Spirit. The end came on October 5, 1813, at Moravian-town. Though the Shawnee had never fought men on horseback, they stood their ground until most of them, including Tecumseh, were killed. To prevent Americans from skinning their chief, his people buried him in an unmarked grave.

Proctor surrendered and later was court-martialed for incompetence. Harrison took Shawnee women and children as hostages and went back to Detroit. By autumn Americans were in possession of Detroit, Fort George, Amhertsburg, and Sandwich. Major-General Wade Hampton was prepared to attack Montréal. De Salaberry's *Voltigeurs* waited in rifle pits layered in rising tiers, a frontier trick.

Hampton unwisely ordered a night attack. His inexperienced men stumbled around in the dark and in the morning were under Canadien guns, the October air reverberating in Iroquois war cries. The terrified Americans turned and ran for the border.

As winter descended the Americans made a second attempt to take Montréal. In bitter cold, the fleet sailed from Sackett's Harbor and feinted toward Kingston, so near the shore that highlanders concealed behind trees killed soldiers on the decks. Prevost established his headquarters in the home of a wealthy German settler, John Crysler. On the morning of November 11, 1813, American landing parties attacked the farm in the belief the defenders were only unskilled militia.

Prevost's men were, in fact, British regulars wearing borrowed overcoats. Despite a bayonet charge, the Americans managed to hold. The commanding officer sent to Hampton for reinforcements. Hampton, who didn't like the officer, refused. Invaders were forced to retreat to a nearby village, French Mills, where they spent the winter before wading home across sloshy ice to avoid spring breakup.

While Prevost's problems were manpower and supplies, American commanders also had difficulties. For one, many militia had enlisted to fight only on American soil or only until the end of the year. As a disgusted colonel observed, "A spirit of subordination was foreign to their views." The New York militia that winter reached the end of their hitch and went home, obliging the United States to withdraw from Fort George. As a parting gesture, Americans burned the pretty town of Newark, two hundred frame homes full of valued possessions, and sent residents into the snow. An American officer who took part was well known to people of

Newark; he was Joseph Willcocks, formerly of the Upper Canada legislature.

British Army and Upper Canada militia took revenge, capturing Fort Niagara and burning and looting Lewiston, Fort Schlosser, Black Rock, Buffalo, and Manchester. Elsewhere along the border, relations remained relatively amicable. Ogdensburg shipped a new printing press to York to replace one destroyed by American raiders. The Royal Navy continued to meet with New England ships at sea.

The curious relationship was fraying, however. In June 1813 the American frigate *Chesapeake* encountered and fought a smaller British frigate *Shannon* almost within Boston harbor. The green American crew was inept. Though the dying captain cried, "Don't give up the ship!" the *Shannon*'s crew, mostly from Nova Scotia, boarded the American ship and towed it triumphantly into Halifax harbor.

Southern Federalists were at loggerheads with the War Hawks as the British blockade of the southern coast brought plantation owners close to bankruptcy. England, worn by the expense of war with Napoleon, was sick of fighting the United States. It was agreed that peace delegations would meet at Ghent. But since Britain would not cease impressment of American sailors, the war in Canada continued anyway.

On April 10, 1814, Napoleon abdicated and the war in the Spanish peninsula ended. Britain got tough. The British blockade was extended to New England, and Wellington's army was posted to Canada. The British foreign minister, Viscount Castlereagh, wanted the British Army to occupy New York, the Ohio Valley, and Maine before peace talks opened.

The British general assigned to the task, unhappily, was Prevost. Wellington, after five days' consideration, refused to take it. Americans dominated the Great Lakes, putting landing parties ashore along Lake Erie as they pleased to burn homes and fields. Some units called themselves the Canadian Volunteers and were made up of Americans who had lived in Upper Canada. The most prominent deserter among them, Joseph Willcocks, was killed in one of the raids.

Wellington's army suffered under Prevost as American leadership improved. Winfield Scott captured Fort Erie on July 3, 1814, and met the British veterans of the Peninsula War in nearby Lundy's Lane, a butchery that lasted one night, settled nothing, and resulted in a thousand casualties.

As preliminaries to the peace talks continued, New Brunswick put in a request for a slice of Maine "so that the important line of communication between this and the neighboring province of Lower Canada by the River St. John may not be interrupted." Castlereagh was willing to oblige. Redcoats landed on the Penobscot coast and on islands in the Passamaquoddy Bay with orders to "occupy so much of the District of Maine as shall ensure an uninterrupted communication between Halifax and Québec."

The landings were almost unopposed. Maine, denied commerce because of the British boycott, was happy to be able to get back to business. Citizens were willing even to take the oath of allegiance to England's king.

Public feeling in Britain was resentful of Americans, who were regarded as opportunists who had taken advantage of Britain's troubles with Napoleon to stab the former mother country in the back. The London *Times* called for a new border to be drawn one hundred miles south of the Great Lakes to teach the Americans a lesson. The world "chastise" appeared frequently in editorials and public addresses.

The Royal Navy, caught in the spirit of revenge, determined to burn Washington to balance the burning of York. In August 1814 the fleet arrived in the Potomac and an army advanced on the capital.

President James Madison fled and the British burned the Library of Congress. Baltimore, forty miles away, saw the flames by night and waited in dread for the attack. But sunken shipping barred the Royal Navy from the harbor so that their cannonballs fell short of Fort McHenry.

A young American lawyer and poet, Francis Scott Key, was on the deck of a British warship eight miles from the target, negotiating a swap of prisoners. By the dawn's early light he saw that the flag was still there. The British gave up the fight.

In Britain, the mood of vengeance changed overnight. People were shocked by the burning of archives, a desecration that dismayed parliamentarians and scholars. While the mortified people berated their government, Americans were more jubilant and united than in any day since the Revolution. The British blockade of New England ended divisiveness and fused the young nation into a whole. The humiliation of the Royal Navy at McHenry and Wellington's army in Upper Canada restored American confidence.

The mood of the peace talks at Ghent reflected the new spirit. Americans no longer were submissive and repentent, and Englishmen didn't speak of chastisement. Henry Clay, one of a distinguished group of American negotiators that included John Quincy Adams and John A. Bayard, had sailed for Ghent expecting to yield the Ohio valley and Maine. Instead he demanded that Britain give the United States Upper and Lower Canada.

In November Britain turned to its hero, the Duke of Wellington, for advice. "I confess that I think you have no right from the state of the war to demand any concession of territory from America," he said. Though the Union Jack flew in Maine, Fort Michilimackinac and Fort Niagara, he observed that England hadn't carried its campaign far into America and had lost two forts, Erie and Amhertsburg, to the Americans. "The state of your military operations, however creditable," he concluded, "does not entitle you to demand any [territory]."

The House of Commons at that moment received the staggering bill for keeping the British Navy and Army active in America. It rebelled. The plan to restore the Shawnee homeland in Indiana and Michigan was abandoned. Alexander Baring, concerned for his wife's estates in Maine, made a moving speech in the House of Commons in which he compared asking America to give up Maine to asking Britain to give up Wales. The British delegation at Ghent accordingly received orders to give the United States everything it wanted except maritime rights to fishing.

Maine was returned to the States, and Fort Niagara and Michilimackinac as well. A boundary west of the Great Lakes cut Selkirk's settlement in half. The North West Company was allowed to keep Fort Astoria on the Columbia, but Britain didn't claim Oregon; Americans could settle there as they wished.

Still, Alexander Baring wrote his friend John Quincy Adams in disappointment. "I wish the British Government would give you Canada at once," he commented. "It is fit for nothing but to breed quarrels."

The Treaty of Ghent was signed on Christmas Eve 1814 as

Andrew Jackson was leading the defense of New Orleans. His victory over the British was one of the war's most decisive. President Madison received a copy of the treaty on February 14, 1815, and it was ratified by a delighted Senate three days later. George Murray, a British general sent to Canada to fire Prevost, walked wearily from New Brunswick to Québec with news that the war was over.

Wellington later gave his opinion that only "the inexperience of the officers of the United States" prevented America from taking Upper and Lower Canada during the War of 1812. Canadians believe that only Wellington's indifference and Prevost's incompetence prevented Canada from acquiring the Ohio valley. Though history books do not agree which side won the war, it is generally accepted that Canada lost the peace.

– 10 –

One Big Company

"The war has given the Americans what they so essentially lacked, a national character founded on a glory common to all," the French ambassador in Washington observed admiringly. Francis Scott Key's poem, "The Star-Spangled Banner," was set to a British tune and became a favorite of military bands.

The national character of the British colonies also underwent change after the War of 1812. Businessmen and settlers who had been inclined to favor republicanism for its optimism and opportunity fell silent. The British colonies rang with anti-Americanism: *freedom* and *liberty* were the words of traitors. Forts along the border bristled with soldiers, and Upper Canada was demanding warships to keep Americans off the Great Lakes.

In 1817 Britain and the United States negotiated the Rush-Bagot agreement by which both countries limited development of navies on the Great Lakes to avoid naval escalation and ruinous expense. New Brunswick was given the Madawaska hinge so vital to its timber export and communication with the Canadas, though a Maine newspaper complained angrily that the state's birthright had been sold. England also took back the island of Grand Manan in the Bay of Fundy, though American settlers there flew the Stars and Stripes in front yards.

The North West Company emerged from the war in collapse. The partners operated by splitting the profits at the year's end, with small concern for a reserve fund. The expensive legal fight with the Earl of Selkirk depleted a company already extended over too much territory. The Nor'westers' London connection, Edward Ellice, failed to buy up the opposition, the Hudson's Bay Company, and in 1820 it appeared obvious to Simon McGillivray, the lame partner who ran the London end, that the HBC was too powerful to defy.

Edward Ellice shuttled between the two giants, and on March 26, 1821, the North West Company agreed to merge with the HBC. Two McGillivrays, William and Simon, and Edward Ellice signed the documents of amalgamation. "Amalgamation!" one Montréal partner exclaimed. "This is not amalgamation but submersion. We are drowned men."

Simon McGillivray almost drowned, indeed, despite his fortune and collection of Rembrandts and Titians. A few years after the "amalgamation" the HBC owned the North West Company's network from Labrador to the Columbia River to the Arctic Ocean. Since it was cheaper and faster to ship furs from James Bay than portage to the St. Lawrence, Montréal for the first time in its two-hundred-year history became irrelevant to the fur trade.

The city's financiers either went broke or diversified. Among the shrewdest was John Molson, who noted Lower Canada's confidence in British army paper money and opened a bank. He plunged into the newest invention, steam engines, and his passenger ship, *Accommodation,* was the first on the river. Peter McGill, in 1817, launched the Bank of Montreal with extensive holdings in land and timber rights.

The era of the fur trade ended for the colonies, but the Hudson's Bay Company entered its golden period. In 1820, just as the merger with the Nor'westers was under way, the HBC sent to Canada a tiny, fussy, vain despot, George Simpson, then in his early thirties, who was to run the Company's empire for thirty-five years.

"The activities of the Hudson's Bay Company in the period 1821 to 1869 deserve an important place in the history of monopolies," historian Harold Innis noted.

Raised in poverty in Scotland by an unmarried mother, Simpson was subjected to harsh discipline as a boy and joined the HBC with a reputation for ruthless efficiency and frugality. His appointment in Canada was expected to be temporary, but he took hold of the sprawling operation with consummate skill and fended off all rivals.

Simpson turned Canada into the Company's private fur farm by application of a blend of corporate genius and sheer terror. He wanted businessmen rather than romantic fur traders, and replaced Nor'westers with his kind of company man. Half the HBC's staff was fired and the rest had salaries cut. Since he was also the government and chief justice of his domain, he jailed or flogged all who complained. He controlled the tribes by withholding gunpowder, without which they couldn't hunt for food. He paid John Jacob Astor an annual fee to keep out of his way and ran off Yankee poachers by shooting at them. Though the HBC did not have authority extending to capital punishment, he hanged offenders anyway.

Simpson's plan for keeping American settlers out of Oregon was to hunt all animals in the area to extinction. He threatened and bullied some settlers in the Red River colony to move to the Columbia River to maintain his claim to the territory, and ordered his factors at Fort Astoria, renamed Fort George, to undersell American traders to drive them out.

A tiny, furious man, he traveled across his domain at breakneck speed with a piper in his canoe to lead him ashore. He transformed half the continent into a model of agribusiness, its hub at Fort Garry on the Red River. Under his direction, furs were carried across the shallow prairie rivers in flat-bottomed boats called York boats. They drew only three feet of water when loaded and were fitted with oversized sails to catch prairie winds. Quick to pick up new technology, he later bought steam-driven paddle-wheelers and hired Mississippi rivermen to run them.

With horses plentiful on the plains, Simpson moved goods in summer in all-wood Red River carts (a Canadien invention) pulled by oxen or small shaganappies bred by the tribes. The carts squeaked maddeningly but were ingenious: a small box suspended between wheels as much as seven feet in diameter could carry eight hundred pounds of freight high and dry over fords.

When Simpson first took up residence in Fort Garry, he followed the example of the Nor'westers and took native women as mistresses. "Bits of brown," he called them. As his fortune grew, his social ambitions dictated something more acceptable to HBC directors. Accordingly, he married a delicate English woman, established her and a piano on the Red River, and banished his mistresses from the community.

He barred "country wives" from his home until his employees took the hint. John George McTavish, a Nor'wester who survived the purges and was trusted by Simpson, evicted the woman who bore his six children and found a wife in England. The centuries-old fur trade practice of miscegenation was ending.

Simpson put a fort in Labrador in 1830 to harvest seals and expanded to San Francisco and Hawaii, where his claim was dubious. He ruthlessly fine-tuned the fur harvest to suit the market and was watchful of depletion. On one occasion when he ordered a region rested to allow animal stock to regenerate, the Slave tribe almost died.

Simpson, with more power than his king, felt an equal among world rulers. When he wanted rights to the Alaskan panhandle, he went to Russia and conferred with the Tsar. In return for a reduced rate for supplies for the HBC's west coast operation and a ten-year agreement that the Company could have exclusive use of the coast from the Columbia River to Cape Spencer on the Beaufort Sea, Simpson rented Alaska to Russia.

Distressed by Americans pouring into Oregon despite his disapproval, "the Little Emperor" built Fort Vancouver on the north shore of the Columbia to halt intruders. Later, he negotiated with four governments over the disposition of Hawaii.

During his long tenure, he never returned to the HBC's directors less than 10 percent annual profit; often it was 25 percent. Obsessive thrift accounted for some of the returns. On Simpson's orders, rotted York boats were burned to recover the nails for reuse, and bags used to ship tobacco to the Red River were recycled as covers for fur bales.

The Red River settlement, attracting Canadiens to migrate from Lower Canada to the more open life of the frontier, nevertheless was wholly owned by the Company. Simpson refused to give farmers a deed for land and extracted rent instead. He banned fur trading for everyone but his own employees. The penalty was to burn down the house of the offender and imprison him without trial, to be released when Simpson felt like it.

Even those who complained loudest agreed that Simpson's toughness worked because he kept out Americans. A Scot fur trader, Alexander Ross, married to a métis and retired to the Red River colony so their children could attend school, wrote that "anarchy and bloodshed" would follow if the HBC released its grasp.

Certainly the community was remarkably honest, a phenomenon which never failed to impress visitors. A Red River métis would follow a departing traveler a hundred miles to return some trifling thing left behind. Wealthy English sportsmen visited Fort Garry for the exotic thrill of the buffalo hunt. When a herd was sighted the entire community—men, women, children, and dogs—piled into a thousand Red River wagons and headed across the dusty prairie.

Military discipline prevailed among the hunters by consent, since order was necessary for maximum effectiveness. Some four hundred hunters could ride through the herd twice and with spectacular accuracy bring down 2,500 animals. Ross wrote that it wasn't unusual to find a knight or baronet "coursing their steeds over the boundless plains and enjoying the pleasures of the chase among the half-breeds and savages of the country." Ross also noted that the herds were shrinking. Though he wondered how the tribes would survive without the staple of their diet, he thought the end of the buffalo would be good for the métis, encouraging them to give up their carefree style and become "a civilized community." The races, once harmonious, were drifting apart. Priests had joined the métis, counseling avoidance of Presbyterian Scots; "an ill-judged step," Ross thought.

The prairie weather in Fort Garry was unbearable for those not inured to it. In 1830 George Simpson's frail and sickly wife could tolerate the winters no longer. The family moved to Lachine, near Montréal, into an ostentatious and ugly house owned by the company. They were just in time to watch the great Canadian rebellion unfold.

— 11 —

The Rebels

The Napoleonic Wars left Britain with two crushing problems: war debts and unemployment. The proximity of coal and iron deposits which gave the island a boost into the industrial age also had meant an end to the usefulness of home workers. Northern factory towns in England were filled with street beggars, but no parish was without groaning rolls of indigents.

At the same time, clearances were continuing in Scotland and overpopulated Ireland had exhausted the soil. When the staple crop, potatoes, failed, people starved.

For the first time, Britain awoke to the knowledge the country was not threatened by underpopulation, as citizens had long believed when they contemplated invasions from teeming France. Instead, they learned that the chaos and riots Thomas Robert Malthus predicted would result from overpopulation. A solution was to export the poor to the nearest colony, Canada. To prime the pump, the government offered free land in the colonies.

In 1823 and 1825, the government sent shipments of Irish indigents to Canada. As well, some 3,000 Scots from Paisley and Glasgow were settled in Perth in Upper Canada. Occasionally landlords paid to move overcrowded tenants, or local societies collected ticket money. "Poor rates are enormously high," wrote Thomas Law Hodges of Hemsted, Kent. "The only remedy is to promote emigration."

The colonies reeled under the burden of the newcomers. A letter to the editor of the *Acadian Recorder* in 1817 noted that nine ships had arrived in Halifax in July with 1,254 passengers and nine more were expected from Londonderry and Belfast with

2,508 more. "What is to become of them, how are they to obtain a subsistence?"

Not all survived the voyage. The means of transport, timber ships, were permitted to carry 240 people—often more—in windowless holds. If winds weren't fair, rations ran out. Of those who stumbled ashore in Saint John, Halifax, or Québec, most of those who could walk went straight to the United States.

Other shipments left Britain for designated parts of the colony. Peter Robinson, son of a Virginia Tory, obtained the job of establishing Irish emigrants in the district around a town he called Peterborough in Upper Canada. London investors formed the Canada Company in 1824 and bought 2½ million acres, settlement of which was supervised badly by a novelist, John Galt. Galt fulfilled the requirements of the company's royal charter to build roads and schools, but couldn't balance the books. He was sacked.

His neighbor, Thomas Talbot, screened applicants according to his prejudices. Highlanders, Quakers, half-pay officers, Americans, and most Irish got the most remote and least-arable land. He transacted no business after noon, reserving the rest of the day for drinking.

Newcomers found work in construction gangs building the latest wonder of commerce, canals. New Yorkers hand dug the Erie Canal in stages, using British loans to finish the link between the Great Lakes and the Atlantic Ocean. That done, eastern factories could ship directly to inland settlers. Montrealers, seeing themselves bypassed again, felt panic. In two years of trying, the Company of Proprietors of the Lachine Canal had been unable to raise money to dredge a channel to connect the St. Lawrence River to the Great Lakes. New York State had invested in the Erie Canal, but Canadiens in the Lower Canada Assembly rejected every attempt English-speaking businessmen made for start-up funds. Canadiens balked because all suggested improvements were upriver in English territory.

The British Army sent survey teams to locate a canal route that would enable supplies to flow into Upper Canada in the event of another war with the United States. To the disappointment of Molson, McGill, and others, the obvious Lachine route was judged too close to the American border to be safe in wartime. The route decided on was four times longer, a sluice between the upper Ottawa River and Lake Ontario called the Rideau Canal. It cost Britain a half-million pounds. Colonel John By of the Royal Engineers supervised the building of it from a headquarters on high ground above the junction of the Ottawa and Rideau rivers, known as Bytown.

Upper Canada, fighting competition from the ebullient United States, sunk itself in debt to build a canal linking Lake Erie with Lake Ontario, the Welland. The Family Compact and other leading businessmen in the Assembly raised investment capital in the United States until costs rose beyond tolerance. To keep control of the canal in Canada, the Tories voted government money for the canal over the protests of many settlers and workers who wanted local improvements instead.

Britain shared the American boom. "Everybody who wishes prosperity to England must wish prosperity to America," the prime minister said in 1820. Forty percent of U.S. imports were purchased in Britain. To keep factories busy, Britain discouraged the development of industry in the colonies and tried to keep Americans from learning how to build cotton mills.

John Strachan, the Anglican priest and hero of the American occupation of York, struggled to maintain "the established church" in Upper Canada, which was filling with Irish Catholics, Scotch Presbyterians, and English and American Methodists. In 1827, exasperated by failure to secure all the clergy reserves for the Church of England, he issued an "Ecclesiastical Chart" which claimed that most of the population of Upper Canada was Anglican, an untruth that inflamed other denominations.

Egerton Ryerson, a Methodist minister and son of a Loyalist, retorted in a furious letter attacking the Family Compact and the governor's group which paid itself high salaries out of Upper Canada's coffers while neglecting roads and schools. Ryerson became spokesman for the underdog and editor of a Methodist paper *The Christian Guardian* published in York.

Lower Canada's two linguistic groups were divided venomously after the war, as New England Tory judges imposed frightful sentences on Canadiens. The House of Assembly appeared irreparably split along the language fault. Young Canadiens, bright, impatient, and frustrated, known as the *Parti Canadien,* tried to have judges impeached, upon which the British governor dissolved parliament.

Louis-Joseph Papineau, fascinated by his readings of English law, led the radical faction and was Speaker of the House. When the *Parti Canadien*'s rejection of canal building became intolerable, Montrealers John Molson and John Richardson appealed to the old friend of the Nor'westers, Edward Ellice, to act. Ellice found no support among the Whigs, though his father-in-law, Earl Grey, was leader of the opposition. He tried the Tories. The Colonial Office was enthusiastic. In 1822 the Union Bill was introduced in Commons, a blueprint for assimilation of French Canada by merging them with rapidly growing Upper Canada and phasing out the French language. Even Charles de Salaberry, who had soldiered for the king, objected. Papineau and John Neilson, a disgruntled Scot journalist, took a petition signed by 60,000 Canadiens to England. Though Montrealers contemptuously described the signatories "Knights of the X," it was an impressive document. Despite all Tory efforts, the British Parliament in the end dropped the bill.

Collisions between Canadiens and the English-speaking minority in the Assembly grew more heated. When the Assembly elected Papineau as Speaker in 1826, the governor again dissolved parliament. Papineau took a petition signed by 87,000 to London and told the House of Commons, "The descendants of the French have no equal rights with their masters of British origin. The history of no other colony presents a similar spectacle of immorality. It is odious that when the laws do not exclude Canadiens from office, that practice should exclude them. They furnish nine-tenths of the revenue and receive barely one-tenth."

A British Parliamentary committee eventually reviewed the complaints. The colonies were factional beyond belief. Cape Breton wanted to separate from Nova Scotia because its delegates were denied seats in the Assembly. Nova Scotia and New Brunswick were fighting over Prince Edward Island. A forest fire in 1825 in New Brunswick destroyed two thousand square miles of pine and killed 160 people, straining relief resources. And the

Hudson's Bay Company was in a shooting war with a free-lance lumberman, William Price, "the father of the Saguenay," over overlapping traplines and timber cutting.

In Upper Canada the differences between the local oligarchy, known as the Family Compact, and its detractors, a disparate group known as "the Reformers," were sharpening. Barnabas Bidwell, a pamphleteer from Massachusetts, moved to Kingston in 1810 to avoid being arrested for misappropriation of funds. He devoted himself to challenging Strachan and other Family Compact figures, notably young Attorney-General John Beverley Robinson, another of the Virginia Robinsons.

Robinson succeeded in having Barnabas Bidwell expelled from the Assembly on the grounds his election was "null and void" because he had served the American government. Bidwell's son, Marshall Spring Bidwell, weathered Robinson's efforts to bar him from the Assembly as well and joined the Reform group, which also included Dr. John Rolph, founder of the colony's first medical school, and a distinguished father-and-son team, William Warren Baldwin, wealthy Irishman, and Robert Baldwin, regarded as an honorable and decent man.

Upper Canada dealt summarily with a Scottish agitator, Robert Gourlay, who in 1817 circulated a questionnaire which among other things asked settlers to list grievances against the establishment. Gourlay, though a British subject, was tried as an alien and banished from the colony. A British officer who sang "Yankee Doodle" while in his cups was stripped of his pension and deported.

A visitor to York in 1824, E. A. Talbot, could appreciate the Tory concern with dissidents. Newcomers from Britain, he wrote, were "indefatigable in acquiring a knowledge of the Rights of Man, the First Principles of Equality, and the True Nature of Independence and, in a word, everything which characterizes an American."

The disparity between the United States and a colony where a British governor could dissolve parliament at will was considerable. The United States drew British emigrants with its energy and bounce. Rochester, New York, "the city of the west" in 1830 had a population of 11,000 and paved streets, while York across the lake was still a village among tree stumps. Every unmarried man who disembarked in New Brunswick walked straight to Maine.

In 1832 the timber ships brought Europe's cholera victims to America. A quarantine station at Grosse Île in the St. Lawrence held 98,000 victims that summer but enough escaped inspection to take the epidemic to every Canadien village along the river. One in ten persons on the St. Lawrence died of cholera, and the colony was swept by a conviction that the disease was a British plan to exterminate the Canadien nation.

John Strachan worked tirelessly in York to nurse victims. The character of newcomers was changing; most were farmers and carpenters who had paid their own passages and arrived with capital. Some English came with a romantic vision of life in the colonies, promoted by travel books extolling frontier life.

Among those who packed up their libraries and spinets in anticipation of adventure and luxury were the Stricklands. The sisters, Catharine Parr Traill and Susanna Moodie, were married to half-pay officers and both wrote voluminously about their experiences. Catharine Traill was plucky. "If you would desire to see your husband happy and prosperous, be content to use the economy and, above all, be cheerful," she advised. Susanna Moodie was not: she felt "the condemned criminal entertains for his cell."

The most vociferous opponent of colonial administration was a gnomelike highlander in a red wig, William Lyon Mackenzie, a Calvinist who maintained a fine wrath against the supple Anglican ethics of Strachan and Robinson. His *Colonial Advocate,* established in York in 1820, became a voice of shrill dissent. In it he described the governor's advisors as "a collection of sturdy beggars, parsons, priests, pensioners, army people, placemen, bank directors and stock and land jobbers . . . a paltry screen to a rotten government." When sons of York's leading families on a summer evening in 1826 dumped the *Colonial Advocate*'s press type in the bay, the courts ordered restitution and rescued the prickly editor from bankruptcy.

Britain's Whig reformers sympathized with the discontent in the British colonies and warned it could result in another American Revolution. Their business judgment, however, dictated caution at allowing unbridled mercantilism in the colonies to threaten the healthy state of Anglo-American commerce.

While they hesitated, another colonial radical developed a following. Nova Scotia's rough-tongued lecher, Joseph Howe, son of an American Tory, wrote the colonial administration in a letter resounding with phrases his father had scorned: "We seek for nothing more than British subjects are entitled to, but we will be content with nothing less."

Howe's popularity among those who opposed the Council of Twelve, Nova Scotia's Tory clique, stemmed from his remarkable defense of himself in March 1835, when he was charged with libeling colonial magistrates in his newspaper, *The Nova Scotian*. His claim on the front page was that magistrates had been "taking from the pockets of the poor" more than £30,000, including a mean levy of £300 a year on the local poorhouse.

Howe, apprenticed at thirteen in his father's printing shop, faced the charges without a lawyer. Despite his lack of formal education, Howe was a brilliant orator. He delivered a speech to the jury lasting six and a half hours in which he listed the perfidities of Halifax magistrates. The jury deliberated ten minutes and returned a verdict of not guilty, after which cheering Haligonians carried Howe home on their shoulders.

The crisis in Lower Canada grew grave. In 1832 three *patriotes* were killed in an election-day melee and the officers responsible for the deaths were found innocent. Incensed, Canadiens in the House of Assembly voted to deny funds to pay salaries to the governor and his staff. In 1834 Papineau took Ninety-Two Resolutions adopted by the Assembly to London. Lord John Russell, a leading Whig reformer, listened as Papineau declared: "It is certain that before long all America is to be republican."

An underground group, the *Fils de la Liberté*, modeled on American revolutionaries, frightened the British establishment and Catholic clergy with talk of overthrowing church and state.

Papineau tried another strategy, a boycott of British goods. Canadiens defiantly wore homespun to show their sympathy. An organized run on banks shook English businessmen, who hired goons to keep Canadien voters away from the polls. In Upper Canada, Mackenzie's virulent insults of Allan Napier MacNab, a leading Tory, caused the furious Family Compact to throw him out of the Assembly. A by-election was called to fill the vacancy. Mackenzie campaigned from the top of a two-story sleigh owned by a tavernkeeper, John Montgomery, and was elected almost unanimously. His opponent received one vote, his own.

When Mackenzie delivered a petition of colonial complaints signed by 25,000 dissatisfied citizens to the Whig Colonial Secretary, Lord Goderich, the peer was not impressed with the leader of Upper Canada's radical reformers. "Five foot nothing and very like a baboon," he sniffed. The two hours he spent with Mackenzie, he commented, were the longest in his life.

Mackenzie, like Papineau, passionately admired American republicanism, the "form of government very fit to prevent abuses of power." His Americanism alienated moderates, Egerton Ryerson and Robert Baldwin. The Tory Assembly was even more affronted and ejected him once more. When he was re-elected, again he was expelled, and when elected once more, was ejected once more.

"Take care you do not end your proceedings by raising him higher and higher in the esteem of the province," warned Jesse Ketchum, a prosperous tanner and supporter of free schools for the poor. In 1835 Mackenzie overwhelmingly was elected the first mayor of the newly incorporated city of York, renamed Toronto.

British Whigs replaced the governors of Upper and Lower Canada with men they hoped would be able to soothe militants. Upper Canada drew Sir Francis Bond Head, a person of haughty vanities ill-suited to dealing with the prickly colonials. He arrived in time for a deepening crisis caused by a depression in the United States, which was soon reflected in the Canadas.

Lower Canada experienced waves of disaster. First was Britain's end run around the Assembly's control of the governor's budget, which left Canadiens without a weapon. Following this a crop failure brought famine and filled poorhouses. Desperation weakened the rule of law and spawned bands of vigilantes, Canadien and English, who roamed the streets. William IV after three years had not responded to the Ninety-Two Resolutions asking for self-government. In March 1837 the Whig Parliament considered a bill rejecting them all, a move interrupted only when William IV died and eighteen-year-old Victoria took the throne.

To the despair of Canadiens, it was clear that Britain would not cease inundating them with English settlers. A new developer, the British Land Company, obtained 800,000 acres east of Montréal, a region known as the Eastern Townships, and announced it planned to put 600,000 settlers on it.

By the summer of 1837, with a financial collapse in the United States and barren fields in Lower Canada, the breaking point was reached. In Saint Ours, a *patriote* stronghold, taverns displayed American eagles and on May 7, 12,000 people gathered to curse Britain. A Declaration of Rights was drafted. One clause belligerently began, "Regarding ourselves as no longer bound except by force to the English government . . ."

The Saint Ours declaration spread along the *patriote* underground. The *Fils de la Liberté* dared to sing the "Marseillaise" openly on the streets of Montréal. A lawyer, George-Étienne Cartier, twenty-three, wrote the movement's anthem, "Avant Tout, Je Suis Canadien." English-speaking Montrealers formed a British Legion as the lieutenant-governor, Archibald Acheson, Earl of Gosford, quietly enlarged his standing army.

Mackenzie was in the backwoods of Upper Canada riding from farm to farm to drum up support against the "wicked and tyrannical government." In Lloydtown, citizens draped the main street with a banner LIBERTY OR DEATH. A Quaker pacifist, Samuel Lount, forsook his vows and spent the summer making pike heads for a revolution that had no guns.

Papineau sent word to Mackenzie on October 9, 1837, that he was ready to fight. Mackenzie called a meeting of conspirators in John Doel's brewery in Toronto. The lieutenant-governor Francis Bond Head had sent almost every British soldier in Upper Canada to help put down *patriotes*. Mackenzie gave a fiery speech urging his followers to take over the deserted city. Except for a small improvised militia that James FitzGibbon, doughty hero of Stoney Creek and Beaver Dam, had organized at his own expense, the government was defenseless. Even so, the militants cautiously decided to delay the attack until December in order to assemble more supporters.

Lower Canada's rebels gathered in the Richelieu valley near the American border. On October 23, 1837, there was a stormy meeting at Saint Charles. Wolfred Nelson, a stocky regimental surgeon married to a Canadien, spoke in broken French, exhorting the *patriotes* to "melt our spoons into bullets." Papineau, depressed, took little part as Nelson outlined plans for a new government.

On November 16, British soldiers sent to arrest rebels were shot from ambush. On November 23 the army arrived in force.

Sir John Colborne, veteran of Waterloo, commanded redcoats hunting for Papineau and Nelson. Colborne sent a messenger, Lieutenant Jack Weir, to notify one of his units to hold up. Weir was captured as Papineau fled for the American border. Though the prisoner was bound, *patriotes* lost control and stabbed him to death with pitchforks. The army, bringing cannons, bombarded the rebel stronghold, a stone distillery in Saint Denis but Canadien marksmen, gloriously excited, beat back the attack.

Redcoats returned on November 25 and in fifteen savage minutes routed the defenders, killing most of them. Inflamed by the discovery of Weir's mutilated corpse, soldiers took frightful vengeance. Saint Denis was burned to the ground and captured *patriotes,* among them Wolfred Nelson, were beaten and paraded to a Montréal prison. Colborne turned his attention to another rebel stronghold, Saint Eustache, west of Montréal and ringed by English settlements. Dr. Jean Chénier, *patriote* leader, was killed in a gallant but futile stand in a church; berserk redcoats then bayoneted prisoners. After burning homes of the rebels, the army moved to peaceful nearby Saint Benoît, hung with white flags, and burned and looted there. Priests refused Catholic burial rites to the slain. Colborne packed the jails of Lower Canada with thousands of prisoners, abused them unmercifully, and hoped the crisis was over.

The postponed rebellion in Upper Canada took notice of the bloody suppression of Papineau's uprising. Mackenzie waited for reinforcements outside Toronto in Montgomery's tavern, a watering place along the old *voyageur* route. FitzGibbon, still lacking military assistance, distributed rifles to citizens and positioned cannons in front of City Hall. On December 4 FitzGibbon scouted the enemy, retreating at the first exchange of shots. He posted a picket commanded by Sheriff William Jarvis, a descendant of American loyalists.

Dr. John Rolph brought Mackenzie news that FitzGibbon was arming. Mackenzie decided to wait no longer. That night his men stumbled into Jarvis' picket. In panic and confusion, both sides fired and ran. The next day FitzGibbon, at the head of a thousand volunteers who had been pouring into Toronto from homesteads in the country, set off to capture Mackenzie. A military band played and citizens lined the newly paved streets and cheered.

Mackenzie's rebels scattered. Mackenzie himself, with a price of £1,000 on his head, waded naked through an icy river on his way to the Niagara border, holding his clothes above his head. He escaped the colony only minutes ahead of his pursuers but dropped a briefcase containing the names of his followers.

That winter Papineau and Mackenzie were heroes in American border towns, in demand at social events. Frustrated jobless men were eager to enlist and invade Canada. Mackenzie established his headquarters on Navy Island on the Canadian side of the Niagara River, where he flew the revolution's flag, a French *tricouleur* with two stars, one for each of the Canadas. Recruits were promised free land in Canada and payment in silver.

A raiding party from Toronto, led by Allan Napier MacNab, scion of a Family Compact family, slipped across the river and set fire to Mackenzie's supply ship, the *Caroline*. Mooring lines were cut and the *Caroline* set adrift to wedge in rocks above the falls. U. S. President Martin Van Buren wakened to the realization that the attack on the *Caroline,* which flew the Stars and Stripes, was an act of war. He ordered governors in Vermont and New York to arrest rebels and assured Britain of his good intentions. Annexation of the colonies, he explained, was "directly contrary to the interests of the United States."

The blameless younger brother of Wolfred Nelson, Robert Nelson, was arrested by Colborne in error and spent a few days of horror in a squalid, overcrowded prison. The experience made a radical of him. He wrote on the wall of his cell, "The English government will remember Robert Nelson" and went to Albany to collect an army. A raid on the arsenal at Elizabethtown, in New York, produced a thousand rifles, with which *patriotes* and Americans in February 1838 mounted an invasion by forty sleighloads of troops. Nelson proclaimed himself the first president of a new Canadian republic but his forces met stiff resistance and were thrown back over the border. Nelson was arrested and confined to an American prison.

Mackenzie meanwhile tried to invade Hickory Island in the St. Lawrence River. A swashbuckling adventurer rejoicing in the name Rensselaer van Rensselaer, twenty-seven, led a small band of rebels against Kingston but his recruits trickled away in the unforgiving February weather.

Gosford was recalled from Lower Canada, glad to be gone from the turmoil, and Colborne took command. The border seethed with talk of war between the Canadas and the United States. English Montréal cried for the blood of rebels held in prison without trial. Robert Nelson was employing his time in captivity to plot a citizen army, Hunters' Lodges (*Les Frères Chasseurs*) that would storm into Canada. Americans who enlisted were blindfolded and taken to hideouts where they swore an oath "never to rest until all tyrants of Britain cease to have any dominion or footing whatever in North America." With unemployment high, Hunters' Lodges were wildly popular; it was rumored that they numbered more than one hundred thousand men.

Gangs of Orangemen and Scots hunted *patriotes* in farms and villages around Montréal, pillaging and burning without restraint. *Habeas corpus* was suspended. Shrines and churches were desecrated.

Britain's new governor arrived in May 1838. He was the radical thorn in the Whig administration, John George Lambton, first Earl of Durham, forty-six, a lean, sallow, ailing millionaire and the ex-prime minister's son-in-law. "Radical Jack," he was called by the British public, who adored him. The Reform Bill of 1832 which widened the franchise beyond landed gentry was drafted in his house. With him was a friend, Edward Ellice, son of the Edward "Bear" Ellice who engineered the sale of the North West Company to the Hudson's Bay Company. Ellice would guide Durham through the shoals of colonial cliques.

Durham was faced with the immediate problem of 161 rebels still in prison. A jury of Canadiens almost certainly would free them, a jury of English almost certainly would hang them. He decided to dispense with trials, free some, and ask others for "confessions." Canadiens responded with orations about justice and liberty. Durham ordered eight, including Wolfred Nelson, to be put in chains by the prison blacksmith and deported to Bermuda. Four months later Durham resigned and left the colony in a huff, indignant at the storm of protest in England over the unauthorized deportation. The governor of Bermuda, insulted that his colony was being used as a prison colony, refused to accept the *patriotes* at first and complained bitterly to his superiors. Piqued, Durham was gone from Lower Canada in September, leaving Colborne in command again.

That month Hunters' Lodges held a convention in Cleveland and agreed to invade the Canadas after the harvest. General Winfield Scott, deeply worried, kept in touch with Colborne; almost every able-bodied American along the border seemed to have joined the Hunters' Lodges; he couldn't trust the militia.

In the Richelieu valley, amid the desolation of burned farmhouses, *patriotes* plotted by night. Robert Nelson, his eyes glittering with frenzy, crossed the border and waited at Napierville for Hunters' Lodges to join him and bring guns. Days passed; they didn't come. The United States, its financial recovery dependent on British banks and the Barings' investments, was firm in patrolling the border. Edward Ellice, that fall enjoying his beautiful seigneury at Beauharnois, noted a suspicious movement of Canadiens around his château. Outnumbered, he surrendered. *Patriotes* looking for guns moved on to the Six Nations reserve at Caughnawaga but were captured instead. Mohawks marched sixty-seven Canadiens to Montréal, where crowds pelted them with rocks all the way to the prison.

Colborne's army easily routed Nelson's unarmed forces, sent Nelson scurrying over the border for safety, and filled Montréal's prisons again with rebels. Martial law was proclaimed as Glengarry highlanders burned a swathe six miles wide through the *patriote* countryside.

Colborne ordered quick trials and sacked judges who protested. On December 18, 1838, five men were hanged at one drop. Condemned men were allowed a final banquet with their wives in the jail corridor. One of them wrote a touching final letter, "My friends and my children shall see better days; they shall be free . . ."

In all, twelve were hanged. Eighty-six more were sentenced to die. Colborne commuted the sentences to exile. Along with a handful of condemned men captured in Upper Canada, they were shackled and led to boats that carried them to the other side of the earth, the merciless prison camps of Australia.

Among those who sailed for Van Dieman's Land was Benjamin Wait, a twenty-four-year-old sawmill operator from the Grand

River in Upper Canada, the only one of the rebels to escape from
prison camp. Wait, chained and frozen to the deck of a prison
ship bearing him down the St. Lawrence, witnessed the miserable
end of the rebellion in Lower Canada, the burning and looting of
patriotes' homes. "Every building that might have afforded the
slightest shelter to man or beast was burned to the ground," Wait
wrote later. "There stood a mother and five children, vainly weeping over the ruins of their home." Colborne thereafter was known
as "Old Firebrand."

Nova Scotia and New Brunswick remained aloof from the rebellion, their contact and interest in the interior colonies slight.
Joseph Howe and J. B. Uniacke, both descended from American
Tories, succeeded in a course of gradualism that in 1837 gave
Reformers a majority in the Assembly. New Brunswick, anxious
to curry Britain's favor because of the timber tariff preference,
took pains not to upset Whigs already too much given, from a
colonial point of view, to talk of free trade.

New Brunswick had grievances over the liberties the British
lieutenant-governor, Howard Douglas, took with timber. Douglas
was skimming off a handsome levy, putting himself and his co-
horts out of reach of the Assembly's authority over revenue. The
timber agent charged with responsibility to keep the funds flowing
was Thomas Baillie, who referred to the colonies' rivers as "my
rivers." Baillie, a rude, imperious man, his appointment secured
by his father's influence in Britain politics, in 1831 was prominent
among Londoners who invested in the New Brunswick and Nova
Scotia Land Company, which made a killing on 350,000 acres in
the colony.

Charles Simmons, Speaker of the New Brunswick Assembly,
furiously brought the colony's complaints to Britain when Baillie
had him arrested for trespassing. To add to his indignation, the
lieutenant-governor announced he would be starting a bank to
rival the Bank of New Brunswick, which Simmons headed.
Tempers frayed when Britain decided the dispute by allowing the
Assembly to collect timber taxes but charged an inflated £14,000
a year for the civil service.

Robert Gowan, editor of the *Courier,* groaned that New Brunswick would be better off asking for equality with slaves in the
West Indies. In 1834 Britain inflamed the sensitive situation in

New Brunswick by appointing a judge, something colonials thought should be done locally.

Pressed by outraged colonials, Britain in 1836 gave New Brunswick what it wanted. A delegation of Lemuel Allan Wilmot, twenty-seven, a lawyer and compelling orator, and William Crane, a wealthy Sackville merchant, convinced the Colonial Secretary, Lord Glenelg, that Baillie should be demoted, the governor's Council widened to include businessmen, and the Assembly given control of previously untouchable Crown timber. Four years of looting the public coffer and giving themselves handsome stands of timber followed, until the assemblymen put the once-affluent colony in debt. While that was going on, rebellion was the farthest thought from their minds.

— 12 —

Durham's Report

The *Inconstant* carried Lord Durham, annoyed and ill, back to England in November 1838 as he and his secretary, Charles Buller, prepared his *Report on the Affairs of British North America*. Durham had spent no time in the Atlantic colonies and visited Upper Canada only briefly (when he visited Niagara Falls and scandalized Toronto Tories by throwing a lavish party to which he invited Americans). Still, he had formed firm judgments in the manner of those who don't stay long enough to be confused by complexities. In the part of his report that dealt with constitutional change—the guts of the conflict in the two Canadas—he had been influenced by exposure to Robert Baldwin of Toronto.

The document he wrote condemned the avarice and poor management of ruling cliques who controlled land grants. Of 17 million acres surveyed in the colony, only one million of poor quality remained. In Lower Canada, only 1.5 million acres of land fit for farming were still vacant. New Brunswick's assemblymen controlled what was left of that colony's land "and keep it in a state of wilderness."

In contrast, the United States had "activity and bustle . . . bookstores . . . newspapers . . . court houses and municipal halls of stone and marble, so new and fresh." British subjects lived "in waste and desolation . . . poor and apparently unenterprising, without towns and markets, almost without roads, living in mean houses."

Durham blamed, in part, the narrow power base in each colony that controlled land, public office, and banks. His solution was rule by elected government, obliging British governors to choose their councils from the majority group in the Assembly: in short, responsible government. The recommendation was considered so radical that the government tried to bury it. Lord Melbourne, Whig leader in the House of Commons, disliking Durham intensely, rejected the document. "The opinion of this country and this government is entirely opposed to independent responsible government," he declared.

The colonies had mixed feelings. Timber kings, a conservative group wary of change, objected. So did Thomas Chandler Haliburton, the Nova Scotian wag known as "Sam Slick," who wrote, "Responsible government is responsible nonsense." Reform-minded workers and settlers rejoiced. In Upper Canada there were Durham Clubs and a Durham Flag. Durham, weak and dying, was hurt by the criticism of his own party. He expressed the hope that "the Canadas will one day do justice to my memory."

His memory is still an anathema to French-speaking Canadiens. In Durham's view, the nationalism of the *patriotes* was a "vain hope." He recommended a merger of Upper and Lower Canada to assimilate the French. "If the population of Upper Canada is rightly estimated at 400,000, the English inhabitants of Lower Canada at 150,000 and the French at 450,000, the union of the two provinces would not only give a clear English majority but one which would be increased every year by the influence of English emigration," Durham wrote. "I expected to find a contest between a government and a people," Durham noted in a sentence which became famous. "I found two nations warring in the bosom of a single state; I found a struggle, not of principles, but of races." The colony's original settlers, he said, "are a people with no history, and no literature."

His report recommended new names; Lower Canada would become Canada East; and Upper Canada, Canada West. They would share equally in one elected Assembly to meet in a place convenient to both. The treasuries were pooled, an injustice to Lower Canada whose Assembly had only a small deficit, while canal-building Upper Canada was deep in debt.

Despite Melbourne's disapproval, Durham's report had support among Whigs and London bankers who had guaranteed canal expenditures in the Canadas. Francis Baring, a member of the finan-

cial firm, was in Melbourne's cabinet. Britain was in a buoyant
mood with young Victoria on the throne. Palmerston, a Tory in
Melbourne's cabinet, prophesied, "I incline to think that she will
turn out to be a remarkable person . . ." The Whig coalition was
tottering as Lord John Russell, colonial secretary, introduced the
Union Act in the House of Commons, incorporating Durham's
blueprint for colonial union but not his radical ideas about
democracy. It passed on July 23, 1840, five days before Durham
died.

Lord Sydenham, Charles Poulett Thomson, destined to be known
by the French as *poulet,* or chicken, was selected as the first
governor-general to preside over the new administration. The
Union Bill maintained British authority over elected assemblies,
but Sydenham was given a budget adequate to create a well-paid
civil service to mollify colonials.

Sydenham picked Robert Baldwin as the united colony's first
solicitor general. Since the language of government was English,
he saw no need to elevate Canadiens. As he explained to Russell,
"There is really not a French Canadian to whom it is possible to
give office." But he recognized he must have a French-speaking
solicitor general to share the task with Baldwin. Making the best
of it, he offered the post to a young lawyer and moderate *patriote* newly released from a British jail. Louis-Hippolyte La
Fontaine turned him down. The representation of Canadiens in
the Assembly was seen as insulting: Canada West, with a much
smaller population, had as many seats, forty-two, as Canada East.

La Fontaine was despondent that Canadiens would be
swamped, since Canada East's part of the legislature would include English Montrealers, who would vote with Canada West.

In the disheartening days that followed the announcement of
the anti-French intent of the Union Bill, La Fontaine was in correspondence with an Upper Canada Reformer, Francis Hincks, a
banker and editor of *The Examiner* in Toronto. Hincks urged the
Canadien to have faith in Robert Baldwin despite Baldwin's acceptance of Sydenham's cabinet post. "Mr. Baldwin is incor-
ruptible," he assured La Fontaine.

The first election under the new constitution was called for the
spring of 1841. La Fontaine, a wealthy man with business con-

nections among English-speaking Montrealers, was open to the hope that a coalition of French *patriotes* and English Reformers might be possible; Canadiens might not be lost after all.

Sydenham blatantly tried to keep French candidates from being elected. He placed polling stations in the heart of English neighborhoods and hired unemployed canal diggers to harass French voters. La Fontaine, concerned for the safety of his supporters, withdrew in his riding of Terrebonne. Baldwin, a great favorite in Toronto, was elected in two ridings.

When the first union Assembly met in June in a Kingston hospital converted for the purpose, Robert Baldwin was the first speaker. He asked Sydenham to dismiss Tories from his cabinet so that the French could be represented. When Sydenham flatly refused, Baldwin resigned as solicitor general and introduced a motion that the governor's council reflect the elected Assembly— ergo, responsible government. When French and English reformers voted together, the motion passed.

Baldwin then asked voters in York riding, one of the two he represented in the Assembly, to replace him as their representative with La Fontaine. In a gesture remarkable in an era when, as Sydenham reported to his Colonial Office, "the French hate the English and would cut all their throats if they could, and the English hate the French and only desire to ride roughshod over them," York voters agreed to be represented by the Canadien *patriote* Louis-Hippolyte La Fontaine.

Sydenham missed the historic moment when La Fontaine took his seat as the member from York. The governor fell off his horse two weeks earlier, suffered lockjaw, and died.

Sydenham's stormy tenure had been long enough to encompass another near-war with the United States, this one over Maine. New Brunswick's governor, replacing the controversial Howard, was Sir John Harvey, a hearty man who loved the good life of costume balls and champagne. Harvey arrived in 1837 and entered enthusiastically in the Assembly's plan to build a railway to haul timber out of the Madawaska. When surveyors began marking the route, Maine reacted in outrage. Washington was asked to reopen negotiations with Britain immediately to establish Maine's claim. In preparation, Maine sent a census taker to count Americans logging in the Madawaska. Harvey had the man arrested. The alarmed governor of Nova Scotia warned the Colonial Office that Harvey was on a collision course with Maine as Harvey sent fifty British timber cruisers up the Aroostook River.

Harvey then reconsidered. He was persuaded by a former colleague in the British colonial service who happened to own the largest sawmill in the disputed territory, and who happened to sell most of his lumber to Maine and Massachusetts. Meanwhile, Governor Fairfield of Maine ordered out the militia. Harvey in return called up the New Brunswick volunteers.

Pubs in the villages along the border were gathering places for idle men awaiting developments. In a tavern in Houlton, an American called for a toast to Maine and a brawl broke out. Someone's arm was broken in the general pummeling. He was the only casualty, as it turned out, of what was called the Aroostook War.

President Martin Van Buren sent Winfield Scott to New Brunswick to handle the dispute: "Peace with honor," he asked. Scott and Harvey got along famously, and agreed that the British should stay out of the Madawaska hinge until the big powers reached a decision. Maine ignored the agreement. American loggers were armed and an American land agent put a cannon on his front lawn. New Brunswickers explained to Harvey that loss of the Témiscouata portage would cripple communications and logging.

Harvey put up a barracks near the portage and sent a note to Governor Fairfield expressing his hope that he wouldn't be misunderstood. When Lord Sydenham heard of the exchange, he exploded and sent two companies of infantry to occupy the Madawaska for Britain. Harvey tried to stop them. When he failed, he sent Maine an apology for their presence, and soon after was reprimanded by a posting to Newfoundland.

Daniel Webster, United States Secretary of State in 1841, learned that an old map used by Benjamin Franklin showed that the Madawaska hinge was first French and then British. Hoping the map would not fall into British hands, he ordered the Maine governor to stay calm. An international commission met to decide the issue. It consisted of Alexander Baring, with the new title of

Lord Ashburton, a committed friend of American expansion, Daniel Webster, who acted as an agent for the Barings in America, and others who supported Maine's position.

Not surprisingly, then, the Webster-Ashburton agreement ("The most foolish treaty ever made," Palmerston called it) favored the United States. Acadien villages on the south shore of the St. John River, the shore on which the route of the New Brunswick-St. Lawrence railway depended, were declared to be in the United States. Though British settlers were homesteading in the fertile Aroostook valley, it went to Maine. Ashburton, who learned of Franklin's map after the partition, expressed relief that it hadn't turned up to spoil the deal for the United States.

Ashburton and Webster also agreed to give the United States 6,500 square miles of the Mesabi and Vermillion iron ore deposits in Minnesota, which Ashburton dismissed as "wild country . . . of little importance to either party." Webster, however, was aware it had "considerable value as a mineral region." Ashburton and Webster threw into the deal an American fort accidentally built on the Canadian side of the line north of Lake Champlain; they moved the border to accommodate it.

In Britain a new Tory Prime Minister, Robert Peel, a rigid opponent of reform, took power. Sydenham's successor in the Canadas, Charles Bagot, was instructed to hold down colonial parliaments. Bagot reached the Canadas, as winter visitors were obliged to do, by crossing through the United States and realized at once that Canadiens had the balance of power in the Assembly.

"The French Canadians, if rightly managed," he advised the Colonial Office, "are the natural instrument by which the government could keep in check the democratic and American tendencies of Upper Canada."

Bagot's notion of good management of Canadiens was to appoint one to supervise Catholic schools, rather than the English-speaking Protestant Britain had hoped for, and to appoint Canadiens as judges and other prominent positions in government. Bagot asked Baldwin and La Fontaine to be jointly attorneys-general, and both agreed. A seamless coalition was formed. Baldwin's Reform party needed Canadien support to achieve its aims to overthrow the Tories, and La Fontaine's Canadiens needed Reformers to avoid assimilation. By putting Reformers and Canadiens in his cabinet, Bagot yielded to the principle of two-level responsible government that both wanted.

The final touch was achieved when the new Assembly of 1842 opened. La Fontaine broke into a passionate speech in French. He was asked to speak the official language, English. He replied, "I distrust my ability to speak English and [I] protest against the cruel injustice of the Union Act in trying to proscribe the mother tongue of half the population of Canada." He continued, in French.

Pressured, La Fontaine worked to achieve amnesty for the rebels of 1837 and 1838. Papineau was in France still scheming to involve the United States in an invasion of Canada. William Lyon Mackenzie, the former admirer of Andrew Jackson's egalitarian principles, was working for Horace Greeley's New York *Tribune* in the Albany press gallery, from which vantage point he found American pork-barrel politics to be no improvement on the Family Compact.

Thousands of young Canadiens, homeless and embittered by the severity of "Old Firebrand's" reprisals against the rebels, left the colony for jobs in Massachusetts factory towns, despite the enmity they created there by working for debased wages.

Governor-General Bagot of the Canadas was dying as another election was held. This time Robert Baldwin was defeated in his riding of Hastings, his supporters beaten by Tories who kept them from the polls. Twenty-five Canadiens elected to the Assembly, one of them a Papineau, immediately offered to resign to create a vacancy for him. The riding of Rimouski was chosen. Homes were hung with bunting and every vote cast was for Baldwin.

Though desperately ill, Bagot continued his efforts to win over Canadiens. He paid out of his own pocket to supply 2,500 Irish Catholic laborers on the Beauharnois canal with a priest, and established the first Catholic bishop in Toronto, Michael Power. At a gala in Montréal, he even persuaded Peter McGill to sit on the same platform as Wolfred Nelson, newly returned from exile and pardoned. When Bagot died in office in May 1843 he was deeply mourned by Canadiens.

His successor, Charles Metcalfe, a veteran of Imperial service in India, loathed the appointment. "I have never undertaken anything with so much repugnancy nor with as little hope of doing well," he confided. He arrived by winter, which obliged him to land in the United States and proceed to his posting by horse-drawn sleigh. He at once set about teaching colonial reformers a lesson. He made a personal appeal to voters in the Canadas to elect Tories who would show decent respect for the Union Jack and Queen Victoria. His intervention had such devastating impact that Canada West's Reformers lost the election and Canadiens found themselves in a legislature dominated by English Tories.

The seat of the Union government was moved to Montréal to be fairer to French-speaking assemblymen. La Fontaine toyed with the cynical idea of a coalition with Tories so that Metcalfe would put Canadiens in his cabinet, but decided against it. Instead, he threatened to resign. Metcalfe offered an inducement to stay amnesty for *patriotes* in exile in Australia, which La Fontaine accepted.

After six years in chains, only thirty-nine were alive to be embraced by weeping relatives who had not expected to see them again. The last man repatriated was Louis-Joseph Papineau from France. His enthusiasm for British government was restored by gains La Fontaine had made in obtaining government appointments for Canadiens.

Metcalfe went home to England in 1845 to die, his face ravaged by cancer. The time was not opportune for such a sick man to be in charge of the British colonies: It appeared the United States was planning another invasion.

The controversy this time was the Oregon territory which Lord Ashburton dismissed in 1842 as "a question worthless in itself." By an understanding reached in the backrooms of the Webster-Ashburton talks about New Brunswick, Edward Ellice and others agreed that the United States would not claim the Hudson's Bay Company's territory in the Columbia valley if Britain would give up Madawaska. The Democratic candidate for the U.S. presidency in 1844, James Knox Polk, ignored the pact. His winning slogan was "Fifty-four forty or fight!" Fifty-four forty was the latitude of the Russian panhandle dipping down the coast from Alaska. The area Polk wanted included all the Hudson's Bay Company trading posts on the Pacific coast.

When the British foreign secretary consulted Ellice, the financier said the HBC could do without Oregon as far north as the

49th parallel. George Simpson fumed. The Company's Fort Vancouver stood on the 45th parallel and he saw no reason to give it up, though Americans pouring over the Oregon Trail were homesteading all around the HBC post.

Simpson had his own plans for "manifest destiny," as Americans called their continental expansion that already had absorbed California, Arizona, Nevada, Utah, parts of Colorado, New Mexico, and Texas. He recommended to the British foreign office that California be annexed to the British colonies. When he was rebuffed he tried to acquire the Sandwich Islands, heart of the Pacific whaling industry, where an HBC trading post was flourishing among American missionaries dedicated to persuading native women to cover their breasts.

Simpson planned to gain control of the islands to sell them to Russia for a naval base. Hawaii's royal family innocently asked Simpson to help the islands remain independent. Simpson discussed the proposal with the Tsar of Russia, his business partner in 1843, and continued on to London to urge Britain to support Hawaiian independence, which it did.

A cousin, Alexander Simpson, unaware that the Hudson's Bay Company's Little Emperor was in France and Belgium signing up more support for Hawaiian rights, took command of a battleship and annexed the Sandwich Islands in the name of the Queen of England. His directness confused everyone, and in the end the United States got Hawaii.

A disappointed Simpson refused to yield to the United States' claims on the Pacific coast. He drafted a military strategy for Britain which included sending an army to the Red River settlement. The redcoats would help him control American competition. The St. Paul Chamber of Commerce had delivered a cargo ship in pieces to the Red River, assembled it there, and was using it to smuggle furs across the border.

The British colonies in America prepared for war. The Assembly of the Canadas approved a militia bill, upon which Étienne-Paschal Taché, one of the last of the *patriotes* of 1837 to surrender, loyally cried, "The last cannon which is shot on this continent in defense of Great Britain will be fired by the hand of a French Canadien!"

Hostilities were averted by the Oregon Treaty of 1846 which

ceded to the United States the Oregon territory to the 49th parallel as Edward Ellice had suggested. A southern dip in the border around Vancouver Island avoided bisecting it. The HBC was consoled with permission to continue trading north of the Columbia.

Wording of the terms of financial compensation to the HBC was vague. Simpson, accustomed to one-man international diplomacy, went to Washington himself to ask Polk to pay him £100,000. After examination of the situation, Simpson concluded that Polk didn't control Congress. He turned instead to a sharp young man, George Nicholas Sanders.

Sanders met secretly with Congressmen, offering bribes for a bill to buy Oregon. Though HBC directors in London were uneasy at the strategy, they could not avoid becoming tangled in intrigues. Congressmen pushed up their price for the bill and asked Britain for more land in the Pacific West.

The Tories dug in their heels. In 1849, when it became obvious that Sanders was ineffective, negotiations were broken off. The United States eventually paid $450,000 in gold, in 1870, for Oregon.

— 13 —

The Railway Ties
that Bind

In the 1830s Britain's Whig Reformers abolished slavery, extended the franchise so that one man in every six could vote, made poor laws more humane, and broadened access to education. Their reforms did not extend to vile conditions in factories or control of exorbitantly high food costs.

The amiable Whig Lord Melbourne put down unrest by sending four hundred labor organizers to penal camps in Australia. A sullen mood of revolt continued. In 1841 unhappy voters turned to the Tories and elected a Conservative majority with Robert Peel as prime minister. Peel, with a middle-class mercantile background, was a free trader. By eliminating tariffs, imported food would be cheaper and industrial products could move easily between the United States and Britain.

The repeal of the Corn Laws in 1846 crushed colonial farmers, dependent on Imperial preferential tariffs. The legislation was hastened by a massive crop failure in Britain. In England and Scotland consequences were severe; bread was beyond the purse of working people. Ireland, with the most dense population of any country in Europe, suffered the loss of its potato crop on which people depended. Potatoes were not only a staple of diet but in many homes were the only food the family had. The potato famine caused a million deaths in poverty-stricken Ireland.

Whole villages emigrated to America to escape. They were packed into reeking typhus-infested ships where 16 percent died during the crossing. Montréal alone counted six thousand orphaned children. The Emigrant Society reported: "From Grosse Island to Sarnia, along the borders of our great river, on the shores of lakes Ontario and Erie, wherever the tide of immigration has extended, are to be found one unbroken chain of graves."

The United States tightened immigration laws, but colonies in America could not exclude British subjects. By the fall of 1847, 32,000 had landed at Québec and 13,000 died there of typhus. Typhus spread as far as the remote colony on the Red River. Half of those who caught the disease died of it, delirious, and with black, swollen tongues that choked them.

Pitiful survivors found land in Canada West. Because they were Catholic, they aroused prejudiced neighbors. Orange societies flared into action; Irishmen fought back with fists and clubs.

Peel's government collapsed in the wake of a backlash against the repeal of the Corn Laws. British Tories were split, bringing Benjamin Disraeli and other Tory dissenters into power. The consequences in Canada had been devastating. Since trade with Britain was at an end, shipyards closed in New Brunswick, timber harvesting stopped, and merchants closed their doors. Five thousand people left the colony for the United States.

Chatham, New Brunswick, depended on its leading citizen, Joseph Cunard, wealthiest man in the colony, owner of mills, shipyards, brickworks, and the first steamship on the Miramichi River, the *Velocity*. In 1847 even Cunard was a bankrupt. An ugly crowd surrounded his ornate mansion where peacocks wandered in the garden. Cunard, a huge man, stuck two pistols in his boot tops, faced the mob, and roared, "Now show me the man who will shoot a Cunard!"

In outrage at the repeal of the Corn Laws, John Redpath, a Montrealer rich from canal building and insurance companies, met with Alexander Tilloch Galt, commissioner of the British American Land Company in the eastern townships, and John Joseph Caldwell Abbott, a young lawyer. With others of like mind, they drew up a manifesto calling for "friendly and peaceful" separation from Britain. Montréal's shops and factories were folding; some 10,000 people left the city for America in the course of the next two years.

"Private property is unsalable in Canada," reported the new governor, James Bruce, eighth Earl of Elgin, "and not a shilling can be raised on the credit of the province."

Canadien *annexationistes* turned to Louis-Joseph Papineau to lead them to union with the United States. The arch-conservative ultramontane bishop of Montréal, Ignace Bourget, was horrified. The movement appeared to him to be led by atheists bent on destroying the church. He launched an appeal to piety that saw a religious revival among Canadiens. Old orders, such as the Jesuits, were restored and zealous new ones created. Shrewdly, Bourget cultivated the friendship of political leaders, particularly La Fontaine.

Lord Elgin, an urbane thirty-six-year-old married to the wealthy daughter of "Radical Jack" Durham, landed in Boston in February 1847, crossed New England, and reached Montréal in time to prepare for the opening of Parliament. He received La Fontaine and complained that the Canadien insisted on speaking French. The point was not lost on the governor; the French language, he realized, was a significant part of *la survivance* and Canadien loyalty to the Crown.

Governors in the other British colonies were also trying to mend the ravages of the repeal of the Corn Laws by showing consideration to the locals. John Harvey, no longer banished to Newfoundland, was in Nova Scotia, dealing with a strident majority of Reformers in the Assembly led by Joseph Howe and J. B. Uniacke. Edmund Walker Head in New Brunswick had an easier time; despite economic hardships, the staunchly Tory Assembly there rejected "the Canadian system," as it called responsible government.

Elgin sought "a policy of neutrality" between warring Tories and Reformers in the Canadas. La Fontaine and Baldwin were losing their following to orators of more radical bent. In Canada East, La Fontaine and his conservative adherents were called *vendus,* sell-outs, and were accused of being interested only in patronage for themselves and those who bribed them. Papineau, a patriarch of sixty, emerged as the leader of radicals who called themselves *les rouges* and sought an independent French nation. The movement's paper, *L'Avenir,* stated, "We only wish one thing, the preservation of our institutions, our language, our laws and our customs."

Elgin feared they would succeed. He warned his wife's uncle, Lord Grey, that Canada might annex itself to the United States. Grey replied easily, "To us, except for the loss of prestige, no slight one, I admit, the loss of Canada would be the loss of little but a source of heavy expense and great anxiety."

In the United States, an annexation movement pressed by northerners and the New York *Herald* was opposed by southern states, who were concerned that addition of antislavery provinces would strengthen northern abolitionists. British colonies were resented for being terminals of an underground railway through which $30 million worth of slaves escaped their owners.

Elgin convened the Canadian Assembly on January 18, 1849, read the opening address in English, paused, and read it in French, a great victory for Canadiens. He placed Baldwin and La Fontaine, whose followers had achieved a majority, in his cabinet. Thus, the Canadas achieved responsible, bilingual government.

A major item of business was a contentious bill to repay Canadiens whose property was destroyed in the rebellion. Upper Canada, now Canada West, had suffered little damage to property; claims were settled speedily. However, Lower Canada, now Canada East, had a staggering reparations bill of £90,000 to cover the cost of entire communities that were leveled.

"No pay to rebels!" English Tories cried. Galleries were packed day after day as the debate raged. Sir Allan MacNab, son of an officer who fought with the British in the Americn Revolution, shouted above the din that Wolfred Nelson had been a "rank rebel" in 1837. Nelson, one of those whose property had burned, replied coldly, "Not to my God."

Baldwin kept control of Canada West Reformers who wanted to bolt and vote with the Tories. In the end the bill was passed by 47 to 18. MacNab and other Tories expected Elgin would veto the bill. Elgin chose to uphold democracy, and on April 25, 1849, signed the Rebellion Losses Bill.

When he left the Assembly a mob pelted his carriage with garbage and stones. The next day Tories smashed windows in the House of Assembly and chopped the Speaker's Throne with axes, setting fires that sent politicians running. One assemblyman, twenty-two-year-old Sandford Fleming, later the father of standard time, slid down a pillar of the second-story balcony carrying a portrait of Queen Victoria rescued from the flames.

La Fontaine's palatial new home was wrecked and his stables burned. A mob hanged an effigy of Elgin and set it on fire. Tories and Orangemen turned out on May 30 when Elgin reconvened parliament and stoned his carriage. One rock weighing two pounds narrowly missed him as his coachmen whipped the horses and escaped. That summer parliament sat with armed soldiers guarding the doors. La Fontaine's home was attacked again and an assailant killed.

On July 4, anti-Elgin merchants hung the Stars and Stripes from shop windows. The British-American League and the Annexation Association, both obsessed with taking the Canadas out of the British Empire, enjoyed a boom in memberships.

Elgin blamed hard times for most of the protest. Reluctantly, he came to the view that the Canadas must find another trading partner, the United States, to replace Britain. He urged Lord Grey to negotiate with Washington for lower tariffs on imports from the Canadas. "Canada cannot be saved unless you force the selfish scheming Yankees to concede reciprocity," he warned.

Baldwin's Reformers, already resentful that he had compelled them to support the Rebellion Losses Bill, were divided further on the free trade issue. A splinter group, led by George Brown, crusty editor of the Toronto *Globe,* opposed Baldwin's alliance with Catholic Canadiens. Brown's followers called themselves pure reformers, or "Clear Grits." Francis Hincks, whose home, like Brown's, was attacked by inflamed Orangemen, emerged as leader of what was left of the Reform party in the legislature.

Hincks was there in part to further his ambitions as a railway tycoon. The expensive canal system that had almost beggared Canada West was obsolete; a mania for railways was sweeping America. Tory leader Sir Allan MacNab was in the forefront in Canada, president, chairman, or director of at least six railway companies. In an unguarded moment after consuming "one of two bottles of good port," he confessed, "all my politics are railroads."

In the British colonies, the two pursuits often were indivisible. Because no investment money could be obtained in Britain or the United States, and few local banks would take such risk, railway entrepreneurs had to rely on government money and therefore on favorably disposed politicians. In 1849 the Canadas led the way with legislation allowing municipalities to invest in railways, with the immediate result that ambitious men ran for public office.

The prosperity in Britain that followed the move to free trade was felt as well in America, and eventually the colonies. The 1850s were a period of confidence and fortune building. Samuel Cunard of Halifax, a tea importer with extensive holdings in Miramichi's timber and Prince Edward Island real estate, ran transatlantic steamships on schedule to carry mail and passengers. In 1854 he endeared himself to Britain by transporting munitions and men to fight the Crimean War against Russia. Peter McGill's Bank of Montreal joined the euphoria and plunged into railways.

Francis Hincks was prime minister of the Canadas in 1851 in a coalition government with Augustin Morin, who subbed for ailing La Fontaine. Hincks tuned the legislative machinery to put government money into private enterprise. Hugh Allan, for one, owner of steamships on the St. Lawrence, received a handsome government contract. A young lawyer from Kingston, John A. Macdonald, sat in the Assembly and watched the deals. They were "steeped to the very lips in infamy," he groaned, "tainted in corruption." Whenever a poorly planned railway collapsed, the government rushed in with a "loan."

A prize was the St. Lawrence and Atlantic Railway from Portland, Maine, to Montréal, built almost entirely on U. S. soil. It was the Canadas' only connection in winter with the Atlantic coast. Indigent Irish immigrants worked cheaply as the colonies went railway-mad. Needing freight to pay for the bustling new track, the colonies desperately wanted trade with America.

Lord Elgin went to Washington, D.C., to negotiate a deal for free trade with balky southern Senators, plying them with good cigars and charm. The Atlantic colonies, crippled by the loss of timber and grain exports to Britain, were willing to give up fishing rights if Americans would establish free trade. Elgin argued in Washington that reciprocity with Canada would not lead to annexation as southerners feared. Instead the colonies would be able to afford to remain British and keep their abolitionist views to themselves.

In 1854 the United States agreed to reciprocity. The decision came during an upswing in the economy. Gold had been discovered in California, New England's factories were expanding, immigration was pushing people west, and railway tracks were going down everywhere.

That year Elgin was replaced by Sir Edmund Walker Head as

governor-general of the Canadas. Head had behaved well as lieutenant-governor in New Brunswick while that colony went through
a frustrating time of trying in vain to get Britain to help build a
railway to Nova Scotia. In his new position, Head presided over
two stormy years as splintered Tories and Reformers tried an
assortment of combinations with Canadiens, also split between
les bleus, or conservatives, and *les rouges,* Papineau's radicals.

Francis Hincks was eclipsed following accusations of graft. Sir
Allan MacNab, the Tory who led the fight against the Rebellion
Losses Bill, happened to be prime minister on the day Canadiens
whipped through an almost-empty legislature a bill establishing
Catholic schools in Canada West. The fury among Orangemen
that greeted the bill helped George Brown's anti-Catholic Grits,
who mounted virulent campaigns against "papists." MacNab-
Morin succeeded anyway in ending the seigneurial system in Canada East, a century after it disappeared in France. MacNab then
departed, accused of graft, extortion, misrepresentation, and thefts
over his activities in the Great Western Railway.

George Brown's collection of Orangemen, farmers, Clear Grits,
Brownites, and Reformers fixed their goals: free trade, fiscal
reform, abolition of Catholic schools, and annexation of the Red
River valley. The Hudson's Bay Company's monopoly was coming up for renewal in 1859. In previous years the Company had
no difficulty demonstrating its value as a benign protector of
the tribes. This time, the HBC faced a parliamentary investigation.

The Red River valley alone was worth the fight. Fort Garry had
prospered despite HBC suppression that drove young people south
to jobs in St. Paul. In 1836 the colony had wrested permission to
elect its own council, though the franchise was limited to English-
speaking whites. Trade with what was about to become the
state of Minnesota was brisk and profitable. Caravans of Red
River wagons left a dust cloud that stretched the whole distance
in summer.

The setting for the parliamentary hearings in London was an
oak-paneled room with a view of the Thames. There Edward
Ellice, George Simpson, and other HBC officials heard accusations that the Company debauched, cheated, and caused the death
of natives. Records proved that the HBC traded huge quantities of

whiskey each year. Peguis, an old chief of the Saulteaux, described seeing "old men who have starved to death within sight of the Company's principle forts." A particularly ruthless factor in Labrador, Donald A. Smith, was charged with genocide of Naskapis, whole camps of whom had died of starvation "without one survivor to tell the tale of their sufferings."

The investigators learned that the act of withholding ammunition from natives was a death warrant since the tribes needed meat to survive. Allegedly because of Smith's sharp practices—he "always showed a balance on the right side of the ledger," his employers said—Naskapis were reduced to cannibalism and drinking the blood of their children. The accused man, wealthy from his share of impressive profits from the Labrador operation, in 1856 was made chief executive officer of the HBC and moved to headquarters in Montréal.

Maps of the HBC's claim were old and contradictory. When the Company refused to provide better maps, Britain sent John Palliser, an Irishman with some knowledge of the plains, to make a firsthand study. Palliser went west in 1857 with surveyors and a University of Toronto geologist, Henry Youle Hind, and spent two years watching buffalo hunts, the goose dance of the Crees, hailstones falling from a summer sky, and crimson flares of an autumn aurora borealis. They dodged Sioux looking to steal their horses and slept in the open in winter with ice on their faces.

Palliser reported the Red River valley was fertile beyond compare but hopelessly cut off from the other colonies. "Look at that prairie," John Gowler, a farmer near Fort Garry, said to him. "Ten thousand head of cattle might feed and fatten there for nothing . . . I could get thirty or forty bushels of wheat per acre year after year . . . but what would be the use? There are no markets."

Palliser believed it would be impossible to build a road or railway from the Canadas to the Red River. In between was solid rock or bottomless bogs. "The egress and ingress to the settlement from the east is obviously through the States," he reported.

The citizens of St. Paul rejoiced, confident that the Red River country eventually would be isolated and annexed to the United States, as Oregon had been. George Brown's Orangemen and Grits were despondent, confined in a colony that seemed destined to have a government controlled by French-speaking Catholics.

They turned their efforts to electoral reform. With English-speaking voters for the first time outnumbering French ones, the Grits demanded "Rep by Pop," representation by population.

In 1856 two men emerged from the tangle of shifting alliances, both moderate Tories and both creditable. One was a Scottish lawyer from Kingston, John A. Macdonald, a lanky, odd-looking man with a bumpy nose, bushy hair, a drinking problem, and considerable charm and wit. The other was George-Étienne Cartier, also a lawyer, descended from a wealthy Montréal family with business ties within the English establishment. Cartier's father, who spelled his son's first name the English way because he named him for George III, was a director in Peter McGill's Bank of Montreal. George-Étienne, lawyer to the Grand Trunk Railway, helped Hugh Allan get government subsidies for his steamships.

Though Cartier was a *patriote* in the uprising of 1837 and, briefly, a refugee in Vermont from British justice, he was no friend of annexationist *rouges*. He found Americans less liberal toward others than any in the world, he said, "except the Chinese."

The Macdonald-Cartier coalition of 1857 was a paste-up that called itself Liberal-Conservative and lived in the nervous middle ground between George Brown's raucous Grits and Papineau's flamboyant *rouges*. Its objective was to build railroads. As it turned out, it had to build a nation to do it.

— 14 —

Confederation

The new coalition was tested during an uproar over the site of a new capital of the Canadas. Following the burning of the parliament buildings in Montréal, the legislature was nomadic, sitting one term in Québec and the next in Toronto. One place provoked Orangemen and the other was repulsive to English Canadians. As well, the expense and inconvenience of moving government documents every year was becoming unbearable.

Sir Edmund Head groaned over the "choice of evils," Montréal, Québec, Kingston, or Toronto. All, he decided, were too close to the border to be safe from an American invasion. Besides, the colony needed to develop its backwoods. His recommendation to Queen Victoria was Bytown, the lumbertown on the Ottawa and Rideau rivers one hundred miles in the bush and renowned for payday binges.

Both Canadas objected. The decision stood. Architects submitted drawings of the proposed parliament buildings on a striking site, a hilltop with a commanding view of the rivers and the rolling Gatineau hills beyond. The winning design was Italianate Gothic, a cathedral-style building of rosy sandstone. When excavation began, contractors discovered the foundation would have to be cut into solid, pre-Cambrian rock.

Reciprocity brought growth to all the colonies. St. John's in Newfoundland had its first paved street, and in 1855 its first elected government. Joseph Howe in Nova Scotia was advocating maritime union of Nova Scotia, Prince Edward Island, New Brunswick, and Newfoundland, a popular idea that even Tory opponents approved. Samuel Leonard Tilley, a rising member of New Brunswick's legislature, saw the scheme as helpful to his main concern, railway building. John Henry Thomas Manners-Sutton, New Brunswick's lieutenant-governor, thought union "a very natural wish, but premature."

Nova Scotia and New Brunswick, building fine wooden ships in such quantities that they were fourth in the world in tonnage, needed a railway network to connect them in trade with the United States. In 1851 the Great Exhibition in Britain's Crystal Palace had featured American manufactured goods, McCormick's reaper, Singer's sewing machine, Colt's revolver, sensations that were drawing population south from the colonies.

While efforts to raise railway money continued, Joseph Howe's attacks on Irish Catholics grew so vicious that his leadership fell into disrepute. A Tory, Charles Tupper, son of a Connecticut Loyalist, became prime minister of Nova Scotia. Both colonies were under the spell of New England's evangelical temperance movement. Leonard Tilley of New Brunswick, with the impressive title of Most Worthy Patriarch of the Sons of Temperance, represented the dries. In 1855 he pushed through the Assembly a bill outlawing liquor. Manners-Sutton, a conspicuous wet, indignantly dissolved the legislature rather than allow prohibition. In the noisy election that followed, the dries resoundingly were defeated. They bitterly regrouped to fight again.

Politics in the Canadas were not yet influenced by the liquor issue. The bloody heads at election time usually were caused by religious differences. Anti-Catholicism was so fierce in Canada West that John A. Macdonald had difficulty holding his seat after his alliance with Cartier; most Orange votes went to George Brown's Grits. But railway building and the new iron industries took some of the heat out of bigotry; there was work for all.

The confidence of the 1850s owed much to stories of fabulous wealth in California's gold field. In 1849, 80,000 fortune hunters went west. When the boom subsided, miners moved north through the mountains, panning the clear streams for silver or gold. In 1856 they struck it rich on the Fraser River in British Columbia, north of Oregon; on the eve of the first snowfall of 1860 they found the motherlode in the Cariboo.

The strikes were on the mainland near the Hudson's Bay Company's Vancouver Island, which was granted to the Company in 1849 in compensation for Oregon. The Company was supposed to put a colony on the island, an expense that Edward Ellice, for one, considered outrageous. Important coal deposits gave the island strategic importance in the British Empire. When Samuel Cunard warned that the United States would grab it unless it was settled, Lord Grey pressured the HBC to establish a colony on Vancouver Island. To pay for it, the HBC sold coal to steamships.

George Simpson was reluctant to spend money transporting English settlers to the island, except for those necessary to maintain Fort Victoria. Gold strikes in California called attention to the neglect. The HBC factor in Fort Victoria was James Douglas, son of a Scot father and a black West Indies mother, who married a métis. A huge man with an explosive temper, in 1851 he was given an additional title, governor of the island, and placed in charge of the tiny developing community.

Douglas ruled in the autocratic style of an HBC factor. In 1856 he was annoyed by instructions to permit an elected Assembly, something foreign to his experience.

In 1857 Douglas notified the Colonial Office that American prospectors were swarming on the mainland. Britain quickly took Vancouver Island from the HBC and made it a Crown Colony. The mainland, however, still belonged to the Hudson's Bay Company, and that's where gold was found that winter.

Douglas had witnessed American settlers taking Oregon from the HBC. He reacted forcefully. Without waiting for authority, he attached the mainland to his mandate, notified Americans they would have to buy mining licenses from him, and placed a British gunboat across the Fraser River to collect.

In the summer of 1858 there were 10,000 men panning for gold between Langley and Yale on the upper Fraser. Douglas kept the upper hand in an uncertain jurisdiction. He wouldn't allow miners to set up their own laws, as they had in California. He ordered Americans to stop bothering the Indians, and established a court to punish miscreants. The judge, who arrived from England fortuitously, was Matthew Baillie Begbie, a formidable Scot who stood six-foot-five.

Begbie controlled the mountain camps while Douglas supervised all traffic in and out of the raw tent city that grew up around his headquarters, Fort Victoria. As 25,000 American miners poured into the Fraser valley, Douglas was in dread that the U.S.

would annex the territory. He made a ruling that Americans couldn't own land. Royal Engineers built mule roads between mining camps, since the rivers were too dangerous to travel. After the Cariboo strike, Douglas blasted a road four hundred miles long out of the shoulders of mountains and paved it with logs, his fabled Cariboo Trail. One imaginative freighter bought twenty-eight camels from a zoo to pack supplies, but the smell of them frightened the mules.

Royal Navy frigates and corvettes stood off the mouth of the Fraser to impress the Americans, but for the most part Douglas and Begbie kept control by the power of their conviction that they were in charge. An effort to hire a low-cost militia made up of escaped slaves, Sir James Douglas' Coloured Regiment, was a mistake. Americans refused to be arrested by a black man. Crime was confined to racial violence. Whites demoralized the natives, fought with blacks, and were vicious to Chinese, who came by the hundreds, pigtails down their backs, to work for half-pay at the dangerous and dirty jobs no one else would do.

Another British judge, Peter O'Reilly, joined Begbie and displayed the same flinty disposition. O'Reilly once assured American miners at Wild Horse Creek, "Boys, I am here to keep order and to administer the law. Those who don't want law and order can git, but those who stay within the camp, remember on which side of the line the camp is. For boys, if there is shooting in Kootenay, there will be hanging in Kootenay."

The Salish tribe, the nation on whose land the gold was found, was debauched with whiskey traded for Salish women. The *British Colonist* of Victoria noted, "Never in all our lives have we gazed upon a scene of more utter wretchedness or hopeless debauchery. The mortality is estimated at one per day for the last year . . . More than half the Salish are gone . . . Slavery has increased. Female slaves are in demand."

Douglas lamented that there were few of British stock in the mix of Americans, Chinese, Mexicans, French, Italians, Germans, and escaped slaves. His mainland capital, New Westminster, was selected with an American invasion in mind. Fears of attack were realized in July 1859 when American troops garrisoned San Juan Island. Douglas had to be restrained from going to war.

By 1862, when the Cariboo gold rush was bringing 5,000

miners a summer into the colony, the first Canadians began to appear in New Westminster and Victoria, many of them merchants.
Their demands for an elected mainland government exasperated
the governor. "The term is associated with revolution and holds
out a menace," he declared. He offered an elected Assembly par-
tially appointed by himself, but Canadians and other British residents objected. Malcolm Cameron, a former member of the Canada West legislature, went to London with an indignant petition
signed by men Governor Douglas dismissed as "a petty Califor-
nian-Canadian clique . . . utterly ignorant of the wants and conditions of the country."

The Colonial Office felt otherwise. Douglas was out of favor.
On top of his intractable attitude toward democracy, there was his
acquisition for himself of valuable land on Vancouver Island, and
his unauthorized expenditure of £100,000 for the Cariboo Trail.
That year, 1864, he retired.

Meanwhile, railway building had reached a fever pitch that
threatened North America's economy. The Canadas were
festooned with bits and pieces of unconnected track, companies in
receivership, villages mortgaged for a precious spur line of track,
and trains falling off flimsy trestles. Two lines were emerging as
contending giants, the Great Western and the Grand Trunk.

The Grand Trunk was in the better position because it had
more directors in the Tory government. Its lawyer, George-
Étienne Cartier, was in the cabinet. One major stockholder, Alexander Galt, was finance minister. Another was the postmaster general who raised the Grand Trunk's mail contract from $25 to
$110 a mile. The Grand Trunk was challenging U.S. railways by
offering passengers in Portland, Maine, transportation to Chicago.
Mystified ticket holders found themselves traveling by way of
Montréal and Canada West.

By the end of the 1850s there was an economic slump. The
government of the Canadas was so divisive it couldn't act. George
Brown proposed a solution, representation by population, by
which Canada West would have a majority. Frightened and angry,
the *parti rouge* under the leadership of Antoine-Aimé Dorion
called for French-speaking people to have an autonomous government, equal but separate from English-speaking Canadians.

Brown was inclined to agree and in the party convention of 1859 the Clear Grits opted for a federated state.

The Atlantic colonies, torn by religious tensions and a struggle between wets and dries, longed for intercolonial railways that would forge "iron bands" to unite the colonies in "one great confederation," in the phrase of the stiff-backed Tory prime minister of Nova Scotia, James William Johnston. Since there were no British loans to build such a railway, track instead ran north and south to the free-trade markets of the United States.

The governor-general of the Canadas, Sir Edmund Head, considered the old goal of American Tories in 1776, union of all the British colonies in North America. The concept seemed more practical since the Hudson's Bay Company's mandate was under fire, and the United States was linking oceans with railway track. Head suggested to the Colonial Office that the union movement, aided by railways, could start in the Atlantic colonies and move west gradually.

In the Canadas, Galt, Cartier, and Macdonald saw colonial union as beneficial for the Grand Trunk railway. Cartier's concern was that Canadiens would be swamped in an English-dominated nation. He was assured the union would be a federation: Canadiens would have autonomy within it.

In 1861 the American South began to secede from the U.S. and guns of the new Confederated States of America fired on a ship carrying the Stars and Stripes. A new President, Abraham Lincoln, declared it unlawful for any state to leave the Union. Both sides prepared for war. The colonies shuddered with apprehension as border states put men into uniform and bought guns. If the Union army turned north, instead of south, it was unlikely that Britain would help; the country was still recovering from the Crimean War and the mutinies in India.

Britain declared itself a neutral in the American Civil War. With Britain's close ties to the cotton plantation owners of Virginia, the position was difficult to maintain. When a British steamer, the *Trent,* was stopped at sea by a Union battleship, which removed two Confederates, conflict was averted only by skilled face-saving on both sides. "One war at a time," Lincoln commented.

The affair of the *Trent* aroused so much alarm in the Canadas that urgent petitions went to Britain for military aid. Seven thousand Crimean veterans sailed that winter. President Lincoln refused to allow them to land in Portland, Maine, to catch a train to Montréal, so they were obliged to walk inland through New Brunswick. Two perished of the cold and exposure.

Alexander Galt went to Washington to receive Lincoln's assurances that the Union army wouldn't invade Canada. He wasn't convinced. In the Canadas, the Assembly was in an uproar over what to do. Members were saying that colonial union was necessary to stand against the States. Cartier was willing, provided that Canadiens had autonomy. His conditions were "that the two provinces co-exist with *equal powers* and that neither should dominate over the other in parliament."

The colonies could not unite unless Britain permitted it. Delegations from the Canadas found in the Colonial Office waiting rooms a delegation from the maritime colonies. The idea of a larger union occurred. A prominent and influential Englishman, Edward William Watkin, had the same notion. Watkin, a Manchester cotton-mill tycoon who visited the colonies in 1860 as one of the party traveling with Queen Victoria's eighteen-year-old son, the Duke of Kent, saw the venture as an opportunity to build a railway.

The Barings' financial house, which had loaned the Grand Trunk some two million pounds and New Brunswick another £800,000, was so deeply committed to colonial railways that union seemed highly desirable. Watkin put his resources to work on the project. New Brunswick's Leonard Tilley was eager to help. He and Watkin vowed to persevere until they could see "the waters of the Pacific from the windows of a British railway carriage."

The Barings made Watkin president of the Grand Trunk, whose finances were still shaky from the strain of absorbing its major rival in the Canadas, the Great Western. The owners planned a railway in the west to compete with American lines. The snag was the Hudson's Bay Company, which still controlled the prairies. The *Globe*'s George Brown had mounted an editorial campaign to annex the HBC's land to Canada West. The terms of the agreement drawn up by Edward Ellice presented a problem:

Canada couldn't have the west until it could afford to defend it from the United States. And the Canadas couldn't even defend themselves.

In one of the most dramatic fateful moments in Canadian history, George Brown decided that he would support the Tories in order to get colonial union. He approached John A. Macdonald, a man he detested, and offered to work with him "to obtain settlement of the sectional question."

The federation movement, patched together for diverse reasons —to make railway fortunes, to be rid of French interference, to obtain French autonomy, to acquire the west—was forged also by events in the United States. The New York *Herald,* ever strident in its view that America should annex the colonies, began advocating force. At the same time, Maine put guns on an island between Eastport and Campobello. In New Brunswick, British sergeants arrived to drill volunteers in the militia.

A major dispute with the Union concerned the free use Confederates made of the Canadas as a refuge and base for spying. There were so many Confederate soldiers in Montréal that the St. Lawrence Hotel hired a bartender who could mix mint juleps. When a Union ship, the *Chesapeake,* was captured at sea by the Confederates, she eluded pursuit by sailing into a Nova Scotia port. A judge set the crew free, making the Union furious.

The Union also was enraged at Britain, which was building ships for the Confederates. The *Alabama,* which had an eleven-month career sinking Union shipping, cost the north dearly. Charles Sumner, an influential U. S. Senator, estimated that the *Alabama* cost the Union $2 billion. If Britain didn't pay, he suggested that the United States should have Canada.

The colonies were ill-prepared. The Canadas, torn by racial dissent, had only a few militia and a handful of British soldiers. The Atlantic colonies had the protection of the Royal Navy, but in the west, the United States had cavalry in the field to control the Santees and Sioux, while the HBC had only factors armed with rifles.

In the spring of 1864 the Canadas had word that the Atlantic colonies were meeting to establish a union. The uneasy coalition of Macdonald, Cartier, and Brown was dismayed and fearful that their plans for a union of all the colonies would be lost. Communication between the colonies was poor, except on the rare occasions when they met in London. Joseph Howe once said, "We have been more like foreigners than fellow-subjects."

The Canadas, therefore, appealed to British governors. Edmund Head was gone, replaced by Sir Charles Stanley, fourth Viscount Monck, who agreed to contact his counterparts in the other colonies with a request, relayed to prime ministers, that a Canadian delegation be allowed to attend the proposed union conference in Charlottetown, Prince Edward Island. The query startled the Atlantic colonies, which hadn't set a date for the meeting. They hurriedly fixed a time and invited the Canadians to attend as observers.

The Canadians left Québec on August 29, 1864, in a steamship, *Queen Victoria,* thoughtfully loaded with $13,000 worth of champagne. The delegation included Macdonald, Cartier, Brown, and Galt, and three junior colleagues, one of whom was the brilliant orator, D'Arcy McGee.

McGee, thirty-nine, five-foot-three, an Irish Catholic with a mop of tight-curled hair, was a recent convert to the benefits of British rule after a youth as a rebel. He escaped from Ireland, was hunted as a traitor, and published a radical newspaper in New York City, *The Nation,* full of diatribes against priests and Englishmen. In his thirties he mellowed, made his peace with the church and the British Empire, and moved to Montréal to become the voice of moderation between his countrymen and Orange Lodges. His gifts at public speaking enabled him to persuade Irish Catholics in Toronto to cease parading on St. Patrick's Day, a ritual that annually provoked Orangemen to mayhem.

McGee's support for colonial union stemmed from his conviction that the United States would swallow the colonies and inflict worse bigotry upon Irish Catholics. He found Canada full of contradictions, a society which was at once "more orderly and more free" than the United States. His growing respect for order caused him to move from the Reform side of the Assembly to sit in the coalition cabinet with the Tories.

The *Queen Victoria* dropped anchor in Charlottetown harbor on September 1, 1864, just as the Atlantic colonies were beginning their session. The first circus ever to visit Prince Edward Island was in town, and the hotels were full. The Canadians were greeted by a party of one, W. H. Pope, secretary to the Prince Edward Island Assembly and an ardent booster of the union movement. Pope, in top hat and tails, rowed out in an oyster boat, "with all the dignity he could," as the Charlottetown *Vindicator* put it, and presented the island's welcome.

The Atlantic delegates politely allowed the Canadians a few minutes to speak. Cartier led off, painting a picture of a great nation, and outlined the plan for each province to control its own culture within a federated state pulled together under a central government that would defend it from aggressors.

When he was done, the Canadians issued an invitation for dinner and champagne on their floating hotel. George Brown, a devoted husband, wrote his wife, "The ice became completely broken, the tongues of the delegates wagged merrily, and the banns of matrimony between all the provinces of British North America have been formally proclaimed."

He was not far wrong. The seaboard colonies were so dazzled by the Canadians that they didn't discuss maritime union further. John A. Macdonald spoke the next day, Saturday, September 3, and described a new sphere of political influence, municipal governments, that were part of the Canadian masterplan. There was a break for the Sabbath, and sessions reconvened on Monday. Alexander Galt gave a breathtaking vision of federated financing which caused delegates to forget that the Canadas were shattered by railway debts.

The meeting was adjourned to Halifax, where Charles Tupper was so carried away as to propose a toast to "colonial union," to which John A. Macdonald responded with a speech that hit three crowd-pleasers—loyalty to the Queen, defense against Americans, and provincial rights. By Monday, September 12, it was agreed that delegates would meet in a few weeks in Québec to draft the constitution of colonial union.

Opposition couldn't form against the breathtaking pace, though Joseph Howe and the *parti rouge* tried. On October 19, 1864, union delegates were seated in a long room in a post office converted for their use in Québec while cold rain beat on the windows. Except for the Canadiens, almost none were native-born; Scots dominated the English-language group. All political parties were represented, though Tories were most numerous. The delegates, most of them bearded and in their forties, wore formal attire—tailcoats and vests with striped trousers and the new seamless silk top hats.

For nine days they argued about the Council, or Senate, or Upper House. They rejected an elected body because it was too American. They wanted something closer to the British House of Lords but they lacked a hereditary nobility. Wealth and political power were the nearest colonial equivalents. The provinces jostled for position in a body so clearly marked for patronage. Canada West secured one third of the membership, Canada East one third, and Nova Scotia, New Brunswick, and Prince Edward Island the final third. The Prince Edward Island delegation, disgusted, was on the verge of revolt.

On the tenth day there was bad news. Confederates who robbed banks in St. Alban's, Vermont, had fled to the Canadas with the Union army under General John A. Dix in pursuit. When a Montréal judge released the Confederates, ruling that under the terms of the Webster-Ashburton extradition agreement political dissenters were excluded from deportation, the New York *Times* fumed, "It may be said that this will lead to war with England. But if it must come, let it come. Not ours the guilt."

Deliberations in Québec continued in a mounting sense of urgency. Canadian militia was sent to the border amid rumors that the Fenian Brotherhood, anti-British Irish rebels fighting in the Union army, were preparing to march on Canada as soon as the Confederacy collapsed.

George Brown led discussion of the central government's legislature, in imitation of Britain to be called the House of Commons. Using a census three years old and estimates of the population change, he fixed Canada East at 65 seats; Canada West, 85. Prince Edward Island was mortified to be assigned only five. Newfoundland, a late arrival to the conference, expressed reservations. A Fenian influence among its Irish citizens was opposed to a colonial union that retained the monarchy.

Macdonald spoke on October 21 on the delicate subject of constitutional powers. He recommended a strong central government to prevent challenges to its authority such as Washington was experiencing. When colonial delegates protested, Macdonald quoted the French liberal Alexis de Tocqueville who visited the United

States in 1835 and shuddered at "tyranny of the majority." Provincial power, Macdonald cried, "would ruin us."

Yet without large measures of provincial powers, French-Canadiens would not enter a union dominated by English-Canadians. For the protection of French-language rights and Catholic schools, Cartier had insisted on provincial autonomy within confederation. The seemingly irreconcilable was adjusted by a provision in the constitution that the federal government would have power over "all matters of a general nature" except those specified as in provincial jurisdiction, while the provinces would administer matters of "private or local nature" not reserved for the federal government.

The category "private and local nature" was intended to cover matters of little importance on the national scene: agriculture, property rights, schools, civil rights, municipal institutions. The "matters of a general nature" reserved for the federal government were commerce (so that railways could be built), defense, shipping, fisheries, trade, and taxation; all the nineteenth-century hardware.

"It makes no matter that it has given these local legislatures very little to do," the Halifax *Citizen* warned a few weeks later. "The legislatures have to meet, and having met, they will find something to do." The editorial predicted that "a sectional legislature under a general congress is only a nursery of sectional feeling, a fruitful factory for local jealousies, grievances and deadlocks to progress." Other analysts speculated that English-language politicians would split in many directions while the French would vote as a bloc and thereby would control the country.

The founding document contains none of the poetical flourishes of human aspiration written into that of the United States. Its authors were not philosophers or men of literature, but lawyers and developers. The closest the language comes to stating a basic principle is in the opening of Section 91, which declares that the British monarch and the Canadian parliament together shall "make laws for the peace, order and good government" of the country.

As weeks wore on in the fall of 1864, every day unseasonably cold and dark with rain, men drank too much. The hotel bills for the fathers of the country amounted to more than $15,000.

Toward the end of the sessions, D'Arcy McGee proposed an

amendment fraught with significance, the right of minorities to denominational schools. Since Catholics were a minority in Canada West and the Atlantic colonies, and Protestants were a minority in Canada East, the clause found support.

On the last day of the three weeks allotted for the Québec Conference, delegates hurriedly disposed of the remaining issues: justice and finance. When Galt explained that all customs duties would go to the federal government, Prince Edward Island, which had almost no other source of revenue, withdrew from the union. The delegates failed to establish a Supreme Court; it was assumed that Britain would continue to control colonial judicial affairs. As well, Britain would handle the new nation's foreign relations, to the chagrin of the delegates.

The final flurry on October 25, 1864, dealt with expansion. Delegates urged that the HBC's territory in the northwest be added to the federation as quickly as possible, and then British Columbia and Vancouver Island. Tilley, Galt, and other railway builders present tacked on references to intercolonial railways.

A remaining detail was the name of the new country. Though they had created a federation, the influence of the southern states crept into talks, and delegates used the word "confederation," which means something else, cooperation between independent bodies. Among the suggested names were Laurentia, New Britain, Cabotia, Britannica, Ursalia, Mesopelagia, Albionora, Borealia, Colonia, Norland, Transatlantia, Hochelaga, Efisga, and Tuponia. Efisga was the acronym for England, France, Ireland, Scotland, Germany, and the Aboriginal Islands; Tuponia stood for The United Provinces of North America.

Though there were one million citizens of French descent living in the colonies which joined, none of the names considered was French. Most reflected the other founding races: 800,000 Irish colonists, 700,000 English, 500,000 Scots, and 200,000 Germans.

To the dismay of the Atlantic colonies, the name that emerged was Canada. The French, to whom it had belonged, were pleased. John A. Macdonald rolled on his tongue "The Kingdom of Canada" and liked the ring of it. When others cautioned that Americans might take offense, it was changed to "The Dominion of

Canada," from the biblical, "He shall have dominion also from sea to sea, and from the river unto the ends of the earth."

When people grumbled about the choice, McGee chided them. "I would ask any member of this House," he declared in the legislature, "how he would feel if he woke up some fine morning and found himself, instead of a Canadian, a Tuponian or a Hochelagander."

Canada it was.

15

An Unpromising Beginning

Reaction to the work of the Québec Conference was overwhelmingly negative. Newfoundland and Prince Edward Island withdrew, leaving only four colonies in the contrivance: the two Canadas, Nova Scotia, and New Brunswick. Joseph Howe, a shameless seeker of patronage, was so incensed that he quit his job as Nova Scotia's Fisheries Commissioner to lead the fight to stop "the Botheration Scheme."

"A more unpromising nucleus of a new nation can hardly be found on the face of the earth," he roared. Charles Tupper found so much opposition in the Assembly that he didn't dare submit the confederation to a vote. Leonard Tilley also faced a storm. He was forced to call an election in New Brunswick and every candidate supporting confederation, including himself, was defeated.

In the Canadas, politicians escaped a similar disaster by not calling an election. They met with rebellious colleagues. Cartier encountered a wall of protest from Antoine-Aimé Dorion's *rouges,* who called him a *vendu,* a sellout. Canadien intellectuals sided with the *rouges.* A young lawyer, Wilfrid Laurier, member of a secret society, the Club Saint Jean-Baptiste, described confederation as a scheme only to enrich Grand Trunk railway shareholders. The *Institut Canadien,* a group of liberals who challenged Bishop Bourget's book banning, was also in an uproar against the plan.

Cartier could not even get his Tory *bleus* to back confederation. He pleaded, "Under the new system Lower Canada will have its local government and almost as much legislative power as formerly," but his followers split when the vote was put. Henri Taschereau, a solid conservative on whom Cartier depended, deserted him, but by putting pressure on some and making promises to others, Cartier obtained a 27 to 21 majority in his party.

The Catholic clerical establishment favored confederation. Bishop Bourget and Cartier had respect for each other's cautious natures. Bourget felt, as Cartier did, that the *rouge Institut Canadien* element was not only politically radical but anticlerical. Both dreaded the radicals more than they did the *anglais*.

Of the four colonies involved, only Canada West wanted confederation, and Canada West swung the weight. In that debt-ridden colony, riddled with failed railways and torn by clashes between Orangemen and Catholics, confederation gave hope of expansion, markets, and protection against American invasion. When the legislature of the Canadas finally met almost five months after the Québec Conference, Macdonald and Brown presented a solid front against the *rouges* and divided Tories of Canada East. Dorion warned, "Our most important civil rights will be under the control of the general government, the majority of which will be hostile to Lower Canada."

The anticonfederation forces were outnumbered in the vote 91 to 33. Among disgruntled losers were twelve Orangemen who predicted that French Catholics would vote as a bloc in the House of Commons and run the country. When they begged Macdonald to submit confederation to an election or plebiscite, he replied, "It would be unconstitutional and anti-British to have a plebiscite."

The next step was to get Britain's approval. Watkin, new majority stockholder in the Hudson's Bay Company as well as head of the Grand Trunk, lobbied in London. His argument was that united colonies stretching from sea to sea would give Britain railway communication with the Orient. "Try for one moment to realize China opened to British commerce," he enthused. "Japan also opened; the new gold fields in our own territory on the extreme west, and California also within reach; India, our Australian colonies . . ."

In the United States, the civil war was ending. Confederates surrendered in April 1865 at Appomattox Court House, and a few days later President Lincoln was assassinated. The British colonies prepared for an invasion by discharged veterans belonging to the Fenian Brotherhood. Macdonald, Brown, Galt, and Cartier sailed for London to beg Britain to defend the Canadas. They were refused.

Opponents of confederation began to waver as rumors reached the colonies of tens of thousands of Fenians marching and drilling along the border. The attack on the village of St. George in New Brunswick was averted only when a British warship, the H.M.S. *Cordelia,* shot off all eighty-one guns, sending sobered Fenians back to Maine. Nervous colonials were yielding to arguments about strength in unity. The anticonfederation government in New Brunswick resigned at the suggestion of the lieutenant-governor, and Peter Mitchell, a delegate at the Québec Conference, formed a new government with Leonard Tilley as provincial secretary.

A railway engineer and inventor, Sandford Fleming, conspicuously surveyed the route of the intercolonial railway that was promised by confederation just as a by-election was called. Tilley wired John A. Macdonald that the proconfederation candidate would win if he had $5,000 more to buy votes. Macdonald obliged, and the man won by a landslide 700 ballots.

The mood of uncertainty and dread worsened when the United States shut down the Reciprocity Treaty's free trade, wiping out markets on which colonial farmers and businessmen depended. Though General George C. Meade was sent by Washington to cool off the Fenians, there were no signs that his efforts were successful. Raids in New Brunswick kept border residents in a state of terror. Tilley asked for more bribe money, "$40,000 or $50,000 to do the work in all our countries" and met with Alexander Tilloch Galt to complete the transaction. Since it was winter, the most convenient location was Portland, Maine.

The founding fathers agreed in Québec that the new nation's capital would be Ottawa, where construction of the theatrical parliament buildings, the largest in the colonies, was almost complete. Final touches on the slate roof and marble interior were expected in May 1866. As the date approached, only New Brunswick had voted on confederation; the other three colonies still did not dare test the electorates.

A joint delegation from the four colonies was expected to go to Britain to ask the House of Commons to approve confederation. With the Fenians expected at any moment and only untrained militia to stop them, Macdonald and Cartier dared not leave the

Canadas. The colonials were shaken that the long Whig regime in the British House of Commons appeared to end with the death of the aged Viscount Palmerston in 1865. With the urging of the Barings, however, the Tories under Benjamin Disraeli seemed just as agreeable to colonial union.

The major Fenian attack on the Canadas came on May 31, 1866, at Niagara. John O'Neill, twenty-five, an Irish rebel, led six hundred seasoned soldiers in Fenian green across the river behind the Fenian flag, a gold IRA harp on green. They captured Fort Erie without difficulty, established the new Republic of Canada there, and celebrated with a Fenian song:

Many battles have we won, along with boys in blue,
And we'll go and capture Canada, for we've nothing else
to do.

A British spy, Thomas Beach, was among the Fenians and kept Canadian authorities informed. Toronto sent six hundred volunteers of the Queen's Own Rifles by paddle boat, but the inexperienced militia was routed at Ridgeway, near Fort Erie. As farmers poured into the Niagara peninsula with pitchforks, pikes, and guns, O'Neill decided to evacuate. Nine Canada volunteers were killed in the brief battle at Ridgeway. The funeral parade in Toronto was a half-mile long.

The strain told on Macdonald, who was drinking heavily. He was shocked when George Brown resigned from his cabinet immediately after the Québec Conference and returned to vilifying Tories in general and Macdonald especially. Macdonald grieved, "We acted together, dined at public places together, played euchre in crossing the Atlantic, and went into society in England together. And yet on the day after he resigned, we resumed our old positions and ceased to speak."

Washington was becoming concerned that the Fenians would trip the United States into a war with Britain. An American warship, the *Michigan,* took O'Neill's fleet of canal boats and barges in tow after the retreat from Fort Erie and arrested the Fenian leaders. Later, they were released. The United States wasn't opposed to annexation, only to the timing. A week later a congressional bill called for "the admission of the states of Nova Scotia, New Brunswick, Canada East and Canada West, and for the organization of the territories of Selkirk, Saskatchewan and Columbia." The New York *News* commented that the United States shouldn't have given up British Columbia in the Oregon purchase.

The British ambassador in Washington made no protest during the Fenian raids on British territory. As Benjamin Disraeli observed, "It can never be our policy to defend the Canadian frontier against the United States. What is the use of colonial deadweights which we do not govern?"

Charles Tupper's efforts to persuade Nova Scotians to accept confederation took no note of Britain's indifference. Love of homeland was sure-fire in a colony of romantic loyalists. Confederation, he declared, would prevent the tragedy of seeing "the British flag lowered beneath the Stars and Stripes." In the winter of 1866 Macdonald went to New York to take a ship for England where confederation would be completed.

The new Tory government was about to adjourn for the Christmas recess. Representatives of the four colonies hired a room in their hotel, the Westminster Palace. John A. Macdonald chaired the sessions, though his high consumption of port resulted in painful burns when his bedclothes caught fire one night and he was sluggish. He was also distracted by the delights of courtship. At fifty-two, widowed when his opium-dosed wife died after a long period as an invalid, he was pursuing the sister of his private secretary after a chance encounter on the streets of London.

Joseph Howe was also in London to oppose confederation on the grounds that it had not been submitted to a vote in three of the four colonies. The new colonial secretary, Lord Carnarvon, thirty-five, a friend of Watkin and the Barings, was on the side of union, persuaded by the powerful lobby of commercial interests. He offered the maritime provinces a sweetener for supporting the union, British money for the intercolonial railway.

Carnarvon hurried the resolutions from the Québec Conference to a printer. Queen Victoria was asked to approve the country's name, Dominion of Canada, and did so. The British North America Act was introduced in the House of Lords on February 12, 1867, for first reading. With Lord Carnarvon's active assistance, it sailed through a second reading and the committee stage where it could be challenged. "We are laying the foundation of a great state," Carnarvon noted, "perhaps one which at a future date may even overshadow this country."

It passed the House of Lords on February 26, 1867, against the distracting background of a battle in the House of Commons over Prime Minister Disraeli's new cabinet. The next day it was introduced in the House of Commons, followed in one day by a second reading. "The measure must be *per saltum* [in one leap]," Macdonald said, "and no echo of it must reverberate through the British provinces until it becomes law." He added confidently, "The Act once passed and beyond remedy, the people would soon learn to be reconciled to it."

The bill caught some attention in the second reading because of Carnarvon's promise that Britain would pay for a railway. Watkin was prepared for that challenge. A transcolonial railway would be good for British trade with the Orient, he said, and was vital for keeping Americans from taking the west. Carnarvon was dropped from Disraeli's cabinet just as the British North America Act emerged untouched from committee stage. On Friday, March 8, 1867, it was passed without debate in an almost-empty House of Commons that filled immediately afterward to discuss the repeal of the dog tax.

The official birth date was fixed for July 1; Macdonald would have preferred July 15 to give the government more time to prepare, but was overruled by Britain. The day dawned auspiciously, bright and warm everywhere in the country, with a national holiday declared and a blizzard of Union Jacks on buildings. In the afternoon there were military parades and picnics. Not everyone celebrated. Halifax shops were hung with black crepe in mourning, and in New Brunswick flags were half mast. The New York *Tribune* commented complacently, "When the experiment [of confederation] shall have failed, as fail it must, a process of peaceful absorption will give Canada her proper place in the great North American republic."

John A. Macdonald, by common consent, took office as first prime minister of Canada. Cartier, the only other contender, could not be considered because Protestants in Canada West, renamed Ontario, would have revolted. Macdonald chose his cabinet according to the regional representation established at the

Québec Conference. To satisfy the ambitions and sensitive feelings of all, it was enormous for such a small nation: five from Ontario, four from Québec, which chose to adopt for the province the name Champlain gave his headquarters, three from Nova Scotia and New Brunswick.

With Macdonald, it made thirteen. The Toronto *Globe* tartly observed, "When the whole business of the United States is transacted by seven cabinet officers, it is surely absurd to appoint thirteen for Canada."

On the day the new government began, Governor-General Viscount Monck strolled from his official residence, Rideau Hall, which he described as a "miserable little house" to the parliament buildings. He was wearing a business suit and was accompanied only by his secretary. Macdonald privately thought the occasion demanded a bit more ceremony.

Monck brought royal favors and titles for the founding fathers. Macdonald got Knight Commander of the Bath, a higher title than Knight of the Bath bestowed on Cartier, Tupper, Tilley, Galt, two Grits from Ontario, William McDougall, and William Howland, whose support of the Tory-Catholic coalition helped placate Orangemen. Galt was so offended that Macdonald received a greater honor that he refused to accept his title and resigned from cabinet. In Britain, Watkin also rejected a title offered for his efforts on behalf of confederation. He thought Cartier's title should have been identical to Macdonald's.

Ironically, the Suez Canal was completed that year, reducing Britain's interest in a railway across Canada as a route to the Orient. The American west was bursting open: Nebraska was admitted into the Union and Oliver Loving completed the first epic cattle drive from Texas north to the railhead. To make the plains safe for wagon trains and settlers, America put an army in the west, cavalry under Civil War General Winfield Scott Hancock. Hancock's junior officers, among them George Custer, were given the task of protecting railways from Cheyennes and Sioux through whose hunting land the track was being laid.

That year as well, 1867, John Stuart Mill argued in vain in Britain that the franchise should be extended to women. Alfred Nobel of Sweden invented dynamite. Karl Marx wrote *Das Kapi-*

tal. And the United States bought Alaska from Russia for $7 million, a purchase Americans viewed as folly.

The first Canadian parliament passed innocuous legislation, such as making lacrosse the national sport. The serious business was a challenge from Nova Scotia, which elected 18 members to the first parliament, Charles Tupper and 17 others committed to taking Nova Scotia out of federation. Joseph Howe, "that pestilent fellow," led furious Nova Scotians into the debate.

D'Arcy McGee, who had fallen from favor in his riding in Montréal because of his conciliatory attitudes on British handling of Irish problems, rallied in Ottawa to help Macdonald fight off the maritime dissenters. On a mild night in April 1868, McGee was putting a key into the lock of his boardinghouse when he was shot and killed, probably by Pat Whelan, an Irishman believed to be a Fenian. The funeral cortege in Montréal was the largest in the city's history, a procession requiring three hours to pass.

Britain put an end to Nova Scotia's protest by ruling it illegal for the province to secede. Joseph Howe had to be content with bartering for a better financial deal. He and Macdonald met in Portland, Maine, to work out details, a cabinet post for Howe and $2 million for the province. Howe took it calmly.

A Québec element objecting strongly to confederation was the literati who offended Bishop Bourget by reading Voltaire and Pascal. Worse, they sided with the republican Giuseppe Garibaldi, who was fighting in Italy to separate church and state. Loyal Canadien Catholics volunteered to fight on the side of the pope. The issue was so volatile and emotional that Bishop Louis-François Laflèche of Trois-Rivières was overcome while blessing departing soldiers and couldn't finish the service.

Bishop Laflèche emerged as even more intractable in his defense of conservative values than Bishop Bourget. Both dreaded exposing their flocks to liberal thinkers, but it was Laflèche who urged Canadiens to avoid learning English to protect the purity of their faith. The obligation to speak English was "the heaviest tax imposed on us by the conquest."

The *Institut Canadien* soon found itself the focus of the struggle between the closed system of *ultramontaine* philosophy and the open-society views of the liberals. In the end, the conflict was macabre: It descended to a fight over a corpse. The dead man was Joseph Guibord, printer of the *Institut*'s yearbook, who died in 1869 and was refused Catholic burial rites.

Guibord's widow, Henriette Brown, took the church to court for refusing the ceremonies and denying her husband burial in hallowed ground. The judgment was in her favor. In 1874, long after Guibord's death, the judicial committee of Britain's Privy Council heard the verdict and agreed with it. Guibord's coffin was taken from the Protestant cemetery through the streets of Montréal to the Catholic cemetery, where the gates were barred on orders from Bishop Bourget. When Bourget was advised that he could not defy the British Privy Council, he opened the cemetery but insisted that Guibord be buried in an unconsecrated part. The French consul at Québec commented that the church's attitude was one of "severity unheard of in our century." Guibord finally was laid to rest encased in cement and scrap iron to prevent devout Catholics from exhuming him.

Orange Ontario took satisfaction in the Guibord incident, which confirmed its view of Catholicism as fanatical demonology. The province was disappointed, however, that confederation had not resulted in annexation of the Hudson's Bay Company territory. George Brown wrote in the *Globe*, "It is unpardonable that civilization should be excluded from half a continent on at best a doubtful right of ownership for the benefit of 232 shareholders."

Both Ontario and Québec were losing population to the United States. Estimates were that 75,000 Canadiens were working in the factories and woods in "the Boston states," despite entreaties from parish priests to stay. Twenty-children families, however, could not be fed and housed on small farms; fecundity was forcing youths into New England because the English-dominated economy at home was closed to illiterate habitants. Ontario's smaller rural families also found existence difficult for poorly educated second generations. Young couples were moving west, competing with Americans for vacant free land beyond the Mississippi.

As a result, the new country couldn't thrive. In the ten years before confederation, a lusty economy and high immigration resulted in a population increase of 33 percent; in the decade after confederation, growth was only 14 percent, much of it due to the birth rate, and industry languished. Canadians were pouring into the United States to enjoy the post civil-war boom.

Steamship companies hoping for transatlantic passengers suffered most from Canada's waning popularity in Britain. Sam Cunard was not affected, since he preferred the profitable runs from Liverpool to New York, and after 1867 no longer stopped at his native Halifax, but Hugh Allan's line was badly stricken. He printed thousands of posters urging Britons to move to Canada, in vain. A survey in 1864 of British tenant farmers, a desirable group, revealed that most had never heard of Canada but all believed that the United States was "the most attractive country in the world."

Canada asked the British government to buy out the Hudson's Bay Company as it had the East Indies Company. The reply was that Britain would not; Canada would have to raise the money itself.

The asking price was going up. Canada offered £300,000, the HBC wanted more, plus the land around its trading posts amounting to 45,000 acres, the heartland of future Canadian cities, and one twentieth of all the fertile lands in the west, giving the Company 6,600,000 acres.

The Canadien, métis, native, and Scot settlers near Fort Garry were not consulted. The colony was filled with rumors that the HBC would not sell, that it would sell to Canada, that Americans would take over. The uncertainty was painful in a community already in turmoil. The American policy of ridding the plains of tribes by the extermination of buffalo herds was a blow to the Red River where people for centuries had depended on buffalo meat for survival. Some turned to farming, though the HBC did not grant land titles and rarely allowed anyone to purchase a farm. Canadiens who had migrated from the St. Lawrence established the pattern of the farms in the traditional ribbon shape streaming back from rivers. Priests from Québec watched over a dark-skinned flock. To communicate with all, they had to learn several tribal languages.

A Methodist missionary, John McDougall, married to a Cree, in 1862 established a post within sight of the Rockies where the mighty Blackfoot nation hunted. He found the fortitude and skill of native people and métis astounding. One buffalo hunter, he said, took seventeen arrows and killed sixteen buffalo, riding his shaganappie bareback at full gallop. Métis sled-drivers carried mail and supplies in winter, running fifty miles a day in temperatures that dipped forty degrees below freezing. "Picked men these were and they knew it," McDougall wrote, "and held themselves accordingly heroes for the time being at every post they touched."

As talks in Britain with the HBC dragged on, the state legislature of Minnesota issued a statement in 1868 that it "would rejoice to be assured that the cession of the North-West British America" was imminent and would "remove all grounds of controversy." Ontario expected a different result. A land speculator and doctor, John Christian Schultz, was in Fort Garry creating a stir, appealing to Protestant settlers to form Orange Lodges and rid themselves of Catholics. He called his group the Canadian Party. They waited for the land rush from Ontario to bring more members.

Survey teams arrived in 1869, uncertain how to handle the curious shaped métis farms. Orders came to survey lots according to the township model used in Ontario. When the team approached the métis farms, however, they encountered resistance. Métis men stood on the survey chain and would not move. Their leader was Louis Riel, an educated twenty-five-year-old just back from Quèbec, able to speak English, French, and four native languages, and emerging as spokesman for the worried community.

That summer the Red River valley was purchased from the HBC by Canada and awaited a lieutenant-governor appointed by Prime Minister Macdonald. The unfortunate choice was William McDougall of Ontario, a rabid Orangeman. Riel declared an emergency and headed a provisional government to negotiate terms of annexation to protect métis farms.

McDougall traveled by way of the United States, reaching Pembina sixty miles south of Fort Garry on October 30, 1869, where he was met by armed and grim métis. A reporter from a St. Paul newspaper observed the governor's humiliation, his panoply "from attorney general down to cooks and scullions" stopped by buffalo hunters and farmers.

Minnesota saw the confrontation as an opportunity for Americans. A railway speculator, Jay Cooke, was ready to bribe Riel to throw in with the United States. Even HBC employees at Fort Garry, accustomed to trading with St. Paul's aggressive businessmen, were not reluctant to see Riel's provisional government raise the Stars and Stripes. William O'Donoghue, a Fenian who saw the métis defiance as a challenge to Britain, replaced the Union Jack with the flag of the United States. Riel firmly restored the Union Jack and fixed an armed guard to watch it.

John A. Macdonald further confused the situation by refusing to pay the HBC until his lieutenant-governor had control of Fort Garry. The money was being held in a Barings bank in London, from where it could be transferred to the Rothschild bank acting for the HBC. Despite the incomplete state of the legal transfer, on December 1, 1869, McDougall declared himself the legal governor of Rupert's Land and the Northwest Territories, issuing the statement from his temporary capital in Pembina, U.S.A.

John Schultz and the Canadian Party staged an uprising on December 7. Riel captured fifty-six and put them in the HBC stockade. One prisoner, Thomas Scott, twenty-seven, an unemployed Irish-born laborer, an Orangeman, and a violent man, spent his time in prison insulting his jailors and early in January made his escape to Portage la Prairie, stronghold of the Canadian Party.

Donald Smith, the infamous HBC factor from Labrador, was the Company's chief in Montréal. Macdonald asked him to intervene. Smith's interest in the Red River settlement was high; he envisioned a corridor of trade from James Bay to St. Paul and planned a railway to join them. He traveled to Fort Garry by way of Chicago and met with Riel in November 1869.

He found Riel calm, dressed in a frock coat, deerskin breeches and moccasins, and the community orderly. Habits of hierarchial command acquired in buffalo hunts served the métis government well. Smith asked Riel to release the remaining prisoners and he did. Riel's Bill of Rights was sent to the Canadian parliament in Ottawa. Riel asked that the Red River be admitted into confederation as a fifth province and that métis land claims and language rights be recognized.

Thomas Scott attempted to lead an attack on Fort Garry but found little support. He made a brazen defiance anyway and was taken prisoner. He abused his guards, who beat him. Riel felt his authority weakening and ordered Scott to be tried by a métis court for insubordination. The next day, March 4, 1870, he was killed by a métis firing squad.

Killing Scott was Riel's fatal error, the only mistake he made in an otherwise reasoned campaign for recognition. Schultz used Scott's death to inflame audiences in Ontario against Riel. He packed Orange Halls and moved people to tears with lurid accounts of Scott's final agony. Ontario demanded Riel's head and posted a reward of $5,000 for his capture. Macdonald was forced to send an army to avenge the murder of Scott.

However, there was no army. Soon after confederation, Britain began withdrawing its forces. Britain agreed to allow the remaining 400 regulars under Colonel Garnet Wolseley, thirty-seven, a veteran of China and the Crimea, to spearhead an expedition to the west. In return, Macdonald promised to be fair about métis land claims. Orangemen in Ontario flocked to enlist but the problem confronting Wolseley was transportation. Since the United States wouldn't allow a British army to travel comfortably by train through Chicago, the assault on Fort Garry would have to wait until spring when the canoe routes and portages would be open.

Macdonald, drinking heavily again, often kept to his bed with a bottle of port at hand. The House of Commons debated Riel's sensible proposals and agreed with almost everything, even the name of the new province, Manitoba. "The postage-stamp province," it was called, since it comprised only 11,000 square miles around Fort Garry. The bill passed on May 12, 1870, shocking Ontario because it didn't include a provision to punish Riel. A militia regiment in Toronto already was subscribed; another, mostly English-speaking, was ready in Québec.

Voyageurs guided the greenhorns over the old fur-trade route, across forty-seven back-breaking portages and through the stripped hunting grounds of starving tribes led by Chief Old Crooked Neck. Ninety-six days after leaving Toronto, they reached Fort Garry. Riel was gone. The disappointed soldiers gave three cheers for Queen Victoria, drank whiskey, were offensive to Catholics, and went home five days later.

Riel was in North Dakota with the Fenian, William O'Donoghue, who was exasperated by Riel's stubborn preference for British rule. O'Donoghue left him and took a petition to President Ulysses S. Grant asking to him to invade Manitoba. Grant ignored him, so O'Donoghue led a small group of Fenians to attack Pembina in the fall of 1871. He was routed by métis.

The Ontario Rifles were posted to Fort Garry to protect the colony. Since most were Orangemen, clashes with the métis were violent. The lieutenant-governor, Adams George Archibald, a maritime lawyer appointed because he supported confederation, wrote Macdonald that the soldiers "seem to feel as if the French half-breeds should be wiped off the face of the globe."

Macdonald asked Britain to decide what to do about the métis in Manitoba. Five years passed without a response but Britain did show more interest in the chronic conflicts between American and Canadian fishermen on the Atlantic seaboard. An Anglo-American commission met in March 1871 to settle claims, especially the United States' demand for reparation for the *Alabama*'s destruction of Union ships during the Civil War. At the Treaty of Washington, John A. Macdonald pressed Canada's claim for damages from Fenian raids. He discovered that neither Britain nor the United States considered him appropriate to the discussions. He wrote Tupper, "The British commissioners have only one idea in their minds, that is to go home to England with a treaty in their pockets settling everything, no matter what it costs Canada."

The New York *World* agreed that in the Treaty of Washington "nearly all the concessions were made by the British side." Macdonald, furious that the United States won expanded fishing rights and that the Fenian raids had not even been mentioned, demanded a guaranteed loan of £4 million by Britain to help build railways. The governor-general of Canada, Lord Lisgar, assured the British government a smaller amount would do.

Macdonald's efforts reopened reciprocity discussion between the United States and Canada. Charles Sumner and others in the U. S. Senate were opposed, believing that if Canada became bankrupt, it could be annexed to the United States peacefully.

President Grant was beseeched by American miners in the Cariboo to take British Columbia into the Union and thereby close the gap between the States and Alaska. Grant suggested to the federal Committee on Pacific Railways that a rail line to British Columbia probably would be sufficient to annex the colony.

Resistance in the colony was led by William Alexander Smith, a maritime-born Canadian who went to California during the gold rush and had his name legally changed to end confusion with other Bill Smiths. He chose the resplendent appellation Amor de Cosmos, which he translated as "lover of the universe." De Cosmos followed the trail of gold north, collided sharply with Governor Douglas when he reached Victoria, and in 1858 established a newspaper to argue his Reform views, the *British Colonist*. He mellowed to become an ardent monarchist and opponent of America. As he saw it, joining Canada was British Columbia's only protection against the United States.

In Britain some feelings ran otherwise. The *Times* observed, "British Columbia is a long way off." If colonists there "think it more convenient to slip into the Union than into the Dominion . . . we all know that we should not attempt to withstand them."

British Columbia was in financial difficulties. As the gold ran out and miners left, there were few customers for the toll roads built at huge expense. A delegate arrived from the east, Hector Louis Langevin, one of John A. Macdonald's cabinet ministers from Québec. Langevin was moved to euphoria by the scenery, promising that Canada would build a railway to British Columbia if that colony would become the sixth province in the Dominion.

De Cosmos led a delegation to ask Ottawa for something more feasible, a wagon road through the mountains. Macdonald's government grandly insisted that it would build nothing less than a railway, the Canadian Pacific. On July 20, 1871, British Columbia joined the Dominion of Canada on condition that a railroad be started no later than 1873. Macdonald promised it would be done.

— 16 —

First,
You Call the Army

The Macdonald government accepted from the start that the Canadian Pacific Railway would be built in the manner of most public works throughout colonial history; the curious, typically Canadian hybrid of public money and private enterprise. The system that evolved in the colony's lean years when outside investors were indifferent had become a fixed practice. Taxpayers tended to accept it as normal. Patriotism expressed itself in such public works as canals through solid rock or railways across muskeg, both seen as testimonials to Canadian ingenuity and grit and properly backed by the government.

In Canada where the natural flow of rivers and commerce is north-south, all lateral efforts east-west are seen as acts of loyalty and defiance.

The daring plan of a new and poor nation to build the longest railway in the world attracted American railway speculators. Chicago's George W. McMullen, Canadian-born son of a Methodist minister, was in Ottawa within days of British Columbia's entry into confederation. Macdonald's promise of free land and subsidies also drew McMullen's associate, Hugh Allan, whose steamship line had made him the richest man in Canada.

Macdonald was determined to keep Americans out of the project and, in any case, much preferred his political associates in the Grand Trunk consortium, Cartier and Galt. The Grand Trunk had the benefit of a promise of British money from Watkin and Barings. Donald Smith and his cousin, George Stephen, a wool manufacturer and director of the Bank of Montreal, were also contenders. Hugh Allan approached them with a view to eliminating some of the competition for the prize, keeping in the background his own connections in the United States with McMullen and three other railway entrepreneurs, W. G. Fargo, Jay Cooke, and W. B. Ogden.

Stephen and Smith lusted for a railway between Fort Garry and Pembina to take HBC furs to American railheads on a year-round basis, rather than waiting for James Bay to thaw. A former Canadian, James J. Hill of St. Paul, already was dickering for the same route. Smith, McMullen, and Allan met in 1871 with Macdonald, who was annoyed to see the American; Allan assured him privately that McMullen would be squeezed out.

Macdonald was facing the country's second federal election and success appeared shaky. Ontario Liberals were gaining strength, using against him his failure to induce the United States to reinstate free trade. Macdonald's masterful campaign stratagem was to turn that defeat into victory. He told voters that to want reciprocity with the United States was to reject Britain. A high tariff wall between the two countries would keep Canada in the Empire, he said, as well as protect Ontario's burgeoning industrialists. The strategy later was known in Tory campaign literature as The National Policy.

Railway speculators were active. David Lewis Macpherson of the Grand Trunk raised $67,000 as a "testimonial fund" for John A. and Hugh Allan pumped money into the faltering campaign to re-elect George-Étienne Cartier, who was dying of Bright's disease. Meanwhile, Britain passed a £2.5 million railway bill for Canada, consolation for the debacle of the Treaty of Washington and pared down on the suggestion of the governor-general from the four million Macdonald requested.

Macdonald unexpectedly favored Hugh Allan over the Grand Trunk. The reason became obvious when Allan was careless with memoranda concerning bribes: $100,000 to Donald Smith; $50,000 for J. J. C. Abbott, a leading Tory in Québec. Cartier asked for more. He had $50,000 for his own campaign, $35,000 for the prime minister's, $22,000 for his Québec associate Hector Langevin. In all "preliminary expenses of the Pacific and various railroads," as Allan described the donations, amounted to $850,000. He dunned McMullen to contribute, and the Chicago millionaire did.

The most damning transaction occurred when Macdonald told

Allan he could be president of the Canadian Pacific and then sent a telegram, "Immediate, private. I must have another ten thousand. Will be the last time of calling. Do not fail me. Answer today. John A. Macdonald."

Macdonald hung on as prime minister in the 1872 election despite an overwhelming swing in Ontario to the Liberals. George McMullen visited the prime minister in Ottawa, showed him Allan's gossipy correspondence and asked to be named president of the CPR instead of Allan. Macdonald, devastated by the extent of the American's involvement in Hugh Allan's bid, put pressure on Allan to repay McMullen $25,000 and sever all connections.

Liberals, smarting from Macdonald's victory at the polls, sent burglars to steal a copy of John A.'s indiscreet telegram to Allan. As the scandal unfolded, an ashen Macdonald consulted the new governor-general, Frederick Temple Blackwood, the fourth Baron of Dufferin and Ava, who was revolted by the mess. He sympathetically allowed Macdonald to delay calling parliament.

When it convened in October, the House of Commons was in an uproar. Donald Smith crossed the floor to sit with the Liberal opposition. The defection finished the Tories. On November 5, 1873, haggard and weaving, John A. announced his government's resignation. Lady Dufferin, sitting in the gallery, wrote, "The announcement was received in perfect silence. The Opposition, directly it was over, crossed the House to their new desks."

The Liberal leader, Alexander Mackenzie, thereby became Canada's second prime minister. A dour Scot stonemason, a prohibitionist, he was in striking contrast to the witty, alcoholic John A. Macdonald. His selection as leader was based in good part on the public perception of him as an honest man, a refreshing change from the capricious ethics of the Conservatives.

Mackenzie could count seven provinces in his domain. Prince Edward Island, awash with ambitious railway fever, had joined a few months earlier on the promise of federal help to pay off its railway debts. Lord Dufferin attended the celebration and noted drily, "I found the Island in a high state of jubilation and quite under the impression that it is the Dominion which has been annexed to Prince Edward Island."

The panic of 1873 launched an economic collapse that blighted North America until 1896. Jay Cooke's overextended Northern

Pacific went broke and New England's textile mills closed their doors. The Central Pacific laid off Chinese crews and the Union Pacific cut back and fired Irish workers. The sudden release of so much cheap labor drove down wages everywhere, a crisis that spread into Canada. The Nine-Hour-Day movement, bitterly fought by George Brown against the *Globe*'s striking typographical union, dissolved. Jobless families begged in the streets and shops went out of business for lack of customers.

Despite the calamity, the new prime minister was determined to keep Canada's promise to British Columbia to begin the railway west. Sandford Fleming, the railway engineer, had completed work in New Brunswick on an unprofitable line through bush, where it was safe from Americans. He turned to the proposed Canadian Pacific. Advance crews examined the inhospitable topography: the rolling rock of the Cambrian Shield north of Lake Superior, boggy lake land west of that, then the vast plains where dangerous Sioux and Blackfoot ruled, and beyond that four hundred miles of mountains on the edge of the Pacific.

One problem appeared to be easing. American buffalo hunters with their magical repeating rifles had almost succeeded in wiping out the buffalo. Buffalo Bill Cody slew 4,000 a year himself. "Kill every buffalo you can," bounty hunters were advised. "Every buffalo dead is an Indian gone."

By arrangement between the British army and Canada, one of Colonel Wolseley's officers remained behind when the regiment left Fort Garry. He was Lieutenant William Francis Butler, and his orders were to determine how large an army Canada would need to keep control of the west while the railroad was built. He called the prairies "the great lone land." He wrote, "One may wander 500 miles in a direct line without seeing a human being or an animal larger than a wolf."

Butler recommended that such an army be well-armed to subdue the Blackfoot nation, "the most savage among even the wild tribes of North America," and that one third should be mounted. To avoid a challenge to the U.S. cavalry across the border, it was decided to call the Canadian army "a police force."

Butler advised Ottawa that the Canadian west was full of American whiskey traders operating forts that flew the Stars and Stripes. His report coincided with news of an incident in the Cypress Hills in Canada, north of the Montana border, where an American posse from Benton had chased Assiniboins, ambushed them, and killed thirty natives.

John A. Macdonald, in one of the final acts before his resignation, created what he named the North West Mounted Police "for the rough and ready—particularly ready" to rid the plains of Americans. The first unit of three hundred volunteers attracted farmers, sailors, university students, veterans of the Riel uprising, and an assortment of unemployed tradesmen. The commanding officer, Lieutenant-Colonel George French, thirty-two, was a British soldier trained at Sandhurst who had no illusions that the police force was anything but a cavalry regiment.

The uniform was a hodgepodge. A red jacket imitated British Army redcoats but was cut like that of a Hussar. Black breeches with a red stripe resembled those of the British cavalry. Cavalry lances were taken from the Light Brigade sacrificed in the Crimean War. Pillbox hats held with chin straps were copied from European artillery dress. When these proved ridiculous in the burning sun of the plains, they were replaced by stetsons of Texas Rangers which the men were forbidden to crease into distinctive shapes.

The unit was ready to move in March 1874 by the only means of transportation available, a U. S. train. They went unarmed, guns packed in crates, and got off at Fargo, North Dakota, to begin closing American whiskey forts. The caravan amused plainsmen as greenhorns straggled across the west drinking from contaminated buffalo ponds, breaking horses' legs in gopher holes, setting up camp so ineptly that tents blew away in storms. When fodder gave out and horses were too weak to walk, the Mounties carried them in oxcarts.

On July 29, the column split into two divisions. Colonel French took the more dangerous command, which searched through Blackfoot territory for the notorious American camp known as Fort Whoop-Up, a heavily armed stockade where infamous American Indian fighter John J. Healy swapped a villainous blend of raw whiskey, red pepper, ginger, and hot water for furs.

French rode into Benton, Montana, to ask directions. Thinking an army would help in controlling restless Blackfeet, traders obliged but sent word to Healy that troops were on the way. French found Whoop-Up deserted and sent his deputy, James

McLeod, to build an army fort nearer the Blackfoot. Risk of conflict was reduced when missionary John McDougall spread Ottawa's $1,500 around to buy peace gifts for the chiefs.

Plains tribes were in a demoralized state. The shortage of buffalo was accompanied by a smallpox epidemic that weakened people couldn't survive. American whiskey brought debauchery and violence. The first news the Blackfoot chief Crowfoot had of the Mounties was good; McLeod emptied whiskey on the ground and put American traders in prison.

Crowfoot, a brilliant strategist and diplomat, went to Fort McLeod to meet the officer for whom it was named. He liked what he saw and gave McLeod the name Stamic Otakan, Blackfoot for Bull's Head. "The law of the Great White Mother must be good when she has a son such as you," the chief told McLeod. "We will obey that law."

When Sitting Bull, great chief of the Dakota Sioux, asked for Crowfoot to bring warriors into the United States to defend their land, Crowfoot refused. Instead, he informed McLeod that if Sioux attacked Mounties, Blackfeet would fight for the Canadians.

In the spring of 1875 Mounties built another fort, this one in the Cypress Hills, and named for its commanding officer, Captain James Morrow Walsh, a Canadian from Ontario. A short distance away, the American plains were boiling with trouble. The Sioux were being driven from their reservation in the Black Hills of Dakota, where gold had been found. Some 15,000 gold-mad prospectors poured into Dakota, throwing up unruly towns with such names as Deadwood and Custer City. Two Sioux chiefs, Crazy Horse and Sitting Bull, were refusing to move to the parched land where Colonel Custer wanted them to relocate.

The North West Mounted Police continued to impress Crowfoot with its toughness. McLeod built another police fort, called Calgary for his home in Scotland. When a Mountie killed a Blackfoot he'd been sent to arrest, McLeod sentenced the soldier to three months of hard labor. When another Mountie failed to find the man he was to bring in, he got the same.

Big, strong, twenty-four-year-old Samuel Steele, a man who loved military life, who fought Fenians when he was sixteen and enlisted to fight Riel at twenty, was in Fort Garry preparing recruits for service in the elite corps. He subjected novice Mounties to winter drills in temperatures that froze their faces, and ordered them to rub salt in saddle sores.

The governor-general and his wife sampled the frontier in the summer of 1874. The Dufferins traveled the *voyageur* route in Nipigon country, portaging eight times in one day and dining one evening on a meal entirely of potatoes, after which they rested from the ordeal in Chicago's Palmer House amid marble staircases, crimson-satin sofas, and bathrooms with hot and cold running water.

The depression grew worse. An estimated 10,000 businesses failed and Canadians streamed to the States, where conditions were slightly better. George Brown went to Washington in a desperate effort to revive reciprocity. He came so close that Nova Scotia and New Brunswick started to celebrate, but the bill was killed in the U. S. Senate. The failure came as a relief to manufacturers in Ontario who feared an influx of low-cost assembly-line American goods would wipe them out.

The old *rouge* faction in Québec was calling itself the Liberal Party, in imitation of the British opposition party. "Liberal" to Bishop Bourget and other clergy summoned up visions of anarchism and atheism. Wilfrid Laurier, a promising thirty-six-year-old lawyer who was emerging as leader of the Liberals, was proof of their suspicions; Laurier once had belonged to the *Institut Canadien,* which defied the church by stocking banned books.

Despite Bourget's opposition, Laurier was elected to the federal legislature in 1877. Mackenzie promptly installed him in the cabinet. To friends who wondered why he hadn't joined the more powerful *bleus* instead, Laurier explained that Canadiens should not become "tools and slaves" of one party.

Prime Minister Mackenzie believed that the appalling economic crisis would be relieved by building the railway across the country. When British Columbia complained about the delay, he promised, "I will leave the Pacific Railway as a heritage to my adopted country." Sandford Fleming hesitated to make a recommendation of a route through the mountains; he could see seven possibilities, all awful. Amor de Cosmos, drifting into madness, no longer was premier of British Columbia. The new leader, George Walkem, a small-town lawyer, insisted that Canada keep its promise to build the CPR.

Edward Blake, a young Ontario Liberal who had been provincial premier, felt just as strongly that the country couldn't yet afford it. He founded the Canada First Party whose goal was to open the west. He dismissed the threat that British Columbia would secede with an offhand, "They know better," infuriating residents of the western province. Lord Carnarvon mediated between the two parties, aggrieved British Columbia and destitute Canada. His verdict was to postpone the CPR until 1890, but build a consolation railway across Vancouver Island in the meanwhile.

The Dufferins went to British Columbia in 1877 amid signs the offended province would leave confederation. Edgar Dewdney, an English surveyor elected in British Columbia to the House of Commons, warned Ottawa that the province was on the verge of joining the United States. The Dufferins discovered he hadn't exaggerated. "The intense longing to become the terminus of the railway possesses the people," Dufferin reported. He returned to Ottawa to recommend to Mackenzie that he scrap Lord Carnarvon's plan and proceed with the Canadian Pacific.

Western land speculators waited for the decision on where the railway would break out of the mountains and require a seaport. Sandford Fleming asked the Royal Navy which inlet it favored. The answer was Burrard, a delta north of the mouth of the Fraser River. Fleming was disappointed, since he preferred Bute Inlet farther north. In the end he recommended both, plus another possibility, the mouth of the Skeena River.

Edgar Dewdney, however, had an inside track on land on Burrard Inlet and lobbied in Ottawa backrooms to choose it. Tenders were let on July 12, 1878, for a rail line that would follow the Fraser to Burrard, where Port Moody overnight became a hub. Mackenzie then rewarded Donald Smith for leaving the Tories by presenting him with the rights to the rail link between Fort Garry and Pembina. Some eighty-three miles of it already were laid. An engine, the *Countess of Dufferin,* was floated down the Red River on a barge to begin hauling supplies to construction gangs.

The cheerful wood-burning *Countess of Dufferin,* the first engine in the Canadian west, was adored in Manitoba as a sign of prosperity. On June 26, 1876, a tragedy struck. George Custer, trying to clear the Sioux out of their Black Hills, ran into an ambush at Little Big Horn Creek. Oglala Sioux under Crazy Horse and Dakota Sioux under Sitting Bull killed 264 soldiers and scouts, finishing off the wounded with Sioux coup sticks, stones tied to braves' wrists.

Sitting Bull and Crazy Horse became separated after the battle. The Dakota chief planned to escape over the border to Canada but couldn't reach Crazy Horse, who died later with a bayonet through his body. His parents buried his heart near Wounded Knee Creek in South Dakota. Sitting Bull and 3,000 Sioux fled to the Cypress Hills, where emaciated tribes were starving for want of buffalo. Sioux lookouts spotted a white soldier and a scout approaching alone. The man was James Walsh of the North West Mounted Police, coming to bring law and order.

Walsh rode into the Sioux camp and took note that many were mounted on U. S. Cavalry-branded horses and had fresh scalps on their belts. Menacing Sioux surrounded him as he explained calmly that he brought protection if they obeyed the laws of the Great White Mother. He slept in a clean lodge and was wakened in the middle of the night by Sioux who asked *what laws?* He said they must not kill, rape, steal, give false testimony, or injure people or property. Then he went back to sleep. In the morning Sitting Bull arrived. "He walks to my lodge alone and unarmed," the Sioux marveled.

The test came next day when six Assiniboins rode into the Sioux camp with stolen horses. Walsh told them they were under arrest. The Assiniboins looked to the Sioux for help. None moved. After a moment of incredulity, they threw down their guns.

Later that summer three hundred Oglala Sioux escaped over the border, robbing as they came. They announced they weren't afraid of the Mounties. Walsh took his entire troop, twenty men, rode into the Oglala camp, reined in before the most imposing lodge and arrested the chief and twenty-one others without taking his gun from the holster. He glared down all who looked argumentative. When he conducted a trial on the spot, found twelve innocent, and sentenced the others to hard labor, he became a fable all over the west.

Crowfoot signed a treaty in 1877 at Blackfoot Crossing, agreeing to keep his nation on a reservation designated by the Great White Mother. The Cree chief, Poundmaker, signed two years later, driven by hunger to take whatever help his nation could get. Big Bear, the last holdout, the greatest Cree chief of his day, was the last to concede; in 1881 he signed.

The final hurrah of the plains tribes was glorious. As Ottawa dignitaries waited under an open-sided tent, one thousand painted Cree, bareback on rugged shaganappies, suddenly appeared on the skyline. They fired guns in the air, gave a chilling war cry, and rode full tilt at the civil service, reining in within yards of the ashen delegation.

Crowfoot believed the Mounties had saved his people. "Bad men and whiskey were killing us so fast that very few indeed of us would have been left today. The police have protected us as the feathers of the bird protect it from the frosts of winter . . ."

In the heart of Cree country, métis displaced from the Red River were finding a new start. After Manitoba's entry into confederation, settlers from Ontario made their life intolerable. There were long delays in granting land title and other signs of administrative hostility. Those who could move did so. On the snaky curves of the broad, shallow Saskatchewan River they started over, once more patiently laying out farms in the distinctive ribbon shape.

Riel was still their hero. Twice he had been elected to the House of Commons, though he was still an outlaw. By 1878 Riel was having periods when he wasn't lucid, his mind filled with visions and religious ecstasy. He took out American citizenship, married a métis woman, and found a job teaching school in Montana.

The communities growing along the Saskatchewan formed a government of their own patterned on the organization of a buffalo hunt. The west's greatest hunter, Gabriel Dumont, was their leader. Dumont, son of two métis, a burly man greatly respected for his wisdom in resolving disputes, was also one of the most affluent. At Batoche he ran the ferry that took passengers and supplies across the placid, muddy Saskatchewan.

Manitoba impatiently awaited completion of the train to St. Paul. In Ottawa, Donald Smith was under attack by the Conservatives he had deserted. The winning tender of his Red River

Transportation Company was $44,000 higher than the second highest bid, a circumstance inviting suspicion. Smith denied he was associated with the Red River Transportation Company. The owners, he said, were Norman Kittson, a former fur trader, and the railway speculator James J. Hill. Charles Tupper, who knew that Smith was a silent partner in the company, was so incensed that he had to be restrained from punching Smith.

Smith was also involved in the astonishing deal the one-eyed James J. Hill juggled, which took the original investors in the St. Paul and Pacific Railway to the cleaners and gained him five hundred miles of finished track, 2.5 million acres of Minnesota, and stock later worth $20 million—all for an outlay of $100,000 cash. Part of the deal was engineered with the help of Smith's Liberal connections in cabinet. Canada gave Smith a ten-year lease on track already built with public money. Another part of the swindle involved getting $500,000 from the Bank of Montreal, which Smith was able to do without the directors' knowledge, since his cousin George Stephen was the bank's president. Hill's profits from that transaction enabled him to build the Great Northern railway across the United States to Seattle, the greatest feat of railway construction in American history.

Alexander Mackenzie delayed the 1878 election on the advice of Edward Blake, waiting for a break in charges of graft and corruption that were being thrown by pious Tories. Their leader, John A. Macdonald, by now sixty-three, wavered between fighting the election on reciprocity or on The National Policy. Charles Tupper carried two speeches with him, one for free trade with the United States and the other for maintaining ties with the motherland.

The maritime provinces were enthusiastic free traders, badly hurt when tariff walls protected Ontario industrialists and drove up prices. Macdonald gambled that he was strong enough in central Canada to win the election despite the maritimes. He picked the antireciprocity platform, and was proved right. His program of keeping out American goods, building a railway, and stimulating immigration rang with confidence. Canadians shattered by the terrible depression straightened their backs and voted for him.

Lord Dufferin was posted to Russia, leaving behind mementos of his cultivated taste. On his suggestion the Canadian clifftop overlooking Niagara Falls was reserved as a public garden, and the historic walls of the old citadel at Québec were restored. His replacement was Sir John Douglas Sutherland Campbell of the Campbell clan, heir to the title of Duke of Argyll, the Marquis of Lorne. Ottawa was thrilled by his prestige and that of his royal wife, Princess Alice, a daughter of the reigning monarch Victoria.

Macdonald felt little enthusiasm for the formal social events the Lornes instituted at Rideau Hall. He was feeling old and spent, and longed for a sinecure. He hoped to be named the first Canadian ambassador to Britain but was reminded stiffly that Britain decided Canada's foreign policy. He inquired if he could be called Canadian High Commissioner. The suggestion, in return, was Special Commissioner. Macdonald was insulted. In the end, the Colonial Office agreed the title would be High Commissioner, so long as the office had no power.

When Macdonald revealed his retirement plan, the Conservative Party was horrified. He was persuaded to remain as prime minister, and the London post went instead to Alexander Tilloch Galt. Galt's chief function would be to recruit British immigrants. If Canada built a railway from sea to sea, the country would need more people to pay for it.

— 17 —

A Very Long Railway

The disadvantage of awarding the contract to build the Canadian Pacific Railway across Canada to the Grand Trunk consortium was that Barings of London, backers of the Grand Trunk, wanted the track to run through the United States. However, the one-eyed American railway tsar James J. Hill agreed to the less desirable all-Canada route, with its thousands of miles of track to be laid through almost uninhabited forest and rock.

John A. Macdonald, widely known as "Old Tomorrow," delayed the decision. Chief Sitting Bull of the Dakota Sioux was creating a problem by refusing to leave the Cypress Hills, and the United States strenuously objected to Canada giving sanctuary to the victor of Little Big Horn. To rid the country of a political liability, Canada refused the Sioux a reservation and aid. General Alfred Terry of the U. S. Army rode to Cypress Hills and promised Sitting Bull a pardon. But Sitting Bull told McLeod of the Mounties, "There is no use talking to these Americans. They are all liars."

Deprived of food and warm clothing, the Sioux nation was dying. After a frightful winter in 1880, all but a handful went south to the waiting U. S. Army. The Mounties promised Sitting Bull and the few families who remained behind that there would be a gift of flour if they would leave. Emaciated and in rags, the last of the Sioux crossed the border under a Mountie escort and were delivered to the U. S. Cavalry. Later Sitting Bull was shot.

With the western frontier secured, Macdonald awarded the charter for the CPR to a group headed by George Stephen of the Bank of Montreal, Richard B. Angus, a cohort of James J. Hill, James J. Hill himself, another ex-Canadian, and John S. Kennedy of New York. Donald Smith, also part of the group, kept a low profile because Macdonald and the Tories hated him.

The prime minister went to London to raise money, but returned empty-handed. Stephen, Angus, Hill, and Kennedy asked Ottawa for more land and guarantees. Macdonald had to yield to them or see the CPR run through Chicago. The provinces belabored Ottawa with complaints, British Columbia because the railway building was so slow, and the maritimes because Macdonald's high tariff forced them to buy expensive Ontario goods. Québec was no longer solid *bleu* as when Cartier was alive; the gingery Liberals under Wilfrid Laurier were gaining adherents among French voters who saw little advantage in a western railway.

Macdonald gambled that finishing the railway, however it was done, would silence criticism. He distributed lavish incentives. Donald Smith was given the government-built Pembina line he wanted, seven hundred miles of Manitoba track valued at $32 million. The CPR syndicate got another stretch of track in British Columbia and a pricey line between Fort William and Selkirk, where boggy ground had swallowed track and engines whole. The syndicate also got $25 million cash from the public coffers, plus 25 million acres of land, tax-free for twenty-five years. Land on which railway stations were built, always in the center of town, was ceded to the CPR forever, also tax-free. The CPR extracted a promise that no other railway would be allowed between its line and the United States border and guarantee of a twenty-year monopoly in the west. Material imported to build the railway was allowed to be tax-free. Also, the CPR was given existing railways east of Ottawa so that the line would run from sea to sea.

George Brown, Macdonald's implacable enemy, wasn't around to complain. Early in 1880 a discharged printer invaded the office of the *Globe*'s editor and shot him in the leg, a wound from which he died a few weeks later. The Liberal party he helped to build poured invective on the Tories' CPR deal, calling it "monstrous." Even the strongly Conservative Toronto *Mail* admitted, "It is not perfect . . ."

The House of Commons was locked in the CPR debates in sessions that thirty times lasted past midnight. Edward Blake, leader of the Liberal opposition, gave a five-hour speech in which the word "corruption" appeared frequently. Macdonald replied imperturbably that opposing the CPR was tantamount to treason, since the CPR was the west's only hope to avoid annexation by the United States. The CPR, he declared, "will give us a great, a united, a rich, an improving, a developing Canada, instead of making us a tributary to American laws, to American railways, to American bondage, to American freights, to all the little tricks and big tricks that American railways are addicted to for the purpose of destroying our road."

With a Conservative majority in the House, the outcome was never in doubt. On February 15, 1881, Governor-General Lorne signed the CPR bill and it was law.

The future of the railway depended on customers. Though Manitoba was growing steadily as settlers moved west from Ontario, the prairies were wastes of buffalo bones known only to Blackfoot and Crees, métis farming on the Saskatchewan, and detachments of Mounties. In the absence of British immigrants, agents desperately looked elsewhere. For the first time Canada advertised in continental Europe. Germans and Swiss were preferred but they went mostly to the States. In the anxiety to fill up the west, some three hundred Jewish refugees from Russian pogroms in 1882 were shipped to Manitoba, though none had any experience farming; most settled in the north end of Winnipeg, Manitoba's largest town.

A flashy swindler calling himself Count Paul D'Esterhazy dazzled Ottawa in 1885 with promises to bring 400,000 Hungarian farmers to Canada. In reality the count was John B. Path, a New York con man. He produced only twenty-eight Hungarian families, all of whom took one look at the bleak, deserted plains and moved to Pennsylvania.

The "Manitoba boom" that struck Ontario in the early 1880s produced as many as 20,000 settlers a year. They traveled on the railway through Chicago and at the end of track, Portage la Prairie, loaded their belongings into squeaky Red River wagons and continued west. Most clustered where CPR track was going down but a few trickled north to the Saskatchewan River where they found métis peacefully farming.

In the province they left, Ontario was thriving under a sanctimonious judge, Oliver Mowat, who was premier for a record twenty-four years. Mowat, a Liberal, tangled with Macdonald over the Constitution. He was obsessed by provincial rights and fought to enlarge them. When Macdonald overruled provincial legislation, as the federal government was empowered to do, Mowat took his case to the Judicial Committee of the Privy Council in Britain, the final authority. The Privy Council, having no grasp of the Constitution's intent to keep power in a centralist state, ruled in Mowat's favor. Piece by piece, it dismantled the Constitution.

By this means Mowat obtained provincial authority over water transportation, and then over licensing taverns, a matter of political concern because Mowat was a dry. The Privy Council also meddled in disputes between provinces. When Ontario and Manitoba could not agree which had jurisdiction of an area around Rat Portage, England decided that Ontario was in the right. Rat Portage subsequently became Kenora.

Meanwhile the CPR was alarmed by the vigor of American railway builders pushing west close to the border. To meet the competition, James J. Hill, Richard Angus, George Stephen, and a new employee, Thomas Lafayette Rosser, an American engineer, met to scrap the proposed route and move the line closer to the border. Rosser pointed out that the decision put track across a treeless desert known as Palliser's triangle. How would he get wood for ties? Hill snapped that was Rosser's problem.

The new scheme was to lay track straight at the mountains and worry later about getting through them. Land speculators hurried ahead of construction gangs, trying to guess the route, buying acres of territory in expectation of selling it dear to the CPR and settlers who would follow. If the CPR found the price too steep, engineers rerouted around the obstacle. Winnipeg, the western jumping-off place for the railway, boomed. In 1881 it had grown from a cluster of taverns not far from Fort Garry to a bustling town with some of Thomas Alva Edison's electric street lights, 108 of Alexander Graham Bell's telephones, and a visiting opera company.

The new project chief of the CPR arrived in the fall of 1881, an American of Dutch and German descent, William Cornelius Van Horne. "A damned Yankee alien," a Winnipeg newspaper noted hospitably. Van Horne's first act was to fire Rosser, who had been dabbling secretly in land speculation. He found Rosser taking his ease in the Manitoba Club. In an argument both men drew guns, astonishing Canadians who went about unarmed.

The Northwest Territories, as the prairies were called, were under the jurisdiction of British Columbia's politician and speculator, Edgar Dewdney, appointed lieutenant-governor by fellow Tory, John A. Macdonald. Dewdney found the land boom in the west impossible to resist. He bought a stark, waterless, treeless piece of the plains called Pile O'Bones, declared it the capital of the Northwest Territories, renamed it Regina for Queen Victoria, and to insure its importance assigned it to the Mounties as their headquarters. When the CPR was obliged to run track to Regina, Dewdney became rich.

Though working conditions were scandalous—crews "herded together like rats in a hole," fired when they were sick or injured, and given food, one observer said, that was unfit for dogs—progress was astounding. With 5,000 men working twelve-hour shifts, five hundred miles of track were laid in one summer. By 1883 the track reached Calgary in the foothills, and work crews saw the mountains marching across the horizon.

An Oblate priest, Father Albert Lacombe, the first Roman Catholic missionary in the west, warned Van Horne that the Blackfoot nation wouldn't tolerate track running through the reservation. Van Horne gave the priest food and tobacco to take to Crowfoot and warn him off. Crees already had discovered it was hopeless to prevent the railway from crossing their reservation. When a Cree chief, Piapot, camped across the route and ripped up surveyors' stakes, Mounties gave Piapot fifteen minutes to move and kicked down his tent pole. Crowfoot considered the odds against the Blackfoot nation surviving confrontation with the CPR and agreed to accept the inevitable.

Another American engineer was laying track in British Columbia. Andrew Onderdonk, a member of a socially prominent New York family and later project chief for the tunnel under the East River to Manhattan, had 10,000 Chinese laborers recruited in Hong Kong to lay track through the mountains. They worked cheaply, one dollar for a twelve-hour day, and tolerated high-risk jobs blasting tunnels in solid rock and building six hundred trestle bridges over gorges.

Unlike the prairies where track was laid at the speed a man

could walk, progress in British Columbia was measured in inches. On a fine day when nothing went wrong, crews could lay only six feet of track. Onderdonk was driven to dizzy feats of imagination. To avoid toll charges on the Cariboo Trail, he lifted a steamboat, *Skuzzy,* on winches held by 150 Chinese on each line and set it down on the upper Fraser River.

Van Horne dealt with the challenge of rock north of Lake Superior by building dynamite factories on the spot. Cost of the nitroglycerine alone ran more than $7.5 million. Some 15,000 men and 4,000 horses toiled on the rock, tormented by black flies six months of the year and arctic cold the rest. Ninety miles of track through a particularly difficult stretch of rock cost $10 million.

The CPR was in trouble after its first year. Stock was offered in New York at a depressed price, and $30 million worth was sold to Americans. John A. Macdonald's Conservative government faced a federal election in 1882 against a background of CPR scandal and financial instability. His tariff wall was proving so advantageous to Ontario industrialists that he could count on their support. When he met some of them in the billiard room of the Queen's Hotel in Toronto, he was promised all the money he needed. Though Liberals complained that he was "debauching the electorate," Macdonald was re-elected with 139 seats to the Liberals' 71.

That year saw another economic downturn. The CPR found few takers when it offered a further round of depressed shares. Alexander Galt, Canadian High Commissioner in London, was disappointed that Britons still showed no interest in emigrating to Canada. Even the government preferred the United States and refused to divert shipments of Irish families destined for New York and Boston.

To make existing track pay, the CPR raised freight rates to a shocking price that united Manitoba farmers in protest. They met in Winnipeg and formed the Manitoba and Northwest Farmers Union, a significant beginning of lifelong western resentment of easterners.

George Stephen went to London to plead the CPR's cause with British bankers who preferred the Grand Trunk. Stephen met with the Grand Trunk's president, Henry Whatley Tyler, a formidable man who had succeeded in making the Grand Trunk one of the most profitable railways in the United States despite the competition of Cornelius Vanderbilt. Tyler told Stephen he would use his influence with British bankers in return for the CPR's track in Ontario and Québec. Stephen declined with regret.

In the summer of 1883 a miracle turned the tide. The depression in Europe drove some British to try the Canadian west. They constructed homes there out of the only building material available, slabs of sod. Holes in the walls allowed for ventilation and a million flies. When it rained, ceilings dripped mud.

Passengers helped CPR revenue somewhat, but costs continued to climb. James J. Hill and his partners quarreled; Hill wanted to abandon the north-of-Superior route and build via Chicago. Stephen balked and Hill resigned. So did the New Yorker, John S. Kennedy. Donald Smith was obliged to take a more visible role as Stephen approached Macdonald for more government help, this time a guarantee of dividends.

Though Macdonald agreed, CPR stock was still unsold on Wall Street. The CPR was so short of funds that crews in Brandon hadn't been paid for three months and there were mutinies all down the line. Macdonald cabled Charles Tupper, who was in London as the new Canada's High Commissioner. "Pacific in trouble," Macdonald told Tupper. "You should be here."

The CPR's financial acrobatics were creative and complex. "To detail the intricacies of the CPR financing would be to write a textbook in arithmetic," one historian groaned on examination of the tangle. Nothing worked; the CPR was in grave danger of collapsing.

An early frost in 1883 nipped crops and brought the threat of famine. "The crops here are almost a total failure," the North West Mounted Police informed Macdonald. "Everything indicates that the half-breeds [métis] are going to be in a very straitened condition before the end of the coming winter, which will probably drive them to an outbreak."

Stephen, who looked a dying man, wrote Macdonald in despair. "Now there is no way in God's earth by which these debts can be paid off but by a loan to the company by the government."

Many felt the government had been generous enough to the CPR. Newspaper descriptions of George Stephen's $3 million mansion in Montréal provoked skepticism of the reality of the

CPR's financial difficulties. Unpaid wages and pay cuts produced an ugly mood in work camps. Tupper returned from London to help Macdonald face the crisis, and in February 1884 they introduced a bill to authorize $22.5 million to save the CPR from a takeover by American creditors.

The House of Commons exploded with Liberal wrath. George Stephen watched the fight anxiously. His Bank of Montreal had advanced the CPR some $6 million on Tupper's signed note that government money would be forthcoming. Onderdonk was also in Ottawa looking for government money. Hector Langevin, Tory stalwart in Québec, led a revolt of French-speaking Conservatives opposed to more help for a railway only Ontario wanted. Macdonald, facing loss of his majority, won them back with promise of subsidies for Québec's railways. The railway bill accordingly was passed on February 28, 1884, mere days before Stephen and Van Horne would have given up.

There was still the problem of finding a route through the Rockies so Van Horne's track could meet Onderdonk's. An American Indian fighter, Major Albert B. Rogers, found it in 1884. Historian Pierre Berton pictured Rogers as he saw the Kicking Horse Pass for the first time, hat off, a quid of tobacco in his cheek, saying "Hell's bells, now ain't that thar a pretty sight," since that comment was Rogers' usual response to the mountain scenery he loved.

Madness swept the work camps as the line neared completion. Near Kicking Horse Pass, crews set aim at the Northern Pacific record and beat it by almost two minutes, laying six hundred feet of track in four minutes and forty-five seconds.

In September 1884 they were through Kicking Horse with the Selkirk range ahead. Base camp on the Bow River was called Holt City for Tim Holt, who ran the CPR general store that sold overpriced goods to construction gangs. Crews lived in tents, ate in tent dining halls, relaxed in a tent billiard parlor, and gawked at affluent guests of a tent hotel. The talk was about Onderdonk's notorious shortcuts: grades sharper than regulations and bridges of wood instead of iron.

Men marveled too about Ontario financier Edmund B. Osler, the CPR's own land developer, and Robert and James Dunsmuirs of British Columbia, father and son who wangled a monopoly on the coal deposits in Vancouver Island in exchange for a railway only seventy miles long. The House of Commons later learned the coal was worth between $100 and $200 million.

The hottest speculation concerned the western terminus of the track. Van Horne upset luckless investors by moving the location from Moody Bay on Burrard Inlet to a larger site on English Bay where a collection of shacks was scattered around a saloon run by John ("Gassy Jack") Deighton, from whom it derived its odorous name, Gastown. As Gastown received the news of its good fortune, it was agreed that the name would have to go. In the end, Vancouver was chosen.

Newcomers from Ontario to the Saskatchewan River, two hundred miles north of track, felt overlooked. Government surveyors hadn't come and their farms were without deeds. After two years of entreaty, Ottawa finally responded. To the dismay of métis, however, the surveyor who came spoke only English and made no effort to visit the narrow riverfront lots where their homes stood.

By the spring of 1884 English-speaking settlers had joined métis in complaining about government neglect. Poor crops indicated that the Crees would starve to death that winter; they feared for their safety. A petition went to Ottawa: "The Indians are reduced so that settlers in many localities are compelled to furnish them with food, partly to prevent them from dying at their doors, partly to preserve the peace of the territory."

Cree chiefs, Big Bear and Poundmaker, roamed the prairies with hunting bands looking for buffalo that had vanished. As autumn neared with no sign of improvement in the situation, settlers agreed that they could influence Ottawa best by becoming a province with an elected representative in the legislature. The west's only province-maker was Louis Riel, founder of Manitoba. The community sent Gabriel Dumont to Montana to ask Riel to help.

Riel was in poor health but agreed. The first impression of him was favorable. He spoke of proceeding cautiously and patiently. That winter, with the condition of Crees becoming desperate, Riel changed. He had visions that transported him into a trance-like state. Priests counseled him to return to Montana. Riel sent word to Macdonald that he would leave if the federal government paid him $35,000 reparation for his land confiscated on the Red River. Macdonald refused to acknowledge the debt and Riel remained at Batoche, his eyes strange and speeches sometimes wild.

By spring Crees were hunting gophers and rabbits to survive. A priest found evidences of cannibalism. Mounties issued meager amounts of food. At Fort Walsh, where 290 lodges were scattered around the post, "They are receiving two days' food to last them seven days." The Stoneys were "mere skeletons."

Louis Riel drew up a proclamation demanding deeds for métis farms, better conditions for tribes, and recognition of Saskatchewan farms and villages as being parts of a French-speaking province. He declared he was ready to fight "a war of extermination" to obtain rights for métis and Crees, a position that abruptly lost him support of most Ontario-born farmers. Prince Albert, an all-English town of seven hundred, rejected rights for French language, law, and religion.

Métis and gaunt Crees joined Riel at Batoche, his headquarters. On March 18, 1885, Riel called on the Mounties to surrender and cut telegraph lines. Word traveled among plains tribes that war was about to begin against the whites. Big Bear, hunting with seven hundred braves, got news that Riel had broken into a general store and was distributing free food. Some braves headed for Batoche, though Big Bear counseled them to avoid trouble.

Starving Crees broke into Hudson's Bay Company stores and deserted farmhouses looking for food. On March 25, 1885, a Mountie detachment rode toward Batoche and at Duck Lake met with Gabriel Dumont, other métis, and some Cree. Shots were exchanged, and the Mounties retreated.

The Mountie superintendent, Leif Crozier, gathered a posse of twenty-five in Prince Albert and took his troop of sixty soldiers to Duck Lake to put down the uprising. Dumont cried, *"Voilà la police!"* and deployed forces on high ground with the Mounties in their gunsights. Under a white flag, Dumont, his young brother, Isidore, and a Cree approached Crozier. Suddenly firing erupted. Crozier shot Isidore Dumont dead and wounded Gabriel. Métis and Cree opened fire and killed twelve of Crozier's men before he ordered a retreat to nearby Fort Carlton, then to Prince Albert.

Big Bear rode into Batoche with one hundred warriors to help Riel. Word of the victory over the invincible Mounties flew across the reservations, igniting hope. Outside Battleford, two hundred of Poundmaker's Crees prowled in war paint, terrifying inhabitants. In Prince Albert, citizens frantically constructed a stockade around the principle building, the Presbyterian church.

Macdonald had warnings from Dewdney that trouble was brewing on the Saskatchewan. "We are not aware of any causes for discontent," the prime minister replied. He was sufficiently concerned, however, to ask the head of the Canadian militia to investigate. The officer was Major-General Frederick Dobson Middleton, fifty-nine, portly, pink-faced, white-moustached veteran of lifelong service for the British Empire. He obtained the posting to Canada only a year earlier as a move to improve his pension.

Middleton asked Macdonald to buy two or three of the latest in military hardware, the American Gatling multiple-firing gun. He then packed his uniform and traveled in civvies by railway via Chicago and back into Canada to Winnipeg where he could wear his uniform again. The circuitous journey illustrated his tactical problem, troop transport. An army might travel through the United States as he had, in civilian clothes, but Americans were unlikely to allow shipment of cannons and Gatlings. If the army went by canoe to Winnipeg, as it did in the first Riel uprising, it would take three months.

Van Horne announced that the CPR would move the troops west. CPR foremen had twenty-four-hour notice to prepare to transport eight hundred soldiers over four gaps in the line totaling about one hundred miles. On a bitterly cold spring day, Torontonians lined sidewalks to cheer the Queen's Own Rifles and the 10th Royal Grenadiers as a military band marched them to the train station. The militia left Kingston in such haste that the men had no winter clothing. The French-speaking 65th Battalion went to the front 2,000 miles away wearing street shoes.

Only Ontario showed enthusiasm for the undertaking. Québec sent one unit, the 65th. In Nova Scotia and New Brunswick employers threatened to fire all who enlisted and the regiment was undersubscribed. The only professional soldiers available were instructors at military schools, all British.

The worst ordeal of the war was getting there. The first gap in the CPR line was at Dog Lake, where a roadbed was so rough that one sleigh tipped thirteen times. The next gap was a trek of seventeen miles over rough ice that cut through thin-soled shoes, after which men traveled on open flatcars exposed to 20° -below temperatures or freezing rain. After that they walked ten miles through knee-deep slush. Beyond that were colonist cars to take them to Winnipeg.

On April 2, eight days after leaving Toronto, the first soldiers were in Winnipeg. Their commander, General Middleton, was already in the field with the Winnipeg militia, the 90th Rifles. That day, Crees looking for food at Frog Lake encountered the Indian agent Thomas Quinn, a college-educated métis. Quinn recognized two of Big Bear's least tractable braves, Traveling Spirit and Imasees, but was confident he could handle the situation.

Residents on their way to Good Friday services in Frog Lake's chapel steered a course around an argument in Cree that developed over taking horses. Traveling Spirit said something to Quinn that the Indian agent rejected rudely. Traveling Spirit raised his gun and shot Quinn dead. The killing released madness, and the Crees shot every man in sight, nine in all, including two Oblate priests. Theresa Delaney and Mary Gowanlock, brides from Québec and Ontario, were taken prisoners after they saw their husbands die.

Big Bear sent a stern message that prisoners were not to be harmed. Johnny Pritchard, a métis descended from a Nor'wester, bought Theresa Delaney's freedom for five horses and $30, and Pierre Blondin, also a métis, put up three horses for Mary Gowanlock. Neither woman was raped.

Fort Pitt was the HBC post nearest Frog Lake. A garrison of twenty-five Mounties there prepared for a Cree attack. Their commander was Francis Dickens, forty-five-year-old son of the novelist Charles Dickens. When Big Bear offered safety to the farm families huddled in a rundown fort, Dickens unhesitatingly trusted him and allowed the people to go. That night Dickens and the Mounties slipped away on a river scow to avoid certain death in the morning.

Canada's governor-general, the Marquis of Lansdowne, contacted the British ambassador in Washington with a request that the U. S. Cavalry seal the western border. Riel, expecting that the United States would use the uprising as an excuse to annex the

Northwest Territories, waited in vain for American help. He was also disappointed that tribes which had suffered famine all winter weren't angry enough to send him warriors. Macdonald shrewdly had ordered Indian agents to release stores of flour and such luxuries as tea and tobacco. Father Lacombe promised Crowfoot that the Blackfoot tribe would be fed, and Crowfoot promised to keep his braves on the reservation.

The uprising therefore was confined to métis and a few Cree. Middleton marched north across thawing prairies. He broke his forces into three columns and sent one under Colonel William Otter of Toronto to Battleford to relieve the siege there. Doubting that the French-speaking unit, the 65th, would fight well against the métis, he sent that regiment to Calgary to round up Big Bear and advanced himself on the rebel stronghold at Batoche.

Dumont prepared an ambush at Fish Creek, and on April 23 caught Middleton in it. The battle was a stand-off. Middleton had the advantage of superior weapons, Winchester repeating rifles and cannons against old single-shot buffalo guns loaded by powder horns, but his green troops were unnerved by the high-pitched whistles by which the invisible enemy communicated.

Otter reached Battleford without a fight and found that Poundmaker's Crees were back on their reservation at Cut Knife Creek, thirty-five miles away. A week later when a Gatling gun was delivered to Battleford, Otter was tempted to try it on the Crees. At dawn he attacked with the Gatling, two seven-pound cannons borrowed from the Mounties and three hundred soldiers. The sleeping camp rallied swiftly. Crees picked up bows and arrows and outflanked the militia, forcing it to withdraw. Poundmaker, like Big Bear uneasy about provoking whites, restrained his braves from pursuing. "Poundmaker was very proud to say that the Crees had never shed the blood of a white man," an English newspaper correspondent had written earlier.

Middleton's Gatling was delivered on May 7 by a flat-bottomed U. S. riverboat, the *Northcote,* which Middleton transformed into a floating fort. Dumont was waiting downriver at Batoche, the cable of his ferry lowered to slice the *Northcote* in half. He gauged wrong and the cable sheared only the mast and funnel, leaving the unhatted ship to float safely away, never to return.

The militia aboard, which included the prime minister's son, Hugh Macdonald, could not persuade the American crew to turn around and fight.

Dumont's troops were deployed in shallow interlocking rifle pits on high ground. For four days Middleton's army tried without success to dislodge them, though métis and Cree were reduced to using unconventional ammunition—stones, nails, buttons, and recycled bullets pried from breastworks. On the fourth day, the Canadians were fed up. Frustrated militia rose up without orders, gave a yell, and ran at the rifle pits.

"We should have lost many lives, and probably our guns, but for the Gatling," a soldier reported. The Colt Firearms Company of Hartford, Connecticut, delivered not only two guns to the pocket war but also a salesman, Captain A. L. Howard, an Indian fighter who had served in the U. S. Cavalry. Wearing the blue-and-gold uniform of the Connecticut State Guard, Howard considered it his duty to give a demonstration under battle conditions. He turned the crank happily at Batoche, firing 1,200 bullets a minute and crooning, "Take that, and that, and that, you devils."

Dumont, thrice wounded, was one of the last to flee the blood-soaked rifle pits. Riel was in a private rapture in which he referred to himself as "David," the Elias of whom Jesus spoke. He drifted away during the battle. Four days after Batoche, soldiers came upon him leaning against a fence, dazed, shabby, wild-eyed, clutching his crucifix.

Poundmaker surrendered a week later, leading his famine-marked people into Middleton's camp. A war correspondent noted that they were "the most pathetic and picturesque procession."

It remained only to find Big Bear. The assignment was given the French-speaking militia in Calgary, which on April 12 left on foot for Edmonton, two hundred miles away. Their commander was a British general, Thomas Strange, who had retired from the Indian army to raise horses conveniently near Calgary. In Edmonton they found sixty-eight men ready to fight. The Edmonton Volunteer Infantry was led by William Stiff, a popular fiddler, and the second in command was Bill Ibbotson, a hardware merchant. They gave the arrivals a fifteen-gun salute and stood smartly at attention. Strange disbanded them on sight.

On May 14,1885, the column moved out of Edmonton looking for Big Bear, rumored to be at Frenchman's Butte where young Crees were testing their courage in the Thirst Dance, the traditional initiation ceremony. The rite required them to skewer their bodies with wooden sticks and hang suspended in silent agony. When the Crees learned of the army's approach, they prepared an ambush of tiered rifle pits at Red Deer Creek. Strange came upon them on May 28 and couldn't shake the defense. Both sides withdrew. Strange sent out a scout—the Mountie Sam Steele.

Steele joined the militia at Calgary, where he was posted to watch Crowfoot and the Blackfoot nation in case the gifts of food failed to keep them peaceful. He came fresh from putting down a strike in the CPR work camp in the Selkirks, where crews hadn't been paid all winter and had suffered heavy casualties in avalanches.

While there, Steele was dangerously ill with a high fever and was expected to die. On the morning of April 1, 1885, he was informed that seven hundred strikers were on their way from Beaver Creek. He threw on his clothes, called for a copy of the Riot Act, took a Winchester rifle and tottered to the bridge over which the mob was coming, his gun aimed belly high.

"Listen to this," he called, opening a book at the page containing the Riot Act, "and keep your hands off your guns or I will shoot the first man of you who moves." He read the Act. "Now disperse at once and behave yourselves," he shouted. They wavered a moment, and then obeyed.

Even the legendary Steele quailed when asked to take a few scouts and find Big Bear, but he stoically did. With forty mounted men, he located five hundred Crees at Loon Lake and madly led a charge. When two Mounties were wounded, Steele raised a white flag: He wanted the Crees to surrender *to him,* and was irritated when they refused. Both sides broke off the engagement as Middleton's army arrived. On July 4 Big Bear rode into Fort Pitt and surrendered his tribe.

The Canadian Army went home. The Hudson's Bay Company, which provided military transportation on the plains, submitted a bill for almost $2 million. The CPR asked for $850,231.32 for train fare. The line was almost finished, but the backers again faced ruin. John A. Macdonald was reluctant to extend another loan, nervous of the political consequences. In June of 1885, with a week to save the CPR, his cabinet debated behind a glass door. Van Horne waited nervously outside. Finally the cabinet agreed to guarantee further funds. The Bank of Montreal released money to cover the payroll. The railway bill was introduced in the House of Commons on June 16, 1885, another $35 million. Passage of the bill went better than Macdonald expected; the CPR had won Ontario by moving the militia west. On July 10 the bill passed with only an hour to spare before the calling of a $400,000 loan that would have put the CPR into receivership.

The homecoming for the conquering heroes was marred by accusations that the French-speaking 65th had shirked the fighting. Since war correspondents stayed with Middleton, activities of the other column went unnoticed. Ontario's Orangemen renewed attacks on Catholics, whetted by tales of Cree and métis atrocities.

Louis Riel was the focus of Ontario's hatred. He was awaiting trial for treason in Regina. The judge and lawyers for both sides were sent from Ontario. The six-man jury was composed of English-speaking settlers. Concerned citizens in Québec raised a fund to send one French-speaking lawyer to aid Riel's defense.

Riel's lawyers argued for a change of venue. This was denied. When the defense pointed out that Riel was a citizen of the United States and should be extradited, the charge was reworded to circumvent the issue. Riel wanted to base his defense on the privilege of necessity, arguing that famine and unresolved métis land claims were responsible for the crisis. He assembled documents to illustrate his point, but none was allowed as evidence.

Instead, lawyers submitted that Riel was insane. William Jackson, a Prince Albert druggist who supported Riel, had entered the same plea, on the advice of his lawyer. The trial was perfunctory. After a half hour, Jackson was sent to an asylum from which he was allowed to escape. Even so, Riel resisted a defense he considered humiliating to his reputation and place in Canadian history. He was not a madman, he maintained; he was a prophet and a patriot.

An Ontario Conservative, D'Alton McCarthy, an Irish Protestant who hated all Catholics, stomped his province calling for Riel's blood. "Either this country will be French or it will be English," he cried. The Toronto *Evening News* reflected public opinion when it said, "We are sick of the French Canadians and their patriotic blabber and their conspiracies against the treasury and the peace of what without them might be a united Canada."

Opponents of the *bleus* of Québec were encouraged by a new liberal pope, Leo XIII, who ordered Québec clergy to stop refusing the sacrament to Catholics who voted for the Liberals. The Riel issue gave Wilfrid Laurier and Honoré Mercier, leader of the provincial Liberals, the cause they needed to demonstrate to voters that the Conservative Party was no friend of Canadiens.

Riel's trial lasted a week. On July 31, 1885, the final day, he rose in his defense. Obliged to use English, he apologized for his clumsiness in that tongue but was nonetheless eloquent. He listed métis grievances and the long history of broken promises to métis and Cree. He asked for a new trial with a full jury of twelve and a competent medical examination to show that he was sane.

The jury considered its verdict for a half-hour and returned with "Guilty." Though the jury recommended mercy, the judge sentenced Riel, who was praying aloud, to be hanged on September 18.

Macdonald was deluged with petitions from Québec to spare Riel's life. Ontario was howling that Riel hang. Meetings there were inflamed by speeches evoking the murder of Thomas Scott. Macdonald decided the wisest course was to appease the richest, most powerful province. "We will have lively times in Québec," he conceded, "but I feel pretty confident that the excitement will die out."

Poundmaker and Big Bear faced quick military courts, which found them guilty. They were shackled in leg-irons by blacksmiths and led into stifling prison cells to serve sentences of three years. Eleven Cree were hanged and thirty-one others sent to prison. All but Poundmaker had their heads shaved, an ignominity he was spared by the intervention of Crowfoot, who had adopted him as a son. Eighteen métis were given sentences of from one to seven years. Two whites brought to trial were acquitted.

Riel's sentence was appealed on the grounds of insanity but doctors gave conflicting testimony. Though Riel had periods of schizophrenic visions, he was often lucid. The Privy Council in Britain refused to hear the case. Tension mounted. French-speaking Conservatives notified Macdonald they would resign if he hanged Riel. "He shall hang though every dog in Québec bark in his favor," Macdonald snapped.

Priests came and went in the cell where Riel prayed constantly. His loyal friend Gabriel Dumont, a refugee in the United States, planned a rescue by pony express but was thwarted when Mounties strengthened the guard around the Regina jail. At eight o'clock on the morning of a bright, cold November 16, 1885, Riel was led to a scaffold. He was pale, his beard long and tangled, but he was calm and sane. He was reciting the Lord's Prayer when the trap was sprung. He dropped nine feet. His heart continued to beat for two minutes.

Flags were lowered to half-mast in Québec. A throng of 50,000 people massed in the Champs de Mars in Montréal to hear thirty-seven speakers. Wilfrid Laurier cried, "Had I been born on the banks of the Saskatchewan, I would myself have shouldered a musket to fight against the neglect of governments and the shameless greed of speculators."

Honoré Mercier, a former *separatist,* shouted, "Riel, our brother, is dead, the victim of fanaticism and treason." Another speaker said, "By killing Riel, Sir John has struck our race at the heart." Montréal's *La Presse* dubbed the Conservatives *le parti de la corde,* the party of the noose.

Canadien politicians had two choices, separatism or federalism. Mercier tended to the former, Laurier the latter; the Liberals were split. In March 1886, when the House of Commons debated the decision to hang Riel, Laurier spoke for compromise between Tory vengeance and Québec separatism. Edward Blake, federal Liberal leader, defied Ontario and spoke for seven hours documenting injustices in Riel's trial. It cost him his political life. As Macdonald expected, he won the vote. French-speaking Tories voted against their leader, but Ontario's Liberals deserted Blake and overwhelmingly supported Riel's execution.

Dewdney quietly arranged amnesty for most rebels still in prison. Big Bear and Poundmaker, broken by a year in the cells after a lifetime in the open, did not long survive their release.

Father Lacombe and Crowfoot traveled to Ottawa to receive official thanks for keeping the Blackfoot nation out of the fighting. With the danger over, food rations to Indians were cut. The North

West Mounted Police was strengthened by 1,000 recruits. The parish of St. Laurent, where the métis land claims remained unrecognized, fell apart. Some métis migrated to the United States, others to the Peace River far from white settlements where they patiently started farming again.

General Middleton left Canada accused of stealing furs from a métis and was appointed Keeper of the Crown Jewels in the Tower of London. Gabriel Dumont, grieving in exile, joined an American wild west show. His act was to shoot glass balls from the back of a galloping horse. On June 7, 1886, he shared a bill in Philadelphia with Buffalo Bill Cody and Annie Oakley.

The CPR was completed as Riel was hanged. The owners gathered to celebrate on November 17, 1885, at a place where the last spike would be driven, high in the Columbia mountain range 340 miles from the Pacific Ocean. Sam Steele was a witness. So was Albert Rogers, discoverer of the Kicking Horse Pass route. He cut the last piece of rail to fit the gap. Donald A. Smith, George Stephen, Cornelius Van Horne, and Sandford Fleming stepped from parlor cars to pose for the photographer.

Fleming had acquired fame as the man who set the world's clocks. Frustrated by the problems of running trains across a continent where every town set time to suit itself, he proposed "terrestrial time," as he put it, by which the world would be divided into twenty-four fixed zones of fifteen longitudinal degrees. Since he was a loyal British subject, he selected as the base line the town of Greenwich on the Thames River in England. His scheme was adopted; the world's first standard time.

The group of CPR builders arranged themselves for the ceremony. Donald Smith, sixty-five and white-bearded, had the honor of swinging the mallet. He and Stephen picked a sentimental name for the site; they called it Craigellachie for a mythical rock dear to their childhoods in Scotland. Smith lifted the hammer, and a hunchbacked photographer from Winnipeg took the picture that has been in every Canadian history book since. The CPR was finished.

— 18 —

Falling Out
with Québec

Macdonald's confidence that after the hanging of Riel "the excitement will die out" in Québec was ill-founded. A provincial election the following year demonstrated how deeply damaged the Conservative Party was: Liberal Honoré Mercier was elected premier.

Macdonald and his wife celebrated the CPR's completion by riding a train across the country to Vancouver. To the consternation of the gentlemen, Lady Macdonald insisted on riding in the cowcatcher scoop in front of the engine to get a finer view of the mountains.

Vancouver was in a sullen, smoldering mood, overflowing with men suddenly unemployed when the CPR was finished. Idle, hungry, angry, they turned on thousands of stranded Chinese who accepted any job however dangerous, unpleasant, or low paid. Leading citizens delivered petitions to the federal government urging that something be done about the Chinese, who were accused of keeping slave prostitutes. Drunks raided a camp of Chinese workers on February 24, 1887, and ran some over a cliff to their deaths.

A Royal Commission on Chinese Immigration investigated charges of debauchery. It discovered that in all of British Columbia there were but ninety single Chinese women among a population of 10,000 Chinese men, proving that stories of widespread slavery were unfounded. The Commission said opium smoked by Chinese seemed no more harmful than whiskey imbibed by non-Chinese. As a concession to British Columbian bigotry, John A. Macdonald set a stiff head tax on all Chinese and barred Chinese,

Mongolians, and Indians from voting, an edict that included even British citizens.

Macdonald, feeling his age after fifteen years as prime minister, selected as his successor a Nova Scotian judge, John Sparrow Thompson, "the greatest discovery of my life." Thompson's political liability, however, was grave. He was married to a Roman Catholic and had converted to that religion, making him unacceptable in Ontario. Macdonald could depend on his National Policy to hold Tory votes anyway. Ontario used the tariff wall to create an industrial boom. Hart Massey's farm implements were gaining world renown for his hometown, Newcastle. Other communities, avid for the jobs factories provided, courted American industrialists to get them to establish plants in Ontario. Since American companies could not export through the tariff wall, the only route around it was a Canadian branch plant. American agents went from town to town searching the best cash bonus, tax easement or land grant in return for an American-owned factory.

Lacking the hydropower which fueled Ontario's blossoming industries, Nova Scotia, New Brunswick, and Prince Edward Island fell into economic despair. Iron ships had replaced the beautiful wooden clippers that had been the maritimers' pride and destroyed the ship-building industry on which they depended. In desperation, W. S. Fielding, Liberal premier of Nova Scotia, introduced a bill on May 7, 1886, to take his province out of confederation.

Separatist feeling was rampant also in Québec, where Honoré Mercier described a French-Canadian nation within America. In a Saint-Jean Baptiste Day speech in 1889, he declared, "This province of Québec is Catholic and French, and it will remain Catholic and French . . . We are now two and a half million French Canadians in America, proud of our past, strong in our present, and confident of our future."

D'Alton McCarthy, an extreme Catholic-hater even among Orangemen, picked the recurring issue of Jesuit estates in Québec as proof of his theory that Catholics were trying to take over the country. His Equal Rights Association enrolled 50,000 members who swore an oath that they would never employ a Catholic or vote for one. Vandals visited the statue of James Wolfe on the Plains of Abraham and toppled it in protest.

Macdonald faced his sixth federal election in 1888 with his National Policy under fire everywhere but in Ontario. Western
farmers and maritimers complained about the high cost of Ontario goods; Québec and Nova Scotia were talking of secession.

Charles Tupper was recalled from London to deal with the crisis in Nova Scotia. He made windy speeches about loyalty to the
Queen, waved the Union Jack, and left the impression that a vote
against Tories was a vote against the British Empire. Voters
overwhelmingly supported the Conservatives, making Premier
Fielding doubtful that his secessionist plan would work. He
dropped it.

Ontario, as expected, voted solidly Tory. Most Liberals, including Edward Blake who had defended Riel, lost their seats. A new
Liberal leader had to be found. Because the party's main strength
was now in Québec, Wilfrid Laurier was selected. A handsome,
graceful man, witty and riveting as a speaker, a philanderer
adored by women, the forty-six-year-old lawyer made an appealing figure. As well, he had demonstrated that he didn't always
support the Québec point of view, which made him palatable in
Ontario.

Manitoba was following Oliver Mowat's example in defying the
authority of the federal government. Despite Macdonald's opposition, the Manitoba legislature passed a railway bill to build a line
to the United States. The Canadian west was attracting Americans. Mormons led by Brigham Young's son-in-law, Charles
Card, bought a half-million acres for a dollar an acre in what
would be Alberta. Mounties promised scandalized neighbors that
no Mormon would be allowed more than one visible wife.

Manitoba's settlers from Ontario outnumbered the French for
the first time. D'Alton McCarthy went west to rally Orangemen.
He stirred up so much heat that in 1890 Manitoba's Liberal government under Premier Thomas Greenway abolished the French
language and support for Catholic schools. At the same time
McCarthy introduced a bill in the House of Commons to ban the
French language and Catholic schools in the Northwest Territories that stretched from Manitoba to the mountains. In Ontario,
Orangemen spearheaded legislation to close Catholic schools in
eastern Ontario.

All three bills were contrary to guarantees for minority education established in the Constitution. Macdonald considered his choices. If he disallowed the legislation under Section 93 of the British North America Act, which permitted the federal government to overrule provincial legislation which contravened the Constitution, Manitoba and Ontario would appeal to the Privy Council, which almost certainly would rule in their favor. If he allowed the bills to stand, Québec would never forgive him.

Passions rose and Manitoba threatened to secede as Macdonald considered the unhappy alternatives. He decided on a compromise. He declared he would allow the Manitoba legislation but the federal government would support Catholic schools in the province. Québec was delighted.

Wilfrid Laurier astounded his followers by opposing Macdonald. Speaking on behalf of provincial rights, he said that invocation of Section 93 put all provincial powers in jeopardy. Charles Tupper argued that Macdonald was trying to hold the country together; Laurier retorted that Macdonald was launching a religious war.

"If I had it in my power," Laurier told the House of Commons, "I would try the sunny way. I would approach this man Greenway with the sunny way of patriotism."

Macdonald's bill passed despite opposition by an unusual alliance of McCarthy's Orangemen, Laurier, and Canadien *rouges*. The Privy Council, however, refused to allow the legislation and invested in the provinces the right to close minority schools, which Manitoba promptly did.

Another crisis concerned clashes in the Bering Sea between American revenue ships and Canadian sealers. When U. S. customs officers arrested Canadians for killing seals on Canadian soil, the dispute was brought to arbitration in Washington. The U. S. Secretary of State, James Blaine, refused to allow a Canadian delegate to attend. Macdonald protested but was advised by Britain that Blaine's decision was reasonable.

Charles Hibbert Tupper, thirty-five-year-old son of Charles Tupper, was allowed as an observer. On his return, he told Macdonald that Canada should never again be represented by the British ambassador in Washington, since he appeared interested only in making "his future residence in Washington as pleasant as possible."

When the United States seized another Canadian sealing ship in the Bering Sea, Britain was provoked to send Royal Navy warships to Esquimalt, British Columbia. In retaliation, the McKinley tariff bill of 1890 cut imports from Canada, a blow felt most by farmers.

On November 7, 1890, the Wall Street stock market crashed, signaling a dip in the long brutal depression, the worst of the century. Drought in the west turned the prairies into a dust bowl. Within a few years an estimated million people left Canada for the United States. A joke of the period was, "What are the only two books in the Old Testament that describe Canada? Lamentations and Exodus."

In Manitoba 40 percent of the homesteaders gave up claims in despair. Entire villages in Québec were deserted, their inhabitants in New England working in factories which depressed wages. When an attempt was made in 1892 to locate 83,000 immigrants who had entered Canada the year before, only 28,000 were still in the country.

Americans renewed talk of manifest destiny—the inevitability of Canada and the United States forming one country. A grouchy, wealthy Oxford don in Toronto, Goldwin Smith, heartily agreed. Smith was fond of annoying descendants of the Family Compact by admiring the logic of continentalism. In any case, he added, Americans already were annexing "the very flower of the Canadian population . . . who leave just as they arrive at manhood and begin to produce."

Many Ontario Liberals agreed. An editorial writer on the *Globe,* Edward Farrer, headed a commercial union movement of small businessmen who faced ruin because of the population drain. Farrer was in touch with wealthy Republicans in New York, among them Charles A. Dana, Andrew Carnegie, John Jacob Astor, Charles L. Tiffany, and Theodore Roosevelt, who in 1892 formed the Continental Union League. When Farrer went to Washington to see Secretary of State Blaine, he was given an immediate appointment. Yet an emissary from Prime Minister Macdonald was advised Blaine couldn't see him for two months.

Ontario Conservatives reacted with such fury that Macdonald was obliged to deny he had tried to meet Blaine. He wrote a ringing disclaimer to newspapers: "As for myself, my course is clear. A British subject I was born—a British subject I will die."

The declaration became the Tory rallying cry as the country prepared for another election, which coincided with celebrations for Queen Victoria's Golden Jubilee. "The Old Flag, The Old Policy, The Old Leader" was the slogan. Farrer, accused of being a traitor, replied with dignity, "The statement that I thought political union with the United States was the manifest destiny of Canada . . . may be a misaken one, but I believed it and I believe it now."

Laurier's Liberals were blighted by charges of disloyalty to the Crown, even though Laurier strenuously disowned Farrer's statement. The aged Macdonald threw himself into the fight. On a raw day in February, he rode in an open carriage to address a rally in Napanee, Ontario, and afterward was too ill to leave his bed. His victory at the polls heartened him and he seemed to revive. But two months later he suffered a slight stroke, recovered from that, and then died of a second stroke on May 29, 1891, at the age of seventy-six.

The long Conservative reign had left the party too divided to select a leader readily. And Tories were hurt by scandals uncovered by one of their own, an upstart Tory journalist from Québec, Israel Tarte. Tarte charged that another Conservative Member of Parliament, Thomas McGreevy, took kickbacks from railway promoters. Though the malfeasance was far from uncommon, the McGreevy affair implicated a bigger fish, Hector Langevin, leader of the Québec Tories.

A New York *Times* reporter who covered the unsavory trial commented, "The Langevin crowd is worse than the Tweed gang ever was." Langevin was exonerated however and McGreevy, who kept loyal silence, received a prison sentence. The Liberals could not gloat. Their Québec leader, Honoré Mercier, was also involved in a $100,000 bribe to the provincial treasurer. The lieutenant-governor called a Québec election. The Tories, promising clean government, won handily.

The federal Tories replaced John A. Macdonald with a compromise, Sir John Abbott, seventy, who had retired to the Senate. "I hate politics," he grumbled. He proved so inept that within a year the Conservatives turned to the Catholic Sir John Thompson.

When Thompson became Canada's fourth prime minister in 1893, Ontario Protestants tried to boycott his cabinet. Thompson disarmed opponents by appointing a leading Orangeman as controller of customs, a patronage plum.

That year saw the bottom of the American depression. The United States dollar sank to fifty-one cents on the world market, 3 million people were unemployed, and one third of all the U. S. railways were in receivership. An infant labor movement was taking shape to fight for job safety, a living wage, and the nine-hour day. Samuel Gompers' powerful American Federation of Labor swallowed the tiny Canadian Trades and Labour Congress formed in 1885. Gompers explained that since most industries in Canada were owned by Americans, Canadian unionists were better served in American unions. There appeared truth in the argument: Canada's biggest strike to date, a nine-month holdout of street railwaymen in London, Ontario, was directed against American owners by an American-based union.

Catholic clergy in Québec considered the union movement anti-church and fought Knights of Labour organizers who were signing up members in Québec and Ontario mills. The traditional weapon of the church, refusal of sacraments, had little effect when working conditions were life-threatening. The thousands of French-Canadians who flocked to join the Knights of Labour made the parent office nervous. Terence Powderley, U. S. head of the organization, complained, "The French are much harder to manage than other people."

Rejected by the church and unwelcome in American unions, beleaguered French-Canadians began to organize independently. In 1891 three strikers were killed at Valleyfield, Québec, by militia sent to keep the cotton mill open. The union grieved over its martyrs and continued to grow.

The most wretched poverty in North America existed in Newfoundland, where every effort to develop the island's resources was thwarted by the mother country. Britain preferred to protect French interests in one third of Newfoundland which Britain had given France. In 1875 Britain closed a lead-ore mine at Port-au-

Prince where Newfoundlanders were working. Later Britain refused to allow Newfoundland to build a railway from St. John's to
the western ferry docks; France complained that the noise of the
trains would frighten the fish. In 1889 Britain closed sixty lobster
factories in the outports because France said they violated an
agreement. The agreement had expired fifty years earlier.

Profit from timber and cod went to Britain, so Newfoundland
remained in a state of constant debt. "The colony was sucked
dry," a correspondent from the London *Daily Mail* observed in
1897. When deposits of copper, lead, and coal were discovered on
the east coast, Newfoundland's hopes were raised. A Montréal
speculator, Robert Reid, offered to build a 548-mile railway to
haul the minerals to the western port in return for a land grant of
2.5 million acres.

Newfoundlanders had no choice. "Local capital is rarely
invested here," one noted bleakly. Construction began under unusual constraints, cloaked in secrecy so that France wouldn't find
out about it and complain to Britain. Two disasters conspired
against the project. The first was the fire of 1892 in St. John's
which burned almost every building in the town of wooden
shacks. Damage, estimated at $20 million, was not covered by
insurance. The second tragedy was a result of the first: The
island went bankrupt in 1894.

Britain was asked to cover the $16 million owed by the govern-
ment, but refused. Both banks closed, leaving the island with little
currency. The premier, William Vallance Whiteway, hurried to
Ottawa to ask Canada to buy Newfoundland. The prime minister
who received him was Mackenzie Bowell, seventy-five, successor
to the talented John Thompson who had died of a heart attack
while dining with Queen Victoria. Bowell, grand master of the
Orange Association of British America, was quickly thrust into
office to give the Tories time to get Charles Tupper back from
London once again.

Whiteway asked $16 million for Newfoundland, the amount of
the debt. Bowell offered $10 million. Bargaining continued until
the men were but $200,000 apart. Neither would budge. In the
end, Britain gave the island $3 million and merchants in St.
John's, the island's "fishocracy," raised the rest in New York and
Montréal.

Reid used this emergency to increase demands for compensations to build the railway. He wanted control of the line, control of shipping, mineral, and timber rights, the telegraph, and St. John's drydock. Whiteway agreed to everything. A St. John's newspaper complained that "the Whiteway party is a shameless gang of boodlers, rogues and jobbers," to which the premier replied that his critics were expressing "crude ideas and decided opinions upon the subject on which they know nothing."

In 1898 Newfoundland finished the railway and celebrated the four-hundredth anniversary of Cabot's landing. Leading citizens rode the train to the end of the line where it linked with ferry boats to the mainland. Whiteway was thrown from office and Reid agreed to give back most of his booty in return for $2.5 million.

With Charles Tupper back from London, the Conservatives were ready for an election. Tupper campaigned on the tried and true Tory platform of loyalty to the Queen and watch out for Americans, but his snap was gone. Despite being French-speaking and a Catholic, Laurier was admired in Ontario for his position on Manitoba's school bill and his fights with bishops. The church campaigned against him in Québec, but Canadiens could not resist seeing one of their own prime minister of Canada. When ballots were counted, Laurier and his Liberals had a creditable majority of 117 to 89.

Laurier demonstrated the benefits of "the sunny way" he had proposed during debates on the Manitoba school question. A young, ambitious Manitoba lawyer, Clifford Sifton of Brandon, drafted a compromise with the help of Québec's Israel Tarte, who had been forced out of the Tory Party. They recommended that Catholic religious instruction be given after regular classes, and that some French be allowed in schools where most students were French.

Soon after, a by-election was held in the federal riding of Bonaventure in Québec. The Liberal candidate, J.-F. Guité, was asked by priests to sign a pledge that he would vote against Laurier's contract. Guité replied, "I am a Catholic and in all questions of faith and morals I am ready to accept without restriction the decisions of my church. In all political decisions I claim the freedom enjoyed by every British subject." The electorate sent him to Ottawa with twice as many votes as the previous Liberal incumbent. The power of the clergy to control federal politics was over.

Laurier addressed himself to the problem of the Canadian population loss to the United States. Though the depression of the nineties ended in 1896, the flow south continued. Canada wasn't holding its native-born population, and newcomers from Europe generally paused in Canada only long enough to get directions to the border. From Ontario to the Rockies there were fewer than a quarter-million homesteaders.

Clifford Sifton brought valuable western expertise to Laurier's cabinet. He cautioned against giving more land to railways and recommended building north-south lines to move people and goods. Also, the west needed a new strain of wheat that would ripen sooner than the favorite, Red Fyfe, which often was caught in September frosts.

At Sifton's suggestion, a government experimental farm was established near Brandon. A young cerealist, Charles Saunders, bent himself to the task of producing seven hundred hybrids to breed the one that would ripen earliest and yield fine, white flour. Saunders learned a shortcut, judging the quality of flour by chewing a handful of wheat kernels.

Clifford Sifton's portfolio in Laurier's cabinet was Minister of the Interior, a responsibility that involved furnishing the interior of Canada with people. He launched an astonishing campaign for such a small country. With most of the U. S. west occupied by homesteaders, he advertised THE LAST BEST WEST, in 7,000 newspapers and on thousands of posters plastered in railway stations across Europe and the States. Families were promised 160 acres of farmland—free.

Germans, Scandinavians, Ukrainians, Slavs of all sorts, and Britons responded. The CPR's colonist cars bulged with a hundred thousand tough European peasants, enured to hard work and hard weather, who spilled out on the plains where the grass grew waist high and the soil was black loam, fertile beyond anything in their experience.

Their introduction to the country's first inhabitants came at railway stations where they unloaded bales of belongings. Crees and Blackfeet, wrapped in filthy blankets, stared at the newcomers. John McDougall, the missionary, grieved for people reduced from proud and free buffalo hunters to loiterers who begged from tourists. "They are in despair," he wrote. "They find themselves robbed of their manhood. They are placed far below the plane conceded to the basest and vilest and most degenerate white people."

Lady Aberdeen, wife of Canada's governor-general in the 1890s, John Campbell Hamilton Gordon, Marquess of Aberdeen and Temair, traveled across the west by train and wrote in her daily journal, "Miserable specimens in dirty, squalid, coloured blankets haunt the railway stations with the object of selling buffalo horns or baskets of feather work. It is a pathetic sight to see what appears to be ghosts of a people of other days . . ."

The flat skyline of the prairies blossomed with grain elevators and the bulb spires of Ukrainian churches. Among the newcomers were nine thousand Doukhobors, considered the finest farmers in Russia, where they were persecuted for being pacifists. Their patron was Count Leo Tolstoy, novelist and humanitarian, who arranged with a Toronto university professor, James Mavor, to find them asylum in Canada. The presence of so many people whose customs were strange and whose language wasn't English came as a shock to Manitoba. "It is revolting in the extreme to think of the blood of such being destined to mix with our good British and French blood to its certain corruption," a Winnipeg newspaper mourned.

The times were good for investors, the country hungry to welcome them. Henri Mercier, "the chocolate king" of Paris, bought Anticosti Island in the Gulf of St. Lawrence for $125,000 in 1895, an island half again as large as Prince Edward Island. Mercier established his own laws in his domain, which he stocked with deer and servants.

The Imperial Oil Company, proprietors of oil deposits near Sarnia, Ontario, needed cash to move a refinery and found it readily enough. Charles O. Stillman, a New Jersey millionaire, put up the money and got a majority of the voting stock in exchange. The American branch plant arrangement was working so satisfactorily for U. S. manufacturers that Laurier's tentative efforts to reopen discussion of free trade were rebuffed.

The influx of diligent farmers in the west severely overtaxed the CPR's freight capacity. By the end of the century bumper crops of wheat were rotting in the elevators. "The hopper was too big for the spout," Van Horne acknowledged. Wheat exports of two million bushels in 1890 rose to seventeen million bushels in 1900.

The Grand Trunk used the situation to insist that another railway was needed across the west. At the same time two hustling promoters in Manitoba, Donald Mann and William Mackenzie, were already at work on a hundred-mile spur line from the CPR to the town of Dauphin, marooned north of track. It proved such a moneymaker that Mann and Mackenzie challenged the Grand Trunk directors and demanded that Ottawa give them the contract for a second continental railway, the Canadian Northern.

Efforts to reconcile the two groups were in vain. Laurier's cabinet included six Grand Trunk directors who urged him to accept their line's bid, but Mann and Mackenzie were heroes in Manitoba. Laurier decided Canada was bounding into a future of plenty and could afford *both*. "I am aware that this plan may scare the timid and frighten the irresolute," he conceded. In 1903 his government authorized the Grand Trunk *and* the Canadian Northern to start laying track.

When critics expressed doubt that a nation of five million could afford so many transcontinental railways, Laurier explained, "At this moment there is a transformation going on in the conditions of our national life which it would be a folly to ignore and a crime to overlook." As a result of his optimism, Canada was to have three lines running west from Winnipeg, two almost overlapping in the Yellowhead Pass, and two eastern lines from North Bay to Ottawa.

Sifton was confident Canada would have a population of twenty million by 1920. "The nineteenth century was the century of the United States," Laurier assured Canadians. "The twentieth century will be the century of Canada."

His optimism did not seem excessive when Canadians learned that northern rivers were running gold. The trail of gold that began in California led to a creek close to the Arctic Circle, in Canada's Yukon River valley. As early as 1878 prospectors found gold nuggets there, but tribes were too militant to allow investigation. A U. S. gunboat armed with a Gatling ended that threat. Americans who followed operated on the assumption that not only Alaska but most of the Yukon was American territory.

Even the American governor in Alaska was unsure where the border really was. Old treaties spoke of the panhandle following "the summit of the mountains situation parallel to the coast." The coastline was deeply jagged, however; if the boundary line was mountains parallel to the deepest inlets, the United States was entitled to a strip of coast one hundred miles deeper than the line of mountains parallel to capes. For Canada the difference was access to the sea.

In the Yukon, which incontrovertibly was Canada's, American prospectors raised the Stars and Stripes and sent mail with U. S. stamps. John J. Healy, the same Montana freebooter who built Fort Whoop-Up in Canada, was in the Yukon in 1896 at Fortymile Creek where he intended to operate a riverboat to bring in American miners.

The small, violent community at Fortymile followed the American frontier tradition and imposed citizen justice. When Healy lost a decision concerning a hired woman, he felt a deep longing for Canadian law and order. He sent a letter to Sam Steele of the North West Mounted Police asking for constables. Steele, chafing under the Mounties' peacetime task of enforcing prohibition, "an insult to free people," passed the request along to Ottawa.

Mounties therefore were on the scene when an American miner, George Washington Carmack, and two Taglish, Skookum Jim and Taglish Charlie, struck gold on April 16, 1896, on a creek that flowed into the Rabbit River, which, in turn, was a tributary of the Klondike. They called their creek Bonanza, which it was, but a fork of the Rabbit, later called Eldorado, was more spectacular; every claim on it was worth at least a half-million dollars.

Word flashed by telegraph around the globe. Within a month, 9,000 frenzied people sailed from Seattle on boats bound for the Alaskan panhandle. In the first year, one million people from all around the world made serious preparations to go to the Klondike; about 100,000 actually went, using every conceivable mode of transportation, including bicycles, the rage of the nineties. A sloop carried 90 Norwegians around the Horn; 200 Australians came from Sydney by steamboat; English peers traveled by yacht with valets to dress them and fine wine to sustain them. Steamship tickets were scalped at $1,500 apiece.

The Canadian government sent a surveyor. Once more, the Canadian border was threatened by Americans. The Mounties summoned the big weapon: Sam Steele.

The Yukon port of entry was Skagway, an American town taken over by a gangster named Soapy Smith. When Sam Steele passed through, noting corpses in alleys and 150 of Smith's armed men fleecing tourists, he described Skagway as "little better than hell on earth." He posted Mounties to guard the Chilkoot Pass between Skagway to the gold fields. On his instructions, no one could climb the Chilkoot through the White Mountains without a customs check and a license issued by the Mounties. The precautions saved the lives of greenhorns who arrived in summer clothing. In winter, temperatures dropped to 40° below and snow drifted sixty feet deep. Mounties collected guns, to the dismay of many Americans who thought a sidearm as necessary as shoes.

Steele reported with satisfaction that "Soapy Smith and his gang dared not show their faces in the Yukon. Everyone went about his business with as strong a sense of security as if he were in the most law-abiding part of the globe."

Strangely, the Yukon was as he described it, law-abiding and peaceful. Though boom towns teemed with gamblers, prostitutes, and swindlers, there was no violence and no stealing, and the Sabbath was observed so strictly a man could be arrested for chopping wood.

Steele established the tone in his handling of the crisis at Lake Bennett, where thousands of would-be miners were jammed above the rapids, waiting for the ice to go. Steele was horrified at makeshift rafts on which people planned to ride the treacherous white water rather than walk the five-mile portage. When Steele arrived, 150 craft already had been smashed and their passengers drowned.

Steele found a high place and addressed the crowd. "There are many of your countrymen who have said that the Mounted Police make the laws as they go along," he announced affably. "I am going to do so now for your own good." By his decree, no women or children rode the rapids and the only boats allowed were those with a pilot licensed by the Mounties. That summer of 1897, 30,000 people traveled the White Horse Rapids without a single loss of life.

Dawson, at the heart of the network of gold-studded creeks, began as a few shacks and in two years was a city of 25,000. On

Sundays an earnest young Presbyterian minister, Robert Dickey, preached a service in the street, standing on a beer barrel. Prostitutes in kimonos lounged on balconies above to hear him.

"It can safely be said that any man, woman or child may walk at any time of the night to any portion of this large camp with as perfect safety from insult as on Sparks Street in Ottawa," Steele bragged. It was true; a miner could leave his poke in an unlocked cabin and return in a month to find the gold untouched.

Tappan Adney, who wrote a book about his experiences as a Klondike stampeder, commented, "There was no real disorder, no shootings, no holdups, none of the things associated with a real live mining camp," yet the Mountie detachment in Dawson consisted of only nine men and a cook.

Most of the Klondike's gold was stripped within three years. Almost $100 million worth found its way to the U. S. Treasury's vaults in Fort Knox. While most countries do not allow foreigners such access to their riches, the Canadian colonial style is passive. A small royalty, based on $15-an-ounce gold, was collected indifferently; in 1980 Canada's royalty on gold was still fixed on a value of $15 an ounce.

The gold strike drew attention to the unresolved dispute about the panhandle border. Teddy Roosevelt, fresh from a Rough Rider charge at San Juan Hill in Cuba and bristling with American triumphs at empire-building, was bullish. An American military machine, ten years in the making, had just taken Puerto Rico from Spain, annexed Hawaii, picked up the Panama Canal, and wiped out Filipino nationalists.

Though some Americans, notably William James and Charles Eliot Norton, professors at Harvard, regretted that America had "taken up her place simply as one of the grasping and selfish nations," Roosevelt pursued a "big stick" policy in the Alaskan panhandle. He sent troops to Alaska in 1903, at which Britain asked hastily for a meeting.

Six men sat down at the Alaskan boundary conference, three from the United States, two from Canada, and one from Britain. The one Englishman voted with the Americans. Outnumbered, Canadians were helpless to prevent the border being moved several hundred miles inland, cutting off half of British Columbia from the sea. Laurier commented that the decision was "one of those concessions which have made British diplomacy odious to Canadian people."

Canada's relations with Britain fluctuated. Laurier's tariff policy giving preference to British goods brought a warm spell. In 1884 Charles Tupper and the irate D'Alton McCarthy were among the founders of the Imperial Federation League, a conference of delegates from British colonies that was hoped to be the basis for free trade and even political federation. The mother country's agenda was somewhat different: Britain wanted the colonies to contribute to the Royal Navy and the standing army. The sessions broke up in a mood of mutual disappointment.

In 1893 there was another crisis in Anglo-Canadian affairs. Britain signed a trade treaty with Germany and Belgium and threw in, for good measure, the preference Canada had voted for British goods. When Canada protested, Britain abruptly lost interest in the Imperial Federation League.

The League resurfaced in 1897, buoyed by the delirious observance of Queen Victoria's sixtieth year on the throne. Laurier attended for Canada what was called the Imperial Conference. Joseph Chamberlain, rising young Colonial Secretary fast outgrowing his socialist youth, chaired the meetings. He stuck to Britain's demand that the members of the Empire help the mother country to defend it. Cried Laurier, whom the Queen had just knighted, "Let the watch fires be lit on the hills and Canada will be the first to respond!"

The watch fires were lit in July 1899, when the British war office asked Canada's governor-general, Lord Minto, for soldiers to fight in South Africa against a Boer uprising. Minto, who served under General Middleton in the Riel campaign, admired Canadians in battle. At his suggestion, three hundred métis and Indians later were hired as pilots on gunboats that took the British Army over the Nile's rapids into the Sudan. He was confident Canadians would respond gladly to the call this time as well.

The South African war, however, was one that divided Britain itself. Many were convinced it was provoked by Cecil Rhodes in order to control South Africa's diamond mines. Liberals in Britain were on the side of Boer independence; so was the German Emperor, confusing his relative, Queen Victoria. When negotiations failed, war broke out in October 1899.

But Canadians wavered. Sam Hughes, forty-five, an Ontario Tory, Orangeman, and militia officer, was a leading hawk in the House of Commons, but he could stir little enthusiasm for a war about which Canadians were uninformed. In January 1900 the issue seemed clearer: The British army had been defeated at Ladysmith.

While Ontario rushed to the flag, Canadiens in Quebéc resisted the call. "We French Canadians belong to one country, Canada," Montréal's *La Presse* declared. "Canada is for us the whole world; but the English Canadians have two countries, one here and one across the sea."

Laurier dared not bring the issue to a vote in parliament, knowing the House would be divided. He used an order-in-council to provide funds to equip a thousand men. For Henri Bourassa, brilliant grandson of Louis-Joseph Papineau and Laurier's likely successor, it was intolerable to send any Canadians to a foreign war. He resigned from Laurier's cabinet.

Donald Smith, wealthy enough from the CPR to afford to buy Canada a regiment, donated the Lord Strathcona's Horse, named for his new title, and hired Sam Steele from the Mounties to lead it. Smith wanted to equip his army with the latest British Army weapon, Lee-Enfield rifles, but Britain refused to sell the guns to colonials.

While Australian and New Zealand volunteers were blended into the British Army, Laurier demanded that Canadians fight together. Canada sent 7,300 men in all to the South African war at a cost of $2.8 million. A British general observed of Steele's unit, "I have never served with a nobler, braver or more serviceable body of men."

Canada's participation in Britain's controversial war broke open old wounds from the hanging of Riel. Ontario and Québec insulted one another. Israel Tarte, who opposed the war, was hanged in effigy in Toronto, and English students in Montréal attacked French-language newspaper offices. Bourassa gave a three-hour speech in the House of Commons, pointing out that a nation with 40 million people was engaged in a war of oppression against 400,000 Boers. Bourassa likened the call for Canadian volunteers to taxation without representation; the war was not Canada's affair, he said. English-speaking Canadians denounced him as a traitor and coward. In 1900 English-speaking women in Montréal indignantly founded a national organization pointedly called the Imperial Order of the Daughters of the Empire, which passed a resolution that Canadian immigration be restricted to those who were "one hundred percent British in language, thought, feeling and impulse."

– 19 –

The Good Years

At the turn of the century, farm families from Europe swarmed to Canada. By 1900 there were 27,000 Ukrainians homesteading on the prairies, people of the steppes who knew how to farm far from water; "stalwart peasants in sheepskin coats," Clifford Sifton called them. The population of Manitoba rose to 225,000 by 1901, and ten years later was almost double that number.

Frail Charles Saunders, the country's patient cerealist, a man who had hoped to spend his life playing the flute and reading French poets, instead entered history as the developer of a strain of wheat that required two weeks less to ripen than Red Fyfe. After years of trying, he developed a strain he called Marquis and it became world famous. By the end of World War I, Marquis wheat added an estimated $100 million to Canadian farm incomes. The London *Daily Express* said of Saunders, "He contributed more to the wealth of his country than any other man."

Passengers packed colonist cars and wheat overflowed freight trains. Railway construction added to the economic boom, putting $775 million in wages and $825 million in materials into Canadian pockets. The government, called upon to bail out railway construction as it had the CPR, found little public opposition. The Canadian Northern received guarantees and the Grand Trunk got cash for a span from Winnipeg to Moncton, New Brunswick.

Factories in Ontario, using the amazing new energy sources of Niagara Falls, churned out consumer goods patterned on products made by their United States parent companies. A shrewd Methodist, Toronto's Timothy Eaton, sent illustrated mail-order catalogues to westerners who spoke no English, and grew rich selling bicycles and stoves from coast to coast.

The longest reign in British history ended when Queen Victoria died in 1901. Her sixty-year-old son became Edward VII. His coronation parade passed under Canada's gift, an arch of prairie wheat costing $33,000 inscribed BRITAIN'S GRANARY. Canada's immigration office in Charing Cross Road helped recruit 65,000 British farmers in a five-year period.

Europe's economy slumped in 1907 and the style of British immigrant changed. Instead of farmers, Canada received unemployed young men by the thousands, many of trade-union background and unsettling to Canadian employers. The west flowered with signs, NO ENGLISH NEED APPLY.

Sifton's immigration campaigns worked wonders. Saskatoon was a general store on the South Saskatchewan River in 1900, a village if you counted the shacks in 1902, a town in 1903, and a city in 1910. The optimism of railway promoters was contagious. British investors plunged in backing Mann and Mackenzie's Canadian Northern, which needed an additional $200 million, and Laurier again bailed out the Grand Trunk, in shock at the cost of laying duplicate tracks north of Lake Superior.

In response to demands from the Northwest Territory, boundaries were moved and in 1905 Saskatchewan and Alberta were made provinces. Edmonton was selected as Alberta's capital. The city had grown so quickly that the new parliament building rose within sight of a decayed Hudson's Bay Company post.

For the first time in the country's history, more people came to Canada than left. In the first decade after the turn of the century, the population rose a third, from four million to six million.

Laurier, re-elected in 1904, faced another confrontation over French-language Catholic schools in the west. Alberta and Saskatchewan insisted on their right to curtail minority education as Manitoba had. Laurier didn't dare ask the Privy Council in Britain to uphold the Canadian Constitution, but again tried "the sunny way" of negotiation. When it proved hopeless, he backed off, issuing some vaguely worded order that parochial schools were desirable and should be provided.

Clifford Sifton resigned from the cabinet in protest. The Conservative leader, Robert Borden, a Halifax lawyer who in 1901 succeeded Charles Tupper, thundered that Laurier was interfering with the rights of the provinces. Ontario's politically powerful Orange societies were agitated. Laurier feared Liberals would lose English-Canadian support and become isolated in Québec. He took back a promise to protect Catholic schools and allowed Alberta and Saskatchewan to do as they pleased about education.

Laurier's most powerful foe in Québec, Henri Bourassa, commented sadly, "I regret to find developing the feeling that Canada is not Canada for all Canadians. We are bound to come to the conclusion that Québec is our only country because we have no liberty elsewhere." French-language newspapers pointed out that Sifton had opened Canada's doors to people of every faith except Roman Catholic, and every nationality except French.

Bourassa's alienation from the federal Liberals was complete. When Laurier cut off Bourassa's access to patronage, he was politically dead. Bourassa's speeches about French identity grew more strident; Laurier seemed more anti-French. When a Québec Liberal, Armand Lavergne, introduced a bill in Commons calling for bilingual stamps and currency, Laurier disowned him.

Canada's immigration policy discouraged all Catholics save those from Ireland, who could not be excluded because they were sent by Britain. The country also took a hard line against nonwhites. Blacks descended from freed slaves had settled around Halifax in Nova Scotia and Chatham in Ontario. Welcomed at first because they were a reproof to the United States, Canadian good will soon wore thin. Blacks were subjected to segregation and abuse. Black Americans migrating to the west were advised to leave: the climate was too rigorous, they were told.

Laurier, anxious to help the railways secure cheap labor, repeatedly disallowed British Columbia's attempts to bar Chinese immigration. When Dunsmuir was made lieutenant-governor of the province, he disallowed such bills himself. The Dunsmuir mines were humming with Chinese workers on half pay. In 1907 Canada allowed 400 Chinese into the country; in 1911, there were 12,000 Chinese immigrants. British Columbia called it "the yellow peril." A fast-rising maritime lawyer, Richard Bedford Bennett, a lawyer for the CPR, won voters by declaring, "British Columbia must remain a white man's country."

East Indians presented a delicate problem since they came with British passports. Laurier created legislation to deal with them. Since ships from India were obliged to stop at Hawaii for supplies, he decreed that no immigrants would be accepted if they made a stop during the voyage.

The forces of racial purity were often at odds with millionaires. When Laurier sent a delegation to Tokyo to ask Japan to contain emigration to Canada to 400 persons a year, it discovered the CPR had retained the Nippon Supply Company to send Japanese workers to Canada by the thousands.

The CPR and other eastern-based cartels continued to fleece western farmers. To meet protests, CPR freight rates were reduced on certain goods by the Crow's Nest Pass agreement of 1897 for which the CPR received $4 million and other government help as compensation. The problem of eastern-owned grain elevators remained. Five companies controlled almost all elevators in the west and set storage prices by agreement. In 1902 angry farmers formed the Territorial Grain Growers' Association. A founder, William Richard Motherwell, said grimly, "The day has gone by for remaining scattered, unbanded communities."

One third of the groaning harvest of the previous year was in elevators awaiting shipment. Motherwell heard men saying, "It's too late for organizing. It's bullets we want." A schoolteacher analyzed the problem. In Canada, bigness counted: The Hudson's Bay Company and the CPR and the grain elevator cartel were illustrations. Therefore, E. A. Partridge explained, farmers needed bigness on their side: The government should control grain elevators and grain terminals.

The Conservatives, looking for western support, took up the cause. In 1910 the Tory government of Manitoba launched a program to nationalize grain elevators. Two years later authority to operate the elevators was given to a farmers' organization, the Grain Growers' Grain Company, created by Partridge, and another rural schoolteacher, Thomas Alexander Crerar. Saskatchewan and Alberta followed with the same blend of government funding and collective control. The Saskatchewan Grain Growers' Association, most militant of farmers' groups, grew to a membership of more than one thousand.

The movement's voice was the *Grain Growers' Guide,* edited by Partridge and steeped in Methodist social gospel. Two clergymen, William Ivens and James Shaver Woodsworth, were leading contributors who filled pages with the doctrine of Christianity as a force for redistribution of wealth. Laurier's "economic imperialism," they said, was causing Ontario to grow at the expense of the west.

Canadians basked in the accomplishments of the Massey-Harris farm implement company, builder of the most advanced harvesting machinery in the world. They claimed a part of the glory for the invention of the telephone by Alexander Graham Bell in Brantford, Ontario, although Canadians had refused to invest money in his gadget. A young New Brunswick promoter, Max Aitken, later knighted as Sir Max and later still made Lord Beaverbrook, was in Montréal in 1907 putting together such mergers as the Canada Cement Company, the Steel Company of Canada, the Canadian Car and Foundry Company, the Dominion Steel and Coal Company, and the Royal Securities Company, all of which brought him sufficient wealth in time to purchase the world's largest newspaper, the London *Daily Express*.

Canada's preference for bigness—big government and big monopolies—reduced diversity and competition. In 1911, 196 Canadian firms merged into forty-one. Gustavus Myers, an American journalist and muckraker who studied the period, later estimated that fewer than fifty men in Canada controlled $4 billion in holdings. Almost all the family wealth could be traced back to the fur trade, timber, and railways.

Low wages and the growing population attracted investors. Early in the century, British financial houses sunk $2 billion in Canada, plunging it in railways, business, and construction. The United States, on the other hand, preferred ownership to investment: with three hundred Canadian branch plants worth a half billion returning profits to the States, Americans were beginning to take an interest in minerals as well. Provinces eagerly pursued purchasers, offering as inducement free land, cheap timber leases, low royalties, tax breaks, and harsh control of labor organizers.

Public protest was confined to the most visible monopolies, such as Bell Telephone, which placed telephone poles wherever it pleased without regard to traffic patterns or aesthetics. When the importance of hydropower was realized in 1903, citizens opposed to more unsightly power lines created a movement for public control of Niagara's hydroelectric generators. Adam Beck, a cigar-box manufacturer in London, Ontario, led the fight and was elected to the Ontario legislature, where he and the Conservative government of Premier James Whitney withstood bribes, slander, intrigue, and court battles to make Ontario hydro publicly owned.

The country's humorists dared to poke fun at men in power. The most irreverent was Bob Edwards, editor of the Calgary *Eye-Opener* which enjoyed the largest circulation in the west. The front page featured photographs of CPR derailments and collisions. On quiet days, headlines proclaimed THERE WERE NO CPR WRECKS THIS WEEK. When the CPR's lawyer, R. B. Bennett, banned the paper from railway newsvendors, Edwards ran a picture of Bennett with the caption, ANOTHER CPR WRECK.

Westerners were bonded on hatred of the east, home of fat profiteers. Farmers followed the newspaper columns of such respected radicals as the Methodist intellectual Salem Bland, whose concept of justice was shaped by the Fabians and Karl Marx. Frustrated urban workers learned organizing from young Brits who had formed trade unions in their native country.

The American west was experiencing a similar wage of agrarian populism and labor unrest. Conservative Samuel Gompers faced rebellion within his AFL for his too-affable relations with owners, as Joe Hill's radical Industrial Workers of the World, the Wobblies, were gaining support in the west. In 1902 a meeting of union leaders in Berlin, Ontario, later renamed Kitchener, resulted in a purge by the AFL of its critics. The exiles formed a new group, the Canadian Labour Federation, which appeared to have little hope against the giant AFL.

Strikes swept the country. The American-led union, the United Brotherhood of Railway Employees, struck against the Canadian Northern when Mann and Mackenzie cut wages and extended the workday. In Winnipeg, 10,000 workers marched in sympathy. The next year the UBRE went on strike in Vancouver against the CPR, which was paying the lowest wages in the railway industry. When a CPR policeman killed a sympathizer in Montréal, a wave of strikes followed. The American AFL ordered rebellious Canadians to return to work or lose their charter.

In Québec, the church's opposition to labor unions was weakening in face of killing conditions in mills and factories. When a few priests in 1902 sided with striking employees of a shoe factory who wanted a safer workplace, the ground was broken for a startling alliance between the Catholic church and labor unions.

In Toronto a young sociologist gained fame for a series of newspaper articles exposing abuses in sweat shops in the garment industry. He was William Lyon Mackenzie King, grandson and namesake of the rebel of Upper Canada, a small, fussy, precise man who later seemed a creditable choice to head a Royal Commission into labor problems.

King's report took a middle ground, condemning both owners indifferent to the lives of workers and militant union leaders. His central recommendation was that the federal government take authority for suppressing strikes and enforcing settlements. Laurier offered King a civil service job in the federal labor department, and later, in 1908, urged him to run for office as a Liberal candidate. After his election, King became Minister of Labor.

The federal government took a heavy hand in fighting labor unions. When miners struck in 1909 in Cape Breton, Laurier sent the army to stop the strike. In Port Arthur, Ontario, police shot two coal handlers, the Deprenzo brothers. The men survived despite twelve bullet wounds and were sent to prison for ten years. King stepped in with legislation forbidding strikes in critical industries. This ended a strike by Alberta coal miners. Balancing the scales, King gave workers legislation forbidding management to fire work forces for trying to organize unions.

Sometimes the federal government used its paramilitary police, the Mounties, to settle disputes. The Trades and Labour Congress complained in 1906 that the RNWMP was "an annex to corporations and companies."

Nevertheless, the country's mood was ebullient and confident. The age of inventions dazzled the world and Canada was not left behind. Guglielmo Marchese Marconi received the world's first transatlantic telegraph message in St. John's, Newfoundland. Manitoba wheat won first prize at the Pan-American Exposition. Horseless carriages were the rage, necessitating speed limits to control recklessness: seven miles an hour. A tiny man who adored bicycles, Samuel McLaughlin of Oshawa, Ontario, son of a prosperous carriage maker, went into partnership with David Buick, an American, to mass-produce the McLaughlin-Buick automobile, ahead of Henry Ford and his wonderful Model T. McLaughlin later sold his company to the American conglomerate, General Motors, and became a multi-millionaire on the proceeds. Asked what was the world's greatest invention, he replied, "Interest."

Railroad gangs working in northern Ontario in 1903 accidentally discovered lunar rock veined with silver. Pieces as large as "stove-lids or cannonballs" lay on the ground. In 1904 Cobalt was a boom town, shipping out silver ore. Because silver was so accessible, agents from Guggenheim and Rockefeller arrived too late to get in on the ground floor. A farmer viewing the excitement over a piece of silver ore remembered where he had seen pink rock like it. He walked a few miles, found the spot, and staked a claim worth $2.5 million. Benny Hollinger, nineteen, stumbled over a nearby vein of gold. When he got it into production, his Dome mine yielded $1 million a month.

Alexander Graham Bell, flying kites in the high winds off the Atlantic at Baddeck, Cape Breton, was dreaming of air travel. He persuaded a New York motorcycle fanatic, Glenn Curtiss, to consider attaching an engine to his giant kites. President Teddy Roosevelt, interested in the military possibilities of aviation, lent the services of Thomas Selfridge of the U. S. Field Artillery. In 1907, Arthur McCurdy, twenty-one, a local engineer, joined them.

In 1908 they formed the Aerial Experiment Association. The Americans left, Selfridge later becoming the first person to die in an airplane crash, but Bell and McCurdy continued work on a lighter-than-air craft. In 1909 McCurdy climbed into a two-seat airplane with the world's first water-cooled engine. Romantically called the *Silver Dart,* McCurdy flew it on a bright February day for a mile at an altitude of thirty feet. Schoolchildren cheered as the *Silver Dart* lifted off the ground, the first manned flight in the British Empire: flown by a Canadian, designed by Canadians, built by Canadians.

McCurdy demonstrated the *Silver Dart* to the Canadian Army, which was not impressed. McCurdy flew at country fairs, hurling oranges at a white sheet to show that airplanes could drop bombs.

His vision of the airplane as a military weapon reflected the world's growing preoccupation with war. Germany's high-quality steel mills and brilliant engineers were producing a navy to rival Britain's. Joseph Chamberlain, British Colonial Secretary, renewed efforts to have the Empire help the Royal Navy. "The weary Titan staggers under the too-vast orb of fate," he intoned. "We think it is time that our children should assist us."

Laurier was unmoved. Nothing was more perfectly calculated for mischief than to ask French-Canadians to pay for the Royal Navy. Henri Bourassa was swaying thousands in Québec with his talk of French independence. He had a new target: British and American industrialists who paid Canadiens half the wages of their equivalents in Ontario factories.

The Catholic Church worried that French-Canadians were being drawn into an English Protestant environment that would corrupt their faith. Jules Paul Tardivel, editor of *La Verité,* which staunchly supported the church, wrote, "It is not necessary for us to possess industry and money. Our mission is to possess the earth and spread ideas." Québec's schools, operated by the clergy, served the church's hope that French Catholics would stay away from English-dominated cities. Stressing dogma and piety, they tended to turn out illiterates who couldn't compete for skilled jobs. Even higher education, reserved for sons of elite Canadiens, produced classical scholars rather than engineers, economists, or scientists.

Though Laurier won the election of 1908, support for the federal Liberals was weakening. Robert Borden's Conservatives swept Manitoba, Nova Scotia, and British Columbia. To win friends in the most western province, Laurier sought to tighten Asian immigration. He asked Britain to furnish him with relevant documents, since Canada lacked any files on matters outside the Empire. Britain replied that British policy on Japanese immigration was none of Canada's business.

The rejection brought to a head a long-standing irritation with British dominance of Canadian foreign affairs, especially those concerning Canada's neighbor, the United States. Communications went by a route described by the governor-general: "Laurier approaches me, I pass on his communication to the Colonial Office, the Colonial Office passes it to the Foreign Office, the Foreign Office to the British Ambassador in Washington, who calls the Secretary of State—and the answer comes back via this long circuitous route to Laurier."

Laurier took the brazen step in 1908 of establishing in offices

over a barber shop what he called the Department of External
Affairs, a euphemism for Foreign Office he hoped would avoid
offending Britain.

By March 1909 the British House of Commons considered a
report that the Kaiser's navy would be more powerful than the
Royal Navy in three years. Canadians loyal to the Crown urged
Laurier to buy a dreadnought or two to help meet the threat.
Laurier suggested instead that Canada build its own navy and
make it available if war broke.

Lord Minto warned Britain before leaving his post as governor-
general in Canada that Laurier "dreams of Canadian independence in a future age." Minto and the Colonial Office were
distressed when Laurier insisted on replacing British commanders of Canada's militia with Canadians. His Naval Bill, introduced in January 1910, was another slight. Laurier proposed
that Canada build its own fleet, five cruisers and six destroyers,
and recruit 3,000 sailors.

Laurier assured Conservatives, "When Britain is at war, Canada is at war. There is no distinction." He had misjudged the
Tories, who found the bill cheeky and tacky. "A tin-pot navy,"
they jeered. Bourassa's *nationalistes* were suspicious that Canada
was readying for a foreign war. Bourassa launched a fighting
newspaper, Montréal's *Le Devoir,* to carry his views. Two supporters, Olivar Asselin and Jules Fournier, went to prison for crit-
icizing the Naval Bill in the radical journal, *Le Nationaliste.*

When Québécois in the House of Commons asked for a plebiscite, English-speaking Canadians furiously defeated the motion,
charging it was treasonous.

The debate overlapped another raw dispute between Ontario
and Québec. When French-speaking parents in Ontario requested
that schools attended by their children be bilingual, even Irish
Catholics fought them. Protesters paraded under the banner, "ONE
SCHOOL, ONE LANGUAGE, ONE FLAG," as much of Ontario called
for a ban on the French language in all schools.

When the Naval Bill passed on April 20, 1910, in the House of
Commons, Québec erupted. *Nationalistes* in the Québec legislature passed a bill requiring the public service to be bilingual
rather than only English. Bourassa counseled calm and moderation. Asselin and Fournier, dismayed at their chief's new mel-

lowness, left *Le Devoir* in disgust and founded a new radical separatist publication, *L'Action Sociale*.

Laurier made a personal inspection of the west, the first Canadian prime minister to travel the country in twenty-five years, and realized that complaints about high tariffs were justified: the cost of manufactured goods from Ontario was outrageous. He sent the Minister of Finance, W. S. Fielding, to Washington to confer with U. S. President William Howard Taft on a reduced tariff wall. Taft offered free trade, which was more than the Liberals dared to accept without losing votes in central Canada.

They drew up an interim step, a draft proposal to maintain the tariff on manufactured goods but allow free trade on natural products such as wheat. At first, it appealed to both Liberals and Conservatives. Tory strategists gradually cooled, worried that it would lead to total reciprocity and ruin Canadian industry.

The Canadian Manufacturers' Association led the protest with an Anti-Reciprocity League. Hugh Graham, rock-ribbed monarchist and anti-American, put $250,000 and the resources of his Montréal *Star* into the fight. Van Horne of the CPR declared he was "out to bust the damned thing." Even Liberal businessmen in Ontario cities came to believe that reciprocity would destroy them.

"VOTE AGAINST NATIONAL SUICIDE," the Conservatives urged. George Foster, a loyal Tory, contributed the phrase, "No Truck or Trade with the Yankees." Sam Hughes in full militia uniform gave speeches about patriotism, the king, the Union Jack, and the motherland. Clifford Sifton turned against his fellow Liberals and announced that reciprocity would close factories and throw thousands of eastern Canadians out of work. Hope for the pact dimmed when the Speaker of the U. S. Congress, Champ Clark, declared that free trade with Canada would lead to the day "when the American flag will float over every square foot of the British North American possessions clear to the North Pole."

Mourned Laurier, white-haired and frail: "I am branded in Québec as a traitor to the French, and in Ontario as a traitor to the English. In Québec I am branded a jingo, and in Ontario a separatist. In Québec I am attacked as an imperialist, and in Ontario as an anti-imperialist. I am neither. I am a Canadian. Canada has been the inspiration of my life."

Laurier, the Liberals, and reciprocity were destroyed in the federal election of 1911. Québec turned against a native son for the first and last time and voted Tory. The west supported the Liberals, but could not outweigh Conservative majorities in central Canada. Robert Borden became prime minister by 134 seats to 86.

The following year Ontario passed Regulation 17, abolishing French in schools. Borden did nothing, knowing the Privy Council wouldn't support the Constitution. When Borden extended Manitoba's borders south to James Bay, an area which took in the predominantly métis community in Keewatin, Québec was dismayed that he didn't try to protect métis schools. Québécois asked him to repeal the Naval Bill. He refused. Tory stock was sunk in Québec.

That year a novel, *Maria Chapdelaine,* written by a Belgian, Louis Hémon, was the rage of Québec. Its appeal came from passages that spoke of French survival and the Québec condition in confederation, such as: "Round about us foreigners came, that we please to call barbarians; they have taken almost all power; they have acquired almost all the money."

— 20 —

The War
to End Wars

In 1913 Canada's Tory prime minister, Robert Borden, met with a young, pugnacious First Lord of the Admiralty, Winston Churchill. Churchill told him that war with the Kaiser was imminent; he asked Canada to donate dreadnoughts. Borden outlined Laurier's plan for a Canadian fleet, owned and manned by Canadians, that would fight with the Royal Navy. Churchill replied that the Navy lacked only big ships, and Canadians were not competent to sail them.

A subdued Borden introduced a Naval Bill in the House of Commons in December. He asked approval to spend $35 million to give dreadnoughts to the Royal Navy. Laurier, leader of the Liberal opposition, demanded a plebiscite; Borden refused. The Liberals filibustered for six months while the Tories sang "Rule Britannia." In the end, Conservatives voted for the bill and the Senate, filled with Laurier appointees, killed it.

Canadian immigration peaked in 1913 with 400,000 pouring into the country. A substantial proportion were young single men from British factory jobs, laid off because of an unexpected slump in the economy. Most went west to find work bringing in the harvest or building railways. Vancouver was growing at a thousand people a month but cities on the prairies collapsed. In Edmonton in 1911 city building lots were sold for $2,000 a front foot; in 1913, 75,000 undeveloped lots were returned for unpaid taxes. For years after, Edmonton's downtown core was a field of weeds.

The Grand Trunk and the Canadian Northern appealed for more money. Failure of the Mann and Mackenzie line would bring down the Canadian Bank of Commerce as well. Borden was forced to grant more guarantees and another $30 million cash.

The Canadian Manufacturers' Association met in Halifax in 1913 and estimated that Canada's railways had cost taxpayers $50,000 for every mile. A small, poor country of only seven million people had supported the cost of three massive railway systems. In the process, the railways drained the country of money, drained its nerve for investment, drained its spunk. Railways left Canadians with a debtor's mentality, sad hoarders who fear financial risk.

Railway layoffs and a sag in construction put unemployed on the streets. In 1913 Ontario had 200,000 men looking for work; in Québec there were 130,000. Rupert Brooke, a poet, visited the two provinces and marveled that their people were so divided.

He wrote, "A stranger is startled by the complete separateness of the two races. Inter-marriage is very rare. They do not meet socially; only in business, and that not often. In the same city these two communities dwell side by side, with different traditions, different languages, different ideals."

As Europe edged closer to war, Borden made Sam Hughes Minister of Militia and Defense. Hughes, the most bellicose politician in the House of Commons, opened with a charge that Canadiens were cowards unfit for military service. By his order the French-speaking 65th Battalion paraded without guns.

Borden approached Woodrow Wilson, President of the United States, and asked for Laurier's 1911 free-trade arrangement, partial reciprocity for farm products. Negotiations necessitated closer contact with Washington, so Borden beefed up the Department of External Affairs.

Then came the assassination at Sarajevo in June 1914. In the escalation that followed, Sam Hughes flew a Union Jack at half-mast in his office, smarting at Britain's slowness to get into action. On August 5, he was thrilled when Britain declared war on Germany. H. G. Wells, British novelist and utopian, also rejoiced. "This, the greatest of all wars, is not just another war—it is the last war!" he cried. "The war that will end war!"

Borden summoned his cabinet and sent a telegram promising Canadians for the British Army. When Britain was at war, Canada was at war. He passed an order-in-council, the War Measures Act, giving himself power of censorship, peremptory arrest and imprisonment, deportation of suspected enemies of the state without trial, and confiscation of property.

The Canadian Navy possessed only two cruisers, which were turned over to the Royal Navy. One, HMCS *Rainbow,* was fresh from a shabby incident in Vancouver harbor where a Japanese ship, *Komagata Maru,* was forbidden to unload 376 Sikhs. By making the voyage directly from India, the Sikhs had complied with the letter of Canadian immigration laws but not the intent. The Canadian cruiser forced the *Komagata Maru* to sail away with all passengers, and British Columbia's premier bought two brand new submarines in Seattle to defend his coast.

Britain took for granted that a declaration of war at Westminster included the entire Empire. The official statement began, "Considering the state of war now existing between the United Kingdom and the Dominions, colonies and dependencies of the British Empire on the one hand and Germany on the other . . ."

The Canadian parliament convened on August 18, 1914. In the first minute the Conservative majority approved a military bill to send 25,000 men to fight the Kaiser. The first to enlist were jobless and homesick men from Britain who had been in Canada less than a year. They were given rudimentary training in a tent camp at Valcartier in Québec and within weeks were in troop ships on the Atlantic. Of the 32,665 men in the oversubscribed first division of the Canadian Expeditionary Force, 64 percent were British-born. By April they were with the British Army in the trenches of France and Belgium.

The sector assigned to the colonies was one of the most exposed parts of the line, a thumb extended into the German trenches near the Belgian town of Ypres. After a winter of shelling, the fields around were barren of vegetation or trees, a nightmare of mudholes in which a company could drown. An officer of the Canadian Engineers examined unprotected ditches in which soldiers lived and found them "paved with rotting bodies and human excreta."

Only days after the Canadians reached Ypres, on April 22, 1915, Germany tested a new weapon of war, chlorine gas. Though British intelligence was aware of its threat, no masks had been issued. Algerians on the Canadian left flank choked in the ghastly green-yellow fog and fled, leaving a three-mile gap through which

Germans attacked with fixed bayonets. Even so, Canadians held the position and in twelve hours suffered 6,000 casualties.

"The Canadians made a stand which was to be remembered as one of the heroic episodes of the war," an American correspondent wrote. The British prime minister, David Lloyd George, saw a use for colonials. "Henceforth," he said, "the Canadians were marked as storm troops."

The news from the front was cheerful. War correspondents who described the reality frequently were jailed. By the spring of 1915 France had lost a quarter of its army, 300,000. Some 60,000 young men died at Ypres alone in April.

Henri Bourassa's *Le Devoir* departed from the joyfully patriotic mood of English newspapers and described the war as "a cooperative crime." Ontario retorted that French-Canadians were shirkers, an untruth. They were enlisting despite Sam Hughes, who vetoed all-French regiments and put French-Canadian volunteers in English-speaking regiments. When the first French-speaking regiment, the Royal 22nd, was authorized over his objections, the ranks filled immediately.

As Bourassa was quick to note, Sam Hughes was surrounded by "boodlers, vampires, the furnishers of bribes and electoral funds." Assorted swindlers and other opportunists descended upon the portly Minister of Militia and Defense looking for military contracts. Though Hughes's devotion to the Empire was above reproach, his judgment was not. He adored the Ross rifle. It was a gun known to jam in continuous use, but it had his blessing. A hundred thousand were distributed to Canadian soldiers who used them at Ypres as clubs.

Soldiers took British Lee-Enfields from the dead, of which there was no short supply. Sir Douglas Haig, the British commander-in-chief, a man some regard as the most bloody officer of this century, once released chlorine gas on a windless day, so that it hung over the British trenches and killed or maimed his own.

In the spring of 1916, 3,000 Canadians were casualties in a suicidal attack on a mound near Saint Éloi. In June of that summer of madness, they were shock troops again at Mount Sorrel, where casualties were 8,000. Then they died in the poppy fields of Flanders and John McCrae, a doctor from Guelph, Ontario, wrote a grieving poem that still makes Canadians weep.

The slaughter extended to the Atlantic where German submarines terrorized shipping. In May 1915, a British luxury liner, *Lusitania,* was sunk without warning off the coast of Ireland with a loss of 1,195 lives, 128 Americans. The incident was used to inflame sentiments in the United States against the Kaiser. Woodrow Wilson wrote a note to the German emperor in such strong language that the U. S. Secretary of State, William Jennings Bryan, resigned in protest.

Bourassa reported on the fortunes being made by munitions manufacturers. In 1916 the American Bethehem Steel Company had profits of $50 million, tax free. Du Pont's profits from the sale of gunpowder increased 200 percent.

Bourassa was making a speech in Ottawa before a hostile audience of jeering soldiers one evening when a sergeant mounted the stage, handed him a Union Jack, and ordered him to wave it. A hush fell as Bourassa put the flag down. He said steadily, "I am ready to wave the British flag in liberty, but I shall not do so under threats." An alert stage manager lowered the curtain and saved Bourassa from the crowd's wrath.

Borden dropped some French-Canadians from his cabinet; they were political liabilities. The House of Commons was churning out military bills as large as $100 million and men were pouring into the army. In 1915, 180,000 enlisted. Women handed white feathers to men still in civilian clothes.

But a third call for recruits was disappointing. With the young Brits gone, quotas set by Sam Hughes were unrealistic. Many Canadians preferred to stay home and enjoy the bliss of full employment as the country's 250 munitions factories worked around the clock and farm work was considered an essential service. Hughes clung to the Ross rifle. When an officer complained that at Saint Éloi frantic soldiers had cut and broken their hands trying to unjam the bolt, Hughes fired the man.

"To win an argument with Hughes, all you needed was a resolute will, a clear mind, a thick skin, and a detachable head," commented Ralph Allen, a war historian of rare gifts.

It took the combined efforts of the governor-general, the prime minister of Canada, General Haig of the Imperial Army, the Imperial Privy Council, and British Colonial Secretary Bonar Law to persuade Sam Hughes to give up the Ross rifle. That done, Borden sacked Hughes.

The Somme campaign ended in only fractional movement. The 140-day battle conceived by General Haig caused more than a million casualties. It began on July 1, 1916, a bright, beautiful morning. By Haig's order, soldiers rose from the trenches and marched as though on parade, rifles at high port, across No Man's Land. Amazed German machine-gunners raked lines that advanced all day, one row of men in khaki followed by another row of men in khaki, row upon row upon row. The sun set on 60,000 British casualties. In northern France graveyards still stretch white crosses as far as the eye can see, each inscribed, *July 1, 1916*. A Newfoundland regiment went to its death that day: of 6,000 men alive and whole in the morning, only 2,000 escaped.

Still the attack continued. When 23,000 Australians and New Zealanders fell, the line was plugged on September 4, 1916, by Canadians. They found a battlefield waist-deep in slime and decomposed corpses, 7,000 dead men per square mile.

Haig ordered an attack on the artillery-blasted village of Courcelette and put Canadians in the spearhead. With the French-speaking Royal 22nd leading, they took Courcelette at bayonet-point, the only victory of the Somme offensive. When the deadly folly was over, 26,000 Canadians were casualties.

The generals asked for more men. Casualty rolls shocked Canada, but in Ontario there was still passion for the cause of king and country. The country was running out of volunteers. Orangemen accused French-Canadians of letting the rest of the country's manhood do all the fighting. Québec, still sizzling over Ontario's Regulation 17 closing French schools, was bitter. Philippe Landry, Speaker of the Senate, snapped, "We shall ask the Mother Country if our children have no other rights than to go and be killed in the service of the Empire."

Landry collected 600,000 signatures on a petition begging Borden to revoke the Ontario school-closing legislation. Laurier added sadly, "Will you refuse us the privilege of education in the language of our mothers and fathers?" The issue was put to vote in the House of Commons, where Borden's refusal to act was upheld. Laurier's Liberals from Ontario threatened to support the Conservatives but their leader warned he would resign if they did.

Of the 250,000 recruits Britain wanted from Canada after the Somme, only 180,000 enlisted. Ontario demanded conscription to fill the quota. Factories fired men to force them into the army and hired women. A British suffragette, Emily Pankhurst, toured Canada making patriotic speeches to women, whom she urged to remind men of their duty.

Pressed by Britain to send more men to the front, Borden called for registration of all men between eighteen and sixty-five as a first step toward conscription. Though the Constitution required a federal election, he declared it would be postponed because of the national emergency. He met Britain's prime minister, Lloyd George, in March 1917, and was invited to sit with the British War Cabinet, a Canadian first. Jan Smuts of South Africa, who also attended, agreed with Borden that the colonies should become involved in British foreign policy relating to themselves. Laurier commented skeptically in the Manchester *Guardian* that Britain hadn't agreed to anything except to listen.

Early in 1917 Canadians were dying at the front in greater numbers than they were enlisting at home. In April they faced Vimy Ridge, an escarpment seven miles long, an anchor of the German line. The Allies regarded it as impregnable. Germans had honeycombed the rocky face with gun emplacements and interconnecting tunnels leading to dining halls, sleeping quarters, and hospitals. Canadians were ordered to take Vimy Ridge.

The attack began before dawn on a freezing Easter morning. Above their heads, other Canadians were involved in the world's first airplane battle. The Royal Flying Corps, a gentlemen's club early in the war entranced with an ideal of honorable conduct and restricted to observing enemy artillery and troop movement, had lost most of its gallant heroes. A new breed, half of them Canadians, went grimly into the sky to fight.

Four divisions of Canadians advanced through snow and sleet toward Vimy, cut through three lines of German trenches, and by mid-morning took the high ground leaving on the gory field 13,000 dead or wounded. "They send us on every forlorn hope," an officer wrote home.

"I hope conscription may not be necessary," Borden said. He inspected the front and in May 1917 announced he would ask parliament to endorse conscription. The United States had entered the war a month earlier. To put an army into the field quickly, Woodrow Wilson ordered Americans to register for the draft. Canada, wrung dry of volunteers, followed Wilson's example. Canadiens violently protested in Montréal, Québec, and Hull and riots caused heavy damage to downtown property.

The Conscription Bill was introduced in June. As Laurier feared, Liberals were split: Québécois lined up with him against the bill, but English-speaking Liberals were for it. By a vote of 102 to 44, English against French, the bill passed in the House of Commons and was approved in the Senate.

Québec boiled with talk of separatism, revolution, and annexation to the United States. In July, 15,000 people in Québec listened as Armand Renaud Lavergne, a Bourassa lieutenant, cried, "If the conscription law is enforced, Canadians have only one choice—to die in Europe or to die in Canada. As far as I am concerned, if my body is to fall on any land, I want it to be on Canadian soil." Arch-monarchist Hugh Graham, owner of the Montréal *Star,* was victim of a bombing of his home. There was a rumor that French-Canadians would assassinate Borden.

General Haig planned his next campaign. In recognition of Canada's contribution, a Canadian was chosen to lead the next Allied assault. He was Arthur Currie, forty-two, a former Vancouver school teacher. His target was Passchendaele, five miles from Vimy. When Haig showed the battle plan to Lloyd George, the prime minister shuddered at prospects of "a ghastly casualty list."

Haig tried cavalry and a relatively new weapon, tanks. Both were mired hopelessly in mud as rain fell steadily for four days and nights. Haig lost a half million men in a futile four months of effort before he abandoned the assault.

Borden meanwhile assembled a Union government which included Liberals who voted for conscription, among them Clifford Sifton. The coalition prepared for a federal election; against them were French-Canadians, standing alone with Laurier. Bourassa returned to his old friend's side to face certain defeat. The Union government campaigned with a vicious slogan, "A vote for Laurier is a vote for the Kaiser." In a country which had suffered heavy casualties, with 6 percent of its total population in uniform, the accusation had devastating effect.

The Church of England declared it was the "sacred duty" of Anglicans to vote Union. French-Canadians said the country had suffered enough and in Québec there were banners *Vive la Révolution!* Even priests signed a statement protesting that "our sons and brothers are sent to the European butchery like so many cattle." English-Canada wasn't united, however, in support of conscription. In the west, farmers fought to protect their sons from being drafted.

Borden, ill, was replaced by an acting prime minister, Arthur Meighen, a silver-tongued speaker second only to Laurier. To assure victory for the Union government, Meighen manipulated the franchise shamelessly. Women were allowed to vote if they had a son, husband, or brother in the armed forces. Immigrants from the Austro-Hungarian Empire lost their vote in case they were disloyal.

In October Canadians were fighting in Passchendaele in bottomless mud that swallowed living men and horses. In one day's action, nine Canadians won the Victoria Cross, the Empire's highest decoration for courage. One, Sergeant Robert Hanna, took command when every officer in his company was dead. In the end Canadians played a major role in the victory at Passchendaele that saw 15,000 Germans taken prisoner.

"If people really knew, the war would be stopped tomorrow," Lloyd George confided to the editor of the Manchester *Guardian*. "But of course they don't know and can't know. The correspondents don't write, and the censorship would not pass the truth."

When the vote came, Canadians overwhelmingly supported conscription. Of Québec's 65 seats in the legislature, 62 seats went to Laurier's anti-conscription Liberals. The Union government included not one French-Canadian.

Québec's despair at being shut out of power aroused ancestral fears that found a champion in a priest, Abbé Lionel Groulx, son of a lumberjack. Groulx was professor of Canadian history at the Université de Montréal, where ardent young nationalists drank in his potent blend of Canadien history, fantasy, piety, and racism.

The draft sent 20,000 conscripted men to the front. A British general who saw the battlefield wept. "Good God," he said, "did we really send men to fight in that?"

The glamorous part of the war was in the sky. When Britain's reckless young ace Albert Ball died at the age of twenty after destroying forty-three German planes, the new idol of the RFC was a Canadian, Billy Bishop, an indifferent pilot but a superb shot. The small young man from Owen Sound ferociously shot down seventy-two planes, five in a single day, to become the leading Allied ace.

Bishop was one of ten thousand Canadians who served in what became the Royal Air Force. The "colonials" showed a natural affinity for solitary combat. Another, Roy A. Brown, was credited with shooting down the great German ace, Baron von Richthofen, known as the Red Baron, and still another, Billy Barker, distinguished himself by fighting alone against sixty Fokkers, six of which he destroyed although his left arm was shattered by bullets and he was wounded in both legs. Another, Stuart Culley, flew a Sopwith Camel four thousand feet higher than it was designed to go and shot down a zeppelin.

On December 6, 1917, North America experienced the worst tragedy of the war, an explosion in Halifax harbor. A Norwegian ship, *Imo,* outward bound with relief supplies, collided with a Belgian munitions ship, *Mont Blanc,* loaded with 2,300 tons of liquid acid, 200 tons of dynamite and 60 tons of explosive acid, with a deck cargo of benzene. Soon after the collision the *Mont Blanc* vaporized and the north end of Halifax was flattened.

Some two thousand people died. Another thousand were mutilated by showers of glass shards or the fire that followed the blast. A ship's anchor was hurled two miles in the greatest explosion in human history to that date. A barn thirty miles away was moved from its foundations. Sailors sixty miles distant thought their ship had struck a mine.

Damage was set at $35 million as Halifax tried to care for homeless, wounded, and orphans. More than $30 million in cash and relief poured in from all over the world. Massachusetts established a relief commission office that paid for clinics, emergency housing, and welfare services.

Americans sailed for Europe in the winter of 1917 to be ready for the German offensive expected in the spring. The Germans already had moved. In March 1918, after nearly four years of fighting from fixed positions on the western front, the Kaiser's Army suddenly rolled forty miles. By summer the astonishing advance brought the Germans back to the Marne, beyond which lay Paris.

"You will advance or fall where you stand, facing the enemy," Arthur Currie told Canadian troops. Conscripts were being rounded up ruthlessly; even farmers' sons with exemptions were herded into troop ships. Germans paid attention to Canadian positions in the line: Where Canadians massed, the Allied attack would begin. Lloyd George wrote in his memoirs, "Whenever the Germans found the Canadian Corps coming into the line, they prepared for the worst." This time Canadians were used as decoys in Flanders while the main assault was launched at Amiens in August. Their part in the German Army's final agonies consisted of breaking the Hindenburg line, after which they slipped along a dry canal and attacked the enemy from the rear. The French-speaking Royal 22nd lost every officer in a maneuver historians regard as one of the most daring and best executed of all Allied campaigns.

General John Pershing's Americans rolled against the Germans at Château-Thierry, Belleau Wood, and Aisne, and finished the second battle of the Marne that ended the German offensive. Canadians suffered another 16,000 casualties in a segment of the front where they faced a quarter of the German Army.

A Swiss intermediary approached Woodrow Wilson on October 2, 1918, and said Germany was ready to ask for peace. The Kaiser abdicated on November 9, and two days later the war was over.

Canada, with a population of 10 million, lost 48,121 men. By contrast, the United States had the same casualties out of a population of 100 million.

The Canadian economy, already reeling from overextended railways, was crippled. British investors withdrew money from Canada to meet the crisis at home, so Canada had to turn to the United States for loans to help to build munitions factories and keep the army in the field. Canadian industry boomed, however; by 1916 one third of Allied shells were made in Canada and shipyards on both coasts operated around the clock to replace U-boat losses.

The emergency was used as an opportunity for the federal government to take over regulation of Canada's banks, a move simplified by their resemblance to British centralist banks with many branches rather than the multiple, uncontrolled, independent banks typical of the American free enterprise system.

The war was financed by loans floated in New York and the issue of government bonds, "Victory Loans," to which Canadians subscribed heavily. Toward the end of the war when the government was forced to consolidate the wasteful duplication of the Grand Trunk and Canadian Northern railways, saving them from receivership by assuming ownership and the debts as well, Ottawa was driven to a desperate "temporary" measure: income tax.

The army came home in 1919 to find the country prostrate with unemployment and inflation. Munitions factories and shipyards closed overnight, throwing thousands out of work just as veterans started to look for jobs. With soaring prices putting food and clothing out of reach of the poor, rebellious men looked longingly at the workers' revolution in Russia which in 1917 overturned a despot and was said to have produced a society of justice and jobs.

The country rumbled with unrest. A suffragette movement, most conspicuous on the prairies, was becoming difficult to ignore. Women wanted to vote so they could elect dries and put an end to alcoholism. As Nellie McClung, novelist and a leading figure in the western feminist movement said, her supporters "had a clear eye, a light hand with cakes, and were not afraid of anything." In 1916 they scored a first victory when they won the right to vote in Manitoba elections.

The same energy ran through the Canadian labor movement, which doubled its membership in two years and by 1919 had 250,000 members. Unionists dared to oppose conscription and in Québec were beaten savagely by soldiers who broke up demonstrations with bullets and bayonets.

Prime Minister Borden clamped down, especially on Canadian unionists who supported the IWW—Joe Hill's Wobblies. Police raided offices in British Columbia where the movement was strong and arrested leaders. The trouble appeared to be contained as the Allies opened negotiations with Germany on a peace settlement. Borden asked that Canada be represented at the talks, which

Britain at first refused. In recognition of Canada's war dead, Lloyd George later conceded that Canada could have a place at the League of Nations, where Borden was so impressive in the negotiations he was later invited to be the British Ambassador to the United States. He declined.

The United States also objected to Canada's presence. The Secretary of State grumbled that he didn't see "why Canada should be concerned in the settlement of European affairs," and was reminded curtly that Canada had suffered more casualties in the war than America.

Borden privately was skeptical of the League of Nations, which he thought an unrealistic vision foisted on the world by Wilson's idealism. Borden's gains on the international scene were offset, however, by increasing unruliness at home. Discharged army veterans, broke and jobless, raged at the country's neglect. With so many looking for jobs, employers cut wages. Workers rebelled. In 1919 Canada had 336 strikes involving 148,000 workers, a record that stood for twenty-four years.

The government called on Mounties to break up the union movement before it turned into another Bolshevik revolution. The last troops to be demobilized came home to riots and head-bashings in June 1919. These were conscripts sent to Russia as part of Britain's attempt to support White Russians and restore the tsar. The Canadians spent miserable months in Murmansk, Archangel, and Vladivostok, watching Russian aristocrats drink champagne among stacks of frozen typhus victims. In March they mutinied, and in June, Borden demanded they be sent home, over the indignant protests of Winston Churchill. The war to end wars was over. In Canada, the war to end unions was approaching its greatest battle.

— 21 —

Hard, Hard Times

Working men met in Calgary in March 1919 to establish what they grandly called One Big Union, OBU, in which all would fight for freedom of speech, release of political prisoners, the right to join any union (even a Communist-minded one), and abolition of capitalism.

Prime Minister Borden was in Europe. He received a cable from the acting prime minister, Sir Thomas White, asking that the Royal Navy send a cruiser to British Columbia to avert the Communist threat of the One Big Union, since there wasn't time to raise a militia and the loyalty of the army was in doubt. Borden replied testily that "as far back as 1885 we attended to our own rebellions."

White was correct in foreseeing a summer of labor unrest. With wages as low as seventeen cents an hour, appalling working conditions, and the cost of food and clothing skyrocketing, trouble was inevitable. It began on May 1, 1919, in Winnipeg when two thousand metal trades workers struck for higher wages and a shorter work week—forty-four hours.

Winnipeg's social-gospel clergymen supported the strikers wholeheartedly. Employers refused to bargain, though wages in Winnipeg were among the lowest in Canada and prices the highest. Within the week, the strike spread to fifty-two other unions. On May 13, a central organizing committee announced that the whole city was on strike: streetcars, mail delivery, newspapers, restaurants, schools, garbage collection, factories; all stopped cold. Police offered to join the strike, but the union committee asked them to prevent looting of deserted shops. By later estimates, half the population of Winnipeg was on strike or was related to a striker; an astonishing display of solidarity that has never been equaled anywhere in the world.

Employers established a command post in the Board of Trade building. Calling themselves the Committee of One Thousand, they issued statements decrying Red rule. On Sundays William Ivens preached to congregations of 10,000 in a public park, since adherents of his Labour Church overflowed all available buildings. His sermons, provocatively entitled, "The Immorality of the Profit System" and "The Resurrection of Democracy," were followed by a collection to aid strikers' families.

The House of Commons met on June 6 just as some Winnipeg employers indicated they were willing to negotiate. Arthur Meighen, Minister of Justice, got fast support for two amendments in the Criminal Code and the Immigration Act. One allowed Mounties to arrest members of organizations designated illegal by the legislation, and the other permitted deportation without trial of anyone believed to be Communist, even British citizens.

The 27th Battalion was so freshly home from the war that it hadn't been disbanded. Soldiers were rushed to Winnipeg by train with cases labeled "Regimental Baggage," containing eight Lewis machine guns. When the veterans learned they would be aiming at Canadian strikers, all but two refused. The Winnipeg police force then was asked to repudiate the strike, but would not. They were fired, and the city found 2,000 unemployed men who would wear armbands proclaiming "Special Constable." They received a princely wage by Winnipeg standards, $6.00 a day.

By the middle of June, stores and factories were open again; workers couldn't afford to stay out any longer. Strikebreakers ran the streetcars as the city returned to normal. On June 17 Mounties and the special police broke into the homes of strike leaders and Methodist clergymen in the middle of the night. The men were put in chains and thrown into prison. "These leaders have plotted to overthrow the government of this country and to establish a Soviet government," Robert Borden declared.

Four days later, in defiance of the mayor's order against demonstrations, 10,000 people marched in silent protest. Near the major intersection of Portage and Main streets, they mobbed a streetcar driven by a strikebreaker. Mounties with bayonets on rifles spilled from a waiting truck. Others rode horses from side streets. They descended with baseball bats on the demonstrators, shooting and swinging; two died on what was called "Bloody Saturday," and scores were severely injured.

Martial law was declared. Deportations began. Men with Slavic names fared worst. Mounties took the view that most Ukrainians were Communists; one man was deported even though he had shown his loyalty at the Somme, where he had been wounded twice. Calm was restored in Winnipeg. People grumbled but they accepted that the government acted wisely. The brutal mop-up continued. Union leaders, prominent Methodists, and radical farmers were arrested. The *Western Labour News* was banned. Union offices were raided and membership lists confiscated.

Ivens was sentenced to a year in prison. He declared to his supporters, "Ideas cannot be crushed, principles never die. Let us all be true to God, true to humanity and true to ourselves, and all will be well." William S. Woodsworth was charged with sedition for quoting Isaiah, "They shall not build and another inherit; they shall not plant and another eat . . . ." Charges were dropped when church leaders protested.

Despite the suppression, western populism grew. Farmers organized a third political party to speak for them, the Progressive Party under a former Tory, Thomas Alexander Crerar. Crerar, once Minister of Agriculture in Borden's Union cabinet, had resigned over tariffs. The new Progressives announced their goals: lower freight rates and tariffs, public ownership of utilities, higher taxes on profits.

Third parties swept provincial and federal elections that followed, as voters registered their criticism of an unresponsive Union government. The United Farmers of Ontario formed the government in that province, and both Manitoba and Alberta elected farmer governments. Labor also formed political parties. In Manitoba, William Ivens was elected as a member of the provincial Independent Labour Party though he was still in jail. Attempts failed to bring farmers and workers together. The farmers, essentially conservative men, found unionists too radical; unions could not forgive farmer juries that sent their leaders to jail after the Winnipeg strike.

Robert Borden resigned in June 1920, to make way for fresh blood in the Tory party. His successor as prime minister was

Arthur Meighen, who the next year called a federal election. The Liberals had lost their leader. Wilfrid Laurier had died in 1919 at seventy-eight and been replaced by the unprepossessing, tiny, stout William Lyon Mackenzie King, master of the middle ground, "the peacemaker."

King had been absent during many confrontations within the Liberal Party during the war, retained by John D. Rockefeller to advise on that magnate's disastrous relations with organized labor. In 1913 Rockefeller put down a strike in his Colorado coal mines by hiring militia armed with machine guns, a tactic that resulted in nineteen deaths, thirteen of them women and children—the so-called Ludlow Massacre. King's recommendation was a compromise both sides accepted: establishment of grievance committees to defuse confrontations. For twenty years it was a blueprint for North American management-labor relations and blunted radicalism.

The new Liberal leader brought fresh and revolutionary ideas about government welfare programs to the 1921 election. Most were set out in his book, *Industry and Humanity,* widely admired for its progressive philosophy by social reformers. He campaigned on the slogan, "Time for Change." King wooed the support of the new third parties. "The farmers' movement is a people's movement and as such the truest kind of Liberalism," he said. "The same is true of labor."

Québécois felt irrelevant, having no friends anywhere. Louis Alexandre Taschereau, Liberal premier of Québec, asked sadly, "Since Québec is so necessary to confederation, is it not deplorable to note its isolation?" Abbé Groulx's disciples were delighted by the drift from Ottawa. Canadiens, they felt, should keep apart from the impure, a category that included all Protestants, Jews, and persons whose mother tongue was not French.

Despite the label, "a group of nondescripts," applied by the Winnipeg *Free Press,* T. A. Crerar's unknown Progressive Party swept the west and sent sixty-five men to the House of Commons. Tories suffered acutely; their leader, Arthur Meighen, was unseated in his own riding. Québec voted for Mackenzie King as the lesser of the evils, since the province would not vote for Conservatives who hanged Riel and imposed conscription. He became prime minister of Canada with a minority government.

The first woman to be elected to the House of Commons sat with the new Progressives. She was Agnes MacPhail, thirty-one, a schoolteacher elected by Ontario farmers.

Though the Tories elected only fifty members, they managed with fast footwork to be named the official Opposition over the more numerous inexperienced Progressives. Mackenzie King, holding fewer seats than the combined Tories and Progressives, courted the latter. He found them divided and unsure. Some wanted lower tariffs, some wanted support for organized labor, some were interested only in freight rates.

The economy was picking up, silencing some of the protest. Women obtained the vote and went back to knitting. Methodists were preoccupied with ecumenism and church union. Trade unions quarreled over leadership, radicalism, and American interference. Crops were bountiful in the west. Only James S. Woodsworth, an intractable socialist, continued to campaign for reform.

Canada learned in the newspapers that Britain was at war with the Turks. Winston Churchill on September 15, 1922, asked Mackenzie King to send troops. King was shaken. "The French-Canadians will be opposed," he predicted; without Québec, the federal Liberals would be lost. But Ontario was ready to go. "If the Turk attacks Constantinople, he attacks Canada!" the Toronto *Globe* cried.

King stalled, though Churchill fumed. Meighen, leader of the Tory opposition, chided him. "When Britain's message came, then Canada should have said: 'Ready, aye, ready; we stand by you,'" he said.

To King's relief, the crisis in the Dardanelles evaporated. Unlike his predecessors, Prime Minister King was a third-generation Canadian who had severed ties to the mother country and placed Canada in a North American context instead. The Canadian delegate at the League of Nations, Raoul Dandurand, reflected King's philosophy when he said, "We live in a fireproof house far from inflammable materials."

Tories accused King of being a traitor to the Crown, but he persevered in a path of disinterest in Imperial conferences and even made demands that the British government leave Canada alone. A historic breakthrough occurred when King forced Britain to allow Canada to negotiate its own fish-war treaty with the United States.

Though Tories objected strenuously to such treason, King won his point. In 1923, fifty-six years after Canada became an independent nation, the country signed its first treaty on its own behalf: The Halibut Treaty, a name that ranks in Canadian history close to the place that the Declaration of Independence holds in the United States.

U.S.-Canadian relations were tested by American prohibition, which was an invitation to larceny for Canadian distillers licensed by the government to bottle spirits for export. A roaring traffic in illicit shipments kept U. S. customs agents sleepless. At night fast motorboats crossed the Detroit River with gin labeled *EXPORT TO JAMAICA*. Smugglers plied between maritime ports on both coasts while on the prairies a hustler named Sam Bronfman used armed convoys of Model-T Fords to take booze to Al Capone in Chicago. Washington indignantly demanded that Ottawa stop the traffic but bribes were fat and payoffs extended all the way from customs clerks to the House of Commons.

Canada was following a hard line with the huge new Communist nation, the Soviet. When famine swept Russia in 1922, Canada refused to extend credit for wheat or seed. King cultivated the United States, which found its neighbor unexpectedly useful. During critical negotiations with Japan for control of the Pacific Ocean, Canada played an influential role in keeping Britain from signing a new treaty with Japan, leaving the way clear for the U. S. Navy. Soonafter, Canada appointed its first ambassador to Washington.

Population growth was almost at a standstill. In the twenties about 1.2 million came to Canada from Britain and western Europe but one million people left Canada for the United States. Immigration from eastern Europe was discouraged in fear that the newcomers would bring communism with them. The postwar Red scare was giving employment to the Royal North West Mounted Police, which otherwise might have been disbanded. The refusal of soldiers and the Winnipeg police to move against strikers caused Ottawa to rethink plans to disband the force. Instead Mounties were given a bigger budget to recruit more men and a new name, Royal Canadian Mounted Police, with a mandate to eradicate subversives from sea to sea.

Studies have shown that the Mountie infiltration of Canadian

unions was so extensive in the twenties and thirties that no local
was without at least one, often a union official. Tim Buck, prominent member of the Canadian Communist Party which numbered
fewer than three hundred, was shadowed night and day. The secretary of the first branch of the Communist Party in Regina was
an RCMP sergeant. In 1921, with deportations running in the
hundreds, Mounties hired Pinkertons from the United States. A
leading clergyman in the Methodist Church discovered that
Mounties had infiltrated even the Labour Church in Edmonton
and had attended 140 church meetings all over the west.

Meanwhile a zealous Canadian Army officer, Colonel James
Sutherland Brown, was making plans for Canada's invasion of the
United States. Using road maps he obtained from U. S. service
stations while disguised as a tourist, Brown designed military
strategy which included the use of soldiers mounted on bicycles
and a cavalry equipped with swords. A flying column from British
Columbia would occupy Spokane and Seattle, while the prairie
strike force took Fargo. The Great Lakes unit would capture Detroit, the Québec phalanx would penetrate the Adirondacks, and
the maritime command would take Maine.

Buster, as Brown was known to friends, was not discouraged
that the Canadian Army consisted of 4,000 men. "It is a difficult,
and on the surface, an almost hopeless task," he conceded when
asked how he thought Canada could defeat the United States. His
commanding officer, Major-General Andrew McNaughton, eventually burned Brown's Defense Scheme No. 1.

The Canadian Army had lost its scruples against mauling Canadian strikers. In 1923 soldiers went to Cape Breton to put down
trouble that followed when the Nova Scotia Steel and Coal Company cut wages 37 percent while keeping food and rent at the
company's stores and houses at the same high price. When
workers struck, John L. Lewis, president of the parent United
Mine Workers of America, denounced them and revoked the
charter. A sympathy strike in Sydney, Nova Scotia, brought the
army there. A machine gun was placed in front of the Bridgeport
Catholic Church, and soldiers told the citizens that anyone who
stepped over a line drawn in the dirt would be killed.

The strike was settled but the company remained closed for six
months as punishment. Parents hunted in the woods for plants

and wild mushrooms to feed hungry children. In 1925 there was a similar tragedy when the British Empire Steel Company, which already had closed eleven mines and put its factories on half shifts, cut credit in company stores. Welfare also was denied and John L. Lewis refused to send strike pay. When scabs arrived to work the factories, there was a riot. Ottawa shipped the army in again with bayonets fixed.

Prime Minister Mackenzie King was finding it difficult to function with a minority government. In the hope that the country would give him more Liberals, he called a general election in 1925. This time it was the Conservatives who improved their position, with 116 Tory seats to 101 for the Liberals. A collection of splinter parties, mostly Progressives, held the remaining twenty-eight seats.

King went to Governor-General Lord Byng of Vimy with a brazen request that he be allowed to form the government anyway with the aid of the twenty-eight outsiders. His aplomb was remarkable, since he had lost even his own seat and had to go through a by-election in a safe riding vacation by a loyal Liberal, Prince Albert, Saskatchewan. Stranger still, the governor-general agreed and King's Québec lieutenant, Ernest Lapointe, faced the angry Tories in the legislature. The price of support by James Woodsworth and other dissenters was that the Liberals bring in old-age pensions. Even so, King doubted he'd have enough votes to survive the Tories' storm over graft uncovered in whiskey smuggling.

Accordingly, only hours before the vote was due, King asked the governor-general to dissolve parliament and allow him to call an election. Lord Byng refused, a decision on whose validity constitution experts still cannot agree. King, furious, declared that governor-generals had no authority to thwart Canadian prime ministers from governing as they saw fit. When Byng remained firm, King returned to the House of Commons, bowed to the Speaker, resigned as prime minister, and moved that the House adjourn.

Arthur Meighen, stunned, rose to speak. King told him coldly that the motion wasn't debatable. "There is no prime minister," he said.

Lord Byng sent for Meighen on June 28 and asked him to form

a Tory government. By promising tariff concessions, Meighen got the support of the crucial Progressive rump and tried to govern. King hit him two days later with a series of Constitutional challenges to his authority. A motion of no confidence passed by a single vote. Byng was forced to allow Meighen to dissolve parliament and call an election.

King campaigned on a simple, easily grasped fact in the welter of constitutional chaos: the governor-general had interfered with a Canadian prime minister's authority. In the election, Liberals were returned with another narrow margin over the Tories. Seven splinter parties claimed 35 seats and again held the balance of power.

Meighen resigned as Tory leader and the party chose another, Richard Bennett, fifty-six, a former CPR lawyer and favorite target of the Calgary *Eye-Opener*'s impudent Bob Edwards.

King attended another Imperial Conference in 1926 in London. Britain hoped to establish a supergovernment of all the colonies and democracies in the Empire. A former British Tory and cabinet minister, Lord Arthur Balfour, author of the documents in which Britain in 1917 promised Jews a homeland in Palestine, chaired the meetings. He described the plan for "autonomous communities" within "a British Commonwealth of Nations."

King, fresh from the confrontation with a British governor-general, was skeptical. He demanded reduced powers for governor-generals and a promise Canada could dispense with the Privy Council to decide Constitutional law. King returned to Canada satisfied he had helped derail the British plan.

He kept his promise to introduce old-age pensions. Times were better; the country could afford them. The Privy Council continued to reshape Canada. It reversed the Canadian Supreme Court in 1929 and ruled that women could be appointed to the Senate. The Privy Council outraged Québec by awarding 100,000 square miles of Labrador to Newfoundland, though Québec's claim to the ore-rich land stretched back three hundred years.

Visitors were bewildered by the contrasts between French-Canadians and other citizens. In 1927 Québécois turned out by the millions to celebrate St. Jean Baptiste Day, which was ignored in the rest of the country, but paid little attention to the observance of Canada's sixtieth birthday, which was given the full fire-works-and-bagpipes treatment everywhere outside Québec. On May 24 English-Canada celebrated Queen Victoria's birthday: *If you don't give us a holiday,/we'll all run away,* schoolchildren chanted. That day French Canada marked the anniversary of Dollard des Ormeaux's fight that saved Montréal from the Iroquois.

The province was cheering a new political hero, Camillien Houde, the mayor of Montréal. Houde rose to leadership of the moribund provincial Conservative party by attacking English bosses. As Houde reminded audiences, one third of Québec's industry was owned by Americans.

Other heroes of the era were Canada's bush pilots who were making the country aware of its last frontier, the north. They were a romantic breed, unfitted for life on the ground after being in aerial combat in World War I. They made a living barn-storming summer fairs in Curtiss biplanes, giving the locals a thrill by taking them for a spin at $2.00 a ride. Some flew people and supplies to outposts on the Arctic Circle over mapless land that had never seen a white man. Since there were no landing fields, they used lakes. In summer they put pontoons on the planes and in winter skis. Winters were the worst; they flew in open cockpits.

Punch Dickins navigated the Barren Lands in 1928 by pure guesswork. In 1929 he landed at Aklavik, an Inuit village on the Arctic Ocean. The most renowned exploit of this most celebrated bush pilot was flying six hundred miles in winter to Fort Vermillion with medical supplies to fight a diphtheria epidemic. When he returned to the airfield at Edmonton, his hands were frozen to the stick.

"Wop" May pioneered a mail flight to Fort Resolution in 1929 with four tons of letters sent by philatelists. Another time May dazzled a baseball crowd in Edmonton by flying low over the field to throw out the first pitch.

Prospectors hitched rides and watched the ground for signs of minerals. None was luckier than Gilbert Labine, who spotted a purple-and-yellow scar on rock, investigated, and staked out Canada's biggest uranium mine. Others wondered if all bush pilots were named Lamb. Tom Lamb and his six sons flew for their own airline, Lambair.

Some pilots scouted whales and others delivered Eaton's catalogues to igloos. The north was full of intrepid men who could survive temperatures of 50° below in unheated, open planes; could land on transparent lakes ringed with rock; could patch holes in pontoons with flattened soup cans; and when necessary could whittle their own propellers. There had been nothing to match 'em since the *voyageurs.*

Another of the country's preoccupations was booze smuggling. When night fell on the Detroit River, sounds of gunfire rose like the cries of crows. U. S. patrols chased power-packed motor launches leaving the Canadian shore with whiskey. Halifax and Saint John sent off merchant ships, gunwales deep in liquor, for Puerto Rico. Mysteriously, they never got past the Hudson River.

In March 1929 two U. S. patrol vessels chased a Canadian schooner, *I'm Alone,* a rumrunner out of Lunenburg, Nova Scotia. After two days, they caught it two hundred miles beyond U. S. territorial limits, arrested the crew, and sank the ship with cannon fire. Ensuing lawsuits took six years to untangle. Finally the United States apologized and paid reparations. The *I'm Alone*'s captain put in a claim for his wardrobe, including a dinner jacket and a collapsible top hat.

President Warren Harding of the United States made a fond comment anyway on Canadian-American relations: "We think the same thoughts, live the same lives, and cherish the same aspirations of service to each other in time of need." There was much truth to this: By the end of the twenties, America owned 56 percent of Canadian industry, controlled two thirds of the unions, and lapped up Canadian whiskey.

The New York stock-market crash of October 1929 destroyed fortunes in the United States, broke banks, and closed factories, mines, shops, and offices. Canada felt the consequences first in the west, which was stuck with a 1928 bumper crop of wheat stockpiled in warehouses, $200 million in grain. When Argentina undersold Canada on the world market, the Winnipeg Grain Exchange effectively collapsed. Wheat dove from $1.60 a bushel to thirty-eight cents.

In 1931 the British pound was almost worthless and the Canadian dollar fell with it. The United States tried to protect its shattered industries by rising tariffs and reducing Canadian exports to one third. The result was a disaster in Canada. The automotive industry, American-owned branch plants from Windsor to Oshawa, turned out 263,000 cars in 1929 and 61,000 in 1932.

Unemployed men went from town to town past factories that were shuttered. They begged food, hunted for scraps in alleys, and rode west in empty freight cars. On the Pacific coast the weather, at least, was kind. Of a population of 10 million, 400,000 were out of work and a million had only part-time jobs. Doctors took fees in chickens, and grocers extended credit. Hungry and ashamed, people lined outside church soup kitchens. Banks foreclosed mortgages and sheriffs took away furniture and nailed boards over doors. Destitute families watched in tears.

Politicians claimed the problem was shiftlessness. President Herbert Hoover in the United States called welfare "unearned income." William Lyon Mackenzie King said it wasn't his concern, welfare was a provincial responsibility under the British North America Act. Though the federal government collected most taxes, it wasn't authorized to dispense welfare. King rashly said he would never give "a five-cent piece" to a province that didn't have a Liberal government. Only Québec and Prince Edward Island qualified.

The country in 1930 turned in despair to a new government, R. B. Bennett's Conservatives. Even Québec voted for a substantial number of Tories; twenty-five. Bennett tried an old Conservative tactic, higher tariffs, but the economy failed to rally.

The tragedy was compounded by a drought in Saskatchewan and Alberta that turned wheat fields to bone-dry dust. The wailing wind across the desert drove people mad. Dust was everywhere, indoors and out. It clogged nostrils and made food gritty. Saskatchewan, the hardest hit, was abandoned by 66,000 people in the early thirties; one in every four farm families. In some areas, one could travel a day and never see an occupied building. The province went broke and asked Ottawa for help to pay relief. Manitoba lost 24,000 people; Alberta, 21,000. The Maritimes were crushed because fish was close to worthless.

Welfare payments in Newfoundland were the lowest, six cents a day; children and the aged starved to death. When people learned of government corruption, a mob descended on the legislature in April 1932 and surely would have lynched Richard Squires, the prime minister, had he not hidden. Bitter Newfoundlanders voted themselves out of democracy. They tried to sell Labrador but found no takers. When the banks failed, Britain took pity and made the island a Crown Colony again.

In the ugly times, Canadiens in Montréal turned on the city's Jewish population living on and near St. Urbain's Street. Abbé Groulx's appeal to racial purity had gained an important disciple, Maurice Duplessis, forty-one, a foxy lawyer who eventually rose to head the provincial Conservative Party. At the Université de Montréal, Groulx's students launched the nationalist *Les Jeune-Canada* which said Canadiens should become "masters in our own house."

Prime Minister Bennett, a millionaire as the result of his CPR connections, appeared paralyzed by the Depression. "I will not permit this country with my voice or my vote to ever become committed to the dole system," he stated, though he wept privately over pitiful letters children wrote of their deprivations. He answered, frequently enclosing five-dollar bills.

Prohibition vanished in the United States and Canadian provinces gradually followed suit, though dries complained bitterly. The government gave assurances that liquor sales would not get out of hand. Beer and booze would be sold only in government stores and taverns would be licensed and inspected by government appointees of the highest probity, in many cases retired police chiefs.

The Tory Minister of Trade and Commerce, Henry Herbert Stevens, was asked to study the price spreads in industry. In 1935 he reported on unprincipled behavior by corporations and suggested the government should control "certain business activities and practices." Stevens, a former stagecoach driver, prospector, and newspaper editor from Vancouver, a self-made man with blunt manners, shocked the Tory cabinet. Forced to resign, he launched a political party of his own, the Reconstruction Party, dedicated to controlling mergers and price fixing.

Radicalism thrived in such desperate times, particularly in the blighted west. Laborers formed the Workers Unity League, which in 1932 had 40,000 members, including Mountie undercover agents. The WUL was involved in a series of strikes in the thirties, all crushed by soldiers or Mounties.

By the fall of 1931, fifty RCMP fired machine guns at demonstrators in Estevan, Saskatchewan, scene of a miners' strike, and killed three. Later, Mounties wrecked homes of strike leaders. Furniture-factory workers in Stratford, Ontario, struck in 1933 and were met by militia and tanks. In 1934, 3,500 workers protesting unsafe conditions in British Columbia's timber industry were attacked by police. Strikers were evicted from their homes and went to prison in irons.

Bennett, who called the strikes "a threat to social order," increased RCMP budgets to handle them. Mounties infiltrated government relief camps where unemployed men were paid twenty cents a day to work in the bush under military supervision. At night weary men groused in bunkhouses about making a better world.

Some provinces found the burden of paying their police forces too much to bear. Ottawa offered to make the swollen ranks of the RCMP available for provincial duty, which was accepted gratefully. In 1932 the force recruited another thousand men and that year 7,647 suspected communists were deported summarily from Canada. Men with Slavic backgrounds dominated the group. Arrested in the quiet hours before dawn, they were hustled to a guarded shed in Halifax to await a ship and then delivered to police in Europe. A number of them sent to Germany later died in Nazi concentration camps. Tim Buck, leader of the Communist Party of Canada, went to prison for five years on evidence of sedition produced by Mounties.

Commissioner James Howden MacBrien of the RCMP observed that when Canada rid itself of foreigners "there would be no unemployment or unrest." Many believed it. Fascism, since it was opposed to communism, had a wide following. Alfred Jones, a magistrate, was cheered by the Toronto establishment Empire Club when he declared that fascism would "fit admirably into our Imperial setting."

Americans elected a new president in 1932, Franklin Delano Roosevelt. When Eugene Victor Debs, socialist labor leader in the United States, was asked why the movement failed in the thirties, his reply was: "Roosevelt." Roosevelt's New Deal measures to provide jobs and put steam in American confidence weakened the opposition of the left.

Frustration with traditional political parties was not diverted by messianic leadership in Canada. In Alberta a Bible-thumping evangelist radio preacher, William Aberhart, picked up a theory called Social Credit from an eccentric Scot, Major C. H. Douglas. In 1935 Albertans elected Aberhart's Social Credit candidates and made him premier, eager to participate in monthly dividends he promised from the tax revenue. As it turned out, Social Credit was just another political party, albeit more honest in the beginning than some. Ottawa disallowed six provincial bills in a row by which Aberhart tried to implement his schemes. Still Aberhart seemed a strong, decent man and remained premier of Alberta until his death in 1943.

Québec also was developing a strong third party. Maurice Duplessis, leader of the provincial Conservatives, was drawn to a breakaway group of radical Liberals who argued that the old federal parties were prejudiced against provincial powers. With them he constructed a new party, the *Union Nationale,* to destroy the strong Liberal government of Louis Alexandre Taschereau that was making deals with British and American industrialists to give away Québec's resources.

Another alternative political party that emerged in the fertile Depression was James S. Woodsworth's Cooperative Commonwealth Federation, a Fabian-socialist mixture of western farmers and eastern intellectuals. The founding documents, drawn up in Regina in 1933 by six Rhodes scholars, dedicated the CCF to "replace the present capitalist system with its inherent injustice and inhumanity by a social order from which the domination and exploitation of one class by another will be eliminated."

To counteract the strong pull of the socialists Mackenzie King moved the Liberal Party to the left. He promised a central bank, unemployment payments, lower tariffs, and the end of restrictions against free speech and assembly imposed after the Winnipeg strike.

Prime Minister Bennett noted the success of Aberhart's radio sermons and Roosevelt's "fireside chats." He used radio to tell Canadians that the government was doing everything it could to help the poor. Though Canadians were not impressed Bennett was awed by the power of the new medium. He won a rare victory, Privy Council approval for federal control of the air, which enabled Ottawa to put private radio stations under government

regulations and to establish a network of government-owned outlets which became the Canadian Broadcasting Corporation. Later
the same ruling enabled the federal government to develop an air-
line, Trans-Canada Airlines (later Air Canada), a spin-off of the
public-owned Canadian National Railway.

Public indifference to the draconian style of the government's
suppression of dissent changed when there was an attempt to
assassinate Tim Buck in prison. Guards at Kingston penitentiary
fired five shots into his cell but Buck miraculously survived. A
western radical, A. E. Smith, was gathering 200,000 signatures on
a petition calling for repeal of the law allowing secret deportations. When the Mounties arrested Smith for sedition, a public
outcry demanded the release of both Smith and Buck.

The government yielded. Buck returned to Toronto and was
welcomed by 17,000 people packed into a gleaming new hockey
rink, Maple Leaf Gardens. Prison-pale and emaciated, he received
the ovation of his lifetime.

By the mid-thirties, British Columbia was putting every resource into a battle to keep indigent Canadians out. Guards
searched freight trains at the Alberta-British Columbia border and
clubbed drifters. Railways strengthened their police forces, but
sympathetic train crews often turned a blind eye to the ragged
men, women, and children who hid in boxcars. Those who filtered
through the blockade to Vancouver found more hostility. In 1935
the homeless had a solution, a protest march to Ottawa.

They swarmed aboard freight trains headed east. They reached
Regina and paused there while their leaders went on to Ottawa to
test the mood of the government. While they were gone, sympathetic citizens in Regina allowed marchers to camp on the football
field and hold a tag day to raise money for food. Prime Minister
Bennett met the leaders in Ottawa and disliked them on sight.
One, Arthur Evans, was known to be a communist; seven others
were not Canadian-born, though two were war veterans.

Mounties attended the talks, during which Evans made some
rash threats. The mayor of Regina was advised to cut off food
supplies to the marchers. On July 1, 1935, Evans called a meeting
in Regina's Market Square. Mounties and local police hit them
with tear gas and clubs. Marchers picked up rocks and threw
them at advancing police. The battle lasted three hours and ended

with a roundup of leaders. The rest of the marchers melted away; in a week they were gone.

As with the aftermath of the Winnipeg strike, Canadians accepted that the decision to stop the march in Regina was proper and the method not intolerable. There was little in the press that wasn't in praise of the police.

Bennett, however, was a man transformed. Influenced by America's euphoric response to Roosevelt's New Deal, he had one of his own. He proclaimed on radio that the capitalist system should "work for the welfare of the people." With an election looming, he rapidly pushed through legislation that had the socialists reeling: curbs on trusts and monopolies, a ban on child labor, a housing program for the poor, unemployment insurance, a mandatory eight-hour working day.

The Privy Council eventually rescinded five of the eight reforms his government passed, ruling in 1937 that the federal government had exceeded its authority. Bennett meanwhile led his Conservatives proudly in the election campaign but encountered cynicism. Liberals suspected that Bennett passed the legislation in full knowledge that the Privy Council wouldn't allow it. Tories were afraid the situation was even worse, that Bennett had become deranged and really did intend to introduce a welfare state. Eight splinter parties competed for voter attention but none seemed more sensible and concerned than Mackenzie King's Liberals, who offered a simple slogan, "King or Chaos," and won a landslide.

Canada's chronic deadlocks over federal and provincial powers had been highlighted by Ottawa's inability to offer social assistance during the Depression. King asked two constitutional lawyers to study "the economic and financial basis of Confederation and the distribution of federal powers." They were Newton Wesley Rowell, a judge from Ontario, and Joseph Sirois, a respected notary from Québec. Rowell and Sirois were to spend three years sorting out the flaws in a constitution gerrymandered by the Imperial Privy Council.

King addressed himself to an interim measure and offered the provinces federal money for their welfare costs. He lowered tariffs on some seven hundred items, which brought prices down. He nationalized the Bank of Canada, promised to build a highway

across Canada, and created a commission to sit as a buffer between the CBC and the government to prevent the abuse of radio
by politicians. Finally he repealed Section 98 of the Criminal
Code which for sixteen years enabled Mounties to deport suspects
without trial.

King's diary, opened on his instructions twenty-five years after
his death, revealed the odd, fussy, dull bachelor to be more than
he appeared. Sexually repressed, he was a spiritualist who doted
on his dead mother and his dog and consulted mediums, the
whirls in his shaving cream, and crystal balls for guidance while
running the affairs of Canada longer than any prime minister in
history.

In 1936 Maurice Duplessis' *Union Nationale* scored a stunning
upset in Québec's provincial election. With the support of the
church, which endorsed his passionate commitment to provincial
rights, Duplessis won seventy-six seats in the ninety-seat legislature and destroyed both the entrenched Liberals and his former
Tory associates. One of his first acts was something the church
wanted, increased police power to suppress dissent.

Union Nationale founders broke away in horror as Duplessis
turned the party sharply right and discarded such election promises as nationalization of hydroelectric utilities and resistance to
foreign capitalists. His Padlock Law which allowed the government to close any premise suspected of harboring a communist
offended people outside the province as well. Woodsworth
protested in the House of Commons, "Twenty times a month they
have trampled on liberties as old as the Magna Carta." Ernest
Lapointe, Minister of Justice and King's trusted Québec lieutenant, took the traditional position of French-Canadian nationalists
and declared that the province had a right to do whatever it saw
fit. As a result of the Padlock Law, Canada's first civil rights
organization was formed in Toronto, the Canadian Civil Liberties
Association.

English-language newspapers accused Québec of being a fascist
state, a charge that gained credibility when Catholic bishops in
Québec issued admiring statements about such Catholic dictators
as Mussolini of Italy, Franco of Spain, and Salazar of Portugal.

In 1935 when Italy invaded Ethiopia, the League of Nations

met in emergency sessions to consider sanctions. Smart money said that the League would not act against the economic interests of its members. The Canadian delegate, Dr. Walter Riddell, a Methodist man of conscience, proposed the League boycott oil shipments to Italy. "The Canadian resolution" was a bombshell. Startled, fifty-one nations voted for the sanctions.

Québec at once saw the vote as a plot against Catholicism. The reaction within the province was so heated that King, always sensitive to the need to keep a Liberal base there, repudiated Riddell. The delegate had no authority to make the motion, he said. Riddell, humiliated, was forced to withdraw. Other nations followed his lead and the motion was rescinded.

The Depression was lifting. In Europe a healthy munitions industry pumped money into the world economy. Britain was making quiet preparations for another war. Mackenzie King was asked if British aircrews could train in Canada. He said no. When Major-General Andrew McNaughton reported on the readiness of the Canadian Army for such a conflict, it was revealed that the country had only enough ammunition for a war lasting ninety minutes.

When King introduced a bill authorizing $10 million for military equipment, MP's asked anxiously if he planned to send troops to Europe. He answered, "I think it extremely doubtful if any of the British dominions will ever send another expeditionary force."

Ian Mackenzie, Minister of Defense, added, "There is no idea whatever of sending a single Canadian soldier overseas in any expeditionary force."

Duplessis, *le chef* as his supporters fondly called him, relaxed. He saw nothing wrong with Canada raising an army to defend itself from communist invaders.

Woodsworth complained that the money would be better spent feeding the hungry. With wheat at fifty cents a bushel and cod a cent a pound, millions of Canadians were still in a desperate condition. The last protest came in the spring of 1938 in Vancouver where the 128-pound Scottish orphan, Robert Brodie, led a sit-in demonstration of jobless men. Brodie, blinded in one eye from police beatings, put demonstrators in the city's leading hotel, its art gallery, and the post office, identifying the enemy as private enterprise, elite culture, and the federal government. Protesters covered all available floor space, politely leaving an aisle for the public to pay a bill, admire a painting, or buy stamps. The George Hotel bought back its lobby for five hundred dollars, which was spent on food. A department store donated socks. The YMCA offered use of its showers. Brodie's weekly, *Sitdowner's Gazette,* was read by thousands, and sympathetic citizens dropped off bags of sandwiches.

Harold Winch, a CCF dockworker slightly deafened by police beatings, offered himself as mediator to end the deadlock, but municipal fathers were in a stony mood. The Mounties and Vancouver police attacked on June 19 behind tear gas. Brodie, conspicuous in an orange sweater, was slashed with riding crops. Firemen who witnessed the brutality and complained were disciplined by the mayor. When a mob collected outside the police station, Harold Winch persuaded them to disperse. Brodie and other leaders went to prison.

The President of the United States visited Canada in the summer of 1938, the first time for a U. S. leader. Franklin Delano Roosevelt met Mackenzie King at Kingston, along with the country's new governor-general, Lord Tweedsmuir, better known as John Buchan, the novelist. Roosevelt spoke of peace and said the United States "will not stand idly by if domination of Canadian soil is threatened."

Later that year British Prime Minister Neville Chamberlain flew to Germany to meet Adolf Hitler. The Nazi leader wanted to absorb Czechoslovakia without interference from Britain and France. Chamberlain appeased and returned with the promise that the world would continue to enjoy peace. But Britain stepped up war production. When Mackenzie King asked for an increase in Canada's "defense" budget, he told French-Canadians that the measure was necessary "against the possibility of external aggression."

The following year, 1939, for the first time in its history, Canada received a reigning monarch, George VI, and his cheerful wife, Elizabeth. The royal couple traveled across the country by train, adored at every stop. The patriotic fervor for Britain alarmed Québec, which was drenched in Union Jacks. Ernest

Lapointe suddenly talked about conscription. He would resign if Canada imposed it. "The best way, the most effective way of helping is not the way that would divide our country and tear it asunder," he warned.

The king and queen departed. The summer was beautiful. Saskatchewan had rain. The Depression was almost over.

— 22 —

Another War
(to End War)

Mackenzie King quietly prepared for war by checking on the 1914 War Measures Act. In August 1939 he discovered that it remained operable by a simple order-in-council; he did not have to consult parliament in order to suspend civil rights, censor the press, and forbid public meetings. Though Canadians had forgotten about it, the War Measures Act of 1914 had never been repealed.

On September 1 Germany swept into Poland. Two days later France and Britain declared war. The Canadian parliament, enjoying the last holiday weekend of the summer, was recalled. King asked for authority to help Britain: What he meant was a Canadian declaration of war on Germany.

The navy consisted of six destroyers and five minesweepers. Canada had taken little part in the escalation of naval power that consumed the military of Britain, the United States, Germany, and Japan. The army of 4,000 men had 23 antitank guns, 14 tanks, and 5 mortars. The Royal Canadian Air Force, a separate unit Britain permitted during World War I when Canadians dominated the Royal Flying Corps, existed mostly on paper.

Parliament debated for three days. The prime minister explained that the country would need munitions and military strength only to protect it from attack. "The present government believes that conscription of men for overseas service will not be a necessary or effective step. No such measure will be introduced by the present administration."

French-Canadians joined other Members of Parliament on September 10, 1939, when Canada declared war on Germany and Italy. The only negative vote came from James Shaver Woodsworth, a snowy-haired sixty-five-year-old leader of the CCF. The pacifist stood alone. The CCF replaced him with a Regina schoolteacher, M. James Coldwell, a dry, patient man.

Mackenzie King consulted the spirit world for guidance. The ghost of his grandfather, William Lyon Mackenzie, appeared to him. The messages were that Hitler was dead. King decided to swear off séances for the duration to avoid "lying spirits."

Factories reopened and the price of wheat climbed. Men idled from threshing gangs in the west were among the first to enlist. Within a few weeks, 55,000 men had joined the forces. The War Measures Act was activated. Some two hundred Canadians of Ukrainian descent were rounded up in the west and put in prison camps without trial. In central Canada, one of the first taken into custody was Montréal's mayor, Camillien Houde, an admirer of Mussolini.

Within two weeks of the declaration of war, Duplessis called an election in Québec. He charged the federal government with using the war as an excuse for dismantling provincial rights. He offered Québec the *Union Nationale*'s protection for "the survival of our popular liberties." Liberals pointed out that the government had promised not to implement conscription and revealed evidence of corruption in Duplessis' administration. The *Union Nationale* went down to defeat. Adélard Godbout, leader of the Liberals, became premier of Québec. Godbout promised to resign "if a single French-Canadian, from now until the end of the hostilities, is mobilized against his will."

The First Division of the army was on the way to Britain on December 10, 1939, the pretense of home defense somehow forgotten. King, accused of paying too much attention to Québec voters, called a quick federal election in January 1940. Robert Bennett was no longer leader of the Tories. In his place was colorless Robert James Manion, veteran of the first World War, a lackluster doctor who was no match for King. Liberals swept the polls with 181 seats to 40 for the Tories, with Québec giving solid support.

The German Army stunned the Allies in the spring of 1940. France's steel-and-concrete Maginor Line, a calcified trench system, was irrelevant as Panzer divisions outflanked it, poured through the Netherlands and Belgium, and entered Paris. Norway fell as Canadian troops were poised to sail from Scotland. Some

Canadians landed in France while the British were fleeing for Dunkirk and were pulled out just before the Germans overran their position.

The question for Canadians was whether their soldiers would fight as a unit. Winston Churchill, Britain's wartime prime minister, was at loggerheads with King and the Canadian general, Andrew McNaughton. Churchill's view of Canadians was that they were good as shock troops, excellent in the air, and fit at sea only in small, disposable ships. The Canadian leader was nervous of taking too many casualties, which would mean conscription. McNaughton irritated British generals by insisting that his soldiers have ample artillery protection. At home, King's policy was to encourage enlistment in the Royal Canadian Air Force and the Royal Canadian Navy rather than the Army, where casualties were heavier.

Britain waited through a summer of suspense for Hitler's invasion. Bank of England gold reserves were shipped to Canada for safekeeping. Mackenzie King quietly slipped a conscription bill through the Liberal-dominated House. It created little stir because it appeared that Britain would fall and troops would be needed for home defense. King and Lapointe promised that no draftees would leave Canada.

A German bomber, apparently by accident, bombed civilians in London's east end in August 1940. Churchill immediately ordered the Royal Air Force to bomb civilians in Berlin. Aerial warfare was profoundly altered. Once confined to military targets, it was now extended deliberately to non-combatants as well. Reprisal bombings of Germany inflicted heavy casualties on air crews. Britain assigned Canadians to carry the brunt of long-range bombing attacks, which created havoc, but contributed nothing to the outcome of the war.

"I don't see why Jerry doesn't bomb Berlin and let the RAF take care of London," a Cockney told Raymond Daniell of the New York *Times*. "We'd both save petrol and we'd be none the worse."

Hitler decided not to invade Britain after all, concerned that Germany did not control the air. That winter, Canada's American-born Minister of Munitions and Supplies, Clarence Decatur Howe, was organizing the production of everything from bullets to aircraft as the country became Britain's arsenal. The greatest achievement of the war, the network of airports across the country where British Commonwealth and Allied aircrews received training, was well advanced.

In the five years of the war, Canada trained 131,000 aircrew, 50,000 of them pilots. Half were Canadians; the others wore shoulder flashes of Norway, Poland, U.S.A., Belgium, Australia, New Zealand, and the Netherlands. A country of 11 million built and equipped 97 bases with 12,000 aircraft.

Canada's navy was made up of little ships—destroyers, minesweepers, and corvettes, the smallest, roughest naval vessels afloat. With loads of depth-charges, they were thin-hulled bombs, but over 90,000 Canadian sailors served in them. Commanded by the Royal Navy, they did the dirty work of escorting convoys across the Atlantic, hunting U-boats, rescuing torpedoed crews.

Though 25,000 Canadians saw action in the air and some 10,000 of them died, they served under Royal Air Force command. No Canadian ever rose to a high level in the RAF command. Canada's military historians have never been able to get a true and clear accounting of their contribution, since they were scattered throughout the RAF from the Hebrides to Calcutta.

The Royal Canadian Navy's only distinctively Canadian unit, which operated out of Newfoundland, was given to the United States by Churchill in the summer of 1941 when Roosevelt expressed anxiety about the safety of American shipping. After that it sailed under U.S.N. command.

Roosevelt urged Mackenzie King to annex Newfoundland, the landfall closest to Europe and jumping-off point for ferry planes to Britain. King put him off, but sent a diplomat to open a Canadian High Commission office in St. John's, the first official link between the island and the mainland in their four-hundred-year history.

C. D. Howe's war production lines gave employment to a million Canadians, including women who wrapped their hair in turbans to keep it out of machinery and put their babies in day-care centers provided by employers and the government. A Wartime Prices and Trade Board monitored prices and wages fairly and kept down inflation. Though there was rationing, Canadians enjoyed a sense of well-being. Some 50,000 women enlisted in support services as military spending rose from a half million in 1939 to five billion by the end of the war. People were buying Victory Bonds, and the money was recycled. The government gave cash to Britain, and Britain spent it on Howe's munitions in Canada.

Germany invaded Russia in June 1941. Canadians in detention camps under suspicion of being communists were released after almost two years' imprisonment. Many promptly enlisted. Québec's clergy found war hard to accept when communists became allies. *L'Action Catholique* maintained, "The greatest peril of the hour is Bolshevism rather than Hitlerism." Still Canadiens were enlisting in great numbers. The first all-French unit was the *Régiment de Maisonneuve*. Within a year, 50,000 French-Canadians were in uniform. Later, *Les Alouettes,* an all-French squadron, flew with the RAF.

The Rowell-Sirois report on the state of the Canadian Constitution was submitted early in 1941. The commissioners noted power was inequitably distributed and said that inequities imperiled the country's survival. The Depression was an illustration: provinces had the authority to provide welfare measures but not the money; the federal government had the money but not the authority. Recommended changes were that the federal government take responsibility for old-age pensions and unemployment insurance, pick up "deadweight costs" of provincial debts, and assist poor provinces with National Adjustment Grants so that the disparity between Ontario and the maritime provinces would be less pronounced, an arrangement to be known as transfer payments.

Mackenzie King called a federal-provincial conference to discuss the recommendations. Ontario objected to wealthy provinces compensating impoverished ones, but Premier Godbout of Québec supported redistribution of income in the national interest. "Separatists, gentlemen, we are not, nor could we be," he declared. "We have made too many sacrifices for Canada. There is not a foot of the soil of the country which has not felt the tread of our people."

Ernest Lapointe died in November 1941 and was replaced by Pierre Joseph Arthur Cardin as King's Québec lieutenant. A few weeks later Japan bombed the U. S. naval base in Hawaii, and attacked the British base at Hong Kong, catching two battalions of Canadian soldiers there. A year earlier Churchill said, "If Japan goes to war, there is not the slightest chance of holding Hong Kong or of relieving it. It is most unwise to increase the loss we shall suffer there." Still, he asked Canada to send troops to Hong Kong.

The battalions sailed from Vancouver October 27, 1941. On Christmas Day, they went to Japanese prison camps, a four-year ordeal that killed three hundred and permanently damaged the survivors.

When Pearl Harbor was bombed, Canada had 23,000 people of Japanese descent living in British Columbia, where prejudice imploded them into a tightly knit, self-reliant community. Most were Canadian citizens, 13,000 born in Canada and 3,000 naturalized. Since 1895 Japanese-Canadians had been forbidden to vote or hold public office. In 1931 the country made an exception for Japanese-Canadians who fought in World War I. Forbidden to enter the professions, Canadians of Japanese descent concentrated their skills in a fishing industry envied for its efficiency and profits.

"The war with Japan was a heaven-sent opportunity to rid the province of the Japanese economic menace forever," a Canadian politician confided. On December 16, 1941, Japanese and Canadians of Japanese descent were compelled to register. More than one thousand fishing boats were seized and auctioned in Vancouver for a fraction of their value. Automobiles were confiscated and Japanese-language newspapers were banned under authority of the War Measures Act.

Three months later the government packed 23,000 people on trains and dumped them inland to spend the rest of the war in ghost towns abandoned a half-century earlier by gold miners. Some were used as forced labor in Alberta's sugar-beet fields or on road gangs. A few considered dangerous were sent to prisoner-of-war camps in northern Ontario and dressed in prison uniforms bearing red targets on the backs. None was guilty of disloyalty to the state; none was charged. Even the RCMP agreed none was a security risk. Still, few Canadians protested.

Mackenzie King was pressed by Roosevelt and Churchill to provide more Canadian soldiers. Both leaders met Joseph Stalin, their unwelcome ally, who demanded an invasion of Europe to draw some of the German Army advancing toward Moscow. They delayed, not displeased at the heavy losses on both sides of the

Russian front, but Roosevelt and Churchill accepted that an Allied landing in Europe was necessary.

Mackenzie King was forced to consider sending drafted soldiers overseas. In January 1942 he announced he would hold a plebiscite to determine if Canadians wanted to release him from his promise to keep draftees at home. As he feared, even the plebiscite bill was divisive. "We are not separatists, but let us not be forced to become separatists," Maxime Raymond, a Québec Liberal, said. Raymond warned that Toronto hawks were "about to forge the nails which will serve to seal the coffin of national unity, and perhaps of confederation."

King, caught, explained ambiguously that he wasn't asking for conscription but for the authority to impose it: "Not necessarily conscription, but conscription if necessary."

Cardin, Lapointe's successor, begged Québec to vote *oui* for the sake of unity. J. Layton Ralston, hero of World War I and Canada's Minister of National Defense, revealed that overseas conscription could be enacted by an order-of-council rather than by submitting the matter to debate in parliament. Québec was suspicious. The result of the plebiscite was a country divided by language. English-speaking Canadians voted 80 percent *yes;* French-speaking Canadians voted 72 percent *non.* Cardin resigned. English-speaking Canadians clamored to see their army in action.

On the morning of August 19, 1942, in broad daylight, Britain put five thousand Canadians on an exposed beach at Dieppe in front of German guns and without prior bombardment from either air or sea. The first wave of men died. British officers sent a second wave, and a third. "Sheer, bloody murder," said a participant. "Mass execution at point-blank range," Lord Lovat, leader of Britain's commandos, called it. "We were sorry for them," a German soldier commented. "It was a mouse going into a trap."

One half of the men who landed that morning became casualties. "No Canadian had anything to do with the actual conception of the plan, the making of the original outline plan for it, or the basic decision to carry it out," Colonel C. P. Stacey, war historian, observed. The slaughter's most plausible explanation was that Churchill wanted to demonstrate to Stalin that an Allied landing in Europe was not possible.

In September 1942 Mackenzie King sent draftees to guard duty in Newfoundland, Alaska, and Greenland to release enlisted men for service in Europe. The cautious move enraged Ralston, the defense minister, who thought King must act on the plebiscite and send draftees overseas. He gave King his resignation privately, but King pressed him to remain.

King's new Québec lieutenant was a sixty-year-old lawyer, Louis St. Laurent, an able administrator who lacked the credibility of his predecessors with Québécois. A racist-clerical party, the *Bloc Populaire,* attracted 37 percent of the ballot in the provincial election by campaigning against overseas conscription and in favor of provincial rights. Godbout's Liberals hung on, though tarred with King's conscription plebiscite.

Anti-French feeling was rising in Ontario, particularly after the long casualty lists of Dieppe. There were ugly incidents when draftees, known as "zombies," clashed with righteous civilians. In a training camp in New Brunswick, a riot between the Dufferin and Haldimand Rifles of Ontario and the Voltigeurs of Québec resulted in one death.

English-speaking Canadians were impatient to see their army in action in spite of the fiasco of Dieppe. Australians and New Zealanders were winning headlines in the African desert campaign against Erwin Rommel and the German Army. General McNaughton was criticized for keeping his army timidly in England while other Commonwealth countries earned the glory, but it was Mackenzie King who kept Canadians out of Africa. He suspected Britain was there only to acquire territory.

Roosevelt and Churchill met at Québec City, sometimes allowing Mackenzie King to share their deliberations. Roosevelt suggested the Canadian Army was "rarin' to go" and asked King to prod McNaughton. Churchill agreed to a small distraction, an invasion of Sicily and Italy. King and Ralston contributed Canadian units though it meant abandoning McNaughton's cherished hope of creating a Canadian Army under his command.

The Canadian First Infantry Division and a tank brigade landed in Sicily on July 10, 1943, and suffered two thousand casualties. On September 3, Canadians went ashore on the toe of Italy and began to fight slowly north through mountains that were natural fortresses. Ralston insisted on adding a headquarters staff so that Canadians could fight under their own officers. When

McNaughton prepared to join his troops, British General Bernard Montgomery told him to stay away. If he landed he would be arrested, Montgomery said. Humiliated, McNaughton offered Ralston his resignation, but Ralston refused to accept it.

Canadians scattered through the Royal Navy and the Royal Air Force made little impact on the public consciousness, but a Canadian Army in the field in Italy was something else. Canada's commitment to the war effort increased measurably. King, encouraged, asked Churchill to send more Canadian soldiers to Italy. British generals preferred to keep Canadians on hold for the landings in France but were obliged to yield. A second Canadian armored division was dispatched to Italy. General Harold Alexander, ground commander in the Mediterranean sector, was incensed. Armor was little use to him in the mountains; he wanted infantry.

"I should be grateful if I can be consulted in future before matters of such importance are agreed upon," he wrote testily. General Dwight David Eisenhower, the genial American selected as Supreme Allied Commander, acknowledged that "political considerations" had prevailed.

The British War Office dismissed General McNaughton, whom it regarded as a boob. Ralston and King went through some formalities to give a semblance of Canadian control to the situation and McNaughton returned to Canada with the burden of a weak explanation that he was ill.

The demoralized Italian Army collapsed under Allied attack, forcing Germany to commit twenty divisions to the front. Canadians met the stiffened line at Potenza, a point of vital importance to the Allies because it threatened U. S. troop landings at Salerno on September 9, 1943. By winter Canadians were fighting in the Adriatic port of Ortona against German paratroopers who had been dropped on commanding hilltops. The Germans withdrew in December. Their commanding officer explained to Hitler, "It costs so much blood it cannot be justified." The campaign is now regarded as a blunder on the part of the British High Command; Canadians suffered 50 percent casualties.

Canada was amazed when Britain asked if Canadians had any recommendations to make to the terms of surrender that Allies would impose on Italy. The unprecedented courtesy caught the understaffed Department of External Affairs unprepared. Diplomats worked through the night and in July 1943 proudly attended a meeting of foreign ministers of the Allied nations, the first time Canada had been included in high-level strategy in seventy-six years of existence.

In the spring of 1943 Canadians took frightful losses in a campaign at Cassino, where Germans held the high ground. In March they broke the Hitler line that protected Rome. In August they fought from house to house in Adriatic towns and cut the German Gothic line. Italy surrendered unconditionally on September 8, 1943. Mussolini fled behind German lines.

Lord Halifax, British ambassador to the United States, visited Toronto to make a speech and dropped a bombshell. After the war, he said, four powers would control world affairs, the Soviet Union, China, the United States, and the British Commonwealth. Britain, braced for waning authority in a new alignment of superpowers, was preparing to reconstitute the British Empire.

Lester Pearson, Canadian ambassador in Washington, D.C., commented, "If we are not careful our international position as an independent nation will be weaker at the end of the war than it was at the beginning."

June 6, 1944, D-Day, dawned on the Allied landings in France. The European assignment for 15,000 Canadians was to hold the flank at a ninth-century village called Caen, where there was an airfield, and then sweep north to dig the Germans out of the harbors of Belgium and Holland, a filthy task. The Toronto *Globe and Mail's* war correspondent Ralph Allen called it "a mean and intimate war."

Germany put seven and a half of Hitler's eight elite panzer divisions against the Canadians at Caen, chewing up lives on both sides. A month later, the Canadians took Caen and pushed along a road straight to Falaise with the British Army, trapping 317,000 Germans between them and the Americans. When the battle of Normandy ended, the heaviest Allied casualties were suffered by Canadians.

That autumn the Canadians were ordered to the marshy Scheldt estuary in the Netherlands, gateway to the Antwerp harbor Eisenhower needed to supply his spring offensive. The campaign was expected to be a slaughter. "We must accept heavy casualties to get quick success," General Montgomery was informed. Word was passed along that more Canadian infantry would be needed in the Scheldt.

The battle of the Scheldt proceeded in icy brine without air support for chilled and exposed soldiers. Ralston visited the front and was struck by the small number of trained fighting men available. He hurried home to tell King that conscripts, who were trained in infantry tactics, should be sent to the front at once.

King stalled. Duplessis' *Union Nationale* government was back in power in Québec, shaking the confidence of King's Liberals. Sending conscripts overseas would mean political death for his party. Tensions between French-Canadians and other Canadians were rubbed raw as casualty lists from the Scheldt dominated front pages. An RCMP officer shot and killed a French-Canadian army deserter. Anti-English feeling ran so high in Québec that a hydro system official was fired because he recommended that French-Canadians should learn to speak English.

King told Ralston that the government would try a high-pressure recruitment campaign rather than send draftees. Ralston argued like a soldier; green troops wouldn't survive long in the Scheldt. King, quirky and paranoid, concluded that Ralston was plotting against him. On November 1 King presided at a regular cabinet meeting, which he opened by placing Ralston's two-year-old resignation on the table. He announced he was accepting it. Ralston, thunderstruck, got to his feet, shook hands civilly all around, and left. King replaced him with a startled Andrew McNaughton.

Pressure was put on draftees to volunteer to go overseas, but the results were negligible. McNaughton addressed troops who booed him. Connie Smythe, bantam owner of the Toronto Maple Leaf hockey team, artillery officer, and passionate patriot, was injured overseas and returned to Canada with stories about cooks being pressed into gaps in the front lines. Tories, who had renamed their party the Progressive Conservatives to show a new peppy attitude, snatched the issue as a vote-catcher. Tory leader John Bracken, moralistic former premier of Manitoba, declared that Mackenzie King was playing with men's lives in order to keep votes in Québec.

King retorted that of the 70,000 draftees in uniform, only 23,000 were French-Canadians. The reality was less interesting than the myth of French cowardice. Canadian generals privately notified King they would resign if conscripts weren't sent overseas. The threat did it. King told parliament on November 22, 1944, that 16,000 conscripted men would be sent overseas.

Two Québec Liberals crossed the floor and sat with the opposition. A popular man, C. G. ("Chubby") Power, overseer of the air-training plan, hero of World War I and a Québécois, resigned from King's cabinet. "I do not believe such a policy to be necessary at this time, nor will it save one single Canadian casualty," he told King. "We have no right to tear this country asunder at this stage."

Louis St. Laurent, who knew of the mutiny of the generals, supported King. Tight-lipped and distressed, he said, "The will of the majority must be respected and it must prevail." But when King asked for a vote of confidence, 34 Liberals, all from Québec, voted against him. English-language Members of Parliament, however, gave him sufficient support to win overwhelmingly.

Of the first 10,000 conscripted men designated to go overseas, 7,000 deserted. An army base in British Columbia had a riot and in Rimouski and Chicoutimi in Québec, mobs set fire to the Union Jack. St. Laurent's handsome mansion was pelted with rocks. Toronto newspapers called on King to restore order with machine guns if necessary.

Of 13,000 conscripts who went to Europe, only a handful faced combat, no better or worse in action than volunteers. The reaction in Québec to their going was surprisingly mild; it appreciated that King had tried. By spring Canadians cleared the Scheldt with fewer casualties than the brass had expected; Germany was almost out of manpower. The Canadians advanced over flooded ground that Eisenhower described as "appalling" through Dutch villages where residents festooned them with flowers. On May 5, 1945, a German general wearily surrendered to the Canadians in a small hotel near the Zuider Zee.

Mackenzie King announced no conscripted men would be sent to fight Japan. There were enough volunteers, 80,000, to meet the needs, he promised.

Though Canada still flew the Union Jack and Canadians traveled under British passports, a shift had occurred. Beginning with the agreement in 1940 between Roosevelt and King to establish a

permanent joint committee on defense, Canada moved by percep-
tible degrees from its traditional place at the end of a British
tether to intense and profitable involvement with the United States
instead. By the end of the war, 70 percent of foreign investment
in Canada was American; C. D. Howe had opened all doors
to United States branch plants and resource developers. British investment, meanwhile, declined to 25 percent.

America and Britain found Canada eager to please. The Allied
chemical and biological warfare testing ground was located at
Sheffield, Alberta, on a site Canada had planned to turn into a
national park. The toxic material was later buried in Canada.
Friendly Britain gave parts of Newfoundland to the United States
for use as air and naval bases. An American military road was
built to Alaska almost entirely on Canadian soil.

In addition, Allied secret agents were trained in Canada at a
charming, secluded farm near Toronto commanded by a Canadian,
William Stephenson, whose code name was Intrepid. One who
trained there was a Brit, Ian Fleming, who later invented the urbane spy James Bond. Stephenson, wealthy from his invention of
the wire-photo machine, also functioned as the discreet link between Roosevelt and Churchill when the two leaders wished to
communicate without the knowledge of their staffs.

By the end of the war, Mackenzie King was accustomed to
shuttling to Washington on one errand or another for Roosevelt
and Churchill. He perceived that Canada's cooperation was taken
for granted by America. "I personally would be strongly opposed
to anything like political union," he wrote in his diary. "It is better to have two people and two governments on this continent than
anything like continental union."

Canada was omitted from the Dumbarton Oaks meeting which
laid down the blueprint for the United Nations, but the oversight
was repaired in time for the founding conference in San Francisco. Canada was assigned to a tier of influence below the five big
nations which had veto power, but found prominence by volun-
teering to be part of peace-keeping armies the United Nations
might send to the world's troublespots. Canadians generally
approved such a role for themselves, seeing it as principled and
useful.

Mackenzie King, reading tea leaves, called an election. His foes in Québec were in disarray; no substantial challenger to the federal Liberal machine had emerged. He was returned to office handily. The surprise was the success of the socialist CCF party, which won 28 seats. In Saskatchewan voters who remembered the dust and grasshoppers of the Depression elected a CCF government. Scrappy T. C. ("Tommy") Douglas, the premier, grinned that he would establish a "beachhead of socialism on a continent of capitalism." Even Ontario voted socialist: factory workers and a developing middle class almost toppled George Drew's Tories.

In the United States, the swing was to the right. Americans rejected the Depression's populism and the New Deal to demand tighter controls of unions, lower taxes, less government interference with business, and less government programs for the poor. Canada, by contrast, emerged from the same Depression to insist on more government support for the disadvantaged and ill, and government control of capitalism.

Americans, their confidence recovered in the prosperity and victories of war, wanted the government out of the way. Canadians, enured to a system that did not reward enterprise and rarely tolerated it, wanted the government to make their lives more secure.

Accordingly, King enlarged the civil service and called a conference to determine how the recommendations of the Rowell-Sirois report could be implemented. His plan was that the federal government would collect most tax money and redistribute it to the provinces according to their needs. Duplessis and Ontario's George Drew would have none of it.

The *Enola Gay* dropped the unthinkable bomb on Hiroshimo in August. After the second one on Nagasaki, peace was signed. Canadians who volunteered for the Pacific were still awaiting delivery of tropical gear. The country counted its dead: 42,000. More than 40 percent of Canadians of military age had served in their country's uniform.

The problem of Japanese-Canadians was an embarrassment. Some 16,000 were still in exile in interior British Columbia; another 7,000 were scattered elsewhere, bearing with them travel permits stamped by police. The United States was making generous reparations to Japanese-Americans similarly abused, but some in British Columbia had another suggestion, send them all to Japan.

Mackenzie King offered Japanese-Canadians two choices, a one-way trip to Japan or their oath to stay "east of the Rockies." Mounties leaned on the former option, distributing deportation papers door to door. Confused, ten thousand signed. A few months later, half requested to rescind the documents. The CCF raised a storm in the House of Commons until Mackenzie King agreed that Canadians of Japanese origin could stay in Canada. Naturalized Canadians born in Japan would be sent back.

The first shipment of eight hundred was ready to leave Vancouver in January 1946. The injustice of their treatment provoked a legal battle, spearheaded by the CCF and civil libertarians in Toronto and Montréal. King took the case to the Supreme Court of Canada. Was it legal to expel naturalized citizens who had not committed a crime? The Supreme Court ruled that it was. An appeal went the customary route to the Privy Council in London, which noted "this was one of the most important cases that has ever come before us," and then judged that the expulsion was legal under the powers of the War Measures Act.

Canada shipped four thousand people to Japan, half of them born in Canada. The country of their ancestry was no more familiar to them than Poland would have been. For five years more, Mounties arrested Japanese-Canadians traveling without a permit. In 1949 the ordeal ended. The government put a stop to harassment and extended to Japanese-Canadians the right to vote, hold office, and educate their children in the professions.

Only a few returned to the coast of British Columbia. The shabby reparations paid for confiscated property had embittered them. A farmer got $7.84 for his truck. One old man was given $140.50 for his house. A trunk of silk kimonos, museum pieces, was valued at fifty cents. The Japanese-Canadians preferred to melt into the industrial cities of central Canada, where they avoided forming ghettos. Next time, they would be more difficult to find.

— 23 —

Uncle Sam Is Here, and Here, and Here

While wartime controls greatly reduced friction between management and labor unions in most of Canada, a particular situation developed in Québec. There, cheap, readily available hydropower created company towns around American, British or English-Canadian mills and pulp and paper factories. Unaffiliated unions dominated by agreeable priests helped keep wages the lowest on the continent. The two American giants of the union movement, the AFL and the CIO, sent organizers to sign up members. The people who came, Americans who did not speak French and not infrequently were Jewish, were viewed by the clergy as atheists and communists.

Trouble began early in the war at Arvida, the world's largest supplier of aluminum for airplanes, where Canadiens were paid between 40 and 60 percent lower than their counterparts elsewhere in North America. The strike in 1941, led by the clergy-dominated *Syndicat National Catholique de l'Aluminum,* was not only for money. Canadiens, who made up 92 percent of the work force, wanted a chance to be promoted. They got assurances only when there was talk of nationalizing the company.

The AFL sent an organizer to concentrate on the low wages. Of Arvida's 15,000 employees, 3,000 took out AFL membership. Though 4,000 Canadiens were members of the *Syndicat,* the AFL went to Ottawa to demand certification as the employees' bargaining agent. Ottawa dispatched an investigator. Like the AFL organizer, he was Jewish. Priests insulted both from the pulpit and Arvida's owners said they would close the plant rather than see the AFL succeed. The AFL retired.

Immediately after the war, management braced for new challenges from the AFL. Trouble came instead from another American union. Some 11,000 members of the United Auto Workers of America left the Ford assembly lines in Windsor, Ontario, to strike for a closed shop. The federal government sent Mounties to break up picket lines. Workers countered by jamming streets with traffic for twenty blocks around the plant. Troops and tanks in the army base at Camp Borden were put on standby. When the Chrysler plant in Windsor joined the strike, a blood-bath appeared inevitable. The government pulled back. A mediator, Judge Ivan Rand, was appointed to find a solution.

He did—the "Rand formula" prevailed in Canadian labor-management disputes. The Rand formula was a typically Canadian non-solution which, also typically, worked. Workers didn't get a closed shop but all those who didn't join the union paid dues anyway.

Union battles in Québec resumed at the Dominion Textile mills in Montréal and Valleyfield. Learning from its mistakes, the AFL this time hired Canadien organizers, one of them a woman, Madeleine Parent. Emphasizing substandard wages, the AFL team lobbied some six thousand workers. The organizers faced opposition from the church, police, and Premier Maurice Duplessis. The plant in Montréal yielded to union demands, but Valleyfield held out.

The company hired strikebreakers and a riot ensued. Maddened strikers tore up sidewalks and pelted police with concrete. Police retaliated with clubs and tear gas. Duplessis ordered the arrest of a union organizer, Kent Rowley, on a charge of sedition. He was held without bail and Madeleine Parent took his place in the line. She was arrested. On the ninety-eighth day of violence the company agreed to a wage increase of twenty-five cents an hour. Rowley served six months in prison.

Abroad, Canada's attention was focused on the emerging United Nations. In 1946 a commission drew up a charter on human rights. A draft was sent to the plenary session of the United Nations. It was signed by all member countries with seven exceptions: Byelorussia, Czechoslovakia, Poland, the Ukraine, the Soviet Union, Yugoslavia—and Canada. The Canadian delegates couldn't sign; in Canada, civil rights are in provincial jurisdiction, not federal. Four days after the list was published, Mackenzie

King ordered mortified delegates to sign, though technically it was illegal.

The Cold War began in Canada only a few weeks after Japan's surrender. A cipher clerk in the Soviet Embassy, Igor Gouzenko, approached the night editor of the Ottawa *Journal* and said he had 109 documents relating to Soviet spy activity in Canada and the United States. The editor said sure, take them to the Justice Building up the street. The security guard there told him to come back in the morning.

Eventually Ottawa recognized that Gouzenko was a real defector with real secrets. Mackenzie King, whose first reaction was that Gouzenko should return the stolen property to his Embassy, notified President Harry Truman of the United States and Prime Minister Clement Atlee of Britain. He was advised to keep the matter quiet. The powers were conferring with the Soviets and didn't want relations disturbed.

Drew Pearson, an American newspaper columnist, broke the story in February 1946. King's cabinet agreed to invoke the ever-useful War Measures Act in secret in order to give the Mounties authority to arrest communists. Police wakened thirteen people before dawn, one a Member of Parliament, Fred Rose, and took them to the RCMP barracks, where they were held without charges, without a lawyer, and without being allowed to contact their families. They were questioned around the clock in six-hour shifts.

The western democracies, aroused by Gouzenko's damning documents, hunted Soviet spies everywhere. A Midwest senator in the United States, Joseph McCarthy, seized the issue to get attention and rode it to power. Americans had the impression well-organized communists in their midst were ready to overthrow the government. In the United States, a wave of poorly substantiated blacklists and Senate investigations destroyed careers and even lives. In Canada the witchhunts took the form of pressure on the National Film Board, suspected of harboring communists because of its sympathetic documentaries about the disadvantaged, and the Canadian Broadcasting Corporation, which was labeled "a Red network." Civil servants with membership in civil liberties organizations were fired on various pretexts. The RCMP Security and Intelligence sections, given unlimited power to find subversive citizens, delivered secret lists of suspects to employers and government officials.

Gouzenko, who appeared at news conferences with a brown paper bag over his head, seemed erratic and unstable. Despite the startling nature of documents he carried from the Soviet Embassy, there was little evidence to convict Canadians of any crime. Fred Rose, the Member of Parliament, and Sam Carr, national organizer for the Canadian Communist Party, admitted they were communists and went to prison.

The CCF concluded it was unwise to describe itself as socialist. Few Canadians could make the distinction between a socialist democrat and a Stalin communist. The CCF Party concentrated on its social programs and in Saskatchewan Tommy Douglas in 1946 introduced the continent's first government-sponsored hospital insurance plan.

Mackenzie King moved his party into social-welfare programs to combat the growing appeal of the CCF. Influenced by Britain's Beveridge Report which advocated sweeping social reform, King offered the provinces federal money if they would introduce Medicare. He brought in unemployment insurance, old-age pensions, and a monthly baby bonus to mothers.

The country had ample financial resources. Under C. D. Howe's direction, American-owned industries were flourishing and exports of American-owned raw materials accelerated. An impressive new export was uranium, the waste product from Gilbert Labine's radium mines in northern Ontario. Believing it to be worthless, Labine stored uranium in the pretty town of Port Hope, on Lake Ontario, until the United States discovered a use for it at Los Alamos.

Canada got an early start in nuclear energy by building the world's second reactor at Chalk River, in Ontario. A Canadian was the world's first victim of an accident in a nuclear power lab. While working in Los Alamos in 1946, Louis Slotin was "tickling the dragon's tail" by poking at radioactive material. His hand slipped and the material fused, the preliminary to a nuclear explosion. Slotin stopped the process by pulling the plutonium apart with his bare hands. His body was shipped in a lead coffin to his parents in Winnipeg.

The next year, the U.S.-owned Imperial Oil Company sank a

drill into a farm near Leduc, Alberta, and stepped back from a gusher. Farmers got ready to celebrate but found the provincial government owned the rights, a legacy of Hudson's Bay Company jurisdiction over minerals, which cannily kept them even when it sold the land.

Ernest Manning, head of Alberta's Social Credit government, thriftily salted away oil royalties but let Americans tap all they wanted. Production jumped in a year from 8 million to 181 million barrels of oil and from 52 to 220 billion cubic feet of natural gas. In return for bearing the costs of exploration and drilling, Americans kept the profits.

Americans also made a strike in the Ungava region of Labrador: iron ore so accessible it blew red in the wind. Mined in an open pit, it couldn't be shipped directly from Sept Isles, a river port, to steel mills on the Great Lakes because of the blocked neck of the St. Lawrence River where it joined Lake Ontario.

Pittsburgh clamored to have a canal rammed through as Ungava's production of cheap iron ore jumped from 2 million to 21 million tons a year. Hamilton, Ontario, which after World War I boasted more American-owned factories, mostly steel mills, than any city in Canada, pressured Ottawa for a canal. Ontario's automotive industry, spread from Windsor to Oshawa and wholly American-owned, also lobbied for the link with the sea and export markets.

The big news was immigration, which had almost ceased in Canada after World War I. The first wave consisted of 40,000 women from Britain and the Netherlands who had married Canadian servicemen.

"The people of Canada do not wish, as a result of mass immigration, to make a fundamental alteration in the character of our population," Mackenzie King assured Canadians alarmed that the country's all-white immigration policies would weaken. British immigrants had preference; George Drew, Tory premier of Ontario, opened a recruitment office in London. Eventually 200,000 British citizens sailed for Canada.

But the country was cutting British ties. In 1947 Canada stopped appealing Supreme Court decisions to the British Privy Council, 80 years after Canada became a nation. That year too Canada issued the first Canadian passports. Mackenzie King got

No. 1. With the decision to have separate citizenship for Canadians, the country was obliged to establish embassies. The Department of External Affairs was enlarged with a crop of bright young men led by Louis St. Laurent and Lester Bowles ("Mike") Pearson, a former history professor and Washington ambassador.

In 1948 Mackenzie King was seventy-four. He had been prime minister twenty-two years, longer than any man in the history of the British Commonwealth. He was exhausted. St. Laurent quietly assumed control of the government as King increasingly kept to himself, communing with his departed mother and grieving over the death of his dog. With the war over, he relaxed his self-imposed ban on séances and was happily exchanging messages with distinguished ghosts, among them Franklin Roosevelt.

To the relief of close associates who knew nothing of his rich secret life but saw deterioration in his judgment, King retired in September 1948. He was replaced as prime minister by the avuncular, shrewd Louis St. Laurent. The succession fixed a tradition for federal Liberals—English would alternate with French. Mike Pearson, St. Laurent's likable deputy, left the civil service for politics and was named the new Minister of External Affairs.

Though Québec supported Liberals in federal elections, the province continued to be charmed by Maurice Duplessis' hopelessly corrupt *Union Nationale* government. *Le chef,* vigorously supported by the dominant right-wing element in the Catholic Church, maintained a political machine well-oiled with patronage. Money for party workers came from American branch plants, lured to the province by Duplessis' assurances that he controlled labor unions.

On February 13, 1949, his power was challenged in a grim company town, Asbestos, Québec, owned by Johns-Manville, an American firm. Workers there in an open asbestos pit which is still the world's largest single source of the carcinogenic substance went on strike. Duplessis, determined to put a quick end to the disturbance, sent one hundred police who beat strikers mercilessly and threw them in jail. The company sued the union and was given a court injunction against the picket lines. The union stubbornly ignored the order and continued to picket. Three months later, on May 5, women with rosaries walked the picket lines, praying. Provincial police on rooftops opened fire with machine

guns and threw tear-gas grenades. With five hundred police reinforcements awaiting orders in nearby Sherbrooke, the distraught
strikers gave up.

The ferocity of the police and the justice of the strikers' complaints created powerful, unexpected friends. Québec's young intellectuals, long aloof from the problems of semi-literate workers,
hurried to Asbestos to help. Among them were Pierre Elliott
Trudeau, a law professor and son of a millionaire whose fortune
was made by sale of gas stations to Imperial Oil, and Gérald
Pelletier, reporter for *Le Devoir,* an expert on the effect of asbestos inhalation. They were joined by a tousle-haired union organizer, Jean Marchand.

Their presence was little noticed. Instead the province was
rocked when two archbishops of the Catholic Church openly took
the side of the strikers. Monsignor Joseph Charbonneau of
Montréal, a man often photographed at the side of Duplessis,
took on state and church. He told his congregation in Notre Dame
Cathedral, "The working class is the victim of a conspiracy which
seeks its destruction, and when there is a conspiracy to crush the
working class, it is the duty of the church to intervene."

Priests stood at church doors to collect donations for strikers'
families. Duplessis sent a furious message to Rome demanding the
pope remove Charbonneau. Soonafter the archbishop was demoted to parish priest. But strikers took heart from him and later,
142 days after the pickets began, Johns-Manville signed a contract granting wage increases and safer conditions.

Trudeau, Pelletier, and Marchand continued to meet after the
heady excitement of the Asbestos strike. Trudeau and Pelletier
founded a journal, *Cité Libre,* the voice of radical protest against
Duplessis' graft and repression. In Ottawa, Prime Minister St.
Laurent took note of the bubbling *rouge* movement. English-
Canada had no cohesion with which to confront such solidarity.
He commissioned a study of Canadian culture, a royal commission headed by a wealthy ascetic, Vincent Massey, brother of the
actor, Raymond Massey.

While Massey listened to poets and professors decry an
avalanche of American books, American radio programs, American magazines, American movies, and American style, Canada
prepared to add another province, the tenth, Newfoundland. After

years as a Crown Colony, Newfoundland was deciding whether to become an independent democracy, join the United Kingdom, or join the United States.

Only a handful wanted to become part of Canada, but one was enough. He was Newfoundland's most popular radio broadcaster, Joseph Smallwood, a chirpy, irreverent journalist with an unquenchable ambition to become a father of confederation by attaching Newfoundland to Canada. While other islanders were transfixed by Americans and the money they flashed at such bases as Gander, Stephenville, and Fort Pepperrell, Joey Smallwood praised old-age pensions and the baby bonus that would flow from Ottawa. Joining the U.S. was dropped as an option.

The Newfoundland referendum of 1948 offered three choices: independence, Canada, or the status quo. By a slim majority, independence won. Smallwood was undaunted. Since more had voted for the combination of the other two, he declared the results inconclusive. A second referendum offered only two options: Canada or independence.

Many Newfoundlanders were so poor they had never been out of debt to the grocery store in their lives. Smallwood promised them food for their children. "MOTHERS—READ THIS!" banners proclaimed. "Confederation is good for children. Confederation is good for mothers. Confederation is good for the family. Once we get confederation we know that NEVER AGAIN WILL THERE BE A HUNGRY CHILD IN NEWFOUNDLAND."

Canada won by only 52 percent but it was enough. When "the last great step of confederation" was announced on March 31, 1949, many Newfoundlanders wore black armbands in mourning. Soon after the baby-bonus checks arrived, they went to the polls to elect their first democratic government in fifteen years. Joey Smallwood and his Liberals rode to victory on the first cash some families had ever seen.

Another development of that year was the creation of an anti-Soviet military bloc, the North Atlantic Treaty Organization. Canada was one of twelve signatories to the pact to keep a combined force in Europe against communist aggression. Consistent with Canada's role in the United Nations, St. Laurent insisted that NATO also have "moral" content in the form of social and cultural cooperation, a stipulation which was included but is rarely observed.

St. Laurent won his first election as prime minister in June 1949, gaining the largest majority in his party's history. Québec supported the Liberals because the kindly man was a native son, and English-Canada did so because he was a sound administrator. The Tories, with only 41 seats against the Liberals' 193, prepared to abandon their new leader, Ontario's former premier, stiff-backed George Drew, who was blamed for the debacle.

That year St. Laurent launched work on the long-promised Trans-Canada Highway. Canadian motorists at last could cross their country without detouring through Chicago. The highway had to overcome difficulties with the Constitution, which St. Laurent avoided by offering the provinces federal money to pay for it. When it was completed in 1962 it stretched 4,860 miles from the Atlantic to the Pacific, a homogeneous road from sea to sea except in Québec where Duplessis wouldn't accept the federal highway markings.

St. Laurent didn't share King's reluctance to allow American military a free hand in Canada. John Foster Dulles, American Secretary of State, was obsessed with a Cold War against the Soviets and the menace of communism. Ottawa was asked to allow a radar screen, the Pine Tree Line, across the north to give warning of Soviet bombers headed for the United States. When this radar line was judged to be useless, another was built farther north, and then another, the Distant Early Warning Line (or DEW Line). Since Canada had no interest in paying for the electronic surveillance, it cost the United States $600 million. Later Canadians were furious that outposts flew the Stars and Stripes and American sentries challenged all comers.

"Whiskey forts all over again," someone grumbled.

The affront was pushed aside when the world learned the Soviets had developed a nuclear bomb. In the Pentagon, generals worked into the night on plans to increase America's nuclear arsenal. A confrontation with communists was brewing in Korea, where the corrupt government of South Korea headed by Syngman Rhee, who was friendly to the Americans, was threatened by communist North Korea.

The invasion of South Korea came on June 25, 1950. The surprise attack carried the North Koreans as far as the port of Pusan. President Harry Truman ordered the U. S. commander in Japan, General Douglas MacArthur to help South Korea. He appealed to the United Nations to send a "police force."

Canada was invited to send troops by the UN Secretary-General. St. Laurent wavered for weeks worried about the reaction of Québec. In the end it was clear that strong anti-communist feelings in the province would endorse action. When the army opened recruiting, 25,000 Canadians volunteered for Korea.

Mackenzie King, seventy-six and ailing, fretted. He noted suspiciously in his diary that the United States was dragging Canada "into as many situations affecting themselves as possible, with a view to leading ultimately to the annexation of our two countries."

Canadians trained at Fort Lewis in the United States under American officers, increasing King's distress. He died on July 22, 1950. The moment he ceased breathing there was thunder and lightning all around his estate, and nowhere else.

Canadians landed in South Korea as the People's Republic of China, Mao Tse Tung's communist government, came to the support of North Korea with 180,000 soldiers. The Canadian contingent, third largest in a United Nations army that included troops from such friendly countries as Britain, Australia, New Zealand, India, and Turkey, fought in South Korea's mountains for a year. The UN regained all territory lost as far as the Imjin River at a cost of 406 Canadian lives.

The war halted while negotiators met patiently under the blue-and-white flag of the United Nations for two years, after which Korea was divided almost exactly as it had been before.

A Canadian icebreaker, *Labrador,* in 1954 sailed through the Arctic from the Atlantic to the Pacific, showing the flag. The voyage reinforced Canada's northern claim, which had lain fallow from the time in the nineteenth century when Britain ceded jurisdiction. A tiny RCMP vessel, the *St. Roch,* pioneered the journey during World War II. With Americans swarming all over Alaska, the Mounties crashed through the ice to demonstrate that the north belonged to Canada.

Most Canadians relied on romantic National Film Board travelogues for a sense of the north, judging it to be a blinding white world where nomadic people hunted caribou, and Inuit, described as "Eskimos," lived in domes of solid ice. Bush pilots of the twenties carried a few civil servants and geologists, and RCAF veterans mapped the tundra from the air. Both activities seemed exotic but irrelevant until the full implication of the DEW Line sunk in. With American flags snapping all over the ice fields, Canadians suddenly realized the north was their front line, beyond which lay the Soviets.

The country tightened surveillance of citizens who might be "a danger to the state." Mounties gave a zealous imitation of McCarthyism. A Winnipeg schoolboy who wrote a letter to a newspaper suggesting that Santa Claus was a communist received a visit and lecture from a Mountie. The government allowed Mounties to deport naturalized Canadians without trial to the country of their origin if the RCMP believed them guilty of "disaffection or disloyalty."

The economic boom continued, allowing Canadians to move to sprawling ranch-style houses in the suburbs where they raised 2.5 children in the *McCall's* magazine ideal of togetherness. "The fatal decades," historian George Woodcock called the period. The groundwork laid by C. D. Howe in bringing American capital into Canada paid off in quantum leaps: In 1945 there was $7.1 billion of foreign investment in Canada; in 1957 there was $17.5 billion, 76 percent of it American. The biggest gains in American ownership were made in manufacturing, where branch plants thrived but produced nothing for export, and in such natural resources as oil and gas.

Vincent Massey's report on Canadian culture identified weak points. Provincially supported universities were slipping in academic qualifications because of lack of funds, he said. Massey was concerned that Canada was saturated with American radio broadcasting and believed the country should be producing its own programs. Further, Canadian literature was starved; without a patron, indigenous arts of all kind were doomed to fade under the competition of mass-market American products.

In reward, Vincent Massey in 1952 was named Canada's first native-born governor-general. His patrician style and slight British accent, then the mark of a cultivated Canadian, was so much like that of two centuries of upper-class British generals that the transition was scarcely noticeable. Though Canada's industrial sector was withering steadily in terms of exports, one glorious exception to the trend was an airplane factory at Malton, outside Toronto, where Canadians were building the Avro Arrow which promised to be the world's fastest combat plane.

George VI of Britain, a mild, decent man, died in 1952 and was succeeded by his glum and dedicated daughter Elizabeth II. St. Laurent led the Liberals to another decisive victory despite rising discontent in the west, where bumper wheat crops clogged storage elevators waiting for customers; U. S. wheat was cheaper.

Central Canada, starved for highrise, needed an army of low-skilled construction laborers and found them in Italy and Portugal. The newcomers concentrated mainly in bustling Toronto where they clustered in neighborhoods dominated by day by women wrapped in black and at night with the fragrance of oregano. Skilled steel workers came from Britain to Hamilton's steel plants, which doubled in capacity to produce skeletons for skyscrapers, and then doubled again.

Alberta's boom depended on the wealth the dinosaur age had deposited beneath its ranchland. A network of pipelines was being built to carry the oil and gas to markets. The first in 1953 linked Edmonton and Vancouver. Howe and St. Laurent negotiated something bigger, a pipeline that would cross Canada and be as glamorous a project as construction of the CPR.

In March 1956 the pipeline bill was introduced in parliament by a proud C. D. Howe. It bore striking resemblances to the building of the CPR. The pipeline would be financed by Canadian Government money and would be owned and controlled by a private company, in this case the American Trans-Canada Pipe Lines. The opposition howled. Conservatives rose in wrath, led by their exhausted leader, George Drew, and a fire-and-brimstone orator from the west, John G. Diefenbaker.

Howe had a deadline in mind, June 5, 1956. He was accustomed to running the Canadian economy as he saw fit under the emergency provisions of the War Measures Act, which had not exposed him to the constraints of the democratic process. Impatiently, he notified parliament that he was tired of the debate and would invoke closure under an ancient, little-used rule. He called for the vote on the night of June 6. Liberals, with their huge majority in the House, voted "aye" and it was law. "A sorry victory," historian Donald Creighton called it.

That summer President Gamal Nasser of Egypt, indignant when the United States withdrew financial help for the Aswan Dam on the Nile River, confiscated Egypt's only economic asset, the Suez Canal. Anthony Eden, British prime minister, responded like a nineteenth-century imperialist dealing with an upstart colonial. Israel was persuaded to attack Egypt to give Britain and France the pretext to intervene and take the Suez back. As the RAF bombed Egyptian airfields and British and French warships steamed toward the Suez, the General Assembly of the United Nations met in emergency session.

Nations of the British Commonwealth were asked to come to the aid of the mother country. St. Laurent demurred. Mike Pearson presented the Assembly with the quintessential Canadian strategy: compromise. On the evening of November 3, 1956, he proposed that a United Nations peace-keeping army be dispatched at once to the Suez to keep the belligerents apart. Nineteen countries abstained from the vote, but Pearson's resolution was accepted unanimously by the rest. Pearson and Dag Hammarskjold, Secretary-General of the UN, put together a military package by buttonholing delegates in the corridors. In forty-eight hours they had an army. A Canadian, General E. L. M. Burns, commanded the troops, who arrived in the Suez in the nick of time to stop the war.

Though Pearson received worldwide praise for his role in solving the Suez crisis, and subsequently became Canada's only recipient of a Nobel Peace Prize, Tories hotly criticized him at the time for betraying Britain.

The Canadian ambassador in Cairo then was Herbert Norman, forty-seven, one of the host of brilliant diplomats who created Canada's External Affairs Department after the war. A Japanese scholar of distinction and a Methodist raised in the tradition of the social gospel, Norman in his youth had admired Marxism, which he described as "a remarkably acute touchstone."

Senator Joseph McCarthy learned from the U. S. State Department that Herbert Norman had belonged to a communist organization during his student years at Cambridge. The information was supplied by the Canadian Mounties, who added that Norman was no longer under suspicion. Still, Norman was named a communist in March 1957 by a U. S. Senate subcommittee. The Canadian Government was silent when queried, though officials knew the accusation was false. Three weeks later Norman committed suicide in Cairo.

When pressed for a comment, President Dwight D. Eisenhower said, "As usual, I shall not criticize anybody."

That year the Canadian Government acted on the recommendations of the Massey Report on Canadian culture. To protect the frail flower of Canadian literature and the other arts from the American deluge, Ottawa established the Canada Council. With a base income derived from $100 million in legacies, the Canada Council launched programs sponsoring writers, dancers, musicians, muralists, actors, filmmakers, weavers, et al., all of whom receive direct grants for travel or study, or indirect grants in the form of subsidies for publishers, opera and ballet companies, orchestras, theaters, and art galleries. "It will contribute to the unity of Canada," a founder promised. The commission controlling broadcasting made a similar rescue attempt, ruling that "Canadian content" had to be protected by radio and television outlets.

George Drew stepped down as Tory leader and the charismatic John G. Diefenbaker replaced him. Diefenbaker, a folk hero in Saskatchewan where he was an inspiring sight in courtrooms defending the underdog, was vain, proud, suspicious of Easterners —especially the Tory establishment of Toronto—and capable of holding a grudge forever.

The pipeline debate soured Canadians on the Liberals. In 1957 they elected Diefenbaker's Progressive Conservatives by a small margin, giving the Tories a minority government. For the first time in twenty-two years, the Conservatives were in power in Ottawa. For the first time, Canada had a prime minister whose heritage was neither British nor French. At sixty-one, Diefenbaker was the oldest elected prime minister in Canadian history.

St. Laurent's Liberals had the option of forming a coalition with the CCF, with which they could ask the governor-general for permission to form a government. St. Laurent, worn and tired, declined. His resignation soon followed and he was replaced by cheerful Mike Pearson, glowing with his accomplishments at the United Nations. Pearson's approachable style and jaunty bow ties were in startling contrast to the somber, formal Liberal leaders who preceded him.

A Toronto corporation lawyer, Walter Gordon, submitted a report concerning American ownership commissioned by the Liberals. Gordon, a man of gentle courtesies, had misgivings about the rapid increase in American ownership of Canadian industry and resources. His study, written in good part by a poet, Douglas LePan, noted that U. S. ownership had doubled in little more than a decade. "Legitimate Canadian interests [are being] overlooked or disregarded," the report stated. Gordon recommended that Canada oblige foreign investors to sell stock to Canadian citizens and appoint Canadians to executive positions.

WHO REALLY OWNS CANADA? asked *Maclean's* magazine, which describes itself as the country's national magazine.

Chafing at the delicacy required to function with a minority government, Diefenbaker in 1958 called a general election. He campaigned like a prophet, his eyes blazing with his vision of opening the north and turning away from crass Americans to the greening of ties with Britain. Canadians loved it. A population swollen by one third since the war also applauded the sprinkling of minorities in his government, which included Ukrainians, Chinese, and Italians, and a woman in the cabinet, Ellen Fairclough of Hamilton, a first.

Canadian voters gave the Tories the biggest electoral victory in history, 208 seats in a parliament of 265. Prairie socialists voted for him, dazzled by the bright promises, and so did Québec, caught in the bandwagon effect and urged by *le chef,* Duplessis himself, to forgive the hanging of Riel and vote Conservative.

Duplessis' animus for Liberals stemmed from his conviction that they used federal bribes to weaken provincial rights. Even Mackenzie King's 1927 legislation to establish old-age pensions was resisted by Québec until 1936. Seeing even the franchise for women as a federalist plot, Québec didn't allow women to vote provincially until 1940. Duplessis opposed Canada Council grants to universities on the same grounds. Students demonstrated in

protest but he maintained that schools were a provincial jurisdiction and their status would be jeopardized if he took federal
money.

Duplessis' rule ended with his death in 1959. The new leader of
the *Union Nationale* was Paul Sauvé, a modern man and prag-
matist, who found a face-saving formula for accepting capital
funds to expand Québec's universities.

John Diefenbaker was ill-suited to power after a lifetime of opposing it. He resented the efficient, pervasive, all-knowing civil
service, which he believed to be loyal to Liberals and secretly
working against his government. He was uncomfortable in meetings with Toronto's suave Tories, whom he mistrusted.

One day, on impulse apparently rooted in dislike of eastern industrial hegemony, he canceled Avro Arrow aircraft production
and ordered that every plane in existence be cut into small pieces.
The Arrow, a surpassingly beautiful, white-hulled supersonic craft
two decades ahead of its time, was the pride of Canadian engineers. Its engine, the Iroquois, was the most powerful in the
world.

When Diefenbaker fired all 14,000 employees, engineers and
designers who had spent ten years building the lovely Arrow dissolved as a working team. Many found work in Houston, Texas,
preparing to put American astronauts on the moon. Diefenbaker's
explanation for the decision was that the Arrow was behind
schedule and costs were over estimates. At $3.75 million apiece,
he predicted there would be no buyers for the Arrow. Ironically,
Canada shopped for an interceptor aircraft twenty years after the
Arrow was destroyed, and was ready to pay an American company
$20 million each for planes inferior to the matchless Arrow.

Diefenbaker's reflexive opposition of the establishment served
him better when he attended his first Commonwealth conferences
in Britain in 1959. The prairie loner gravitated naturally to delegates from Third World nations. He aligned Canada with African
and Asian nations in opposition to the all-white governments of
South Africa and Rhodesia. A vote of censure supported by Canada caused South Africa to resign from the British Commonwealth.

The legislation of which Diefenbaker was most proud was a Bill
of Rights. Though the document had no legal significance because

Canadian courts have no constitutional authority over civil rights, it made a handsome wallhanging in the office of the Canadian Civil Liberties Association. Diefenbaker was attentive to the needs of the west. His sale of wheat to the People's Republic of China for cash relieved groaning grain elevators but raised hackles in the U. S. State Department.

After obstructing for generations all Canadian efforts to get American cooperation to build a seaway in the St. Lawrence River, the United States finally yielded, alarmed by threats that Canada would do it alone. Port cities of New York, New Orleans, and Boston successfully lobbied in the past to block the proposal, which would create rival seaports on Great Lakes' cities. Washington was pushed to support the St. Lawrence Canal by the clamor from Pittsburgh and other inland industrial cities who wanted access to Labrador's iron ore. American ports were mollified by assurances that the canal would not be dredged deep enough for the large ocean carriers. Canada failed to get Washington to relent on that, or to allow the route to be toll-free to keep down the cost of imports; the United States insisted on high tolls so that U. S. railway freight rates wouldn't be undercut.

The St. Lawrence canals were opened in the summer of 1959. President Dwight Eisenhower presided on behalf of the United States and Queen Elizabeth II for Canada. A delighed Diefenbaker was in attendance. On a morning deep in mist, the queen's immaculate yacht, the *Britannia,* slowly passed along a line of ships from three navies, U.S., Royal, and Royal Canadian, their bulks looming silently one by one out of the fog. The Seaway officially was open.

The defense budget, the Seaway, and Canada's dismal trade balance were sinking the federal government in debt, but impoverished southern Europeans saw it as a land of plenty. In 1957 immigration peaked at 282,000. In Toronto whole neighborhoods were transformed by shops and restaurants redolent with the flavors of Calabria and Macedonia. Canada's industrial heartland received most of the newcomers: Ontario drew 35 percent, Québec 30. French-Canadians were distressed that few immigrants to Québec wanted their children to speak French; parents sent them to English schools instead.

Québec's brief fling with the federal Conservatives ended.

Diefenbaker showed no interest in French-Canadians. His "maize amees" caliber of French was egregious and patronizing, and his failure to appoint a Québec lieutenant was taken as an insult. The province was cheered, however, when a French-Canadian, Georges Vanier, a war hero from a distinguished Québec family, was appointed governor-general of Canada, the first francophone in the position.

The *Union Nationale* government didn't long survive the death of Duplessis. The Montréal newspaper *Le Devoir* assigned reporters to investigate the party's long record of corruption. In short order, every member of Paul Sauvé's cabinet had a lawsuit for libel against the paper. Even the Catholic Church was alienated from the party after the Asbestos strike. In 1960, after sixteen years in power, the *Union Nationale* government was defeated narrowly by Jean Lesage's Liberals.

The socialist CCF Party underwent a facelift designed to emphasize its new ties to the union movement. The Canadian Congress of Labour endorsed the party, which renamed itself the New Democratic Party and chose a new leader, spunky Tommy Douglas, premier of Saskatchewan.

The Social Credit Party, which governed Alberta and British Columbia, had failed to interest easterners except for a burning group of zealots in Québec. In 1961 the party cultivated the offshoot by making Réal Caouette, a colorful, flashing-eyed fanatic, its deputy leader.

Jean Lesage's victory over the rotted but entrenched *Union Nationale* owed much to his ability to recruit new blood in the party. His most notable acquisition was Québec's most popular journalist and broadcaster, the superbly bilingual, quick-witted, and charming René Lévesque. Lévesque was elevated to the cabinet as Minister of Natural Resources. His most substantial achievement in that portfolio was to nationalize hydroelectric power, seizing it from British and American private owners while paying handsome reparations.

Lesage's bright Minister of Education, Paul Gérin-Lajoie, undertook similar reforms in Québec's antiquated church-run education system. As part of what one observer dubbed "the quiet revolution," Gérin-Lajoie introduced contemporary maths and sciences, raised elementary school standards, infused high schools with technology, and launched post-secondary education that dealt with more than classics. The church was aghast.

Asked about the reforms, Lévesque replied, "What's the result? A nation awake, in full swing, fed up with being seen as a museum, as 'the quaint old province of Québec.'"

The province bounced with books, plays, poems, and folk songs about French-Canada's heritage, the artists bolstered by Canada Council grants and employment in the federal government's Radio Canada and National Film Board. French-Canadians living outside Québec, known as francophones to distinguish them from non-French, who were designated anglophones, stirred after years of assimilation enforced by all-English schools. In Moncton, New Brunswick, home of Acadiens and Canadiens from Québec, a protest movement grew when the mayor refused requests to provide municipal services in French.

A *rouge* movement, the *Rassemblement pour l'Indépendance Nationale* (RIN) attracted hot young separatists to the leadership of Marcel Chaput, who wrote the handbook of the radicals, *Pourquoi Je Suis Séparatiste*. Chaput declared that history intended that North America have an independent French-speaking country. Separation from Canada would complete Québec's natural destiny.

English-Canada was unaware of the forces sweeping Québec. John Diefenbaker's troubles with the young American President John Kennedy, who plainly found the Canadian prime minister ridiculous, were more engrossing. Some of the conflict stemmed from Canada's participation in the North American Air Defense Command (NORAD), a largely American military operation with headquarters in Colorado Springs. The NORAD alliance permanently damaged Canada's credibility with Third World nations, who stopped believing that the country operated independently from the United States.

James Minifie, a Canadian journalist in Washington, D.C., wrote, "The conviction is growing in many quarters that the subordination, or appearance of subordination, consequent to this top-heavy integration—this horse-rabbit pie with one horse and one rabbit—deprives Canada of one of the strongest weapons in its armoury, its leadership of the middle powers in the councils of the world."

Howard Green, a Tory Minister of External Affairs, a farmer with little polish but a genuine commitment to disarmament, found his efforts at the United Nations greeted with skepticism. Diefenbaker, ever touchy in matters of face, became a balky partner in dealings with NORAD.

Diefenbaker preferred the view north, where the Canadian frontier had become a lively crossroads for geologists, surveyors, weather-watchers, Mounties, bush pilots, Americans running the DEW Line, civil servants, romantics, outcasts, missionaries, and tourists. Alert, the most northern settlement, was the jumping-off place for visitors to the North Pole, a few hundred miles beyond.

The heavy traffic disrupted Inuit hunters who had survived for centuries in one of the world's least hospitable regions. The tribes, whom tourists mistakenly called Eskimos, proved to be as readily demoralized by liquor and welfare handouts as any other native people in North America. The Alcan highway construction crews brought liquor to the north in quantities, beginning the destruction of what had been close-knit, supportive family life. By the fifties, tuberculosis and diphtheria had all but wiped out some hunting bands. Infant mortality for all Canadian tribes was among the world's highest, and life expectancy less than forty years. Doctors reported that violence, brain disease, depression, and suicide were destroying an entire people. Canadians of European stock scarcely noticed; during World War II Ottawa effected an economy by closing schools on the reservations and no one commented.

Young native militants began creating waves. Native protest organizations, slow to develop in a tradition which did not honor authoritarianism, were torn between those who wanted the tribes to save themselves by returning to their origins and others who thought the solution was modernization, between the patient ones willing to endure a hundred government studies and the impatient who would tolerate not one more, between young and old, between women and men.

Diefenbaker's dream of the north, an apocalyptic vision of millions of people living in solar bubbles, had failed totally to consider that the north already was inhabited by thousands of people living in hell.

Diefenbaker had to abandon his plan to spend $50 million on

northern communities as the country's economy sagged. The Canadian dollar was pegged at ninety-two cents and the country borrowed heavily to cover its debts. Administrative costs were mounting along with the trade deficit but Diefenbaker hoped to solve his problems with more government spending. His decision put him in conflict with the governor of the Bank of Canada, James Coyne, who favored a tight money policy. Coyne's speeches about the menace of American economic domination rankled the prime minister. Diefenbaker asked for Coyne's resignation. When Coyne refused, Diefenbaker pushed parliament to sack him, a shabby deed that many found distasteful.

Diefenbaker also quarreled with the provinces over tax-sharing and other issues no longer clear in the Constitution. His conflict with British Columbia over the Columbia River created enemies for him there. The federal government wanted to build dams on the river, which rises in Canada and flows through the United States, and keep the power in Canada, but British Columbia and the United States objected. Premier W. A. C. Bennett (known as "Wacky") of British Columbia claimed that his province had the right to sell Columbia River hydroelectric power to the States and spend the profits. Ottawa was blocked; the Constitution didn't protect the federal government's interests.

When U. S. President John Kennedy visited Ottawa in 1961 to mend fences with the prickly prime minister, he made a graceful comment: "Geography has made us neighbors. History has made us friends. Economics has made us partners. And necessity has made us allies."

Diefenbaker's hope of improved Anglo-Canadian trade was dashed when the motherland turned instead to the European Common Market. An irritated Diefenbaker attended a Commonwealth Prime Minister's Conference in London in 1962 and was lampooned as a doddering old fool by the merciless British press.

In October 1962 a U. S. spy plane detected Soviet missile sites in Cuba. President Kennedy gave Canada a half-hour warning and put North America on war alert. Diefenbaker, furious at the slight, retaliated by saying that Canadian forces wouldn't be part of the NORAD standby. In asking for a parliamentary investigation of the Cuban situation, he inferred that Kennedy was lying.

The tension between the two nations already was formidable

because Diefenbaker was delaying the decision to allow the United States to put nuclear warheads on its Bomarc-B missiles snuggled into two sites, one at North Bay in Ontario and the other La Macaza, Québec. The missiles were part of NORAD defense, which hoped to protect America's industrial heartland by shooting down Soviet bombers over Canada. Diefenbaker's hesitation at completing Canada's commitment to NORAD and allowing the warheads to be installed created space for a fine righteous debate about disarmament and moral leadership, into which Canadian opinion-makers and opinion-holders plunged joyfully.

Diefenbaker was unimpressed that the decision to put missile sites in Canada was made by President Kennedy and Prime Minister Harold Macmillan of Britain at a meeting in Nassau in December 1962. "More and more nuclear deterrent is becoming of such a nature that more nuclear arms will add nothing material to our defense," Diefenbaker commented stubbornly.

The Pentagon was incredulous that Canada would take a position in favor of unarmed missiles. The Tory Party was divided; a resolute "dump Dief" movement was growing, led by the president of the Conservatives, Dalton Camp. The Liberal strategy in the confrontation was to take the pro side on nuclear weapons. Mike Pearson startled followers with an announcement that he was in favor of the warheads and nuclear bombs for the RCAF Starfighters in NATO.

A retiring U. S. general, Lauris Norstad, called a press conference in Ottawa and informed Canadians that if they didn't accept the warheads, they were welching on their NORAD commitment. Diefenbaker said he wasn't rejecting the warheads, he was only asking for more discussion. Kennedy could stand him no longer. Through the Secretary of State, he issued a cold rebuttal of Diefenbaker's arguments and declared bluntly that the Canadian Government didn't have anything "sufficiently practical" to contribute to the discussion.

Three members of Diefenbaker's cabinet resigned. Two days later the Commons voted no confidence in his government and he was forced to call an election. Kennedy sent a campaign expert to help the Liberals.

Pearson's slogan, "Sixty Days of Decision," promised two months of resolution in contrast to Diefenbaker's bumbling style.

The Tories deserted Diefenbaker and he stomped the country alone, at his best as the underdog but helpless against the swing against him. In April 1963 Canadians elected a Liberal minority government, 128 Grits against 96 Tories.

The Social Credit Party shared a surprising 24 seats between an Alberta wing headed by Robert Thompson and the flourishing French-Canadian wing under Réal Caouette. The coalition of Albertans and French could not survive the nuclear warhead crisis. The west was in favor of them; Québec was not. Caouette separated from the Albertans and vowed his *Creditistes* might take Québec out of Canada.

Unrest among Québécois could no longer be ignored. Caouette's opportunistic separatism was one of many signs the province was ready to explode. Accordingly, Liberals and Conservatives geared up to make federalism more attractive. They made campaign promises to make the federal civil service bilingual for the benefit of citizens whose mother tongue was French. The promises were dismissed as electioneering. The only way the civil service could be bilingual would be to hire francophones, since anglophones almost never learned the other language. No Canadian seriously believed the government would go that far.

Mike Pearson's "Sixty Days of Decision" proved an embarrassment. The press labeled his administration the "do nothing parliament." His friend Walter Gordon, the finance minister, produced a budget based on an ambitious plan to take control of Canadian industry from Americans. It was attacked as outrageously naïve and Pearson forced Gordon to withdraw it. In truth, American investment was producing jobs and a living standard that kept Canadians among the world's leading consumers. "The most northern banana republic in the world," some Canadians commented ruefully.

They were beginning to notice the price of American ownership. Elsewhere, small countries lured the multinationals with promises of cheap, nonunion labor and low taxes. Northern Ontario towns, dependent on a single industry, turned into ghost towns overnight if branch plants closed. When General Electric decided to make television tubes elsewhere, a thousand people in London, Ontario, were out of work.

The extent of the American presence made sober reading. The

United States' control had risen to more than half of Canadian industry, almost 100 percent of Canadian oil and gas, 97 percent of the automobile and automotive parts industry (the country's largest industry), and more than 90 percent of rubber products.

"It is probable that we have already advanced too far along the road to economic union with the United States for turning back to be possible," the Toronto *Globe and Mail* reflected. "They need our resources, we want their standard of living. We are already dependent on them in defense. Geography weds us, language weds us, culture weds us. To turn back now would be to drop Canadians far down the scale of prosperity, to retard our development drastically, to invite mass emigration of Canadians who refused to accept such deprivations, and perhaps to drive the United States to take by force—economic, rather than military—certain of our resources."

President Kennedy met with Prime Minister Pearson at Hyannisport in 1963. "He'll do," the President told aides. The two leaders agreed secretly that Canada would accept nuclear warheads. On New Year's Eve a shipment of them arrived at La Macaza in Québec labeled "special ammunition."

— 24 —

Québec

Young people out of step with their governments were the phenomenon of the sixties. In Québec youth could make a clear case.
They lived in a society ruled by people who didn't speak their language, who dismissed them with contempt, who would keep them
and their children in second-rate jobs with third-rate incomes. Of
the two choices, change English-Canada or leave it, the course of
mature men of a philosophical bent was to work for change on
the federal level. The choice of a twenty-year-old was to take
Québec out of confederation, by violent means if necessary.

Three Québécois, Pierre Elliott Trudeau, Jean Marchand, and
Gérald Pelletier, veterans of the Asbestos strike, gathered often in
Pelletier's kitchen. The problem with changing English-Canada
was that French-Canadians in the federal government were often
a poor lot, weak and even venal. Better men would have to enter
politics to reform government: Them. The Liberal party, the political vehicle for aspiring French-Canadian politicians, was the
obvious choice.

The three were joined sometimes by René Lévesque, who dis-
agreed with their plan. French-Canadians, he said, should work
inside Québec for change or risk becoming pawns of the English
establishment. Trudeau was fascinated by the acclaim Lévesque
received through his appearances on television. Lévesque helped
him arrange an audition, but Trudeau was unimpressive.

Trudeau's *Cité Libre,* voice of the intellectual left, hammered
on the theme of foreign domination of Québec's commerce. The
tone was too polite to suit some. A rival, more radical paper,
Parti Pris, appeared in 1963 and was snapped up by students at
the Université de Montréal, the hotbed of separatism. Lévesque

alone of the Lesage cabinet spoke to the mood of powerful resentment that was finding expression in the pubs in Montréal's French-Canadian quarter, where singers, writers, and broadcasters gathered.

Lévesque, a tiny man who as a child was beaten up regularly by English bullies in his hometown of New Carlisle in the Gaspé, warned a Toronto audience in 1963, "Outside Québec, I don't find two great cultures. I feel like a foreigner."

The angriest *séparatistes* joined the militant *Front de Libération du Québec,* the FLQ, heavily infiltrated with Mounties and their informers. Aided by undercover Mounties, as it later was revealed, FLQ stole dynamite and placed bombs in the bright red mailboxes of Her Majesty's mail service in the wealthy Westmount section of Montréal where the English lived, thus making a statement against Canada and English bosses in one blast timed to go off at night when no one would be hurt.

Prime Minister Pearson's Irish-potato face and disarming lisp charmed voters despite his inept start. Québec's turmoil seemed little more than the work of cranks as the rest of Canada enjoyed a picture of itself reflected in a folksy, good-hearted prime minister addicted to the Dodgers.

A favorite story fondly repeated at the time concerned a red telephone in the prime minister's office which connected with NORAD headquarters in Colorado Springs and was reserved for emergencies. One afternoon it rang. Pearson, who was chatting with Paul Martin, his Minister of External Affairs, hunted through desk drawers to find the phone he absentmindedly had put aside. "My God," Martin gasped, "do you realize this could mean war?"

Replied Pearson, hunting in a closet, "No, not if we don't answer it."

Pearson quietly rid the country of some of its colonial trappings, which were red flags to Québec *séparatistes.* Government documents no longer were stamped "Dominion of Canada." Instead they were headed "Government of Canada." The ex-prime minister, John Diefenbaker, an ardent traditionalist, was apoplectic at each betrayal of the monarchy but nothing raised him to such quivering rage as the Great Flag Debate.

Pearson announced that Canada would have a flag of its own in time for its hundredth anniversary in 1967. Until that point Cana-

dians flew the Union Jack, or a Red Ensign with the Union Jack
on the fly, or (in Québec) a blue-and-white *fleur de lis*. Pearson
held a competition and invited Canadians to submit designs. The
House of Commons rocked to filibustering orations about the
motherland and men who had died for the Old Flag. The contest winner, not unexpectedly, was a maple leaf, a decorator's
design of red and white. It was run up a flagstaff on Parliament
Hill on February 15, 1965, almost ninety-eight years after Canada became a nation.

Pearson proposed "cooperative federalism" to adjust the Constitution to government programs never envisioned in the nineteenth century. Québec's premier, Jean Lesage, accepted federal
funds for pensions and health care but insisted that Québec would
administer the programs as it saw fit. In a series of "First
Ministers" conferences, ten provincial premiers and Pearson,
Lesage rejected twenty-nine federal-provincial cost-sharing programs that he felt violated his authority. He vetoed Pearson's plan
to bring the Constitution home from Britain and redraft it.

Lesage's belligerence owed much to the hot wind of separatism on his back. Québécois wanted their premier to be tough
on provincial rights, to stand up to the English. A young Marxist,
Pierre Vallières, a writer on the staff of Trudeau's *Cité Libre,* quit
the journal and joined the FLQ, whose activities were claiming
headlines. The group set dynamite in an armory on March 7,
1963, and a few weeks later toppled Wolfe's monument from its
pedestal on the Plains of Abraham.

The dangerous tactic had its first casualty when a night watch-
man found a bomb behind an army recruitment center, picked it
up out of curiosity, and accidentally detonated it. In May, ten
postboxes in Westmount exploded without harming anyone, but
when a demolition expert attempted to remove one that had
failed to go off, the trigger device slipped and he lost his left arm.

The editor of *Le Devoir,* Claude Ryan, was disturbed by the
polarity developing. He produced a "third option," a position neither *séparatiste* nor *federaliste*. A craggy-faced, brooding man, a
devout Catholic, Ryan's response in part was shaped by his recognition of the church's ancient debt to British protection. His
design was semi-sovereignty for Québec within Canada; the best
of both worlds. "Canada," he wrote in 1964, "is accepted not as a

last resort from which one would like to be liberated, but as a valuable political reality which one wants to improve."

Pearson resurrected the ultimate Canadian solution, a long government study. The Royal Commission on Bilingualism and Biculturalism, known as the Bi and Bi Commission, was headed by anglophone Davidson Dunton, president of Ottawa's Carlton University, and francophone André Laurendeau, of *Le Devoir*. The task they undertook was investigation of English-French relations at the federal level. At bottom, the assignment was to keep Québec from separating.

In 1964 Pearson introduced the Official Languages Act, which made bilingual federal services obligatory wherever more than 10 percent of the population spoke one of the two official languages. Overnight, Québécois had the inside track on thousands of government jobs. René Lévesque was unimpressed. "As long as one goddamn French-Canadian remains on the soil of Québec, there isn't a chance of integrating us into the hybrid, bicultural monstrosity that you dream of," he told English-Canada.

Trudeau, Pelletier, and Marchand, rejecting what they saw as narrow parochialism, were ready in 1965 to enter federal politics. They ran in the third federal election in almost four years of minority-government administration. The Liberals were returned with yet another uneasy margin, 131 to 97 Tories, but this time brought Trudeau, Marchand, and Pelletier with them.

Brilliant Trudeau, a former law professor, was made Pearson's Minister of Justice. Canadians had never seen a politician like this one. He was a bachelor who dated stunningly beautiful women. He was expert at solitary sports: scuba, downhill skiing, highboard diving, mountain climbing. He was a world traveler, an aesthetic. He was also inscrutable, mysterious; a mystic.

In Trudeau's first year in the justice portfolio, he overhauled the country's antique divorce and abortion laws and legalized homosexuality between consenting adults. "The state," he grinned, "has no business in the bedrooms of the nation."

Walter Gordon, exiled from political life for his budget's failure in the Pearson cabinet, remained concerned by the extent of American investment. He presented a report to government, *A Choice for Canada: Independence or Colonial Status,* which was considered another embarrassment for the Liberal party.

Canada celebrated its hundredth birthday in 1967 with euphoria and delight. Montréal's World's Fair site, known as Expo, was the centennial's main attraction. Built by the ambitious mayor, Jean Drapeau, Expo was a vaulting achievement of architecture and design that attracted 50 million people. Peter C. Newman wrote in the Toronto *Star:* "This is the greatest thing we have ever done as a nation . . . if this little sub-arctic, self-obsessed country of 20,000,000 people can put on this kind of a show, then it can do almost anything."

"We [are] now entering a new and happier period in our history," agreed Robert Fulford in *Saturday Night.*

When Queen Elizabeth visited Québec, riot police protected her from seeing young francophones protesting her presence. The new premier was Daniel Johnson, leader of the resurgent *Union Nationale,* returned to office as part of a backlash against Lesage's impious reform of education. Lesage's Liberals lost their most popular candidate, René Lévesque, as well. Lévesque put his plan for Québec sovereignty to a vote at a Liberal convention. When it was defeated 1,500 to 7, he quit.

Asked what Québec wanted, Lévesque replied, "A homeland for a people; *patrie!* A nation in the fullest sense of the word."

Charles de Gaulle of France visited Expo, stood on a balcony above a deliriously applauding crowd in Montréal, and mischievously cried, *"Vive le Québec libre!"* The country was appalled but Québec *séparatistes* rejoiced.

Lévesque became the catalyst for nonviolent *séparatistes,* who formed a new political party of the left, *Parti Québécois.* In English-Canada it was dubbed the PQ; in Québec, *les Péquistes.* A poll showed 10 percent of Québec's people supported Lévesque's separatism. He declared that in five years he would have a majority.

As the year of the centennial was ending, Progressive Conservatives rid themselves of the leader some considered a political liability, John George Diefenbaker. He was replaced in September 1967 by a shy, warm, almost diffident man, Robert Stanfield, a "Red Tory," and former premier of Nova Scotia whose family fortune came from an underwear factory.

Pearson, disheartened that his party couldn't get a majority government under his leadership, delivered a final piece of legislation entrenching the rights of the French language in the federal government and resigned. "What is at stake is no less than Canada's survival as a nation," Pearson told delegates to a conference on the Constitution. His legislation extended as far as his jurisdiction permitted. It obliged post offices, government documents, packagers of all kinds, including soup cans, airlines, and CBC radio and television outlets to use both official languages equally. Ottawa had no authority, however, over schools, a sore point. In New Brunswick where some communities were more than half francophone, children went to school in English only; Ontario had all-French villages with all-English schools; French pockets of Manitoba could speak French only at home.

Pierre Trudeau's suggestion that the provinces yield authority over civil liberties to the federal government was met with rejection. Premiers assumed Trudeau meant to use civil rights as a tool to make French obligatory in schools.

Pearson stepped down as leader, pleased with a free-trade pact he signed with the United States by which the automotive industry was continentalized. Because Detroit's production costs were lower and its range of models larger, Canadians were buying the American product, with the result that Canada's auto-trade deficit in 1965 was $768 million. Pearson threatened to subsidize an all-Canadian car industry, at which point negotiations for the auto pact became serious. With 500,000 Canadian jobs at stake in the golden horseshoe from Oshawa to Windsor, Ontario, Pearson won Washington's agreement to wipe out the tariff and redistribute production to eliminate duplication. Canada was given heavy gas-gulping cars, popular in the sixties, and overnight wiped out the trade deficit.

The new Liberal leader, suiting the party's policy of alternating francophone and anglophone, was Pierre Elliott Trudeau. English-Canada expected that Trudeau, an avowed anti-separatist, would put Québec in its place. He inherited, by his own admission, "a county that was falling apart." He shrugged, and added, "French-Canadians used to say that it was not worth the trouble of going to Ottawa since we're being persecuted and hounded out of office."

His remedy was to force bilingualism on a huge reluctant Ottawa bureaucracy. Even the country's highest mandarins of the civil service, all anglophones, were advised to learn French or be eclipsed. The government paid for immersion French in Ottawa language centers which processed a thousand civil servants a year. While they struggled with irregular French verbs, motivation to succeed was assured by throngs of bilingual francophones zipping up to the top in every ministry.

Trudeau called an election in 1968, and crossed the country to adulation called Trudeaumania. His nonchalance, his indifference to accepted political strategy of campaign promises, his air of mocking superiority, his jackknives off motel diving boards, were in dazzling contrast to the earnest awkwardness of Robert Stanfield. Liberals swept the election with 155 seats to 72 for the Tories.

The issue of American ownership of the Canadian economy continued to dominate. A young socialist economist, Melville Watkins, created a sensation in 1968 with a report, *Foreign Ownership and the Structure of Canadian Industry,* a damning document. Trudeau groaned that a business partnership with the United States was like being a mouse in bed with an elephant. Financiers were alarmed by the wide interest in the Watkins report. "Very strong nationalist feelings are arising," noted one John Devlin, chairman and president of a tobacco empire. "I hope sanity will prevail at the federal level."

Meanwhile the Canadian economy glowed. Trudeau spread a network of youth hostels to serve the hippie generation, grew his hair long, and wore sandals in the House of Commons, provided government money for poor-people conferences, folk festivals, and co-op housing. The Company of Young Canadians, an internal replica of the American Peace Corps, attracted bright young idealists who believed good works could transform the lives of Saskatchewan métis, Cape Breton miners, and Toronto drug addicts. Through the Canada Council, there was boundless money for improvisational theater, sculptures made from Styrofoam cups, and poems arranged in geometrical patterns.

Some of the creative energy that flowed into counterculture newspapers and health-food stores came from Americans who migrated to Canada to avoid the Vietnam War. American refugees poured over the border for the first time since the War of Independence and were impressed by the cleanliness of the streets, the absence of muggers, and the exhilaration of Trudeau's swinging participatory government.

They marched in demonstrations shouting "Hell No, We Won't Go," while Canadians carried placards that proclaimed END CANADIAN COMPLICITY. Canada, while receiving Vietnam War resisters amicably, was selling $300 million worth of munitions a year to the Pentagon and using its representatives on the UN observer team in Vietnam to spy for the American Army.

Québec youth was reading Pierre Vallières' *Negres Blancs d'Amerique* (*White Niggers of America*) and preparing a revolution. The FLQ leader wrote the book while he and Charles Gagnon languished in a prison in New York, arrested while protesting at the United Nations that Canada was mistreating Québécois under the UN's charter on civil rights. Vallières and Gagnon were extradited to Canada, where they were put in prison to await trial, without bail, for one year, in the case of Vallières, and two for Gagnon. Though both were found innocent of the charges, they served a total of four years in prison.

Terror bombings by the FLQ decreased markedly with the arrest of Pierre-Paul Geoffroy, charged with responsibility for thirty-one bombings. Geoffroy was sentenced to 124 years in prison.

Pierre Trudeau attended the St. Jean Baptiste parade in Montréal in 1968 and was barraged with stones. He kept his seat in the grandstand as police closed in on *séparatistes*. After that, police budgets increased dramatically to permit more recruitment and purchase of anti-riot equipment from the United States.

Police were braced in October 1969 for violence that accompanied a strike of Québécois cab drivers against the English-owned Murray Hill limousine service, which enjoyed a monopoly on airport transportation. The confrontation resulted in a shooting death, an undercover policeman.

That month Daniel Johnson's *Union Nationale* government produced a language bill to compel children of immigrants to attend French-language schools. Studies showed that the French language was on the decline in Québec; Lord Durham's nineteenth-century plan to assimilate francophones was becoming a reality under the impact of anglo economy, American television, and a sharply fallen birth rate in Québec, now the country's lowest.

René Lévesque's *Parti Québécois* was growing. A significant new member was Jacques Parizeau, later Québec's finance minister, who concluded the Canadian Constitution was "madness." "Eighty percent of all public works are conducted by the provinces and municipalities without any influence by the central government," he said. He reasoned that separatism was merely a matter of finishing the process.

In the Québec election in the spring of 1968, one in every four voters supported the *Parti Québécois*. Because the separatist vote was scattered, the results didn't reflect its strength. Instead, the Liberals swept to power with a majority led by Robert Bourassa, a dapper man with patent-leather hair and a rich, well-connected wife.

The FLQ seethed with frustration. On October 5, 1970, members of the Libération cell of the FLQ drew up in a black taxi before the handsome stone residence of the British trade commissioner in Montréal, James Richard Cross, known as Jasper to his friends. Cross was surprised and taken prisoner, a symbol, the FLQ said, of "British economic imperialism." The kidnappers demanded release of FLQ members jailed after two botched attempts of a similar nature. They listed other conditions, among them the publishing of the FLQ manifesto and safe conduct to Cuba or Algiers for hostage-takers.

Trudeau declared that the demands were unacceptable, but left the door open for negotiations. Both the Toronto *Star* and Claude Ryan's *Le Devoir* advocated concessions to save Cross. Trudeau relented and allowed the FLQ manifesto to be read on radio. It was reprinted widely in French and English but not always in its entirety. Few anglophones knew that it described Trudeau as a *tapette,* a homosexual.

Robert Bourassa, unperturbed, went to New York for an important meeting with American investors to raise money for a James Bay power project. Trudeau continued with plans for a visit to the Soviet. Jérôme Choquette, Bourassa's justice minister, appeared ready to grant clemency to the kidnappers. Three FLQ members, part of the Chénier cell, named for the *patriote* head of the 1837 rebellion, concluded the strategy to bring world attention to the movement was failing. They kidnapped Pierre Laporte, member of Bourassa's cabinet and second-most-important provincial Liberal.

Trudeau warned wealthy Montrealers they might be next. Bourassa and Mayor Jean Drapeau of Montréal asked for guns to put down the revolution. Drapeau described a "seditious plot and apprehended insurrection" as rumors swept the country of an army hiding in the hills. Laporte wrote pitiably to Bourassa, "You have the power to dispose of my life."

"We will not let a minority group impose its will on society by violence," Trudeau replied sternly. The kidnappings stung, an affront to his pride in his leadership of Québécois. On October 12, the Chénier cell issued its last communiqué "before the execution or liberation of Pierre Laporte." Trudeau sent the army, five hundred soldiers in combat uniforms, to stand guard with FN rifles in the streets of Ottawa and Montréal.

Lévesque met with Claude Ryan, both shaken by the conviction the FLQ was capable of killing the hostages if Trudeau pushed too hard. On the evening of October 14, they issued a statement urging moderation. Trudeau saw his tough position eroding. He was edgy and pugnacious. A CBC television encounter with Tim Ralfe showed a glittering-eyed prime minister who called civil libertarians "bleeding hearts" and added, "All I can say is, go on and bleed. But it is more important to keep law and order in the society than to be worried about weak-kneed people who don't like the looks of . . ."

Ralfe interrupted, "At any cost? How far would you go? How far would you extend that?"

"Just watch me," Trudeau replied grimly.

For reasons still not clear, Trudeau had prepared months earlier to invoke the War Measures Act. All was ready when Governor-General Roland Michener was roused from sleep in the middle of the night, October 14, to sign the document that put the country on a wartime basis and suspended civil liberties. In the hours before dawn, Montréal police arrested anyone they chose. People were manacled, pushed into armored vehicles, and taken to jail for interrogation. Police were not required to have warrants or even demonstrate reasonable grounds for the arrests; suspects were not allowed to notify families or contact lawyers.

Among those scooped up were Pauline Julien, folk singer, her teenage children, and a sister who happened to be visiting; Vallières and Gagnon; Gerald Godin and Nick Auf der Maur, journalists. Many of the 497 people taken into custody were members of the *Parti Québécois,* a legal, nonviolent political party that had attracted 24 percent of the Québec vote.

Most were released after weeks in prison and "some brutality," as Jérôme Choquette put it. Only eighteen were ever convicted of anything.

Trudeau explained to the House of Commons on the morning of October 15 that the War Measures Act was necessary because a state of "apprehended insurrection" existed. Asked to describe evidence of such a threat, he refused. He has never since elaborated on his reasons and is testy with questioners.

The United States endured the assassination of a President, a civil rights leader, 4,300 bombings by terrorists, 43 deaths and 384 injuries from clashes, and $21 million in property damage in a fifteen-month period prior to April 1970 without tampering with civil rights. In Canada, two kidnappings resulted in a state of war.

Debate raged in parliament all that day as Robert Stanfield's Progressive Conservatives and Tommy Douglas's NDP accused Trudeau of overreacting. Stanfield declared that the War Measures Act "denied citizens their freedom for no crime except their political opinions." He said, "That is repugnant to every ideal that we have ever held about free speech."

On the night of October 16, the Chénier cell killed Laporte, strangling him with a religious neck chain he wore. His body was found in the trunk of a battered car near an airport.

When debate resumed in parliament Monday morning on the War Measures Act, opponents found themselves out of step with their shocked countrymen. No other government act in Canada's history ever received such overwhelming public support as the War Measures Act. According to a Gallup poll, close to 90 percent approved Trudeau's decision. The NDP and the Canadian Civil Liberties Association, which continued to insist that invocation of the restrictive act appeared unjustified, lost members.

Some 30,000 Americans who had moved to Canada under the impression the country was a haven of civil rights woke up to appreciate they had erred. One of them, Edgar Z. Friedenberg, author of the best-selling *Coming of Age in America,* reflected on the situation from his university post in Halifax. "I found it especially embarrassing," he wrote in *Ramparts* magazine, "to be forced to confront the fact that Canadians enjoy far fewer and weaker formal civil liberties than Americans do."

After two weeks of police bungling, puzzling to those aware of the extensive Mountie infiltration in the FLQ, a member of the Chénier cell finally was apprehended and led police to others. On December 3, 1970, police surrounded a house where James Cross was a prisoner. The Libération cell asked for transportation to Cuba in return for surrendering their hostage unharmed. They were provided with a police escort to the airport and exile. Cross, who endured fifty-nine days of captivity with icy calm, later said his kidnapping was "a case of six kids trying to make a revolution."

Trudeau produced new legislation, the Public Order Act, a somewhat weaker version of the War Measures Act. Parliament endorsed it with relief. Only one man, a United Church minister from Prince Edward Island, Tory David MacDonald, dared to vote against it.

The country was calm in the aftermath of the kidnappings. The War Measures Act was directed mostly at Québécois, and anglophones relaxed, sure that *séparatistes* had been taught a lesson. A U.S. tanker, *Manhattan,* dominated the news. Without prior notification to Ottawa, it twice crossed the Arctic in Canadian waters. Canadians were singularly aroused and immediately extended offshore coastal claims from three miles to one hundred miles.

Tension centered over Canada's claim to a pie-shaped wedge of the north extending to the North Pole, an area of vast potential for oil and gas discoveries under the polar seas. The United States objected. Ottawa suddenly demonstrated a fascination for scientific inquiry in the regions, sending scientists to live on the ice under exceedingly large Canadian flags. One of them, Joseph B. MacInnis, a doctor and adventurer, donned a wet suit and was the first man ever to descend voluntarily under the polar icecap. There, he found a discarded Pepsi-Cola can.

Trudeau convened another First Ministers conference in Victoria, B.C., in 1971 to discuss the perennial issue, the Canadian Constitution. This time the sessions reached the brink of victory. English-language provinces conceded the issue of providing

French-language services, and Robert Bourassa seemed prepared to accept federal authority in Québec. But at the very moment when it appeared the British North America Act would be withdrawn from Britain and rewritten to suit a federated Canada, Bourassa had second thoughts. His chief advisor, Claude Morin, a man of outstanding intellectual gifts, warned that Ottawa would control Québec's social services and slowly destroy Québécois autonomy.

"Pretty well all the fields that determine a society's future," he said, listing youth programs, culture, urban affairs, communications, regional development, and adult education, were already in federal hands, turning the province into a "docile and obedient regional administration." Bourassa announced he would not sign.

The mess of intergovernment overlap produced two hundred federal-provincial committees that tried to sort out the varying jurisdictions. Of 482 contacts between federal and provincial delegations in a year, 117 concerned environment alone.

Trudeau's visit to the west coast bore other fruit. That winter he married Margaret Sinclair, twenty-two, daughter of a British Columbia Liberal who had been a member of Pearson's cabinet. Wide-eyed, a dewy flower child, shy, and photogenic, Margaret Trudeau ended speculation about Trudeau's prolonged bachelorhood. In the next three years, she gave birth to three handsome sons, two of them born on Christmas Day.

Though Tories complained about the cost of the enormous staff Trudeau built—clever, sophisticated men with Harvard backgrounds—the prime minister's office for the first time thronged with francophones and Québécois held powerful posts in his cabinet. Canadianization of the country continued, though John Diefenbaker thundered and sputtered his opposition. Queen Elizabeth's face disappeared from the ten-dollar bill and was replaced by John A. Macdonald's. (The back of the bill is an American-owned oil refinery.) By means of intimidation and cash bonuses, nine thousand anglophone civil servants were speaking passable French.

Behind the scenes, the Royal Canadian Mounted Police had orders to destroy the *séparatistes* by any means. Its Security and Intelligence division recruited francophones for undercover work in Québec and, for good measure, infiltrated all organizations engaged in dissent, from native rights groups to the NDP arch-nationalist Waffle splinter. The force reported to the federal Solicitor General Jean-Pierre Goyer, but appeared to be suspicious of government as well. Goyer later testified before a royal commission that the RCMP didn't tell him it was breaking the law.

In November 1972 Goyer was replaced as solicitor general by Warren Allmand. The RCMP subsequently bugged one of his conversations. Because Trudeau visited communist countries in his youth as a world traveler, the RCMP also maintained a file on him.

On the night of October 6, 1972, Mounties and other police staged a burglary of a *sépartiste* newspaper, *L'Agence de Presse Libre du Québec,* stole ten cases of documents and destroyed them though there was nothing in the office to link the paper with illegal activity. The "dirty tricks" squad, G Section, issued forged manifestos ostensibly from the FLQ urging violence, stole dynamite to give the illusion of dangerous activity, and kidnapped friends of *séparatistes* and beat them into agreeing to become informers.

When G squad had difficulty placing wiretaps in a barn where *séparatistes* planned to meet, the Mounties simply burned down the barn. In January 1973 they broke into the headquarters of a legitimate political party, Lévesque's *Parti Québécois,* and took the membership list for copying. They warned Premier Bourassa that he might be kidnapped. The premier hired bodyguards.

"It never crossed my mind that the RCMP could conceive of using a criminal act," Goyer later protested.

While G squad was creating the appearance of violent revolution in Québec, most English-Canadians were preoccupied with the country's economy. President Richard M. Nixon in August 1971 took the United States off the gold standard and raised the tariff wall. Canada was caught at a moment in its economic history when it was exporting more to the United States than it was importing; a first.

After a century of trade deficits, Canada had a surplus in the years from 1969 to 1971. James Reston commented in the New York *Times,* "When by a series of accidents they [Canadians] sold more to the United States than they bought, they were suddenly stunned by Secretary of Treasury John Connally, who told them this would not do and they would have to shape up."

Branch plants began to disappear. The country had become dependent on export of its natural resources. Few worried about it. The National Energy Board in 1971 assured the country that their reserves of oil would last 923 years, and reserves of gas were sufficient for 396 years. As Canada's manufacturing sector declined, Richard Gwyn of the Toronto *Star* expressed concern. In the 1950s Canada exported 24 percent of minerals and metals in raw form, he wrote. By the 1970s it was shipping 42 percent "in the same state they come out of the ground."

Gwyn warned, "Our economy is as immature, as non-competitive except in raw materials, as it was soon after World War II. About our only growth industry is bureaucracy."

Alberta, a growing rival to Ontario as the country's wealthiest province, slipped off its Social Credit Government in 1971 and replaced it with Progressive-Conservative businessmen. Premier Peter Lougheed, a former football player, announced that the province would store some oil and gas royalties in a creation he called the Alberta Heritage Fund. Lougheed also served notice that Alberta would not tolerate interference with profits by Ottawa.

Trudeau led Liberals into a federal election in 1972 on the theme, "The Land Is Strong," and praised multiculturalism and diversity. His boosterism was unconfined. His Canada Day message explained that Canadians "are identifiable because of our moderation and our affability, our tolerance of others, and our acceptance of change."

He narrowly escaped defeat. Liberals elected 109, Conservatives 107. The New Democratic Party headed by David Lewis, Rhodes scholar who helped found the CCF, had 31 seats and the balance of power. Lewis chose to prop up Trudeau rather than Stanfield, so Trudeau limped back into the prime minister's office. Pressure from the socialists obliged Trudeau to pass legislation creating a government-owned oil industry, PetroCan, which gave Canadians a presence in their own oil fields. All three leaders, Trudeau, Stanfield, and Lewis, lobbied enough support in their ranks to win a free vote abolishing capital punishment for a trial period.

At the prodding of the NDP, Trudeau created a watchdog committee to review American takeover of Canadian firms, which were running at between 175 to 200 a year. Dian Cohen, a Montréal economist, predicted accurately that the committee was a toothless "non-event." Canadians, it turned out, could not afford the luxury of rejecting American money.

The government took a tougher position against branch-plant U.S. magazines by ruling that advertising in magazines not owned and produced in Canada would not be eligible for deduction as an income-tax expense, a measure aimed transparently at repackaged Canadian editions of *Time* and *Reader's Digest*. American magazines continued to thrive anyway but the legislation was a boon to Canadian magazine publishers. *Maclean's,* flagship in the industry, later became a weekly. Its editor, Peter C. Newman, lunched with Walter Gordon, patron saint of economic nationalism. With economist Abraham Rotstein, they launched the Committee for an Independent Canada, a patriotic organization dedicated to Canadian control of its industry and resources.

The Committee for an Independent Canada took aim as well at Canadian education, drenched in American professors, American textbooks, and American attitudes. Some faculties, notably sociology, geography, and political science, were forced to expand so rapidly—to accommodate the postwar baby boom—that American professors outnumbered the scarce supply of Canadians. In Canadian bookstores, 97 percent of publications on the magazine racks were imported, and so were 98 percent of all paperbacks.

"Is it too much to ask that Canadian children be taught about their country and its literature from books written and published by Canadians?" asked Doris Anderson, editor of *Chatelaine,* a magazine aimed at women. Only 2 percent of textbooks used in Canadian schools were Canadian.

The consciousness-raising of the Committee for an Independent Canada coincided with clashes between Canadian enterprise and the U. S. State Department. A Montréal subsidiary of Studebaker-Worthington, Inc., of Harrison, New Jersey, had an offer to sell twenty-five diesel locomotives to Cuba, a deal legal under Canadian laws but not permitted under U. S. trading with the enemy regulations. With $18 million and 1,800 Canadian jobs depending on it, Ottawa told the company to go ahead. President Richard Nixon fumed—he hated Trudeau in what Henry Kissinger described as Nixon's mistrust of elegance and intelligence—but the sale eventually was made.

"How many people lie awake at night worrying about a massive locomotive attack from Cuba?" asked the Montréal *Gazette*.

William Porter, United States ambassador to Canada, fumed at the rising tide of anti-Americanism. He was particularly incensed that Canada belatedly had decided to restrict oil and natural gas exports to the United States. Canadians awoke one morning to learn that they had been misled about infinite reserves of both resources. In truth, Alberta might be dry before the end of the century.

Canada is both an oil-exporting and oil-importing country, an anomaly that results from its merciless geography. Since western oil and gas pipelines don't extend beyond the rich markets of Ontario, eastern Canada relies on oil imported chiefly from Venezuela at OPEC prices. To keep the expense bearable in the politically sensitive Maritimes and Québec, Ottawa subsidizes imports and forces Alberta to sell to Canadians at half the world price.

The long Liberal regime in Ottawa and the increasing complexity of federal administration resulted in deep-grained habits of bureaucratic secrecy and autocracy. Trudeau and his advisors found it simpler to function without bothering parliament or the country about the details. Gerald Baldwin, elderly upright Tory from Alberta, devoted himself to attaining a freedom of information bill. By his estimate, 80 percent of all government documents were labeled secret, even those containing such innocuous information as the stress level of bridges or a study of nursing homes. One of the most serious of the hidden papers concerned Canada's participation in an international uranium cartel which illegally fixed prices. At the first hint of a leak, Trudeau got an order-in-council which made it a crime for anyone in Canada to discuss any aspect of the uranium deal. Penalties ranged to $10,000 in fines and five years in prison. Canadians learned some of the damning facts through U.S. freedom of information accesses.

Canadians tolerated the ban, as they did an appeal court's reversal of a jury's acquittal, something not seen in English courts in centuries. The victim was a Montréal doctor, Henry Morgentaler, who was accused of performing abortions in his clinic rather than in a hospital, as the law requires. A French-Canadian jury found Morgentaler innocent but the Québec Supreme Court reversed the decision and sent the doctor to prison, a great hardship for a man who had been in Nazi concentration camps. Morgentaler was charged with another abortion and a second French-Canadian jury returned a verdict of not guilty. Again the Québec Supreme Court overthrew the verdict. Morgentaler remained in jail until he suffered a heart attack.

Trudeau, chafing under the constraints of a minority government, called an election in 1974. This time he campaigned with his wife, Margaret, who had been shielded from public scrutiny since their marriage. She proved a stunning asset. In Vancouver she told voters in a high-school auditorium that the prime minister had taught her a lot about loving, an endorsation he received with equanimity.

Robert Stanfield, an honorable, humorous man with an unfortunately dour expression, stuck to the advice of his aides and campaigned on a platform of bad news. He said the economy was in trouble and could be rescued only with a tough program of wage and price controls. Trudeau scoffed and won the election with a majority of 141 over a poor showing by the Tories, 95.

The losers changed their leaders. David Lewis, defeated in his own riding by a woman who campaigned against abortion, was replaced as head of the NDP by a political scientist from the automotive center of Oshawa near Toronto, Ed Broadbent. Robert Stanfield retired, leaving Tory heavyweights deadlocked. The compromise choice was Joe Clark of Alberta, a man of such unprepossessing manner that the media dubbed him Joe Who? His wife, a feminist and law student, annoyed some when she announced she would be known by her own name, Maureen McTeer.

Soon after the election, Margaret Trudeau checked into a Montréal hospital with what was described as a nervous breakdown.

A year later, Trudeau conceded that Stanfield had been right about the economy. Unemployment was rising, the Canadian dollar was sinking, industry was collapsing. Canada's trade deficit in

manufactured goods reached $10 billion, much of it caused by the
U.S.-Canada auto pact, which was souring for Canada as North
Americans turned away from gas-guzzlers. Rising OPEC oil
prices were costing the federal government dearly in subsidies for
the Atlantic provinces, and the expensive, overgrown civil service
was becoming a crushing burden in such a small country. Trudeau's fondness for Harvard Business School technocrats resulted
in 474 top-level civil-service positions in Ottawa in 1976 that
paid more than their Washington, D.C., equivalents.

The program to make the government bilingual was another ex-
travagance. Described in the west as "pushing French down our
throats," it cost taxpayers an estimated $324,364 to teach one
anglophone cabinet minister to speak fractured French.

In 1976 Montréal proudly hosted the Olympics in a magnificent
stadium whose construction was riddled with graft, a specialty of
the city's monument-builders. Québec, with one of Canada's
highest unemployment rates, mortgaged its future with an ambitious project, the James Bay hydroelecric power plant. Construction began in bitterness as Cree and Inuit protested the invasion of their land. The tribes eventually settled for $225 million in
reparations and the right to self-government. Early estimates of
the project were $6 billion; in 1976, six years later, costs were
$17 billion and rising. That year 40 percent of all U.S. debt capi-
tal flowing into Canada was earmarked for James Bay, future supplier of hydro for New York State.

A fateful clash erupted over language rights, this one the
request by air-traffic controllers in Québec to speak French to
Québécois pilots. Canada's commercial airline pilots, almost all
of them anglophones, panicked, convinced that they would have
to learn French or be replaced. They mounted a shrill campaign,
claiming that bilingual air-traffic controllers would be a menace to
passenger safety, and fed reporters distorted stories of near-
collisions over Québec. When they went on strike, the country's
commercial air traffic was grounded.

Inconveniences to passengers, freight, and mail were blamed on
Québec. Trudeau bowed to pressure from English-Canada and
ordered a review of the situation. His old comrade from the Asbestos strike, Jean Marchand, quit the cabinet in disgust. Qué-

bec's pilots and controllers broke away from their English-dominated associations and formed *L'Association des Gens de l'Air du Québec*.

The inquiry subsequently reported that there was no threat to air safety if controllers spoke to pilots in their mother tongue; in fact, the reverse was true. The controversy deeply rankled in Québec and came to be seen as the crowning incident that made *séparatistes* out of moderates.

Robert Bourassa's response to concern that the French language was dying out was Bill 22, which required immigrant's children who weren't fluent in English to attend French schools. Though English-Canada found it obnoxious, the *Parti Québécois* objected on the grounds that it didn't go far enough to make French "as soon as possible, the language of communication, work, commerce, and business." Anglophone businesses, banks, and trust companies, shocked by a bill they saw as invading English-language rights, began to move offices from Montréal. Westmount's mansions sprouted For Sale signs, with few takers. A Toronto hockey crowd booed when an announcement on the public-address system was repeated in French.

Prices and inflation continued to climb, but wages were pegged at 7 percent. Corporate profits, however, rose by an average of 137 percent before taxes. With 10 million workdays lost through strikes, Canada, in 1975, was the world's second-most strike-torn country. A particularly devastating one was that of 22,000 postal workers, who stopped mail delivery until the government gave them the raise they needed.

Trudeau began to dismantle welfare services provided in better times and adjusted the shared-funding system that had enabled the creaking Constitution to function. Instead of earmarking funds for such services as Medicare and day care, the federal government turned over a lump sum to be used as provinces saw fit. The immediate result was a decided gain in provincial autonomy and some decrease in welfare and health budgets.

The dismay felt by those at the bottom of the social scale created some stir, but the country was engrossed by the drama unfolding in the north, where native people and environmentalists were fighting to stop the building of a pipeline down the Mackenzie River valley. American oil companies who owned oil and gas drillings in the Arctic proposed to build the pipeline in order to supply Americans with oil and gas. The territory over which the pipeline would pass was fragile tundra inhabited by migrating caribou herds and native tribes whose land claims had never been settled.

Trudeau met criticism by establishing a royal commission of one, Thomas Berger, a judge of the British Columbia Supreme Court, and former leader of the B.C. NDP. Berger, a quiet courteous man, conducted hearings all over the north and listened to everyone who wanted to speak. Using a bush plane and, sometimes, dogsled or canoe, he traveled the north and attentively heard from trappers, scientists, Marxists, oil tycoons, toothless tribal matriarchs and chiefs.

"There is no doubt in my mind that if a pipeline is built, they might as well kill us," George Erasmus, president of the Indian Brotherhood of the Northwest Territories, told Berger.

Half of Canada's land mass was involved in the controversy, directly or indirectly. Every Canadian, it seemed, had an opinion. Berger's recommendation was to delay construction along the Mackenzie route for at least ten years.

Prime Minister Trudeau and President Jimmy Carter signed an agreement to build a pipeline costing an estimated $8 billion from Alaska's Prudhoe Bay down the Alcan Highway to the American border, where it would split to connect with San Francisco and Chicago, taking American gas to American buyers. The luscious contract was awarded to a Canadian company, Alberta's Foothills Pipe Line, which looked in vain for venture capital; the Alaskan gas the pipeline delivered was considered too costly.

In April 1978 parliament passed Trudeau's Northern Pipeline Act, designed to prevent construction of any part of the transport line until all the money was in place.

Westerners fumed at the obstruction. They regarded Trudeau as their natural enemy, an easterner who was trying to rob them of their long-delayed affluence, and a French-Canadian easterner at that. Their fury found an outlet in such objects as cereal boxes, which were printed in both French and English as the federal law demanded. Post offices designated POST OFFICE—BUREAU DE POSTE made them livid. Keith Spicer, the country's commissioner of official languages, gave them ammunition when he admitted frankly that $400 million spent on French lessons for Ottawa civil servants might better have been invested in French classes in primary school. The enforced bilingualism, he said, was a "country-wide catastrophe."

"English-Canadians no longer care whether Québec separates," Richard Gwyn concluded in the Toronto *Star*.

Québécois faced a provincial election in the autumn of 1976. René Lévesque's *Parti Québécois* played down its separatist roots and campaigned on the issues of good government and social reform. Lévesque promised that what he mildly called sovereignty association, rather than the harsher word separatism, would not happen without a referendum's approval.

Trudeau gave little support to the struggling provincial Liberals and their leader, Robert Bourassa, discredited by scandals concerning the Olympic Stadium. Claude Ryan of *Le Devoir* unexpectedly advised voters to support *les Péquistes*. On November 15, 1976, they did. The separatist *Parti Québécois* won a landslide victory, all but wiping out the Liberals, and English-speaking Canadians woke up to a country perhaps poised on dissolution.

— 25 —

The Referendum

A subdued English-Canada watched the ecstatic victory celebration of the *Parti Québécois* in the Paul Sauvé Arena in Montréal. Television cameras caught faces shining with tears and luminous joy as supporters greeted René Lévesque, the new premier of Québec.

The tone of some comment the next day was one of bewilderment and hurt. Government service had been opened to Québécois, government offices were bilingual, groceries sold TOMATO KETCHUP KETCHUP AUX TOMATES. Patronage had been ample: Mirabel, a superfluous inconvenient airport north of Montréal, had adopted a white elephant as its symbol because it was costing taxpayers a million dollars a day. What else did Québec want? Some said maybe it was the War Measures Act. It was Trudeau's fault; he was too rigid.

Trudeau dismissed the possibility that the PQ victory indicated Québec wanted to separate. He seemed detached and indifferent, but suddenly millions of dollars were available for unity television spectaculars, unity celebrations on Parliament Hill, unity book festivals, unity conferences, unity essay contests, and a unity train, the American Freedom Train used in the U. S. bicentennial, which was renamed and reupholstered with stuffed bears and the sound of the loon. And, of course, there was a royal commission on unity called the Unity Task Force.

René Lévesque's first major speech after the PQ victory was before New York bankers who were worried about their investments in Québec. He told a banquet room packed with financiers that Québec's aspirations were identical to those of the founding fathers of 1776, a comparison his conservative audience found unappealing.

Trudeau picked a scapegoat to account for the stunning PQ victory. He said voters had been swayed by newscasters on Radio Canada who were *séparatistes* and he ordered an investigation of their partiality. Media figures from English-Canada joined a Québécois protest meeting in Montréal, which was not the kind of unity Trudeau had in mind. The investigation later decided the accusation was untrue.

Some Tory politicians suggested that English-Canada should be ready to negotiate if Québec really wanted to leave. The Conservative leader, Joe Clark, forced them to retract. The strategy that was emerging everywhere was Trudeau's: Lock the door.

The Unity Task Force crossed the country in search of harmony and was subjected at every stop to harangues against Canada and other Canadians. Acadiens in New Brunswick complained that they didn't have French-language schools or French-language courts, though in some communities they numbered 90 percent of the population. The Atlantic provinces were upset about poverty that dated from confederation. The west resented Ontario, which produced most of Canada's costly manufactured goods under the protection of a tariff and shipped them to prairie consumers with high freight charges tacked on. Ontario's industry, vulnerable to the rising cost of oil and gas, resented Alberta's efforts to raise the price. In the north, where the Yukon and Northwest Territories still had no vestige of self-government, the grievances were with Ottawa's insensitive bureaucracy.

The suspicion grew that the only Canadians interested in unity were in Ontario, which needed the markets, or in the federal Liberal party, which needed Québec to get elected.

"If we can work out a just and equitable confederation, I'm all for it," commented Silver Donald Cameron, a journalist in Cape Breton. "But if we can't, and Québec pulls out, I'm prepared to contemplate independence for the Atlantic provinces as well."

The ravages of Canadian geography were central to the discussion. The United States could physically survive if, say, Texas left the union, but Canada is a lateral nation; if a bead drops off, the necklace is broken. American investors, requiring a one-piece Canada for their security, sided with the federalists. In the White House, Zbigniew Brzezinski, President Carter's Security Advisor, was mindful of the background paper he prepared for the U. S. State Department in which he used his experience as a student at Montréal's McGill University to explain his theory that the rest of Canada would join the United States if Québec separated.

In February 1977 Trudeau addressed a joint session of the U. S. Congress and Senate. He declared that separatism was "a crime against the history of mankind." Press attention during the visit to Washington was diverted by the flaky behavior of Margaret Trudeau, who attended a formal reception in a short dress and with a run in her stocking.

The illegal activities of the Royal Canadian Mounted Police were emerging in two royal commissions, a federal one appointed by Trudeau, the so-called McDonald Commission, and the one in Québec, the Keable Commission, both known by the names of their chairmen. When the Keable Commission appeared on the verge of involving Trudeau's cabinet, and Trudeau himself, in the Mountie misdeeds in Québec, Canada's Supreme Court stopped it on the grounds that the provincial inquiry was exceeding its jurisdiction. Tories and the NDP, scenting blood, hammered at Trudeau in the House of Commons question periods. The prime minister wasn't ruffled. He maintained that a government shouldn't supervise police closely.

Both opposition parties dropped the issue abruptly when they opened their mail from constituents, almost all of whom were outraged that anyone had dared to criticize the RCMP. When the McDonald Commission found that the Mounties had been opening first-class mail illegally, the reaction of Canadians was to change the law to save Mounties from embarrassment.

A morning tabloid, the right-wing Toronto *Sun,* which regularly hints that Trudeau is a communist agent, was served with warrants under the Official Secrets Act, a move seen as Trudeau's revenge. Canadians who worried that something was going wrong with their traditional freedom of speech were jolted to learn that freedom of speech is an American tradition; Canada has no comparable law.

Trudeau offhandedly remarked in the House of Commons that media self-discipline "is always the preferred course, failing which, of course, discipline has to be imposed upon them."

Lévesque attended his first summit federal-provincial conference in a cheery mood. He and Trudeau measured each other, both impeccably affable. When English-language premiers criticized the PQ's plan to strengthen Québec's language laws, Lévesque sardonically offered to enshrine minority language rights in his province if the nine anglophone provinces would do the same. Only one, New Brunswick, was ready to recognize the other official language.

Bill 101, the *Parti Québécois* language bill, ordered that all public signs and billboards in the province be written in French only, and all children from out of the province attend French schools. Businesses with more than fifty employees were required to conduct their affairs in French. A food-market chain, Steinberg's, asked permission to label shelves in predominantly English neighborhoods in that language and was refused.

Lévesque conceded that Bill 101 was "an imperfect tool, sometimes a cruel tool to many people," but insisted it was necessary to prevent erosion of the French language. The statement was not entirely accurate: more recent studies demonstrated that the trend to assimilation had been reversed even before the *Péquiste* election.

When the Canadian armed forces moved a crack paratroop regiment from Alberta to a base in Ontario, and the defense budget included armored vehicles designated "for domestic use," Canadians worried that Trudeau meant to keep Québec in federated Canada by force. Historian Kenneth McNaught pointed to the reaction of the United States to secession of the South and commented, "It would be improper to permit our present debate to continue on the assumption that peaceful secession of the province of Québec from the union of Canada is possible."

Trudeau delayed setting a date for a federal election, disturbed that opinion polls showed his popularity at low ebb. Urged to make concessions to Québec, he curtly refused. If Québec were treated differently, he said, Alberta would want special status, too, and then British Columbia, and finally there would be no central government left.

An indifferent economist, he had no programs with which to meet the country's rising inflation and unemployment problems, part of a worldwide trend. Though his composure remained intact he appeared tired and depressed. Claude Ryan, editor of *Le Devoir,* suddenly entered politics. Concerned that Lévesque and Trudeau had polarized the separatism debate, he offered himself as leader of the provincial Liberals with his "third option," increased power for all provinces within a Canadian federal state. Trudeau gave Ryan a chilly welcome as both Liberals postponed airing their differences in the interest of fighting Lévesque.

In the face of the prohibitive costs and the west's animosity, Trudeau dismantled the civil service bilingualism programs. Many counted the effort a disaster, but an honorable one. Léon Dion, a member of the 1965 royal commission on bilingualism and biculturalism, told *Maclean's* magazine sadly that the program "far from leading to linguistic peace has aggravated animosity between anglophones and francophones."

Solange Chaput-Rolland, a spirited member of the Unity Task Force, agreed. "I used to extol the virtues of speaking two languages, but I will never bother to fight for that anymore. We live in two islands of unilingualism."

William Johnson, a federalist Québécois and the Toronto *Globe and Mail*'s Québec correspondent, feared the consequences of that attitude. "Canada under double unilingualism will not survive twenty years," he predicted.

The Liberals gloomily watched their candidates topple in a ripple of by-elections. In Saskatchewan, the party was wiped out in a provincial election. Indications were that the party didn't exist west of Manitoba.

Margaret Trudeau celebrated the couple's eighth wedding anniversary by becoming notorious. She hung out with the Rolling Stones in a Toronto hotel and went on to become a media celebrity who prattled about lewd encounters with Ted Kennedy and Prince Charles. The Trudeaus separated, Pierre keeping custody of their three sons. Both were silent about their relationship. His opponents withheld public comment or criticism for reasons of taste and judgment: In the area of his marital problems, Trudeau had Canada's sympathy.

Lévesque went to France where Québec's lavish embassy rivals

Canada's. The President of France awarded him the Legion of Honor, a medal the President had denied Trudeau.

Though Canadians are baffled by the turgid complexity of the Constitution, they began to realize that reforming the British North America Act was the only way to put the country back together. The Unity Task Force recommended changes that would create proportional representation so that Canadians who vote substantially for losing candidates would not be excluded in the House of Commons. The proposal would permit Tories from Québec and Liberals from Alberta to sit in the government, thereby avoiding the divisive distribution of power that exists under the present system. Others suggested Senate reform as a way to achieve minority representation. Another First Ministers Conference of premiers and Trudeau met to go over the same ground. There were twenty-two major areas to be addressed; there was complete agreement on none.

By the spring of 1979 Trudeau could not postpone an election any longer. Joe Clark, thirty-nine, the awkward and vague Tory leader, campaigned with an arsenal of promises to cut government spending, end government secretiveness, and mend federal relations with the provinces. Trudeau, shaking off all omens and advice, stuck to the one issue that interested him, Canadian unity.

Voters were more concerned with their shrinking dollar and the mounting problems in unemployment. After sixteen years in office, the federal Liberals were deposed on May 21, 1979, and Joe Clark became prime minister with a minority government. Clark, speaking French competently, was sensitive to Québec's mood. Since Québec had elected only two Conservatives, he gave his cabinet some French-Canadian balance by bringing Québec Tories out of the Senate. But it was disquietingly obvious that almost everyone in office was English and almost everyone in the Liberal opposition was French.

Clark gave his government the summer to find its way to the unaccustomed seats of power. The country appeared to run exactly as well, or badly, when it had no parliament as when it did. In addition to meeting Ottawa's smoothly entrenched civil servants, Tories also considered strategy. Outnumbered in the House of Commons by the combined opposition, they would have to govern with the consent of one of the two small parties, the NDP or the Québec *Créditistes*.

Trudeau appeared listless. Soon after parliament resumed in October, he announced his retirement to take effect at the next Liberal convention. Lévesque produced a White Paper outlining sovereignty association; Trudeau didn't rise with his old fire to dispute it. The PQ document, released in November 1979, was a blueprint for separation. Québec would be autonomous in its government, laws, citizenship, and passports; the "association" part of sovereignty association came in sharing with Canada currency, inland navigation, and trade. The border would be open for free circulation of people and goods.

"We Quebeckers are a nation," the White Paper declared, "the most firmly anchored nation on this continent . . . It is vitally important that from now on this home be completely ours."

Clark wrestled with the numbing problem of finding a compromise beween Alberta's insistence on raising energy prices and Ontario's anxiety to keep prices down. Since the premiers concerned, Peter Lougheed and William Davis, were both Tories, the argument split Clark's party as well. The powers of Alberta and the federal government were in exquisite balance. Alberta had the right to set its own price for oil and gas consumed within the province but couldn't control the export price. The federal government would have to get Alberta's agreement in order to impose a bigger tax bite, or else Lougheed threatened to shut off the pipelines and "let Ontario freeze in the dark."

Clark negotiated an agreement giving Alberta an increase of $4 a barrel in 1980, with an escalation until 1985 when it would still be less than the 1980 OPEC price. Lougheed accepted it reluctantly. Canada's cheap oil and gas resulted in wastefully high consumption, he said. Americans in border cities filled their automobile tanks with cheap, plentiful Canadian gas. Ontario's William Davis, on the other hand, was aghast at the $4-a-barrel increase. He said it would cost thousands of jobs in marginal industries. Davis asked why Canadians should pay world prices for their own oil, and cast aspersions on Lougheed's patriotism.

The new Tory government introduced its first budget to the House of Commons, a belt-tightener that required Canadians to pay eighteen cents a gallon more for gasoline. The Tories, confident they could weather the storm it produced, had misjudged the country's mood. The party's thirty-eight weeks in office had been marked by a spirit of amateurism and inactivity that was distressing in such a period of crisis. On December 14, 1979, the astonished Tories were ousted by the combined Liberal-NDP-*Créditiste* opposition. Prime Minister Clark, seemingly unconcerned, was obliged to call another election.

Trudeau kept his party in suspense for a few days before announcing that he would withdraw his resignation and remain as leader for the campaign. The Liberal strategy was to use Trudeau sparingly. Except at the end when his humor and moral certainty seemed restored, he made few appearances, read prepared speeches with no interest or inflection, refused a television debate with Clark and Ed Broadbent, the NDP leader, and treated the press with more than his usual disdain.

The campaign was marked by a Tory flirtation with free trade that would have made John A. Macdonald reach for the bottle. John Crosbie, Clark's Minister of Finance, a millionaire from Newfoundland whose humor had a cutting edge, hinted that his government would attempt to extend the auto pact's free trade to include all trade with the United States. "If we're going to be dominated by anyone," he said, "I'd prefer it be the Americans rather than anyone else."

The Toronto *Star* reeled; a headline stated FREE TRADE COULD END US. "We would get the ordinary jobs in mining, oil and gas production, and pulp and paper," an editorial claimed. "The Americans would get the top jobs in designing and producing computers, automated machinery, and micro-electric products." Most Canadian economists agreed with that assessment. Of Canada's exports, 70 percent of which went to the United States, most were raw materials; of Canada's imports, 70 percent of which came from the United States, most were manufactured goods. By increasing their production only 10 percent, American branch plants in Canada could wipe out the insignificant Canadian-owned industry.

Québec prepared confidently to continue the flow of resources-out and computers-in. At James Bay the world's largest hydroelectric power plant swung into production, exporting electricity to New York. The remote location made the site untenable for the tourist trade but the plant was a remarkable attraction, taller than the Great Pyramid of Egypt and more than a mile long.

Claude Ryan, leader of the Québec Liberals, released his so-called Beige Paper in January as the federal election campaign was cresting. His much-anticipated third option came as a shock to English-Canada. Ryan called for abolition of the monarchy and the Senate, an increase in provincial powers to make them equal to the federal government, and guarantees that both official languages would be respected in every province.

"The primary and most urgent source of anxiety for the future of Canada comes from a problem as old as federation itself, the relationship between the two founding peoples," Ryan wrote. "It is evident that the only reasonably satisfactory relationship is one which is based on equality, an equality accepted by both parties."

Though the spirit of the document differed greatly with Lévesque's sovereignty association, the intent of Ryan's "renewed federalism" wasn't much different. Where Lévesque would create two sovereignties, Ryan would have eleven. Either way, factionalism would run rampant.

A mood of fatalism gripped many Canadians. The country made little sense. It was patched together in the beginning out of disparate pieces left over from the French Empire and the American Revolution, its people rejected by both. In 1867 it lurched into nationhood without asking those concerned if nationhood was what they wanted, because most of them didn't.

If railways hadn't been invented, Canada wouldn't have been invented either; the flag should show a locomotive, not a maple leaf.

The economy was defeated from the start by the unconscionable geography. The country never could, and never did, afford itself. Canada began by begging money from one foreign country, Britain, and wound up with most of its assets sold at knockdown prices to another, the United States.

The country's devotion to heavy-handed authority was useful when the government was run by British Army officers in order to repel invasions, but unsuited for growth and flexibility in a modern world; the result was an apathetic citizenry and a national police force that behaved like some foreign power's army of occupation.

Some Canadians thought: If separation comes, *let it;* something better might emerge out of the ruins.

The winter gloom of such despair was lifted by a bolt of good news. Canada's ambassador in Iran Kenneth D. Taylor, hid six Americans in his embassy in Teheran for three months, protecting them from the infamous hostage-taking at the U. S. Embassy. The world learned of it when Taylor successfully smuggled them out of the country disguised as Canadians. Americans were deliriously grateful, and said so in sky-writing and drinks on the house. Canadians were reminded of their good-guy virtues, the qualities displayed when Mike Pearson solved the Suez crisis and stopped a war—namely, a cool head under stress, decency, compassion, and a survivor's instinct for preservation.

René Lévesque announced the date of the separatist referendum, May 20, 1980, and the wording of an ambiguous question. Québec would be asked to vote *oui* or *non* to allow its government to negotiate with Ottawa for sovereignty association.

The referendum was an onion, a conundrum, a serpentine, Jesuitical plot. It meant everything; it meant nothing. Interpretation depended on the perspective of the person peeling the onion. First, there was the question itself, an admission perhaps that asking Québec directly if it wanted to separate would have resulted in flat rejection. Then, there was speculation about the real meaning of the eventual result. A *oui* might mean no; Québécois might want to scare Ottawa into making concessions that would make Québec happy enough to stay in federation. On the other hand, a *non* vote might actually mean yes if one anticipated that failure to support separation (if one believed that the referendum really meant to test *séparatiste* sentiment; the mind reeled) would make English-Canada impossibly smug and irritating, until Québec was provoked enough to leave.

The federal election day was February 18, 1980. From the moment the polls closed in Newfoundland, there was no doubt of the outcome. Pierre Elliott Trudeau was back as prime minister and the Liberals had a majority government, good for five years.

Western Canada was in shock. Not one Liberal was elected west of Manitoba. All the west's Members of Parliament were in the impotent Tory and NDP opposition.

Joe Clark submitted his resignation, as the Constitution requires, to the governor-general, Ed Shreyer, former NDP premier of Manitoba. The ceremony took place in a hospital room where His Excellency was recovering from emergency surgery on an ulcer.

Trudeau announced that Canada would support President Jimmy Carter's boycott of the Moscow Olympics. In other respects relations between the countries were failing. Canada and the United States were waging another battle in the centuries-old Fish War. A Rhode Island Senator, Claiborne Pell, stood in the way of Senate ratification of a treaty signed by Trudeau and Carter in 1978 after two years of negotiation. The fish treaty established quotas in certain disputed coastal waters, but New England thought it was shortchanged on the scallops.

Accordingly, spanking new American fishing boats were cleaning up the scallops, in retaliation for which Canadian fishing boats started exceeding Canadian treaty quotas on cod, haddock, and yellowtail flounder. Geoffrey Stevens of the Toronto *Globe and Mail,* Fish War correspondent, estimated that no more than eight people in Washington and Ottawa understand the intricacies of what was going on.

At the same time the U. S. Senate went ahead with appropriations for the Garrison Dam in North Dakota, an irrigation project that would back polluted water into Manitoba, and President Carter's announcement of a switch to coal presaged acid rain in Canada that would kill the lakes. The Acid Rain War, that one was called. The Television Commercial War concerned the blackout in Canada of commercials on American programs, with the substitution of Canadian ones. Border television broadcasters in the U.S. demanded that President Carter do something awful to Canada.

On May 20, 1980, a huge turnout in Québec thronged to the polls to vote *non* to separation. Sixty percent to 40 percent, they rejected the overture to secession. A disconsolate Lévesque accepted the decision with grace and said he would bargain in good faith at future constitutional conferences. The people of Québec, he observed wearily, had "cleanly given federalism another chance."

English-Canada's euphoria with the outcome of the referendum didn't survive the week. British Columbia and Alberta, with combined surpluses bigger than the national deficit, enough to buy Canada and give it away, were preparing for a bare-knuckle fight with Ottawa over energy jurisdiction. By July 1980 matters had reached a crisis. Premier Bill Bennett of British Columbia and Premier Peter Lougheed of Alberta headed an unprecedented joint meeting of their cabinets which discussed strategy behind closed doors.

Their first move was a shot across Ottawa's bows. They issued a statement which declared they would not tolerate any federal export tax on energy, the effect of which would be the "capture . . . of the sale price of a *provincial* resource." (Italics implied.)

Federal Energy Minister Marc Lalonde, the smartest and least-liked member of Trudeau's cabinet, simultaneously informed the House of Commons he was raising the price of gasoline.

Trudeau appeared to be in a hurry. He said if the provincial premiers couldn't agree on an amending formula for the British North America Act by September 1980, he'd patriate the Constitution anyway. Though government leaders at both levels of government assigned themselves a rigorous schedule of meetings, it seemed unlikely there would be a consensus on any substantive matter beyond provincial participation in selecting the Supreme Court, some changes in family law, and the decision to keep the monarchy, which Lévesque did not oppose on the grounds that it was irrelevant.

Meanwhile, Alberta's Foothills Pipe Line company, unable to raise what had become a $23 billion price tag to build a gas pipeline from Alaska to San Francisco and Chicago, applied to Ottawa for permission to build a piece of it, the lucrative southern end. The proposed section, however, would carry Canadian gas to the United States, a departure from the original intention that only Alaskan gas would be involved.

The House of Commons was in an uproar when the Liberals announced that Foothills would be allowed to proceed. The opposition claimed that the decision to export a non-renewable resource was irresponsible and perhaps illegal as well, under the terms of an earlier act of parliament which required all the pipeline money to be in place before construction began on any of it. Energy Minister Marc Lalonde replied that neither accusation was true. And there the matter sat, another Canadian controversy in a brooding summer of eroding goodwill.

A singularly bright moment was achieved on July 1, 1980, Canada's one hundred and thirteenth birthday, when the entire country attempted to sing the new lyrics of "O Canada," which that day was proclaimed the official national anthem. The previous lyrics repeated the line *we stand on guard for thee* five times, which was judged to be excessive for a song possessing only eight lines.

The new lyrics were the result of seventeen years of consultation and fourteen government bills. Suggestions that the English lyrics be translated from the original French ones were dismissed; the French lyrics go on about carrying the cross and protecting *nos droits,* our rights. Instead, the revised English version eliminated three *we stand on guard for thee*. The lines substituted were given long and serious consideration in the hope of avoiding offense to women, racial minorities, or atheists.

A choir assembled on Parliament Hill to sing the national anthem before a vast holiday crowd. A dispute over which national anthem should take precedence, the English or the French one, was resolved with typical Canadian ingenuity. The choir was divided in half and sang both versions simultaneously. The platform party, which included Governor-General Shreyer and Prime Minister Trudeau, sang in the language of choice. Those who preferred the English lyrics used song sheets. The crowd, moved and bemused, sang the French version or one of the many English versions, as it pleased.

In September 1980 the ten provincial premiers met with Prime Minister Trudeau in Ottawa for a final try at agreeing on an amending formula to give Canadians an all-Canada Constitution. Trudeau's position had hardened; concessions offered at earlier conferences had been withdrawn. The premiers, particularly those with energy resources at stake, were furious. The only one to give Trudeau full support was, predictably, Ontario's William Davis.

The conference ended with the usual speeches of recrimination.

A few weeks later Trudeau announced that he would act unilaterally and request Westminster to amend the British North America Act and give it to Canada. Opposition leader Joe Clark used strong language. Trudeau's high-handedness, he said, could bring about "the end of this country, Canada." Premier Davis urged fellow Tories to disregard their leader, Clark.

In October the premiers met again, this time in Toronto and without Trudeau. They called a press conference to announce that nine of them opposed Trudeau's action and five of them would take the federal government to court to dispute his right to tamper with the Constitution without their agreement.

Britain's Prime Minister Margaret Thatcher viewed the boiling controversy with horror. With domestic problems enough of her own to face, she was appalled that her government was about to be dragged into the interminable Canadian wrangle about the Constitution.

The two views of Canada were, indeed, irreconcilable. Federalists, led by Trudeau, who was aching to give Canada its own Constitution and then resign, saw a powerful Ottawa as essential to nationhood; provinces, except for Ontario which benefits most from federation, believe that Ottawa has no right to dictate what they will do with their gas or their oil or their minorities or their communication systems or their schools or . . . anything.

"We don't want to leave Canada," Alberta's Peter Lougheed informed Joan Sutton of the Toronto *Star*. ". . . it's more a matter of being pushed out the door."

Bibliography

Abella, Irving, Ed. *On Strike, Six Key Labor Struggles in Canada 1919-1945.* Toronto: James Lewis and Samuel, 1975.

Aberdeen, Ishbel Maria Majoribanks. *Canadian Journal,* Ed. John Saywell. Toronto: Champlain Society, 1960.

Adachi, Ken. *The Enemy that Never Was, a History of the Japanese Canadians.* Toronto: McClelland & Stewart, 1976.

Adams, Ian. *The Real Poverty Report.* Edmonton: Hurtig, 1971.

Adler-Karlsson, Gunnar. *Reclaiming the Canadian Economy: A Swedish Approach Through Functional Socialism.* Toronto: House of Anansi, 1970.

Allen, Ralph. *Ordeal by Fire, Canada 1910-1945.* Vol. 5, Canadian History Series, Ed. Thomas B. Costain. Toronto: Doubleday Canada, Ltd., 1961.

Allen, Richard. *The Social Passion, Religion and Social Reform in Canada 1914-1928.* Toronto: University of Toronto Press, 1971.

Armstrong, F. H. "William Lyon Mackenzie, First Mayor of Toronto: A Study of a Critic in Power," *Canadian Historical Review,* 1967.

Arthur, Eric. *Toronto: No Mean City.* Toronto: University of Toronto Press, 1964.

Aster, Sidney. *1939: The Making of the Second World War.* New York: Simon and Schuster, 1973.

Atwood, Margaret. *Days of the Rebels 1815-1840.* Editor-in-Chief, Toivo Kiil. Toronto: Canada's Illustrated Heritage, 1978.

————. *Survival, a Thematic Guide to Canadian Literature.* Toronto: Anansi, 1972.

Bailey, Thomas A. *A Diplomatic History of the American People.* Third Ed. New York: F. S. Crofts & Co., 1946.

Batten, Jack. *Canada Moves Westward 1880-1890.* Editor-in-Chief, Toivo Kiil. Toronto: Canada's Illustrated Heritage, 1978.

Berger, Carl, Ed. *The West and the Nation: Essays in Honour of W. L. Morton.* Toronto: McClelland & Stewart, 1976.

Bergeron, Léandre. *The History of Québec, a Patriote's Handbook.* Toronto: NC Press, 1971.

Berton, Pierre, Ed. *Great Canadians, a Century of Achievement*. Toronto: The Canadian Centennial Library, 1965.

———. *Historical Headlines, a Century of Canadian News Dramas*. Toronto: The Canadian Centennial Library, 1967.

———. *Invasion of Canada 1812–1813*, Vol. 1. Toronto: McClelland & Stewart, 1980.

———. *The Klondike Fever*. New York: Alfred A. Knopf, 1958.

———. *Klondike, The Last Great Gold Rush 1896–1899*. Toronto: McClelland & Stewart, 1958.

———. *The Last Spike*. Toronto: McClelland & Stewart, 1971.

———. *My Country*. Toronto: McClelland & Stewart, 1976.

———. *The National Dream*. Toronto: McClelland & Stewart, 1970.

———. *The Wild Frontier*. Toronto: McClelland & Stewart, 1977.

———. *The Wild Frontier, More Tales from the Remarkable Past*. Toronto: McClelland & Stewart, 1978.

Bishop, W. J. *The Early History of Surgery*. London: Oldbourne Science Library, 1960.

Bissell, Claude, Ed. *Great Canadian Writing, a Century of Imagination*. Toronto: Canadian Centennial Library, 1966.

Bliss, J. Michael, Ed. *Canadian History in Documents, 1763–1966*. Toronto: Ryerson Press, 1966.

Blyth, Jack A. *The Canadian Social Inheritance*. Toronto: Copp Clark, 1972.

Bothwell, Robert, Ed. *Policy by Other Means, Essays in Honour of C. P. Stacey*. Toronto: Clarke, Irwin, 1972.

Braithwaite, Max. *The Hungry Thirties 1930–1940*. Editor-in-Chief, Toivo Kiil. Toronto: Canada's Illustrated Heritage, 1978.

Brault, Lucien, Ed. *A Century of Reporting: The National Press Club Anthology*. Toronto: Clarke Irwin, 1967.

Brebner, J. B. *Canada: A Modern History*. Ann Arbor: University of Michigan Press, 1970.

Briggs, Harold E. *Frontiers of the Northwest, a History of the Upper Missouri Valley*. New York: P. Smith, 1950.

Broadfoot, Barry. *The Pioneer Years, 1895–1914*. Toronto: Doubleday Canada, Ltd., 1976.

———. *Ten Lost Years, 1929–1939*. Toronto: Doubleday Canada, Ltd., 1973.

Brown, Caroline. *An Unauthorized History of the RCMP*. Toronto: James Lorimer & Co., 1978.

Brown, Dee. *Bury My Heart at Wounded Knee*. New York: Holt, Rinehart & Winston, 1970.

———. *The Year of the Century, 1876*. New York: Charles Scribner's Sons, 1966.

Brown, George W., Gen. Ed. *Dictionary of Canadian Biography*, Vol. I, 1000–1700. Toronto: University of Toronto Press, 1966.

———. *Dictionary of Canadian Biography*, Vol. IV, 1771–1800. Toronto: University of Toronto Press, 1979.

————. *Dictionary of Canadian Biography*, Vol. IX, 1861–70. Toronto: University of Toronto Press, 1976.

————. *Dictionary of Canadian Biography*, Vol. X, 1871–80. Toronto: University of Toronto Press, 1972.

Brown, Lorne. "Breaking Down Myths of Peace and Harmony in Canadian Labour History," *Canadian Dimension*. 1977.

————. *An Unauthorized History of the RCMP*. Toronto: James Lorimer & Co., 1978.

Brown, R. Craig. *Canada 1896–1921, a Nation Transformed*. Toronto: McClelland & Stewart, 1974.

————, Ed. *The Canadians, 1867–1967*. Toronto: Macmillan of Canada, 1968.

Brunet, M. *French Canada and the Early Decades of British Rule, 1760–1791*. Ottawa: Canadian Historical Association, 1963.

Bumsted, J. M., Ed. *Canadian History Before Confederation*. Georgetown: Irwin-Dorsey, 1972.

Burns, R. M., Ed. *One Country or Two?* Montreal and London: McGill-Queen's University Press, 1971.

Callwood, June. *The Naughty Nineties 1890–1900*. Editor-in-Chief, Toivo Kiil. Toronto: Canada's Illustrated Heritage, 1978.

Cameron, Silver Donald. "O Atlantica! We Stand on Guard for Thee!" *Saturday Night*. September, 1977.

Careless, J. M. S. *Canada, the Story of Challenge*. Toronto: Macmillan of Canada, 1963.

————, Ed. *The Canadians 1867–1967*. Toronto: Macmillan of Canada, 1968.

————. *Colonists and Canadiens 1760–1867*. Toronto: Macmillan, 1971.

————. *"The Union of the Canadas" The Growth of Canadian Institutions 1841–1857*. Canadian Centenary Series. Toronto: McClelland & Stewart, 1967.

Carroll, Joy. *Pioneer Days 1840–1860*. Editor-in-Chief, Toivo Kiil. Toronto: Canada's Illustrated Heritage, 1978.

Cashman, Tony. *The Best Edmonton Stories*. Edmonton: Hurtig, 1976.

Cattermole, William. *Emigration: the Advantages of Emigration to Canada*. Toronto: Coles Canadiana Collection. Reproduced, 1970.

Chafe, J. W. *Extraordinary Tales from Manitoba History*. Manitoba Historical Society. Toronto: McClelland & Stewart, 1973.

Chambers, Captain Ernest J. *The Royal North-West Mounted Police, a Corps History*. Toronto: Coles Canadiana Collection. Reproduced, 1972.

Charlesbois, Peter. *The Life of Louis Riel*. Toronto: NC Press, 1975.

Churchill, Winston. *A History of the English Speaking Peoples,* Vol. 3. New York: Dodd, Mead, 1958.

Clark, Samuel Delbert. *The Developing Canadian Community*. Toronto: University of Toronto Press, 1962.

————. "The Frontier and Democratic Theory." *Transactions of the Royal Society of Canada*, 48 (1954), Series III, Section 2.

Coles Canadiana Collection (no author). *The Story of Louis Riel*. Toronto: Reproduced, 1970.

————. *The Backwoods of Canada, 1836, Letters from the Wife of an Emigrant Officer*. Reproduced, 1971.

Collins, Robert. "The Age of Innocence 1870–1880." Editor-in-Chief, Toivo Kiil. Toronto: Canada's Illustrated Heritage, 1978.

Colombo, John Robert, Ed. *The Mackenzie Poems*. Toronto: Swan Publishing, 1966.

Connell, Brian. *The Plains of Abraham*. London: Hodder & Stoughton, 1959.

Cook, Ramsay. *Canada: A Modern Study*. Toronto: Clarke Irwin, 1977.

————. *Canada 1896–1921, a Nation Transformed*. Toronto: McClelland & Stewart, 1974.

————, Ed. *The West and the Nation: Essays in Honour of W. L. Morton*. Toronto: McClelland & Stewart, 1976.

Corrective Collective. *She Named It Canada* (*Because That's What It Was Called*). Vancouver, 1971.

Costain, Thomas B. *The White and the Gold; The French Regime in Canada*. Garden City: Doubleday & Company, Inc., 1954.

Cowan, Heen I. *British Immigration Before Confederation*. Canadian Historical Association. Booklet №22.

Cowley, Robert. "The Bloodiest Battle in History," *Horizon*. Summer, 1972.

Craig, Gerald M. *Upper Canada: the Formative Years 1784–1841*. Canadian Centenary Series. Toronto: McClelland & Stewart, 1963.

Creighton, Donald. *Canada's First Century*. Toronto: Macmillan, 1970.

————. *Dominion of the North: A History of Canada*. Toronto: New Ed., Macmillan, 1962.

————. *The Empire of the St. Lawrence*. Toronto: New Ed., Macmillan, 1956.

————. *John A. Macdonald: the Young Politician*. Toronto: Fourth Ed., Macmillan, 1968.

————. *John A. Macdonald: the Old Chieftain*. Toronto: Fourth Ed., Macmillan, 1968.

————. *The Story of Canada*. Toronto: Macmillan, 1971.

Cross, Michael, Ed. *Policy by Other Means, Essays in Honour of C. P. Stacey*. Toronto: Clarke Irwin, 1972.

Crowe, Harry S., Ed. *A Source Book of Canadian History*. Toronto: Longmans, 1959. Rev. Ed., 1964.

Desbarats, Peter. *René, a Canadian in Search of a Country*. Toronto: McClelland & Stewart, 1976.

Dickey, Robert M. *First Missionary to the Klondike*, documents of the Methodist Church in Canada.

Doughty, Arthur G. *The Cradle of New France, the Story of the City Founded by Champlain*. London: Longmans, Green & Co., 1909.

Douglas, David C., Ed. *English Historical Documents*, Vol. X, 1714–1783. Bristol: University of Bristol, 1952.

Drysdale, Patrick, Ed. *Dictionary of Canadianisms.* Toronto: W. J. Gage Ltd., 1967.

Dufferin, Marchioness of. *My Canadian Journal.* Toronto: Coles Canadiana Collection. Reproduced, 1971.

Earys, James G. *In Defence of Canada, from the Great War to the Great Depression,* Vol. I. Toronto: University of Toronto Press, 1961.

———. *In Defence of Canada, Appeasement and Rearmament,* Vol. II. Toronto: University of Toronto Press, 1961.

Eccles, W. J. *Canada Under Louis IV 1663–1701.* Canadian Centenary Series. Toronto: McClelland & Stewart, 1964.

Edmonds, Alan. *The Years of Protest 1960–1970.* Editor-in-Chief, Toivo Kiil. Toronto: Canada's Illustrated Heritage, 1978.

Fergusson, C. Bruce. "The Expulsion of the Acadians," *Dalhousie Review* XXXV, 1955.

Ferns, Henry. *The Age of Mackenzie King.* Toronto: James Lorimer & Co., 1976.

Firth, Edith G., Ed. *The Town of York 1815–1834, a Further Collection of Documents of Early Toronto.* Toronto: University of Toronto Press, 1966.

FitzGibbon, Mary Agnes. *A Veteran of 1812, the Life of James FitzGibbon.* Toronto: Coles Canadiana Collection. Reproduced, 1970.

Flanagan, Thomas. *Louis "David" Riel: Prophet of the New World.* Toronto: University of Toronto Press, 1979.

Frankfurter, Glen. *Baneful Domination.* Don Mills: Longman Canada Ltd., 1971.

Franklin, Stephen. *A Time of Heroes 1940–1950.* Editor-in-Chief, Toivo Kiil. Toronto: Canada's Illustrated Heritage, 1978.

Frye, Northrop. *The Bush Garden, Essays on the Canadian Imagination.* Toronto: Anansi, 1971.

Fulford, Robert. "How English Canada Came to be Oppressed," *Saturday Night.* June, 1972.

Gagnon, Jean-Louis, Ed. *A Century of Reporting, the National Press Club Anthology.* Toronto: Clarke, Irwin, 1967.

Galbraith, John S. *The Little Emperor, Governor Simpson of the Hudson's Bay Company.* Toronto: Macmillan of Canada, 1976.

Godsell, Patrician, Ed. *Letters and Diaries of Lady Durham.* Toronto: Oberon Press, 1979.

Golden, Aubrey. *Rumours of War.* Toronto: New Ed., James Lorimer & Co., 1979.

Gordon, Walter L. *A Choice for Canada.* Toronto: McClelland & Stewart, 1966.

Granatstein, J. L. *Broken Promises: a History of Conscription in Canada.* Toronto: Oxford University Press, 1977.

———. *Canada's War: The Politics of the Mackenzie King Government, 1939–1945.* Toronto: Oxford University Press, 1975.

Grant, George. *Lament for a Nation.* Toronto: McClelland & Stewart, 1972.

Gray, Hugh. *Letters from Canada 1809.* Toronto: Coles Canadiana Collection. Reproduced, 1971.

Gray, James H. *Booze.* Toronto: Macmillan of Canada, 1972.

————. *Red Lights on the Prairies.* Toronto: Macmillan of Canada, 1972.

Guillet, Edwin C. *The Great Migration: The Atlantic Crossing by Sailing Ship 1770–1860.* Toronto: University of Toronto Press, 1963.

————. *Pioneer Settlements in Upper Canada.* Toronto: University of Toronto Press, 1933.

Haggart, Ronald. *Rumours of War.* Toronto: New Ed., James Lorimer & Co., 1979.

Hall, Roger. "An Imperial Businessman in the Age of Improvement: Simon McGillivray After the Fur Trade." *Dalhousie Review,* Vol. 59, No. 1. Spring, 1979.

Halpenny, Francess G., Gen. Ed. *Dictionary of Canadian Biography,* Vol. IV, 1771–1800. Toronto: University of Toronto Press, 1979.

————. *Dictionary of Canadian Biography,* Vol. IX, 1861–1870. Toronto: University of Toronto Press, 1976.

————. *Dictionary of Canadian Biography,* Vol. X, 1871–1880. Toronto: University of Toronto Press, 1972.

Hannan, Leslie F. *Canada at War: The Record of a Fighting People.* Canadian Illustrated Library. Toronto: McClelland & Stewart, 1968.

————, Ed. *Maclean's Canada, Portrait of a Country.* Toronto: McClelland & Stewart, 1960.

————. *Redcoats and Royalists 1760–1815.* Editor-in-Chief, Toivo Kiil. Toronto: Canada's Illustrated Heritage, 1978.

Hardin, Herschel. *A Nation Unaware.* North Vancouver: J. J. Douglas Ltd., 1974.

Harris, R. *Canada Before Confederation: A Study in Historical Geography.* Toronto: OUP, 1972.

Hayne, David M., Gen. Ed. *Dictionary of Canadian Biography,* Vol. II, 1701–1740. Toronto: University of Toronto Press, 1969.

————. *Dictionary of Canadian Biography,* Vol. IV, 1771–1800. Toronto: University of Toronto Press, 1979.

————. *Dictionary of Canadian Biography,* Vol. IX, 1861–1870. Toronto: University of Toronto Press, 1972.

————. *Dictionary of Canadian Biography,* Vol. X, 1871–1880. Toronto: University of Toronto Press, 1972.

Heidenreich, Conrad. *Huronia, a History and Geography of the Huron Indians 1600–1650.* Toronto: McClelland & Stewart, 1971.

Hibbert, Christopher. *Charles I.* London: Weidenfeld and Nicholson, 1968.

Hill, Douglas. *The Opening of the Canadian West.* London: Heinemann, 1967.

Hind, Henry Youle. *Narrative of the Canadian Red River Expedition of 1857.* Edmonton: Hurtig, 1971.

Hitsman, J. M. *Broken Promises: A History of Conscription in Canada.* Toronto: Oxford University Press, 1977.

Hofstadter, Richard, Ed. *Turner and the Sociology of the Frontier.* New York: Basic Books Inc., 1968.

Horwood, Harold. *Beyond the Road: Portraits and Visions of Newfoundlanders.* Toronto: Van Nostrand Reinhold, 1976.

————. *The Colonial Dream 1497–1760.* Editor-in-Chief, Toiv Kiil. Toronto: Canada's Illustrated Heritage, 1978.

————. *Newfoundland.* Toronto: Macmillan of Canada, 1969.

Hutchison, Bruce. *The Incredible Canadian.* Toronto: Longmans Green, 1952.

Inguarta, José E. "The Merchants of Montreal at the Conquest: Socio-Economic Profile," *Histoire sociale-Social History,* Vol. III, No. 16. Ottawa: University of Ottawa Press, November, 1975.

Innis, Donald Quayle. *Canada, a Geographic Study.* Toronto: McGraw-Hill, 1966.

Innis, Harold. *The Fur Trade in Canada.* Toronto: Rev. Ed., University of Toronto Press, 1970.

Innis, Mary Quayle, Ed. *Mrs. Simcoe's Diary.* Toronto: Macmillan of Canada, 1965.

Jenness, Diamond. *Indians of Canada.* Ottawa: Fourth Ed., National Museum of Canada, 1958.

Jessen, Merrill, Ed. *English Historical Documents,* Vol. IX. American Colonial Documents to 1776.

Keenleyside, Hugh. "How British Columbia Was Almost Annexed by the USA," *Canadian Dimension.* November, 1971.

Kesterton, Wilfred, Ed. *A Century of Reporting, the National Press Club Anthology.* Toronto: Clarke, Irwin, 1967.

Kilbourn, William, Ed. *Canada: A Guide to the Peaceable Kingdom.* Toronto: Macmillan of Canada, 1970.

————. *The Firebrand.* Toronto: Clarke, Irwin Canadiana Paperback, 1956.

————. *The Making of the Nation, a Century of Challenge.* Toronto: Canadian Centennial Publications, 1965.

King, William Lyon Mackenzie. *Industry and Humanity.* Toronto: University of Toronto Press, 1973.

Kirk, Russell. *The Conservative Mind.* New York: Avon, 1953.

Knightley, Phillip. *The First Casualty.* New York and London: Harcourt Brace Jovanovich, 1975.

Labaree, Leonard Woods. *Conservatism in Early American History.* Yale Lectures, 1947.

Lamb, W. Kaye. *Canada's Five Centuries: from Discovery to Present Day.* Toronto: McGraw-Hill, 1971.

Langton, Anne. *A Gentlewoman in Upper Canada, The Journals of Anne Langton.* Toronto: Clarke, Irwin Canadiana Paperback, 1967.

Lawrence, D. H. *Studies in Classic American Literature.* New York: Viking Compass, 1961.

Laxer, James. "Lament for an Industry," *The Last Post.* December-January, 1971–72.

————. *The Liberal Idea of Canada.* Toronto: James Lorimer & Co., 1977.

Laxer, Robert. *The Liberal Idea of Canada.* Toronto: James Lorimer & Co., 1977.

Lévesque, René. *An Option for Québec.* Toronto: McClelland & Stewart, 1968.

Lipset, Seymour Martin. *Agrarian Socialism.* New York: Doubleday Anchor Books, 1968.

————. *The First New Nation.* London: Heinemann, 1964.

————, Ed. *Turner and the Sociology of the Frontier.* New York: Basic Books, 1968.

Lipton, Charles. *The Trade Union Movement of Canada 1827–1959.* Montréal: Canadian Social Publications, 1966.

Loomis, Stanley. *Paris in the Terror.* Philadelphia and New York: J. B. Lippincott Company, 1964.

Lord, Walter. *The Dawn's Early Light.* New York: W. W. Norton & Co., 1972.

————. *The Good Years, from 1900 to the First World War.* New York: Harper & Brothers, 1960.

Lower, Arthur R. M. *Canadians in the Making, A Social History of Canada.* Toronto: Longmans Green & Co., 1958.

————. *Colony to Nation.* Toronto: Longmans, Fourth Ed., 1969.

————. *Great Britain's Woodyard, British America and the Timber Trade 1763–1867.* Toronto: McGill-Queen's University Press, 1973.

————. *History and Myth: Arthur Lower and the Making of Canadian Nationalism.* Vancouver: University of British Columbia Press, 1975.

Lower, J. A. *Canada: An Outline of History.* Toronto: Rev. Ed., McGraw-Hill Ryerson, 1973.

Lukasiewicz, J. *The Railway Game.* Toronto: McClelland & Stewart, 1976.

Manceron, Claude. *Twilight of the Old Order.* New York: Alfred A. Knopf, 1975.

Manning, Helen Taft. *The Revolt of French Canada 1800–1835: A Chapter in the History of the British Commonwealth.* Toronto: Macmillan of Canada, 1962.

Matheson, Gwen, Ed. *Women in the Canadian Mosaic.* Toronto: Peter Martin Associates, 1976.

McArthur, D. C., Ed. *A Century of Reporting, the National Press Club Anthology.* Toronto: Clarke, Irwin, 1967.

McCourt, Edward A. *Saskatchewan.* Toronto: Macmillan of Canada, 1968.

MacDermot, H. E. *One Hundred Years of Medicine in Canada (1867–1967).* Toronto: McClelland & Stewart, 1967.

McDiarmid, Garnet. *Teaching Prejudice.* Toronto: Ontario Institute for Studies in Education, 1971.

Macdonald, Norman. *Canada—Immigration and Colonization 1841–1903.* Toronto: Macmillan of Canada, 1966.

McDougall, John. *Parsons on the Plains*. Don Mills: Longman Canada, 1971.

———. *Pathfinding on Plain and Prairie*. Toronto: Coles Canadiana Collection. Reproduced, 1971.

McKay, W. A. *A Century of Reporting, the National Press Club Anthology*. Toronto: Clarke, Irwin, 1967.

Mackenzie, William Lyon. *The Mackenzie Poems*. Toronto: Swan Publishing, 1966.

McNaught, Kenneth. "Canada's Rebels Put on Trial," *Globe and Mail*, May 24, 1975.

———. *The Pelican History of Canada*. Toronto: Rev. Ed., Penguin, 1975.

———, Ed. *A Source Book of Canadian History*. Toronto: Longmans 1959; Rev. Ed., 1964.

MacNutt, W. S. *The Atlantic Provinces: The Emergence of a Colonial Society 1712–1857*. Toronto: Canadian Centenary Series, McClelland & Stewart, 1965.

———. *New Brunswick, a History: 1784–1967*. Toronto: Macmillan of Canada, 1963.

Métis Association of Alberta. *Many Laws*. Edmonton: Canindis Foundation, 1970.

Minifie, James. *Peacemaker or Powder-Monkey: Canada's Role in a Revolutionary World*. Toronto: McClelland & Stewart, 1960.

Monet, Jacques. *The Last Cannon Shot, a Study of French-Canadian Nationalism 1837–1850*. Toronto: University of Toronto Press, 1969.

Morison, Samuel Eliot. *Samuel Champlain, Father of New France*. Boston and Toronto: Little Brown and Company, 1972.

Morris, Audrey Y. *Gentle Pioneers*. Toronto and London: Hodder and Stoughton, 1966.

Morris, Richard B., Ed. *Encyclopedia of American History*. New York: Harpers, 1953.

Morton, Desmond. *The Canadian General, Sir William Otter*. Toronto: Hakkert, 1974.

———. *The Last War Drum*. Toronto: Hakkert, 1972.

Morton, William L. *The Canadian Identity*. Madison: University of Wisconsin Press, 1961.

———. *The Kingdom of Canada: A General History from Earliest Times*. Toronto: McClelland & Stewart, 1963.

Mowat, Farley. *Tundra*. Toronto: McClelland & Stewart, 1973.

Myers, Gustavus. *History of Canadian Wealth*. Toronto: James Lewis & Samuel, 1972.

Neatby, H. Blair. *The Politics of Chaos, Canada in the Thirties*. Toronto: Macmillan of Canada, 1973.

Neatby, Hilda. *Quebec: The Revolutionary Age 1760–1791*. Toronto: Canadian Centenary Series, McClelland & Stewart, 1966.

Newman, Peter C. *Renegade in Power: The Diefenbaker Years*. Toronto: McClelland & Stewart, 1963.

O'Neill, Paul. *The Oldest City: The Story of St. John's, Newfoundland.* Erin: Press Porcepic, 1975.

Orkin, Mark M. *Speaking Canadian English, an Informal Account of the English Language in Canada.* Toronto: General Publishing, 1970.

Ormsby, William. "The Problem of Canadian Union 1822–1828," *The Canadian Review,* 1958.

Ostry, Bernard. *The Age of Mackenzie King.* Toronto: James Lorimer & Co., 1976.

Patterson, E. Palmer II. *The Canadian Indian, a History Since 1500.* Toronto: Collier-Macmillan, 1972.

Patterson, Graeme. "An Enduring Canadian Myth: Responsible Government and the Family Compact," *Journal of Canadian Studies,* Vol. 12. Spring, 1977.

Peden, Murray. *Fall of an Arrow.* Toronto: Canada's Wings, 1979.

Penner, Norman, Ed. *Winnipeg 1919, the Strikers' Own History of the Winnipeg General Strike.* Toronto: James Lewis & Samuel, 1973.

People's History Collective. *People's History of Cape Breton.* Halifax: P.O. Box 1282, North Postal Zone, 1971.

Phillips, Alan. *Into the Twentieth Century 1900–1910.* Editor-in-Chief, Toivo Kiil. Toronto: Canada's Illustrated Heritage, 1978.

Porter, John. *The Vertical Mosaic, an Analysis of Social Class and Power in Canada.* Toronto: University of Toronto Press, 1965.

Porter, McKenzie. *Overture to Victoria.* Toronto: Longmans Green & Co., 1961.

Pratt, David. *Teaching Prejudice.* Toronto: Ontario Institute for Studies in Education, 1971.

Raddall, Thomas H. *Halifax: Warden of the North.* Toronto: McClelland & Stewart, 1948.

————. "How General Washington Lost Canada," *Maclean's* magazine, September 14, 1957.

Rasmussen, Linda. *A Harvest Yet to Reap, a History of Prairie Women.* Toronto: The Women's Press, 1976.

Rasmussen, Lorna. *A Harvest Yet to Reap, a History of Prairie Women.* Toronto: The Women's Press, 1976.

Reid, J. H. Stewart. *A Source Book of Canadian History.* Toronto: Longmans, Rev. Ed., 1964.

Rich, E. E. *The Fur Trade and the Northwest to 1857.* Toronto: Canadian Centenary Series, McClelland & Stewart, 1967.

Ricker, J. C. *Canada: A Modern Study.* Toronto: Clarke, Irwin, 1977.

Rioux, Marcel. *Québec in Question.* Toronto: James Lewis and Samuel, 1971.

Robinson, Helen Caster. *Joseph Brant.* Toronto: Longmans, 1971.

Ross, Alexander. *The Booming Fifties 1950–1960.* Editor-in-Chief, Toivo Kiil. Toronto: Canada's Illustrated Heritage, 1978.

————. *The Red River Settlement: Its Rise, Progress and Present State.* Edmonton: Hurtig, 1972.

Rotstein, Abraham. *The Precarious Homestead*. Toronto: New Press, 1973.

Royal Bank of Canada. *A Conspectus of Canada, Centennial Year 1967*.

Russel, Andy. *The Rockies*. Edmonton: Hurtig, 1976.

Ryerson, Stanley. *Unequal Union*. Toronto: Progress Books, 1968.

Savage, Candace. *A Harvest Yet to Reap, a History of Prairie Women*. Toronto: The Women's Press, 1976.

Saywell, John T. *Canada: A Modern Study*. Toronto: Clarke, Irwin, 1977.

Schirmer, Daniel B. *Republic or Empire: American Resistance to the Philippine War*. Cambridge: Schenkman Publishing, 1972.

Schull, Joseph. *Ontario Since 1867*. Toronto: McClelland & Stewart, 1975.

———. *Rebellion, the Rising in French Canada 1837*. Toronto: Macmillan of Canada, 1971.

Senier, Hereward. "Quebec and the Fenians," *Canadian Historical Review*, 1967.

Smiley, Donald V. *Canada in Question: Federalism in the Seventies*. Toronto: McGraw-Hill Ryerson, 1972.

Smith, Denis. *Bleeding Hearts . . . Bleeding Country*. Edmonton: Hurtig, 1971.

Smyth, John. *The Story of the Victoria Cross*. London: Frederick Muller, Ltd., 1963.

Sosin, Jack M. "The French Settlements in British Policy for the North American Interior 1760–1774," *Canadian Historical Review*, 1958.

Stacey, C. P. *Quebec, 1759, The Siege and the Battle*. Toronto: Macmillan of Canada, 1959.

———. *A Very Double Life, the Private World of Mackenzie King*. Toronto: Macmillan of Canada, 1976.

Stanley, George F. G. *The Birth of Western Canada: A History of the Riel Rebellion*. Toronto: University of Toronto Press, 1961.

———. *New France: The Last Phase 1744–1760*. Toronto: Canadian Centenary Series, McClelland & Stewart, 1968.

Steele, Samuel B. *Forty Years in Canada*. Toronto: Ryerson Archives Series, McGraw-Hill Ryerson, 1972.

Stephenson, William. *Dawn of the Nation 1860–1870*. Editor-in-Chief, Toivo Kiil. Toronto: Canada's Illustrated Heritage, 1978.

Stewart, Walter. *Shrug: Trudeau in Power*. Toronto: NC, 1971.

———. *Strike!* Toronto: McClelland & Stewart, 1977.

Symington, Fraser. *The First Canadians*. Editor-in-Chief, Toivo Kiil. Toronto: Canada's Illustrated Heritage, 1978.

Symons, R. D. *Where the Wagon Led*. New York and Toronto: Doubleday & Company, Inc., 1973.

Taylor, Stephen. *Beyond the Road: Portraits and Visions of Newfoundlanders*. Toronto: Van Nostrand Reinhold, 1976.

Tivy, Louis, Ed. *Your Loving Anna, Letters from the Ontario Frontier*. Toronto: University of Toronto Press, 1972.

Trigger, Bruce G. "The French Presence in Huronia: The Structure of Franco-Huron Relations in the First Half of the Second Century," *Canadian Historical Review*, 1968.

Trudeau, Pierre Elliott. *Federalism and the French Canadians*. Toronto: Macmillan of Canada, 1968.

Trudel, Marcel. *The Beginnings of New France, 1524–1663*. Toronto: McClelland & Stewart, 1973.

Tupper, Charles. *Minutes, the Charlottetown Conference*. Public Archives of Toronto.

Turner, John Peter. *The North-West Mounted Police 1873–1893*, Vols. I and II. Ottawa: King's Printer, 1950.

Vallières, Pierre. *White Niggers of America*. Toronto: McClelland & Stewart, 1971.

Wade, Mason. *The French Canadians*, Vol. I, 1760–1911; Vol. II, 1911–1967. Toronto: Macmillan of Canada, Rev. Ed., 1968.

Wait, Benjamin. *The Wait Letters*. Erin: Press Porcepic, 1976.

Waite, P. B. *Canada 1874–1896, Arduous Destiny*. Toronto: McClelland & Stewart, 1971.

Wallace, W. Stewart, Ed. *The Macmillan Dictionary of Canadian Biography*. Revised by W. A. McKay. Toronto: Fourth Ed., Macmillan of Canada, 1978.

Waller, Adrian. "Explosion, The Great Halifax Disaster of 1917," *Reader's Digest*, December, 1977.

Warkentin, John. *Canada Before Confederation: A Study in Historical Geography*. Toronto: OUP, 1972.

Warner, Oliver. *With Wolfe to Quebec*. Toronto and London: Collins, 1972.

Watkin, E. W. *Canada and the States: Recollections 1851–1886*. London: Ward, Lock & Co., 1887.

Wheeler, Anne. *A Harvest Yet to Reap, a History of Prairie Women*. Toronto: The Women's Press, 1976.

Whitelaw, William Menzies. *The Maritimes and Canada Before Confederation*. Toronto: Oxford University Press, 1966.

———. *The Quebec Conference*. Booklet #20, Canadian Historical Association.

Wiebe, Rudy. *The Scorched Wood People*. Toronto: McClelland & Stewart, 1972.

———. *The Temptations of Big Bear*. Toronto: McClelland & Stewart, 1974.

Woodcock, George. *The Canadians*. Toronto: Fitzhenry & Whiteside, 1979.

Woodham-Smith, Cecil. *The Great Hunger*. New York and Evanston: Harper & Row, 1962.

Young, Christopher, Ed. *A Century of Reporting, the National Press Club Anthology*. Toronto: Clarke, Irwin, 1967.

Zaslow, Morris. *The Opening of the Canadian North 1870–1914*. Toronto: Canadian Centenary Series, McClelland & Stewart, 1971.

1901 editions of the T. Eaton Catalogues. Toronto: Musson Book Company, 1970.

Sessional Papers 1896 ♯61, Report of Royal Commission on the Sweating System, Archives of Canada.

Canada's Special Resources: *The Piecemeal Surrender*. *Last Post*. Special Report, 1971.

Index

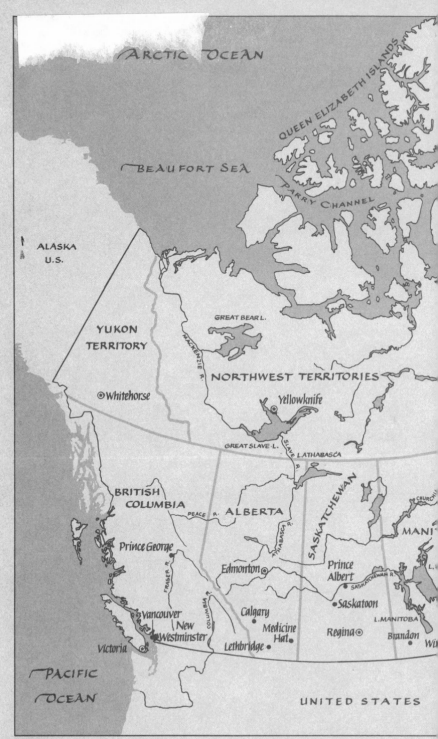